HUEY LONG'S LOUISIANA

ALLAN P. SINDLER

Huey Long's Louisiana

STATE POLITICS, 1920-1952

THE JOHNS HOPKINS PRESS
Baltimore and London

The Johns Hopkins Press, Baltimore, Maryland 21218
The Johns Hopkins Press Ltd., London

Standard Book Number (clothbound edition) 8018-0596-1
Standard Book Number (paperback edition) 8018-0597-X

Originally published, 1956
Second printing, 1962
Third printing, 1966
Fourth printing, 1970
Johns Hopkins Paperbacks edition, 1968

To Lenore AND *My Parents*

Preface

PERHAPS the profusion of literature on Huey Long best indicates why the study of recent Louisiana politics scarcely has begun. The flamboyant figure of Huey Long, the Louisiana Kingfish, has bedazzled commentators who otherwise would have attempted to examine, more or less systematically, the underlying structure and process of state politics. It seems fair to suggest that most earlier writers, by implicitly adopting a "great man" view of politics, have fallen short of a full understanding both of Louisiana politics and, necessarily therefore, of Huey Long as well.

This book represents no more than a beginning step in what seems to me to be the worthwhile effort of taking the subject of Louisiana politics out from under the dominating shadow of Huey Long. My central concern is with the form and content of Louisiana's one-party bifactional politics during the period 1920–52. The major political events of those three decades have been arranged and interpreted. The rise and dominance of the Long faction have been analyzed in the broad framework of a continuing movement of class protest having origins in nineteenth-century Louisiana and extending beyond the death, in 1935, of the Kingfish. The extent to which Louisiana's bifactionalism approaches the operating efficiency of competitive two-party politics has provided another focal concern of the study. As an inevitable, though somewhat incidental, by-product of my core objective, some new perspectives for the judgment of Huey Long have been developed.

Much remains to be done in the way of comprehending recent Louisiana politics. If this study, by mapping the terrain in detail and offering some guideposts, contributes to that end, its essential purpose will have been served.

The obvious hazards involved in any interpretation of recent politics require a few words on the approach and methods of my inquiry. As a political scientist not native to Louisiana I have no partisan axe to grind relative to the two major factions, Long and anti-Long. If I criticize both more frequently than I praise either it reflects my belief that democratic politics lies neither in one-man rule in the name of the people nor in oligarchic rule in the name of good government.

In addition to my reliance upon the customary materials of scholarship, I have made extensive use, though with simple statistical techniques, of primary-election data on a parish (county) and ward basis and of roll-call data on state legislators. In addition, highly useful information was secured through informal questionnaires and personal interviews. Such efforts, of course, can minimize but never eliminate the controversial quality inherent in a study of recent politics. It is the reader's right to judge the degree of success or failure achieved.

Though mine is the sole responsibility for what follows, I should like to acknowledge my indebtedness to many persons and organizations for their aid and courtesy. A research training fellowship from the Social Science Research Council enabled me to explore original source materials and to interview many knowledgeable political observers in Louisiana for a period of one year. Several staff members of Louisiana State University were unfailingly helpful to me: Homer L. Hitt and Rudolf Heberle of the Department of Rural Sociology; the late Kimbrough Owen and Emmett Asseff of the Department of Government; Perry F. Boyer of the College of Commerce; and Reid Grigsby of the Agricultural Extension Service. Joseph P. Nelson of the office of the Secretary of State of Louisiana gave generously of his time to help the author obtain unpublished election data. I am indebted also to Edgar B. Stern and Monte Lemann of New Orleans for personal courtesies and for aid on a phase of the project.

Miss Lucille May Grace, a veteran elective state official, kindly allowed me full use of her scrapbook collection of press clippings covering state politics from 1930 to 1951. Library privileges were granted through the co-operation of Mrs. Tom Atkinson of the Louisiana State Library in Baton Rouge; Garland W. Taylor of the Howard W. Tilton Memorial Library at the Tulane University, in New Orleans; and John Hall Jacobs of the New Orleans Public

Library. A special word of appreciation is due T. N. McMullan and the late Mrs. Ruth Campbell, respectively chief circulation librarian and librarian in charge of the Louisiana Room at the Louisiana State University Library, in Baton Rouge.

I owe much to those natives of Louisiana, representing all factional hues, who responded openly and thoughtfully in interviews and questionnaires to my many requests for information and interpretation. While a list of those "formally" interviewed appears in the bibliography, none of their observations which have been quoted in this study are specified as to source beyond the general attribution "informant." This procedure has been followed, not to create an aura of mystery, but simply to keep faith with a pledge I made to each interviewee.

Some special obligations should be recorded. Edward W. Stagg, Baton Rouge correspondent of the New Orleans *Item*, offered his astute observations on Louisiana politics to the author over a period of many months in 1951–52. Val C. Mogensen, Executive Director of the Bureau of Governmental Research, in New Orleans, made available many of the studies of that organization and took a lively interest in parts of my investigations. I gratefully acknowledge my debt to William Y. Elliott of Harvard University for encouraging my long-standing interest in Southern politics, and to V. O. Key, Jr., also of Harvard, for a critical reading of an earlier version of the study which helped me greatly in the revision necessary to produce this book. I should like to thank the *American Political Science Review* for permitting me to draw upon an article of mine in the September, 1955, issue for use in portions of the concluding chapter of this study.

My deepest obligation is to my wife, Lenore, who fully shared in the varied tasks, tedious as well as challenging, that go to make up scholarly inquiry.

Allan P. Sindler

Acknowledgments

FOR PERMITTING ME to quote from various newspapers, articles, and books, I am indebted to the following persons and publishers: *The American Mercury,* Hodding Carter—"Huey Long: American Dictator," in Isabel Leighton (editor), *The Aspirin Age* (Simon and Schuster); Baton Rouge *Morning Advocate* and Baton Rouge *State-Times* (Capital City Press); Bureau of Governmental Research, New Orleans, Louisiana; Earle J. Christenberry, holder of the legal copyright on the *Louisiana Progress* and on the *American Progress;* Harnett T. Kane—*Louisiana Hayride* (William Morrow and Company); Alfred A. Knopf, Inc., V. O. Key, Jr.—*Southern Politics;* J. B. Lippincott Company, Carleton Beals—*The Story of Huey P. Long;* Russell B. Long permitted my use of quotations from Huey P. Long—*Every Man a King* (National Book Company); Louisiana State University Bureau of Government Research, Emmett Asseff—*Legislative Apportionment in Louisiana;* Louisiana State University Press, Rudolf Heberle, *The Labor Force in Louisiana,* Roger W. Shugg, *Origins of Class Struggle in Louisiana, 1840–1875,* T. Lynn Smith and Homer L. Hitt, *The People of Louisiana;* New Orleans *Item;* New Orleans *States* and New Orleans *Times-Picayune* (The Times-Picayune Publishing Company); New York *World-Telegram and Sun—World Almanac;* Pelican Publishing Company, Thomas O. Harris—*The Kingfish;* Public Affairs Research Council of Louisiana, Inc.; Shreveport *Journal* (Journal Publishing Company, Inc.); Shreveport *Times;* University of Alabama Press, Alexander Heard and Donald S. Strong —*Southern Primaries and Elections.*

Contents

Tables

Figures   Unless otherwise noted, all figures are quartile maps which display the results obtained by a quartile ranking of parishes by the proportion of the popular vote each cast for the candidate named.

HUEY LONG'S LOUISIANA

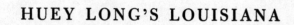

CHAPTER 1

The setting for recent politics

IN EXPLANATION of his rise to power, Huey Long often observed, "Just call me *sui generis* and let it go at that." That self-characterization, while accurate, fell short of a full explanation. Longite politics was an outgrowth of class tensions which Longism undoubtedly intensified but did not create. In the perspective of history, Longism represented the third major attempt of rural lower-class whites to challenge the dominant alliance of conservative planters and urban upper classes.

An understanding of recent Louisiana politics thus requires an awareness that the interaction of social classes in nineteenth-century Louisiana built up a potential of political conflict which failed to come to a head prior to Huey Long, principally because of racial preoccupations and the events of Reconstruction.[1] The selective commentary that follows seeks to support and illustrate that core judgment. Attention is directed to the crises of Secession and of Populism and to the more recent manifestation of control by conservatives exemplified by the statewide power of the Choctaw machine of New Orleans.

Ante-bellum Louisiana and the crisis of Secession

Rural planters and the men of commerce in the city, though comprising but 3 per cent of the free people of the state, controlled the greater part of the economic wealth and political power of ante-bellum Louisiana.[2] Within the agricultural world, the cotton and

---

[1] This evaluation of Louisiana history relies heavily upon Roger W. Shugg, *Origins of Class Struggle in Louisiana, 1840-1875* (Baton Rouge, 1939).
[2] *Ibid.*, 6–120, is the source for the following data and discussion.

sugar parishes[3] of the Delta were the center of the plantation system, the Black Belt, and of commercially successful agriculture. The Black Belt, with one-quarter of the free people, had two-thirds of the slaves and one-half of the assessed wealth outside New Orleans. By 1860, although more than two-thirds of the agricultural properties enumerated by the census were less than one hundred acres in size, Louisiana was properly regarded as a state of great plantations. Planter-owned land constituted nearly seven times that used in farming by lesser rural whites. The value of plantations, even excluding slaves, greatly exceeded that of farms, while the value of sugar and cotton crops raised for a world market dwarfed that of farmer subsistence crops. This rural upper class was allied with its counterpart in New Orleans, the latter controlling the credit, legal, and transportation factors essential to the economic life of a slave plantation system.

The poorer rural whites, in 1860 constituting one-third of the white people outside New Orleans, were restricted to small holdings in the oak and pine upland areas, remote from transportation and commercial markets.[4] They were responsible for but one-fifth of the total cotton production and had barely one-ninth of the state's assessed wealth. In 1860, rural and urban nonslaveholders, each group about equal in numbers, comprised 71 per cent of the white population. Both the distribution of slaveholdings and the outnumbering of plantations by smaller landholdings support the conclusion that a majority of rural free people had no direct stake in the retention of the institution of slavery.[5]

In the decade before the Civil War the slaveholding plantation system, already possessed of disproportionate economic power, steadily encroached upon the nonslaveholding economy by increasingly restricting the economic opportunities of both farmers and laborers. By the 1850's, after the pressure of immigrants had sent land prices soaring, inferior public lands—capable at best of sustaining a subsistence economy—comprised the bulk of cheap land available.[6] Dur-

---

[3] The term "parish" is the Louisiana equivalent of the political subdivision "county" common to the other states of the nation.

[4] For a discussion of the misuse of the "poor white" concept, see Shugg, *Origins of Class Struggle*, 20–24; A. N. J. Den Hollander, "The Tradition of 'Poor Whites,'" in W. T. Couch (ed.), *Culture in the South* (Chapel Hill, 1935), 403–31.

[5] See Shugg, *Origins of Class Struggle*, 76–78, for a fuller treatment of these conclusions.

ing that same period the price of slaves rose out of all proportion to the market price of cotton, making it more difficult for farmers to become planters. The Negro in slavery also caused free white labor to suffer, for to the latter were relegated the casual and accessory tasks of the plantation system. It is significant that white immigrants from Ireland, not Negro slaves, cleared the roads, drained the ditches, built the levees, and dug the canals.

The ruling alliance buttressed its economic predominance by political control so successfully that one authority has characterized antebellum Louisiana as a "government by gentlemen."[7] Under the Louisiana Constitution of 1812, the property qualifications for suffrage, the method of apportionment of Senate seats, and the failure to re-apportion House seats until 1841 combined to empower the Black Belt at the expense of both New Orleans and the white belt.[8] When the constitutional convention of 1845, under the influence of Jacksonian democracy, abolished all property qualifications for voters and candidates, the planters succeeded in changing the basis of the apportionment of Senate seats from registered electors to total population, including slaves. While the Black Belt thereby retained control of the Senate, other changes placed the New Orleans delegation as the balance of power between farmer and planter in the House.[9]

Rural distrust of New Orleans in the 1852 constitutional convention served to persuade city delegates to support the planters' demands for an even more disproportionate share of legislative seats. At first prepared to resist the Black Belt's proposal to adopt total population as the basis for the allocation of House as well as Senate seats, the New Orleans delegation reconsidered and consciously cast its lot with the planters after the rural delegates had attempted to restrict the city's share of House seats to a maximum of 25 per cent.

---

[6] Harry L. Coles, Jr., "Some Notes on Slaveownership and Landownership in Louisiana, 1850–1860," *Journal of Southern History*, ix (August, 1943), 381–94, suggests somewhat different conclusions than Shugg on the question of land ownership and its distribution in Louisiana in the 1850's.

[7] The characterization is the title of the fifth chapter in Shugg, *Origins of Class Struggle*, 121.

[8] *Ibid.*, 122; Emmett Asseff, *Legislative Apportionment in Louisiana*, Louisiana State University Bureau of Government Research (Baton Rouge, 1950), 10.

[9] The following analysis is drawn from Shugg, *Origins of Class Struggle*, 125–34, and from Asseff, *Legislative Apportionment*, 16–18.

In return for city support, planters agreed not to enact limitations on the number of House seats assignable to any single parish.[10]

Although, as Shugg suggests, city delegates may have acted on the belief that continuing immigration eventually would bring about the predominance of New Orleans, the 1852 settlement made the planters, with whom the urban upper classes had close business and social ties, supreme.[11] Table 1 sets forth the details of Black Belt supremacy under the 1852 Constitution. "Thus arose the conservative alliance of wealth, personal and real, urban and rural, that dominated Louisiana through the legislative representation of slave property."[12] Compared to other Southern states the uniqueness of the Louisiana situation lay not in the composition of its governing class but in the fact that only in Louisiana was the Black Belt able to secure the adoption of total population as the basis of representation in both houses of the Legislature.

TABLE 1. The Political Dominance of the Black Belt in Ante-Bellum Louisiana: Relative Strength of Black Belt, White Belt and New Orleans Subsequent to the Re-apportionment of 1854

	% Total Pop.	% White Pop.	% Electors	% Reps.	% Senators
Black Belt	55.4	36.5	42.9	52.3	53.1
White Belt	18.5	21.3	23.3	21.6	31.3
New Orleans	26.1	42.2	33.8	26.1	15.6
Total	100.0	100.0	100.0	100.0	100.0

SOURCE: adapted from Emmett Asseff, *Legislative Apportionment in Louisiana*, Louisiana State University Bureau of Government Research (Baton Rouge, 1950), 23.

The interplay of party conflict in ante-bellum Louisiana did not neatly parallel the extension of planter power evident in the development of legislative apportionment systems. The National Republicans and their successors, the Whigs, lost effective control of the state's politics by 1843 and rapidly disintegrated after the introduction of the slavery issue into national politics. Many members of the Whig party, whose core areas of support included New Orleans and

[10] For a fuller discussion, see Shugg, *Origins of Class Struggle*, 139–42.
[11] *Ibid.*, 141.
[12] *Ibid.*

the plantation lands, turned to the Know-Nothings; others joined the Democrats. Yet the ascendancy of the Democratic party, which attracted the allegiance of most small farmers and city workingmen, never threatened the fundamentals of the slave society and the plantation economy. It is in view of the pervasiveness of planter beliefs that Shugg concludes,

> For Louisiana was governed by gentlemen. It made no great difference to the majority of people whether power belonged to . . . Democrats or Whigs, the country or the city. . . . While planters held the upper hand, filled many offices, and set the tone of public opinion, city lawyers occupied the larger share of offices, represented the merchants, and withal served their planting clients as well. Judah Benjamin was a symbol of the union of interests which dominated Louisiana: he was a lawyer and a planter, first a Whig and finally a Democrat.[13]

That ante-bellum Louisiana was "governed by gentlemen" does not, by itself, necessarily suggest the existence of class tensions. The character of public policy must be investigated. A note on the inadequacies of public education provides ample evidence to support the conclusion that the Louisiana elite ruled more in the image of unenlightened self-interest than of a broader public interest.

Planters felt no obligation to underwrite a system of free public education either before or after that governmental obligation was adopted in the Constitution of 1845. From 1811 to 1845, the "public schools" of the state consisted of those parish academies and schools to which the state granted funds conditional upon the free instruction of a designated proportion of indigent pupils.[14] Stigmatized as pauper schools and therefore shunned by rich and poor alike, these schools hardly began to satisfy basic educational needs. In the thirteen years 1818–31, for example, state expenditures for education totaled $354,000; in 1834, there were only 1,500 children in the public educational system.[15] After 1845, Whiggish devotion to economy in government frustrated administrative implementation of the grand principle of free education. Residents of the poorer rural parishes thus were the chief victims of the illiberal educational policies of a

---

[13] *Ibid.*, 155.

[14] Edwin D. Fay, *The History of Education in Louisiana* (Washington, 1898), 27, terms the 1803–45 era as the "beneficiary period" in recognition of this policy.

[15] T. H. Harris, *The Story of Education in Louisiana* (New Orleans, 1924), 10.

state governed by gentlemen. In the decade before the Civil War, for example, scarcely one-third of the educable rural whites attended school.[16]

By objective standards, then, ante-bellum Louisiana contained the ingredients for class struggle. Whether conflict actually would develop, however, depended upon the extent to which both sides subjectively were aware of their different and rival class positions. Class conflict failed to develop because considerations of race and caste overshadowed those of class as the voices of abolitionism rose in the land. All classes of whites assumed a common defensive and aggressive posture, and the social philosophy of the planters became the accepted creed. The dominance of the upper classes thus was made legitimate.[17] The ability of this cohesive, articulate, and aggressive minority to control the destinies of the free people of Louisiana was tested in the crisis of Secession and its aftermath, in which the upper classes won the battle, lost the War, and ultimately gained the peace.

The inherent limitations of judgments based largely on analysis of electoral data, together with the possible inaccuracy of the particular electoral data on Louisiana's secession,[18] prohibit an exact assessment of the role of planters in Louisiana's decision to join the Confederacy. The data do permit inferences, however, on the more modest problem of whether the Secession movement provided evidence of class antagonisms. For the latter reason the major political events in Louisiana in 1860–61 briefly will be reviewed, first descriptively, and then analytically.

The fires of sectionalism that blazed in South Carolina only flickered in Louisiana. The economic interests of wealthy Louisianians, whether in sugar protected by tariffs or in commerce dependent upon the export trade of the entire Mississippi valley, had developed in them a national outlook. The Louisiana Legislature, for example, condemned South Carolina's attempt to nullify national law in 1832–33. But Louisiana was also a Southern state, susceptible to a closing

[16] Shugg, *Origins of Class Struggle,* 74.
[17] *Ibid.,* 30–31.
[18] Although not legally challenged in its own day, Shugg, *Origins of Class Struggle,* 163–64, notes that the official returns in the convention election of 1861 were suppressed for three months after the election. In view of the slim majority accorded Secession, a little doctoring might have gone a long way. In the absence of any proof of fraud, this study assumes the accuracy of the published figures.

of the ranks in answer to the fiery attacks of abolitionists, the morality of Stowe, and the violence of John Brown. The development of secession sentiment in Louisiana reflected those dual strands. During 1859, Louisiana newspapers gave little attention to the issue of slavery and less to secession, but in the course of the following year the bulk of the state's press undertook the advocacy of outright secession.[19]

Conflict within Louisiana's Democratic party, particularly between factional rivals John Slidell and Pierre Soulé, helped propel the state toward disunion. Slidell, the more powerful of the two politicians, endorsed Buchanan's support of the presidential candidacy of Breckinridge and became an "immediate secessionist." The minority faction, led by Soulé, espoused the national viewpoint of Douglas and subsequently urged "cooperationism" with sister Southern states as the alternative to immediate secession. The remnants of the former Whig majority in the state either had gone over to the Democrats with Senator Judah Benjamin in 1856 or, in New Orleans, had taken over the Know-Nothings and controlled city elections until 1860. These ex-Whigs remained moderate to the end, supporting Bell and the Union rather than immediate secession.

In Louisiana, as elsewhere in the South, the presidential contest lay essentially between Breckinridge and Bell. Although there was a discernible difference between the secession policies of the two, the Bell and Breckinridge camps in Louisiana each attracted both secessionists and unionists. Any correlation, therefore, of presidential voting with secession sentiment, as will be shown shortly, requires careful handling. The November, 1860, presidential election gave victory to Slidell and the extreme Democrats: Breckinridge had 22,681 votes; Bell 20,204; and Douglas 7,625.

That the national election of Lincoln served to harden secessionist views in Louisiana is indicated by the editorial comments of the New Orleans *Daily Picayune*, an anti-secessionist organ. "Since the announcement of the election of the chief of sectionalism to the office of the Presidency, public opinion in Louisiana has undergone a very important change. The movement in other Southern States, as well as the haughty, threatening, overbearing attitude of the North, has had a marked influence in hurrying forward what may truly be

[19] John C. Merrill, Jr., "Louisiana Public Opinion on Secession, 1859-1860," Unpublished Master's thesis, Louisiana State University (Baton Rouge, 1950), 38.

denominated a revolutionary sentiment in this State."[20] On December
10, Governor Moore, at Slidell's direction, convoked the General
Assembly which issued a call for the election of a convention on
January 7, 1861, to determine the continuation or disruption of
Louisiana's membership in the Union. It should be noted that this
action was taken in violation of the requirement of Article 141 of the
Constitution of 1852: that the question of a convention be submitted
to popular vote.[21] Since the convention seats were allocated on the
basis of the existing distribution of seats in both chambers of the
Legislature, the Black Belt retained its advantageous position relative to New Orleans and the white belt.

Two well-defined points of view were expressed clearly and frequently during the month-long campaign following the call for a
convention. Cooperationists argued for the exploration of alternatives
of action less drastic than secession; Secessionists rejected anything
less than immediate secession. There can be no claim, of course, that
support of Cooperationism was equivalent to a firm commitment to
the pro-Union position. Nevertheless, the difference in degree between Secessionist and Cooperationist proposals closely approached
a difference in kind when it is recalled that South Carolina seceded
on December 21, 1860. For these reasons, there should be no serious
quarrel with the utilization of convention voting data as an index of
secessionist and anti-disunionist attitudes.

In the convention election of January 7, 1861, the Secessionists
secured 83 seats on the strength of 20,448 votes, the Cooperationists
only 47 delegates on the basis of 17,296 votes. Governor Moore chose
to interpret the results as a unanimous endorsement of secession.
"The vote of the people has since confirmed the faith of their Representatives . . . that the undivided sentiment of the State is for immediate and effective resistance, and that there is not found within her
limits any difference of sentiment, except as to minor points of expediency in regard to the manner and time of making such resistance,
so as to give it the most imposing form for dignity and success. . . ."[22]
Yet, in spite of Moore's interpretation and in spite of the fact that
four more Southern states had seceded from the Union in the interim

---

[20] December 10, 1860, as quoted by Jefferson D. Bragg, *Louisiana in the Confederacy* (Baton Rouge, 1941), 21.

[21] Shugg, *Origins of Class Struggle*, 166–67.

[22] Quoted by Bragg, *Louisiana in the Confederacy*, 28.

between the election of delegates and the meeting of the convention in Louisiana, the Cooperationists were able to muster 47 votes at the convention in support of a moderate proposal calling for a conference of Southern states. The Secessionists, however, remained in firm control of the convention: the Ordinance of Secession was adopted by a vote of 113–17. By refusing (84–43 vote) to submit the Ordinance to the judgment of the people the convention took the second revolutionary step on the road to revolution itself.[23] Finally, the con-

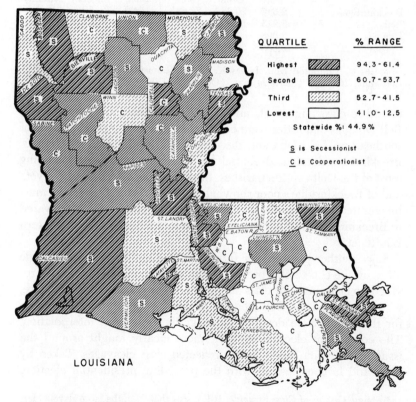

FIGURE 1. Quartile map: proportion of parish vote cast for Breckinridge electors, presidential election of 1860, and designation of subsequent Secessionist and Cooperationist parishes, 1861.

SOURCE: same as that for Table 2.

[23] Shugg, *Origins of Class Struggle*, 166–67.

vention arrogated to itself the legislative power during the state's
two months of awkward independence until Louisiana became a part
of the United Confederacy.

Analysis of the presidential election of 1860 in Louisiana (see
Table 2 and Figure 1) reveals a somewhat confusing pattern with

TABLE 2. The Louisiana Vote in the Presidential Election of 1860

	Orleans	Other	State	% State	Parishes Carried by Majority	Plurality
Breckinridge	2,645	20,036	22,681	44.9	29	8
Bell	5,215	14,989	20,204	40.0	3	6
Douglas	2,998	4,627	7,625	15.1	0	2
Total	10,858	39,652	50,510	100.0	32	16

SOURCE: computed from James K. Greer, "Louisiana Politics, 1845-1861,"
Louisiana Historical Quarterly, XIII (October, 1930), 641.

regard to class alignments and secession sentiments. The combined
Bell-Douglas majorities were confined largely to the planter areas of
southeastern Louisiana and the commercial center of New Orleans.
Breckinridge dominated central and northern Louisiana, including
most of the Delta cotton parishes. In view of the closeness of the vote
and of Breckinridge's poor showing in New Orleans, his victory must
be credited in part to Slidell and his rural machine, which delivered
to Breckinridge most of the votes of the Red River section in western
Louisiana.

Since neither planters nor farmers nor urbanites were of a single
mind on the choice of a president, the election of 1860 by itself provided no clear proof of class alignment.[24] Those observers, therefore,
who interpreted the Bell-Douglas majority vote as a moral triumph
for the Union were destined to be guilty of hopeful interpolation.
The convention election of 1861, more clearly fought around the
issue of secession, more clearly reflected class cleavages. Taken by
itself and in combination with the preceding presidential election,

[24] Shugg, *Origins of Class Struggle*, 161, insists that " . . . the large slaveholders
. . . were the most fervent sectional patriots." A glance at Figure 1 indicates that
the Black Belt parishes of St. Mary and Concordia were in the third quartile of
support for Breckinridge, while Carroll barely made the second quartile. Each of
the three parishes gave considerable support (over 40 per cent) to Bell. Shugg's
judgment fails to account for the anomaly of Madison Parish, for the stand of the
other Sugar Bowl parishes, and for the evident conversion to Southern sectionalism of many small farmers in north Louisiana.

analysis of the convention election yields conclusions pertinent to our present concern with class alignments.

In the convention election the Cooperationists gained majorities in twenty parishes, while the Secessionists carried the remaining twenty-eight. As Figure 1 indicates, Cooperationism was supported by the cluster of parishes in southeast Louisiana (Orleans excluded), which represented the arena of Soulé and the seat of conservative Whigdom, by the Florida parishes,[25] and by scattered parishes in northern Louisiana. The other parishes in the state returned Secessionist delegates to the convention. A reading of Table 3, which summarizes the data on parish behavior in the presidential and convention elections mapped in Figure 1, provides additional insights. It

TABLE 3. Parish Voting Behavior in the Presidential Election of 1860 and the Convention Election of 1861

| | No. of Parishes in Each Quartile of Support for Breckinridge, 1860 | | | |
	High	2nd	3rd	Low
28 Secessionist parishes, 1861	11	8	7	2
20 Cooperationist parishes, 1861	1	4	5	10
Total	12	12	12	12

SOURCE: Figure 1.

will be seen that two-thirds of the Secessionist parishes had been in the upper half of all parishes in support of Breckinridge, while three-fourths of the Cooperationist parishes had been in the lower half. When Table 3 is read in the other direction, the highest relationships appear in the extreme quartiles: all but one (Caldwell) of the twelve parishes in the highest quartile of support for Breckinridge subsequently went Secessionist, while all but two parishes (Madison and Orleans) in the lowest quartile of support for Breckinridge supported Cooperationism.

The foregoing analysis permits the conclusion that the reaction of Louisianians to the crisis of Secession suggested a class basis for political alignment, albeit a very incomplete and fuzzy class basis. White farmers in the uplands and on the sandy soils of some of the northern and Florida parishes clearly were hostile to the policy of

[25] A historic term still in current use which refers to the parishes of Washington, St. Tammany, Tangipahoa, Livingston, St. Helena, East and West Feliciana, and East Baton Rouge in east-central Louisiana.

immediate secession. That hostility led to defection from Slidell in
the Red River section, was voiced within the convention by the anti-
slavery delegate from Catahoula, and was affirmed during the War
by the high rate of "draft-dodging" among the poorer whites of
Catahoula and the Florida parishes.[26] The planter-commercial alliance, for its part, displayed considerably less cohesion than would
be expected in terms of an uncompromising class interpretation of
Secession. After a notable lack of unity in the presidential election
the Mississippi Delta cotton planters, at least, closed ranks in support
of Secession. Neither Breckinridge nor disunion, however, attracted
the loyalty of most of the sugar parishes. Perhaps the most significant
clue to why Louisiana went Secessionist and to the limits of a class
analysis lies in the support of Secession by those parishes which, on
the basis of objective evidence, should have been Cooperationist.

There would seem to be little supporting evidence, therefore, for
the view of Louisiana's secession that holds a "planter plot" to be the
heart of the matter.[27] The milder verdict of Roger W. Shugg is more
tenable: ". . . [the coercion and precipitate actions of the slavehold-
ers] indicated successful minority pressure, rather than a conspiracy.
. . . It was this minority which led the majority of people out of the
Union, not by conspiracy but by the exercise of powers they had
always possessed, in behalf of the slaveholding philosophy which
had become the creed of the South. The majority of people in Louisiana were either opposed to or indifferent to secession, but altogether
helpless in any event to resist it. . . ."[28]

Nonetheless, the crisis of Secession was not resolved without a
hesitant and partial expression of class consciousness by white farmers who resisted the clamor for immediate secession. Though obscured by the imperative of racial honor during Reconstruction, this
fuzzy class consciousness reappeared in sharper focus as Populism
and, though suppressed anew, ultimately found its voice in the person of the Louisiana Kingfish.

[26] Shugg, *Origins of Class Struggle*, 178, and Shugg, "A Suppressed Cooperationist Protest Against Secession," *Louisiana Historical Quarterly*, xix (January,
1936), 199–204.

[27] For an exposition of this view, see the six articles by Lane C. Kendall, "The
Interregnum in Louisiana in 1861," *Louisiana Historical Quarterly*, xvi–xvii
(1933–34).

[28] Shugg, *Origins of Class Struggle*, 169. Shugg's conclusions appear to be
more moderate than his commentary on the presidential election of 1860.

Post-bellum Louisiana and the crisis of Populism

The shared experience by Louisiana whites of subjection to Republican adventurers, supported by the vote of the Negro, snuffed out whatever class tensions might have been developing in antebellum Louisiana. However, the common resistance of whites to Reconstruction, successfully concluded in 1877, should not obscure an important difference in class attitudes and tactics. While the battle for racial supremacy early alienated the mass of whites from Republican rule, the upper classes resented more the economic ills and the looting of public funds occasioned by Radical government. It was only after their serious attempts to enlist the Negro in common cause met with failure that the upper classes adopted white supremacy as the rallying cry in the struggle for self-government.

The manner in which racial fears undercut lower-class radicalism may be illustrated by reference to the short-lived Louisiana Constitution of 1864.[29] Under Lincoln's "ten per cent plan," the Free State party defeated the Conservatives in gubernatorial and constitutional convention elections covering nineteen southern Louisiana parishes under Union control. The Free Staters desired to re-create Louisiana in the image of the loyal non-planter and non-merchant classes, but their flexibility of action was always restricted by their racial anxieties. Thus the Free Staters advocated that the basis of representation in the convention should be white population, a criterion at once designed to end planter domination, to reassert urban power within the state, and to ignore the Negro.

The Constitution of 1864, framed under the auspices of the Free State party, was distinguished by urban labor and rural farmer reforms, while pro-Negro measures were included only as a consequence of pressure exerted on the reluctant convention by General Banks and Governor Hahn. Thus the delegates early passed, and later rescinded, a resolution prohibiting future state legislatures from enfranchising the Negro, and provided for free public education on a non-segregated basis only after seriously considering a proposal for separate racial taxation. The constitutional reforms of 1864 were stillborn, however, because the disfranchisement of the Negro displeased

[29] The following account is adapted from John R. Ficklen, *History of Reconstruction in Louisiana (Through 1868)* (Baltimore, 1910), 45–87, and Shugg, *Origins of Class Struggle*, 196–211.

the Senate of the United States.

The racial preoccupations which circumscribed class reform in 1864 also moved lower-class whites to support the returning Confederate leaders. But the restored Democrats soon stumbled fatally, for the planters' demands upon the labor of his ex-slave were more repugnant to Northern Republicanism than the racial prejudice of white farmers and laborers had been. Louisiana's enactment of a Black Code, its rejection of the Fourteenth Amendment, and the Orleans race riot of 1866 aroused the ire of Congressional Radicals and brought about the dismal period of military reconstruction.

The high fiscal costs of Reconstruction induced by Republican misrule stimulated men of means to cast about for effective ways by which the rascals could be ousted from office. The state property tax rate climbed from 3.75 mills in 1866 to 21.5 mills in 1871, while the state's debt increased from $10,000,000 in 1860 to $29,600,000 in 1872, with another $12,000,000 of bonds authorized though unissued.[30] The flexibility of upper-class tactics contrasted strongly with the Negrophobia of poorer whites. In New Orleans, for example, businessmen contemplated running Negro candidates for city and Congressional offices to displace white Republicans.[31] Some of the former Whigs vainly attempted to gain control of the Republicans by infiltration.[32] The conservatives went so far as to invite the Negro to form a new organization with them, based upon a guarantee to the Negro of equal civil, political, economic, and legal rights.[33] When these tactics proved fruitless, the men of wealth closed ranks with their white brothers and joined in the cry of white supremacy. It was only after the conservatives found themselves unable to control the Negro in his exercise of political power that they allied with common whites to overthrow the Republican beneficiaries of that suffrage.

The Reconstruction status of the Louisiana Negro proved no great barrier to the restoration of white dominance. The radicalism of the Radicals had been a shallow affair, directed to the perpetuation of their own power and not to the advancement of their Negro partners. In spite of their numerical strength within the Republican party,

[30] Shugg, *Origins of Class Struggle*, 228.
[31] T. Harry Williams, "An Analysis of Some Reconstruction Attitudes," *Journal of Southern History*, XII (November, 1946), 480.
[32] *Ibid.*, 481.
[33] T. Harry Williams, "The Louisiana Unification Movement of 1873," *Journal of Southern History*, XI (August, 1945), 349–69.

Negroes played a subsidiary role to white leaders, who utilized them as pawns in the lucrative business of politics.[34] True, under the Constitution of 1868, Negroes gained the right to vote, to hold office, to attend tax-supported schools on a non-segregated basis, and to mingle on equal terms with whites. But in the inevitable clash between legislative fiat and an ingrained way of life, the latter was triumphant. The Constitution of 1868 thus widened the racial breach. Practical measures to aid the Negro, such as the freedman's dream of forty acres and a mule, were ignored by this "radical" convention. By not encouraging the Negro to own farmland, Republicans assured the overthrow of both the party and the Negro once the artificial prop of federal power was removed. At the same time, grandiloquent assertions of racial equality coupled with bi-racial occupancy of public offices offended those whites likely to be most tolerant of the continued exploitation of men of wealth in the state.

After the withdrawal of federal troops from Louisiana, the Democrats issued a call for a constitutional convention in 1879, to which ninety-eight Democrats, thirty-two Republicans and four others were elected. The delegates drew lessons from Reconstruction experience that were more obvious than exact. Antipathy to Republican misrule was extended to hostility toward their progressive legislation, and the syllogistic conclusion reached was that economy and conservatism were the hallmarks of good government. The powers of the state legislature were rigorously circumscribed to prevent a repetition of past excesses, while the appointive powers of the governor were heightened to permit wholesale displacement of Republican officeholders. By unduly curbing the necessary powers of state government, the convention foolishly placed restrictions on the Democratic future in the name of the Republican past.[35] In particular, the

[34] P. B. S. Pinchback, a leading Negro Republican, voiced the disappointment of his race with Republican leadership in the convention of 1879. "For a while we were admitted into the general council chamber, and some little respect was paid to our wishes, but gradually a line of demarkation was drawn between our rulers and ourselves that reached a distinct color line within our party, which took shape and assumed formidable proportions soon thereafter between the two races in the State." New Orleans *Daily Picayune,* June 10, 1879, as quoted by Alden L. Powell, "A History of Louisiana State Constitutions," Louisiana State Law Institute, Constitution Revision Project, Explanatory Notes and Materials for the Projet of a Constitution for the State of Louisiana (Baton Rouge, 1950), I, 141.

[35] Consult Powell, *loc. cit.,* 139–76, for a detailed study of the Constitution of 1879.

organic law of 1879 hampered the ability of contemporary government to deal effectively with the unrest in the 1880's which culmi-
nated in the crisis of Populism.

The political uprising of Louisiana's tenant and small independent
farmers during the 1890's was a consequence of the post-bellum continuation of the depressed status of the poorer whites. The unwillingness of the Democratic party, in either Louisiana or the nation, to
satisfy urgent agrarian demands propelled Louisiana farmers in
strange new directions. Sectional insularity was abandoned for an
alliance with Western agriculturalists. Concern for the maintained
subordination of the Negro was sacrificed implicitly by the creation
of a rival party and by explicit action through the recruitment of
Negro voters as allies against the Democrats. But though the farmers'
tactics of fusion with some Negroes, with Republicans, and finally
with Democrats bespoke a new clarity and flexibility of political
expression on their part, those gyrations ultimately betrayed the
farmers themselves. With the candidacy of Bryan in 1896, the Democrats reclaimed the agrarian bolters, and shortly after Bryan's defeat
the united white classes put Satan behind them by disfranchising the
Negro, their common pawn in politics.

The basis of Populist protest in Louisiana, as Shugg analyzes it,
stemmed from the post-bellum perpetuation of the plantation system
through the credit device of the crop-lien and through the absolute
increase in both the number of plantations and in the acreage controlled by them. High rates of tenancy, of overseer management, and
of absentee ownership were the natural products of an economic
system where the large estate remained the primary basis of agricultural production.[36] Many of the white farmers on poor soils turned
to lumbering and to livestock, while others tied themselves to the
commercial cotton economy spawned by the plantation system. The
capacity of small farmers to survive the vicissitudes of the crop-lien
system, however, often was greatly inferior to that of the planter. By
1894, after years of declining prices, cotton tumbled to a new low
of 4.3¢ a pound. The credit panic of 1893 and the flood ravages of
the Mississippi and Red rivers in 1891–92 additionally depressed the
agricultural economy.[37] It was the cumulative impact of these eco-

[36] Shugg, *Origins of Class Struggle*, 234–313, particularly 236–37, 241.
[37] Melvin J. White, "Populism in Louisiana During the Nineties," *The Mississippi Valley Historical Review*, v (June, 1918), 4.

nomic forces which drove the farmer to seek remedial benefits through politics.

By 1875, the Grange had attained its maximum Louisiana strength of about ten thousand members, drawn largely from the northern uplands and the Florida parishes. Dissatisfaction with the Grange's political passivity caused its rapid decline in Louisiana by the late 1870's. Throughout the 1880's the Knights of Labor attracted some support, particularly among farm laborers, sugar workers, and the urban work force of New Orleans. The highest membership reported by the Knights for this period, however, was 3,539 in 1886.[38] The Farmers' Alliance was considerably more influential in Louisiana than either the Grange or the Knights. Originating in Texas in 1876, the Alliance swept eastward, organizing and educating the farmers, and gradually assumed the character of a pressure group within the Democratic party in many Southern states.

The willingness of Democrats to accede to agrarian demands was tempered by their conviction that farmers would not endanger the maintenance of white supremacy by creating a rival party. That view was realistic. Farmer agitation up to 1890 in Louisiana had confined itself to working within the Democratic party, and the separatist politics later undertaken always was handicapped by the nonco-operation of segments of the Alliance. Continued Democratic rejection of farmer proposals, however, served to move more aggressive farmers toward third-party activities. In the Congressional election of 1890, the Alliance men of the Fourth Congressional District, embracing roughly all of north-central and northwestern Louisiana, replied to fraudulent Democratic nominating tactics by holding a rump convention at Natchitoches. Though the Alliance candidate was defeated in 1890, and again in the Congressional election of 1892, by the latter date the Populists were fully organized, had challenged Alliance leadership, and had entered politics on their own.

The 1892 state election provided no index of farmer influence because the dominant issue was the fate of the Louisiana Lottery Company, an unusual experiment in state-sanctioned gambling.[39] That issue so split the Democratic party that two Democrats, one anti-lottery and the other pro-lottery, ran in the general election. In pro-

---

[38] Frederic Meyers, "The Knights of Labor in the South," *Southern Economic Journal*, VI (April, 1940), 483.

[39] An able account of the Lottery is that of Berthold C. Alwes, "The History

test against the Alliance's support of anti-lottery Democrats, farmer delegates from the Florida parishes and southwestern and northern Louisiana put forward an independent Populist slate. The Populists ran a poor fifth in the general election, securing less than 6 per cent of the total vote cast, and carrying only the hill parishes of Catahoula, Grant, Vernon, and Winn.

The more usual tactic of Louisiana Populists, similar to the agrarian protest movement in other Southern states, was to ally with the other minority party, the Republicans. Although such an alliance was struck in Louisiana for the temporary purpose of the fall election of 1892, it continued through the state election of 1896. The 1892 arrangements revealed the main areas of strength possessed by each: the Populists ran candidates in the Fourth, Fifth, and Sixth Congressional districts, the Republicans in the Second and Third; and both parties supported an independent Democrat in the First District. The Democrats, nonetheless, easily carried the state for Cleveland and captured all Congressional seats. The fusion of minority parties added only the Republican parishes of St. Charles, St. James, and St. John to the Populist strongholds of Winn, Grant, and Lincoln. In the 1894 Congressional election, the Populists carried ten parishes in the uplands and Florida parish sections.

By the time of the 1896 state election, the stage was set for a widespread revolt against the Democratic party and its dominant faction. Agrarian discontents were intensified by severe droughts in 1895 which affected southwest and north Louisiana. The sugar planters, alarmed by Cleveland's tariff policies, aligned with the Republicans. And in New Orleans, civic reformers entered a mayoralty candidate against the nominee of the city machine.

The Democrats nominated Governor Foster (the anti-lottery Democrat in 1892) for re-election on a platform which straddled the silver issue, of concern to farmers, and supported a constitutional amendment on suffrage which was opposed by the Orleans machine.[40] Populists, Republicans, and sugar planters, after considerable fric-

of the Louisiana State Lottery Company," *Louisiana Historical Quarterly*, xxvii (October, 1944), 964–1118.

[40] The suffrage amendment provided for an educational test with the alternative of a property qualification and permitted future legislative revision without the requirement of electoral approval. The Orleans machine, deserting the state administration on the issue, opposed the measure as harmful to its Negro and immigrant supporters.

tion, agreed on a state ticket headed by John Pharr, a Republican sugar planter from St. Mary Parish. Although each of the elements of the coalition was opposed to the suffrage amendment, their unity derived far more from a desire to defeat the Democrats than from their adherence to a common program.

Table 4 reports the results of the gubernatorial election, at which, incidentally, both the suffrage amendment and the machine mayoralty candidate in New Orleans were defeated.

TABLE 4. The Louisiana Vote in the Gubernatorial Election of 1896

	Orleans	Other	State	% State	Parishes Carried by Majority
Foster (Dem.)	26,330	89,886	116,216	57.0	33
Pharr (Pop.-Rep.)	21,683	66,015	87,698	43.0	26
Other			176	0.0	0
Total	48,013	155,901	204,090	100.0	59

SOURCE: adapted from Alexander Heard and Donald S. Strong, *Southern Primaries and Elections* (University, Alabama, 1950), 75–76.

Two circumstances operated to augment the Democratic vote. Many Populists undoubtedly resented the alliance with Republicans in a state office contest. In St. Landry Parish, for example, some Populists allied with Democrats. Second, the Democrats used roving bands of "regulators" in the upland parishes as part of a general and somewhat successful effort to manipulate the Negro vote. It is instructive to observe that in spite of Democratic endorsement of the suffrage amendment, designed in part to curtail Negro voting, Foster carried twenty-three of the twenty-seven parishes in which the total of colored registered voters exceeded that of the whites. Observing the strength of Pharr in the upland parishes, one newspaper commented that if ". . . the Republicans [had] held their own in the Negro parishes and polled the Negro vote they claimed, it would have been a Democratic defeat."[41]

Figure 2 reveals the areas of the state most receptive to and most hostile to the Populists. The small-farmer parishes in the north-central uplands and in the Florida parishes, which had provided the core membership of the Grange, continued to be the backbone of agrarian protest. Post-bellum migration of small farmers to southwest

[41] New Orleans *Times-Democrat*, editorial, July 21, 1896.

Louisiana and to the second tier of parishes bordering on the northeast Delta parishes explained Populist appeal in those sections. The Sugar Belt's support of Pharr should be understood as a reaction to the tariff stands of the national parties. Anti-Populist areas included the Red River and Mississippi River deltas, the Felicianas, two of the sugar parishes, and the parishes containing the urban centers of Shreveport, Alexandria, Monroe, and New Orleans.

Elements of continuity in political alignments are suggested when parish behavior in 1896 is compared to that of 1861. In both elections

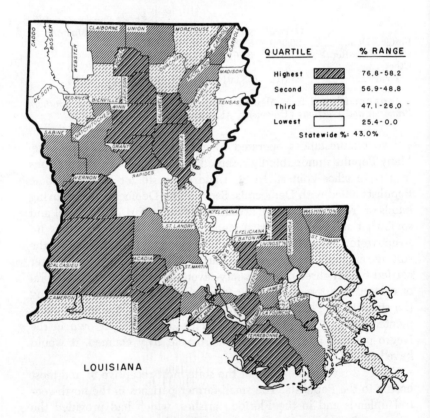

FIGURE 2. Quartile map: proportion of parish vote cast for Pharr, Populist-Republican candidate, gubernatorial election of 1896.

SOURCE: same as that for Table 4.

the sugar planters placed their unique economic concerns above all other considerations. Of the twelve north Louisiana parishes in the upper half of all parishes for Populism, eight had voted for Cooperationist delegates and four for Secessionists. Of the thirteen parishes in the lowest quartile of support for Populism whose boundaries in 1896 were the same as they were in 1861, eleven had been for Secession and but two for Cooperationism.

Though the parish patterns uncovered for the 1896 election are marred by some deviations, it may fairly be inferred that Populism brought to a head the expression of class antagonisms in considerably less fuzzy fashion than had the crisis of Secession. Particularly worthy of note is the development of planter-farmer and rural-urban observable differences in voting behavior, for these factors loom large in understanding the patterns of support of and opposition to Longism in recent Louisiana politics.

Louisiana Democrats were impressed sufficiently by the Populist showing to grant significant concessions to them in preparation for the presidential election of 1896. The Democrats adopted a silver plank and formally allied with the Populists, granting them one-half the electors to enable them to support Tom Watson for vice-president on the Bryan ticket. Discounting the demoralization likely to follow in the wake of such abrupt changes in political bedfellows, Populist leaders predicted that the future of their party would be enhanced by the fusion.[42] But though the silver Democrats overwhelmingly carried Louisiana for Bryan, the presidential election of 1896 marked the decline of Populism as a separate party in both Louisiana and the nation. Subsequent to the 1900 state election, Louisiana Populists failed to enter either a state or Congressional ticket.

The rapid disintegration of the Populist party was traceable in good part to the new willingness of Democrats to write agrarian reforms into the Constitution of 1898. That document created, among other things, agencies to regulate railroads and banks, a State Board of Appraisers to assess utility companies, and a State Board of Agriculture and Immigration. To the cheers of both Democrats and Populists, the new Constitution also effectively brought about the disfranchisement of the Negro. By the latter action Louisiana participated in what one writer has termed "one of the paradoxes of South-

[42] See, for example, the *Louisiana Populist*, October 9, 1896.

ern history," namely, "that political democracy for the white man and racial discrimination for the black were often products of the same dynamics. . . . The barriers of racial discrimination mounted in direct ratio with the tide of political democracy among whites. . . ."[43]

By the close of the century, then, Louisiana seemingly had achieved class harmony within one big party, unified by considerations of race. Populism, the clearest political expression of class conflict in the 1800's, was defunct.[44] The Negro was barred from political participation. But those who expected the latter "reform" to purify politics and to encourage white political division along class lines were guilty of unwarranted optimism. Maintenance of the political sterility of the Negro precluded the development of a democratic politics based upon healthy competition between parties. Exclusion of the Negro from politics gave rise to a number of interrelated consequences, including a dulling of issues, decreasing voter turnout, continued control of the party by the same kind of inner clique, and a divorce of the state from national issues and politics. It was thus no accident that the controlling force in state politics in twentieth-century Louisiana prior to Huey Long came to be the city machine of New Orleans.

The Choctaws of New Orleans and pre-Long Louisiana

Ever since its inception in 1897 the Choctaw Club of New Orleans has been an organization of professional politicians seeking to retain control of the city-parish government.[45] Known more familiarly as the "Ring," the "Choctaws," or, after a factional tiff in the early 1920's, as the "old regulars," this durable organization has constituted, in

[43] C. Vann Woodward, *Origins of the New South: 1877–1913* (Baton Rouge, 1951), 211. The Louisiana convention adopted a "grandfather clause" in preference to entrusting parish registrars of voters to administer an "understanding" clause in discriminatory fashion.

[44] The support accorded Eugene V. Debs in the presidential election of 1912 indicates the continuing latent radicalism of the Populist areas. Debs received over 5,000 votes in Louisiana, mainly from the western and north-central parishes where the lumbering–small-farm complex prevailed. Socialist sentiment in Louisiana was an outgrowth of the ruthlessness of lumber combines and the proselyting of the International Workers of the World (Wobblies).

[45] The city of New Orleans was co-extensive with the parish of Orleans. The Commission Council was the governing body of both and was, therefore, both a state and a municipal agent for all purposes of local government.

effect, a Democratic machine comparable in methods and objectives to the urban machines in some of the non-Southern states. An investigation into the successful operation of the Ring in city politics is not directly relevant to the concern of this study and, in addition, has already been undertaken in an illuminating, if now somewhat dated, published work.[46] Of greater pertinence here is the presentation of material indicating how the Choctaws became the controlling force in state politics and noting the consequences for public policy of that control.

The prominence of New Orleans in state politics was the natural outcome of its number of voters and its share of seats in the Legislature and in the state central committee of the Democratic party. In state primary elections the New Orleans vote constituted over 20 per cent of the state vote. Within the Legislature, Orleans was allocated 20 of 100 representatives and 8 of 39 senators.[47] A similar proportion of the membership of the governing party committee was granted to the city. City action, therefore, particularly if cohesive, frequently could be decisive in the election of state officials, the referenda on constitutional amendments, in the consideration of legislation, and in the framing of party rules.

The dominance of the Choctaws in state politics was the inevitable outcome of Orleans' dependence upon and vulnerability to the actions of the governor and the Legislature. The constitutions of 1898 and 1921, following the 1879 model, were niggardly in grants of power to parish and municipal governments. Local affairs, as a consequence, were thrust into the arena of state politics. To protect their hegemony in city politics the Choctaws thus were compelled actively to concern themselves with the election of friendly or at least nonhostile governors and state legislators.

[46] George M. Reynolds, *Machine Politics in New Orleans, 1897–1926* (New York, 1936).

[47] From 1880 to 1920 the main under-represented areas in both the Legislature and the Democratic State Central Committee were the secondary urban parishes of Caddo, East Baton Rouge, Calcasieu, Rapides, and St. Landry, while the rural parishes were over-represented. In the absence of re-apportionment since the adoption of the Constitution of 1921, these trends have been accentuated. In the pre-1921 period, however, Orleans was not deprived by apportionment of the full strength of urban allies, for the other cities of the state were then controlled by agricultural or raw-material manufacturing interests. The pattern of "New Orleans versus the country parishes" thus was accurate demographically as well as politically for the pre-1921 period.

Entry of the Ring in state politics injected one-sided elements of durable organization into the one-party system which enhanced the machine's statewide power. The cohesive Choctaw delegation, entering into transitory alliance with first one, and then another, group of legislators, was able to prevent the enactment of legislation it deemed repressive and, somewhat less consistently, to secure the passage of measures advantageous to its interests. One common tactic consisted of the Ring's skillfully electing to support some country-parish bills not affecting its interests in order to develop sufficient country-parish backing for its own measures. To secure Ring support, rural legislators, in their turn, often excluded Orleans from coverage by inclusion in their bills of what came to be a familiar legislative clause, "parish of Orleans excepted."

In addition to directing the maneuvers of the city's legislative delegation, the Ring caucus endorsed slates of candidates in every election involving the voters of New Orleans. For state-office primaries the implications of Choctaw support were hidden by the elaboration of a ritual designed to blunt country-parish dislike of the statewide power of the city machine. The Ring never openly entered a gubernatorial candidate of its own nor endorsed one early in the campaign. Customarily, after a period of watchful waiting, the Choctaws quietly would enter into the necessary understandings with that candidate who was not hostile to them and who appeared to have the likeliest prospects of winning a plurality of votes in the country parishes. Shortly afterwards, the Ring publicly would announce its endorsement.

The ritual then began. The Choctaw-supported candidate would assure the voters that the machine's endorsement had come unsolicited and had been accepted without conditions. Rival candidates, many of whom had sought Ring support in vain, would proclaim their independence and label their more fortunate competitor as "the tool of the city machine." There followed the retort from the Ring candidate that the Choctaws, by endorsing him, had sought only to climb on the bandwagon of the one candidate certain to win. Such traditional campaign oratory served to obscure the fact that many potential candidates checked with the Choctaws before deciding whether or not to run, and that the Choctaws in effect created a state ticket through their endorsements of candidates for each state office.

The results of gubernatorial primaries, however, made it quite clear that the Ring's support, more often than not, was helpful to victory. From 1900 to 1924, the Choctaws supported the successful gubernatorial candidacies of Heard, Blanchard, Sanders, Pleasant, and Fuqua. When the Ring itself was made a major campaign issue, as in the primaries of 1912 and 1920, its influence declined and its candidate lost. Such temporary defeats by transitory "good government" movements never seriously threatened the hold of the machine. To affect the Choctaws' control of patronage in critical fashion required sustained attack over time, for the Ring had at its disposal city, parish, and state sources of patronage. As a consequence of its fortified position the machine survived reform assaults and proved to be the hardiest of the many organized political groups opposed to Huey Long.

While the Ring emerged usually as victor in the running battle between city and country, its conservative imprint on public policy helped to develop the reservoir of intense dissatisfaction which the Kingfish tapped in his rise to power. The Ring aligned itself openly with the top civic and business organizations of the city and respected their wishes in legislative matters.[48] The interests of private utilities were catered to so thoroughly that it required the heavy-handed actions of Governor Long in 1928 to make natural gas at cheap rates available to the residents of New Orleans. In state policy the Choctaws opposed the passage of employers' liability laws, of bills to create a state agency to regulate public utilities and to provide for rural homestead taxation exemptions, and of the federal income tax amendment. It is not surprising, therefore, to discover that the plantation parishes of East Carroll, Madison, and Tensas consistently supported Ring-backed gubernatorial candidates. The dominant influence of the Choctaws in state politics, after all, continued the tradition of upper-class control.

It is not very much of an exaggeration to conclude that under Ring and planter control Louisiana approximated a civic vacuum. The sound and fury of politics represented little more than empty tilts for power among officeseekers possessed of a common conservatism. If it promised little to the ante-bellum farmer whether Whig or Democrat occupied the statehouse, it promised less to the farmer, at the turn of the century, which Democratic faction assumed control.

[48] Harold Zink, *City Bosses in the United States* (Durham, 1930), 331.

Dominant state economic interests had little to fear in the way of "unsafe" politics. Those groups likely to challenge the rule of the upper classes either were politically dormant or were controlled by conservative elements, as in south Louisiana and Orleans, or were divided by mutual suspicions, as in the case of the farmers of Protestant north Louisiana and Catholic south Louisiana.

Yet there had developed in nineteenth-century Louisiana increasingly well-defined class antagonisms which, if the appropriately charismatic leader appeared, could stimulate another attempt at protest politics by lower-class whites. Huey Long, *sui generis* or no, thus must be understood in the context of the origins of class conflict in Louisiana. The persistent appeal of Longism in recent Louisiana politics owes as much, if not more, to repressed class bitterness as it does to the makeshift liberal policies of the Longs. Political control by lower-class leaders for the better part of the last two decades has not yet dulled class resentments founded on the rankling awareness of a century of discrimination.

Some relevant data on the people of Louisiana

While the origins of Longism lay in the development of class tensions in ante- and post-bellum Louisiana, Longism itself developed in the period since 1920. It is necessary, therefore, for the reader to be acquainted with at least those characteristics of recent Louisiana which might be said to constitute the raw materials of state politics. The most pertinent categories of demographic data include types of farming and industry, urban and rural distributions of population, racial proportions, and the bi-religious division of the state into Catholic south and Protestant north. The task of presenting the necessary information is greatly simplified by the availability of other studies which concern themselves directly with presenting and interpreting census and other data on the foregoing topics.[49]

[49] Basic demographic material is available readily in T. Lynn Smith and Homer L. Hitt, *The People of Louisiana* (Baton Rouge, 1952), and in Homer L. Hitt and Alvin L. Bertrand, *Social Aspects of Hospital Planning*, Louisiana Study Series No. 1 (Baton Rouge, 1947). An analysis of industrial areas and the labor force is contained in Rudolf Heberle, *The Labor Force in Louisiana* (Baton Rouge, 1948). Useful additional information is in Stanley W. Preston, "Survey of Louisiana Manufacturing, 1929–1939," *Louisiana Business Bulletin*, VIII (December, 1946), 5–30, and in William H. Baughn and William D. Ross,

Most of Louisiana consists of lowlands. "From an elevation of nearly 500 feet on its Arkansas border, Louisiana slopes gently southward to desolate coastal marshes that dissolve into the Gulf of Mexico. The entire area has an average altitude of only 100 feet; one-third of the surface is only half as high, and actually lies below the banks of rivers running through it. This immense lowland is saved from flood by levees from ten to fifty feet in height, which extend over 1700 miles in length."[50] The wanderings of the Mississippi have produced not only marshlands and swamps but also rich soils which flank its course from the Delta parishes to the Sugar Bowl. From northwest Louisiana the Red River flows southward to join with the Mississippi, and together they have created a Y-shaped drainage basin consisting of fertile alluvial soils.[51] Most of north Louisiana (other than the alluvial areas) and the northern half of the Florida parishes (the Felicianas and East Baton Rouge excepted) consist of hilly lands of inferior soils. Prairie lands blanket most of the southwestern parishes, while a wide strip of marshland runs across the southern part of each of the parishes bordering on the Gulf.

The temperate region of the state lies north of the junction of the Red and Mississippi rivers and supports a cotton economy similar to that of neighboring Eastern states, an economy ranging from plantation commercial agriculture to subsistence farming. Heavy rainfall south of Rapides Parish discourages cotton culture but, in combination with tropical heat, facilitates the growth of rice, citrus fruits, and sugar cane. The cultivation of the latter crop, however, perhaps derived more from governmental tariff policy than from climate. While the diversity in the agricultural world should not be minimized, the gulf between hill farmer and cotton planter justifiably may be stressed as the intra-agricultural cleavage most relevant to an understanding of state politics.

With reference to types of industry, Louisiana has lacked an adequate proportion of high-productivity manufacturing industries which contribute the most to per capita income and to the tax coffers of the state. Louisiana's potential of cheap labor has not been suffi-

"Changes in the Louisiana Manufacturing Economy Between 1939 and 1947," *Louisiana Business Bulletin*, XIII (April, 1951), 7–83.
[50] Shugg, *Origins of Class Struggle*, 3.
[51] *Ibid.*, 4.

cient to counterbalance its lack of raw materials and its remoteness
from markets for purposes of attracting industry. In such circumstances the capacity of Louisiana to sustain the welfare politics of
Longism has rested in good part on the willingness of its political
leaders to tax the businesses exploiting the varied natural resources
of the state. In addition, through the port of New Orleans, Louisiana
has retained commercial and shipping activities of importance to its
economy.

The imbalance within Louisiana industry may be gauged by noting the proportions of the working population engaged in primary
industry (agriculture, fishing, and forestry) and in manufacturing,
in Louisiana and the nation, for 1940 and 1950. In Louisiana, the
percentages for primary industry in 1940 and 1950 respectively were
33.2 and 18.3; the national proportions were 18.8 and 12.4. The
Louisiana proportions for manufacturing in 1940 and 1950 respectively were 12.9 and 15.1; the national percentages were 23.4 and
25.9.[52]

Louisiana has had not only an inadequate share of manufacturing
in general but also an inadequate share of the kinds of manufacturing that add most to the value of the product made and to the income
of the workers employed. In both 1939 and 1947, Louisiana's major
industries, measured in terms of production workers, were, in order
of importance: lumber and products (except furniture); food and
kindred products; paper and allied products; chemicals and allied
products; petroleum and coal products.[53] All of the foregoing were
raw-material oriented industries, the first three of them representative of Southern industries in which the manufacturing process
added little to the value of raw materials. The foregoing data help
explain why—to take 1939 figures as an example—per capita income
of Louisiana's employed labor force was only 70 per cent of the
national figure, its median wage or salary income but 60 per cent of
the national median.[54]

The centers of secondary industry (manufacturing, building, min-

[52] For 1940 data, see Heberle, *The Labor Force in Louisiana*, 17; for 1950
data, the *1950 Census of Population*, Vol. ii, Characteristics of the Population,
Part I (United States Summary), Table 132, and Part 18 (Louisiana), Table 84.

[53] For 1939 data, see Preston, "Survey of Louisiana Manufacturing," *loc. cit.*,
24; for 1947 data, consult Baughn and Ross, "Changes in the Louisiana Manufacturing Economy," *loc. cit.*, 34.

[54] Heberle, *The Labor Force in Louisiana*, 19.

ing) were in New Orleans and adjoining Jefferson Parish, Shreveport in Caddo Parish, and Baton Rouge in East Baton Rouge Parish. In 1940 those three centers together accounted for nearly one-half of the total secondary industry labor force and for more than one-half of the total value of products and of the total value added by manufacture.[55] However, considerably less than one-third of the four-parish work force was employed in secondary industry. Other lesser industrial areas included the parishes of Calcasieu, Ouachita, and Rapides.

The centers of industry, as might be expected, were also the centers of urban population. Under the narrow definition of "urban" used in the 1940 Census,[56] the only completely urban parish was Orleans, and the only other parishes a majority of whose population was urban were Ouachita and Caddo. Under the broadened definition of "urban" used in the 1950 Census, the parishes of East Baton Rouge, Jefferson, Lafayette, Calcasieu, Iberia, and St. Mary also have been classified as predominantly urban.[57] Rapides Parish, one-third of whose residents lived in Alexandria, and two-thirds in the "metropolitan area" of Alexandria, still failed to be classified as predominantly urban under the new census criteria.

In 1940, though New Orleans (with a population of 494,537) was the largest city in the South, Louisiana was 58.5 per cent rural and 41.5 per cent urban. Of the rural population, 61.5 per cent were rural-farm (36.0 per cent of the state population of 2,363,880), concentrated mainly in the cotton regions of the uplands, the upper Delta, and the Florida parishes. The rural-farm population constituted a majority in thirty-four parishes and from one-half to one-third the population in eighteen additional parishes. Twenty-three parishes had no urban area at all, though that total unrealistically included Jefferson, St. Bernard, and West Baton Rouge, each of which was a satellite of an urban area.

The last three decades in Louisiana have been characterized by a

[55] Preston, "Survey of Louisiana Manufacturing," 30.

[56] In the censuses of 1920, 1930, and 1940, "urban" was defined as all persons residing within the limits of incorporated centers having 2,500 or more inhabitants. Smith and Hitt, *The People of Louisiana*, 20.

[57] *1950 Census of Population*, Part 18 (Louisiana), Table 12. As Smith and Hitt, *The People of Louisiana*, 20, comment, the Census in 1950 included within the urban population the people residing in the thickly settled zones immediately outside the corporate limits of cities having 50,000 or more inhabitants, and those residing in unincorporated centers of 2,500 or more inhabitants.

relative decline in rural-farm population and a relative increase in the proportion of urban population. From 1920 to 1950, the proportion of rural-farm population to total population has declined from 43.6 to 21.2 per cent; the 1950 Census classified Louisiana as 54.9 per cent urban.[58] The proliferation of urban areas has made invalid, from a demographic standpoint, the long-heard cry of "New Orleans versus the country parishes." In 1940, the combined population of the fifty-three urban areas other than New Orleans roughly equalled that of Orleans. In 1950, in good part because of the changed definition of "urban," 61.2 per cent of the state's urban population were reported as living elsewhere than in New Orleans.[59]

With reference to racial proportions, about one-third of the state's population was classified as Negro in 1940 (35.9 per cent) and again in 1950 (32.9 per cent). Although the Negro generally was more rural in residence than the white, there was no clear inverse relationship between race and urbanity. In 1940, for example, while Alexandria, Lake Charles, Monroe, and Shreveport had a higher proportion of Negroes than the state had, the reverse was true for Baton Rouge, Bogalusa, Lafayette, and New Orleans. The 1950 data showed that roughly one-half the Negroes, as compared with about three-fifths of the whites, were urban in residence.[60]

The Negro population was unevenly distributed throughout the state. There were relatively small proportions of Negroes in the rice, truck farm, swamp and marshland areas of south Louisiana, in the eastern Florida parishes, and in the piney woods and hills of north Louisiana. High Negro concentrations of population were characteristic of the plantation economy of the Delta areas, of the bluff districts of the Felicianas, of the upland cotton areas in DeSoto, Claiborne, and Morehouse parishes, and of the Sugar Bowl.

In Louisiana, as in most of the South, the distribution of Negro population is an important datum for understanding the differences in white reaction to the recent gains of the Negro on the political, educational, and legal fronts. No matter where the Negro resided, however, his income and level of living usually was considerably lower than that of the white. For that reason, if for no other, the very

---

[58] *1950 Census of Population*, Part 18 (Louisiana), Table 10. Louisiana's population in 1950 totaled 2,683,516.

[59] *Ibid.*, Tables 10 and 12.

[60] Smith and Hitt, *The People of Louisiana*, 38.

recent entry of the Negro in Louisiana politics may be expected to contribute to the durability of a politics of lower-class protest.

Perhaps Louisiana most sharply diverged from other Southern states in the matter of the religious affiliation of its people. Although the methods employed in the 1936 Census on religion left much to be desired,[61] the data revealed contrasts too sharp to be attributable solely to error. In 1936, the state was nearly solidly Christian in faith, with roughly equal numbers affiliated with Catholic and Protestant churches. Fifty-four of the sixty-four parishes were either more than two-thirds Catholic or more than two-thirds Protestant. The geographic concentration of religions was no less striking: the Florida parishes, west-central, and northern Louisiana were largely Protestant (mostly Baptist or Methodist), while the rest of south Louisiana was mainly Catholic.

The sections of south Louisiana containing the highest proportions of Catholics roughly coincided with the sections of French cultural domination.[62] A more exact notion of the limits of "south Louisiana," with its French and Catholic referents, is provided by the following description.

It resembles a large triangle whose base consists of the Gulf of Mexico. One side is bounded by a straight line running from the southwestern tip of the state to the junction of the Red and the Mississippi rivers, and the other side is bounded by a straight line running from the latter point through the city of New Orleans to the Gulf of Mexico. Except for a considerable French population in Avoyelles Parish and other French communities dotted along the Red River as far north as Natchitoches, relatively few French-settled localities lie outside the area so described, and relatively few non-French aggregates are included within the limits set forth.[63]

In 1930 and again in 1940, the number of Louisiana French was estimated at about 44 per cent of the native white population.[64]

The use of "Creole" and "Cajun" as interchangeable descriptive

---

[61] The Census of Religious Bodies undertaken in 1936 restricted its inquiry to church organizations in lieu of enumerating the population and, therefore, in the case of Louisiana, undoubtedly understressed Protestant strength while recording more accurately the number of Catholic affiliates. The 1946 Census of Religious Bodies remains unpublished. Consult Smith and Hitt, *The People of Louisiana*, 128–30, for a fuller discussion.

[62] *Ibid.*, 47–49, for a more extensive treatment.

[63] *Ibid.*, 49.

[64] *Ibid.*

terms for the French people of Louisiana, though frequent, is in error. The Creoles are descendants of the early Spanish or French settlers and comprise part of the social aristocracy in New Orleans and other cities.[65] The Cajuns are the descendants of the Acadians who fled persecution in British Nova Scotia in the mid-eighteenth century to resettle in Louisiana under the protective arm of the French government. Of the Catholic faith also, Cajuns differ greatly from Creoles in their lower level of living and in their concentration in rural, and sometimes inaccessible, sections of south-central and southeast Louisiana. Cajuns, in fact, have been described as "the largest unassimilated nationality group in America."[66]

The religious and cultural contrasts within Louisiana have led to the frequent application of the framework "north Louisiana" and "south Louisiana" to many fields of study, politics included. Some differences in political behavior between the two sections are observable. The factional loyalties of many south Louisiana parishes during the period 1920-52 were less consistent than the loyalties of other parishes in the state. Although Louisiana natives refer to "the mercurial French temperament" by way of explanation, a more persuasive reason might refer to the more tight-knit political organization in many south Louisiana parishes and localities. Insofar as the folklore of politicians may be relied upon, it would appear to be not extraordinary for a candidate who secures the support of the leaders of a Cajun community to garner a healthy majority of the votes cast in that community.[67] The shifts in factional alliances from one election to another indulged in by these local leaders, if such occur, would help explain the more erratic political behavior of south Louisiana.[68] Yet another factor which ought to be mentioned is the frequently heard accusation that electoral fraud is of greater scope

[65] In Louisiana, the term "Creole" has no reference to the offspring of interbreeding whites and Negroes.
[66] Harlan W. Gilmore, "Social Isolation of the French Speaking People of Rural Louisiana," *Social Forces*, xii (October, 1933), 82.
[67] A Protestant informant stated to the author that the best district judges were elected by the south Louisiana parishes with the highest rates of illiteracy. The explanation offered was that a majority of people followed the choice of their community leaders, and that the latter sought to support superior candidates for judicial office.
[68] The following comments by Earl Long, in 1932, suggest the manipulability of south Louisiana voters: "There are very few people in north Louisiana that can not vote as they please. The French people in south Louisiana are fine,

and frequency in south Louisiana than elsewhere in the state.[69]

French Louisianians are asserted to have great respect for personal liberties, among which most emphatically are the rights to drink and to gamble. These two liberties, therefore, are enjoyed openly and never, as is alleged of north Louisianians, behind the barn door. Indeed, the hypocrisy of the uplander is too much for the Gallic mind: "in north Louisiana," so the saying goes, "a wet will vote dry, while in south Louisiana a dry will vote wet." Gambling, though illegal under state law, frequently plays a major role in parish politics in south Louisiana and helps account for the usual dominance of the sheriff in the political organization of the parish. The problem of gambling also frequently underlies the skirmishes between parish politicos and governors over the grand principle of "home rule."

The bi-religious division of the state also has given rise to some political "rules of thumb." One old saw, for example, many times nicked but to date unbroken, cautions that only a Protestant seriously may aspire to the office of governor of Louisiana. While the occupants of the Executive Mansion since 1920 have been of the Protestant faith, it should be noted that experienced Catholic politicians in 1924, 1932, and 1952 waged serious campaigns for the governorship.[70]

Generally speaking, neither an aggressive Catholicism nor anti-clericalism has been the norm of state politics, but on occasion religious differences have provided a basis for political division. Examples of the latter situation would include the gubernatorial primary of 1924, in which the Klan issue was of moment, and the recurring referenda on the liquor question. Whether the foregoing examples of observable differences in the political behavior of the two sections

---

generous, polite, very courteous, but they are easier to work on and play on their sympathy than they are up in north Louisiana. In north Louisiana when they get against you they are against you. In south Louisiana they will soften up." United States Senate, *Hearings of the Special Committee on the Investigation of Campaign Expenditures,* 72nd Congress, 2nd Session (1932), 814.

[69] An editorial in the Baton Rouge *State-Times* of March 23, 1937, commented with reference to a recent judicial invalidation of one of Huey Long's election laws, "No one in politics should want more than an honest count of votes, but unfortunately, as the governor well knows, many people do, particularly in South Louisiana." An astute south Louisiana observer estimated to this writer that "currently [1952] one-third of the votes of from five to seven Cajun parishes are purchasable."

[70] The most recent addition to the list is deLesseps Morrison, Catholic mayor of New Orleans, who waged an unsuccessful campaign as the leading anti-Long candidate in the 1956 gubernatorial primary.

merit retention of the "north-south Louisiana" framework for political analysis is somewhat doubtful. A suspicion remains that terms of proven value in demographic studies may have been extended uncritically to the field of politics on the faulty expectation of equal utility.

Some ground rules for the game of Louisiana politics

One final topic remains for the reader to be acquainted with before the events of recent Louisiana politics can be fully appreciated. That topic, discussed in this section, concerns information on suffrage, nominations, elections, and party machinery, which, in sum, comprise the most important of the ground rules for the game of Louisiana politics. To a considerable extent the description offered fits the entire period 1921–52. Any additional significant changes in these ground rules not noted in this section will be discussed within the chronological treatment of state politics in the chapters that follow.

The most conspicuous effect of the suffrage provisions in the 1898 and 1921 constitutions, together with the adoption of the white primary in 1906, was to bring about the virtual disfranchisement of the Negro.[71] To vote in any given general election or primary, the individual had to apply personally and meet the registration requirements enumerated in the Constitution. Louisiana's version of the common Southern drive to deprive the Negro of political influence constituted, in essence, the empowering of parish registrars of voters to administer registration requirements in a racially discriminatory fashion. This technique was supplemented by the Democratic party's adoption of a white primary in a state where the general election merely ratified the results of the preceding primary. The racial effect of these devices was clear: in March, 1940, for example, there were 653,087 literate registrants and 49,826 illiterate or disabled registrants of the white race, compared to 884 and 13 Negro registrants in those two categories respectively.[72] Now that the Negro in very recent years has entered actively in state politics, due to judicial overthrow of the foregoing devices, the cumbersome registration

[71] Article VIII, sections 1–6, of the Constitution of 1921 contains the suffrage provisions.

[72] *Report of the Secretary of State to the Governor of Louisiana,* 1939–40.

procedures in Louisiana should be critically re-examined.

The Constitution of 1921 was framed under the auspices of the "good government" administration of Governor Parker and, therefore, contained provisions on registration aimed at curtailing the influence of the Orleans city machine. Those reform provisions were largely ineffective. The Ring saw to it that their immigrant supporters paid their poll taxes, while a grant of power to the governor to appoint the Orleans registrar of voters proved to be a two-edged sword. While reform governors thereby might reduce registration fraud in the city, governors in alliance with the Choctaws could accomplish exactly the opposite result. It might be noted in this connection that the power of the governor, through a state registration board, to remove parish registrars of voters also could be abused for factional gain. Although its purpose was to permit the ouster of registrars too lenient on Negro registration, Huey Long, for example, used that authority to remove the registrar of Iberville Parish apparently because his law partner happened to be an anti-Long state senator.

In the absence of meaningful party competition, Louisiana's Democratic party organization should function neutrally with reference to intra-Democratic factionalism. And, in fact, factional aggrandizement behind the mask of party neutrality has been the exception rather than the rule in recent Louisiana politics. No doubt much of the explanation lies in the detailed statutory regulation of party activity which restricted the discretion of party officials. However, where discretionary authority was retained by the party, the fact that the governor's wishes usually were respected by party committees has led to occasional factional misuse of party machinery.

By law the state central committee could select national convention delegates itself or provide for their selection by a state convention. In practice the former procedure has been followed, with but one convention (1940) being called from 1928 through 1952. Customarily the governor has "controlled" the state's delegation to the Democratic National Convention. The same law applied to the Republican party and, in practice, their delegates have been selected in state, district, and parish conventions controlled by the Old Guard faction. Thus neither party has allowed the party rank and file much say in the selection of national party delegates.

The state central committee also was authorized to determine which national party ticket constituted the slate of the Louisiana

Democratic party. That authority has lost its rubber-stamp characteristic in recent presidential elections. In 1948, the States' Rights bolters persuaded the state central committee to bless the Thurmond-Wright ticket with the rooster, the emblem of the Louisiana Democratic party. In 1952, Governor Kennon refused to acquiesce in the "loyalty oath" propounded at the Democratic National Convention on the legal grounds that only the state central committee, not the party delegation to the national convention, had the power to commit the state party to a national ticket.

On occasion, the death of a nominee prior to the general election placed significant power in the hands of the particular party committee concerned. In 1933, for example, when faced with the foregoing situation, a Congressional district party committee subservient to Huey Long designated a Long partisan as the nominee rather than hold another primary election as required by law. The governing party organ also was empowered to determine the qualifications of nominees for state office whose right to run was challenged by an elector. In the middle of the 1952 gubernatorial campaign, the state central committee was called upon to pass judgment on the claim by one candidate that another candidate was ineligible to run. It was evident to those who watched the party committee proceedings, including this writer, that Governor Earl Long played an influential, if not a dominant, role in the committee's decision.

In a similar fashion, state laws governing the conduct of party primaries have permitted only occasional abuse on the part of any of the factions composing the Democratic party. By the terms of the 1906 compulsory primary law, later incorporated into the Constitution of 1921 and modified by the primary law of 1922, political parties had to secure nominations for state and local offices, and for Congress, by direct primary election.[73] In recognition of the crucial importance of the primary in a one-party state, the primaries were conducted largely at public expense and low assessment fees encouraged candidacies at all political levels. Detailed public regulation confined the discretion of party officials with reference to the conduct of primaries to the specification of qualifications for candidates and voters.

---

[73] Towns with a population of less than 5,000 were exempt from the provisions of the mandatory primary law. Nominations for special elections were conducted in the same manner as those for regular elections.

Although the regulation of the primary machinery aimed at fair play for all candidates and factions, defects within the system were exploited skillfully by some to the detriment of others. One significant defect arose from the fact that throughout most of the period of recent Louisiana politics candidates for local office controlled the selection of poll commissioners and watchers in the gubernatorial first primary, and, until 1940, in the second primary as well.[74] From a gubernatorial candidate's viewpoint, the presence of officials in polling places who were "friendly" to him was considered to be a deterrent to the perpetration of electoral irregularities on behalf of any of his rival candidates. Particular significance was attached to equitable representation in those precincts containing sizeable proportions of illiterate voters who, under state law, were entitled to the assistance of poll commissioners in casting their ballots. One effect of this provision was to give relatively greater representation in more precincts to those candidates and factions possessed of a statewide organization and allied with local candidates in many parishes. To secure such disproportionate representation, a well-financed state faction could enter a large number of non-serious candidates in various primaries for local offices. That device, known as "dummy candidates," plagued Louisiana politics before, during, and after Huey's reign and, notwithstanding remedial legislation enacted in 1940, remains a current problem.

A novel exploitation of a loophole in the procedures governing runoff primaries provided another example of factional abuse. In a one-party state runoff primaries are designed to secure majority endorsement for elective public officials in a manner comparable to the function of the general election in competitive two-party states. In Louisiana, if no candidate for public office secured a majority of the vote cast in the first primary, then a runoff or second primary between the two leading first-primary candidates was mandatory. One exception permitted candidates for the minor state offices, in the event that no gubernatorial runoff was held, to win party nomination by plurality vote. In the 1944 state campaign, several Longite candidates for minor state offices, each of whom had secured a plurality of the first-primary vote, sought to have the Longite gubernatorial candidate withdraw from the race so as to make applicable to their

[74] Act 79 of 1922 and Act 46 of 1940. For additional discussion, see below, p. 276.

candidacies the foregoing exception. Although their attempt failed, that exception to the general rule subsequently was repealed.[75]

The Democratic party in Louisiana holds two distinct sets of primaries, each set, of course, followed by a general election. The following dates of the primaries held true for most of the period of recent Louisiana politics. A primary election for state officials and some parish officials (including state legislators, sheriffs, assessors, clerks of court, coroners, police jury and other ward officials) was held every four years on the third Tuesday of January, followed (after a runoff primary, if necessary, had been held five or six weeks after the first primary) by a general election on the first Tuesday next following the third Monday in April. A primary election for Congressional posts and some district and parish officials (including judicial offices, state and parish school boards, district attorneys, and public service commissioners) was held respectively every two years and every four years on the second Tuesday in September, followed by the general election on the same day as the national election in November.

The character of the offices to be filled in the January primary has helped to make possible the Louisiana development of a ticket system linking together candidates running for state and parish offices in a manner approximating a party slate in non-Southern states. The hope that primaries held at a different time than the gubernatorial primaries would take elective judges and educational officials out of factional politics has met with some limited success. It might be noted also that the dates of the primaries could be changed, and on occasion have been changed, by simple legislative action. This has led to the suggestion, as yet not adopted, that the dates of the primaries be fixed in the Constitution, so that subsequent changes would require the support of extraordinary legislative majorities and ratification by the people at the general election following the close of the

[75] Act 60 of 1944, which simply repealed section 79 of Act 46 of 1940, presumably was intended to forestall the occurrence of situations like that threatened in the interim between gubernatorial primaries in 1944. The method of simple repeal of section 79, however, proved defective. After the gubernatorial first primary in January, 1956, at which Earl Long was nominated, the Democratic State Central Committee declared the leading first-primary candidates for the lesser state offices, two of whom lacked majority support, to be the party nominees. In the litigation which followed, the Louisiana Supreme Court unanimously supported the Committee's action and interpretation of the law. New Orleans *Times-Picayune*, February 8, 1956.

legislative session concerned.

The capacity of the Democratic party to monopolize recent Louisiana politics rested in relatively slight part on benefits derived from law.[76] For the most part the very dominance of the Democratic party was its most effective weapon against the Republicans as a party. Those individuals who permitted their Republican leanings to lead them to register as Republicans found themselves isolated from the mainstream of state and local politics. In state politics, the battle of factions within the Democratic party substituted for the contest between parties. In presidential politics, in the light of the moribund character of state Republicanism, the Democratic party was more tolerant of the crossing of party lines by its party members. The fact that statutory regulation of party applied with fine impartiality to Republicans and Democrats alike, therefore, should not obscure the disparity of strength between them. The suggestive finding that the number of voters affiliated with the Republican party in Louisiana has more than tripled from 1940 to 1954 loses its power of suggestion when the respective figures of 1,573 and 5,772 voters are inserted. In 1940, registered Democrats totaled 701,783, and in 1954, 860,977.[77]

An appraisal of recent Louisiana politics thus must concentrate on factional politics within the Democratic party. While many Louisianians are fond of asserting that their durable bifactionalism has been equivalent to a two-party system, the fact remains that factions have not been treated, either in public status or public regulation, in the same manner as party under Louisiana law. The examples presented earlier in this section suggest that in a one-party state, where factional lines have become firm and durable, the necessary distinction between party organization and factional organization at times may become blurred. Louisianians would do well, therefore, to adapt their laws to conform to the reality of one-party factionalism rather than to maintain the fiction of a two-party system. Such action would go far toward the political neutralization of party machinery and primary procedures originally intended.

[76] The Republican party met the legal qualifications for recognition as a party throughout the 1920–52 period. For a knowledgeable interpretation of the various legal devices by which the Democratic party sought to prevent defection by its party members or by party candidates, consult V. O. Key, Jr., *Southern Politics* (New York, 1949), 428–38.

[77] *Report of the Secretary of State to the Governor of Louisiana*, 1939–40, 1953–54.

CHAPTER 2

Reform and reaction in the 1920's

PARKER, LONG, AND THE CONSERVATIVES

THE PRECEDING CHAPTER has argued that the latency of class antagonisms in nineteenth-century Louisiana provided more than a backdrop to the rise of Huey Long; historical class conflict comprised the deep emotional and symbolic content of Longism itself. Similarly, Huey Long was the fountain neither of corruption nor of progressivism in recent Louisiana politics. Many of the tactics and issues associated with Longism had their origins in the immediate pre-Huey period of politics. These observations invite a revaluation of the Louisiana Kingfish in the broad context of the historic continuum of class hostility and of the legal framework of political power already examined, and of the nature of politics immediately preceding Huey's rise to power, to which we now turn our attention.

The gentleman as reformer, 1920–24

The administration of Governor John M. Parker, a gentlemanly reformer elected in 1920 largely on his pledge to end Ring rule of the state, witnessed the development of political issues which were to aid Huey Long in his 1924 and 1928 bids for the governorship. Parker's failure to subdue the Choctaws preserved the issue of "machine rule" for Huey's exploitation during his campaigns. The Governor's mishandling of state regulation of natural gas production, particularly his inability to persuade the utility companies to supply Orleans with cheap natural gas, similarly played into Long's hands. The decision of the constitutional convention of 1921 to finance highway construction by pay-as-you-go taxation permitted Long to champion the politically more appealing policy of state bond issues.

Finally, the reaction of business and planter interests to the adoption of a state income tax and to Parker's moderate proposal to tax industries exploiting Louisiana's natural resources betrayed their selfish shortsightedness for all to see and for Huey to attack.

By applying fully his patronage authority within Orleans Parish, Governor Parker helped to bring about the defeat of Choctaw Mayor Behrman in the city election of September, 1920. The fruits of victory soon were lost, however, by apathy and petty factionalism within the city reform camp. Anti-Choctaw provisions inserted in the Constitution of 1921 met with little practical success in operation. Parker's own leaders in New Orleans, after opposing the inclusion in the Constitution of compulsory city civil service, never acted upon the milder provision permitting Orleans' adoption of a merit system which was endorsed by the convention. Both the Governor and city reformers were as blind to city vice and gambling as the Ring had been. As a consequence of the ineptitude and disintegration of the anti-machine forces, Behrman recaptured City Hall in the mayoralty campaign of 1925.

Governor Parker also mishandled two facets of the natural gas production problem in the state. Despite his conservationist leanings, Parker did not curtail effectively the wasteful use of natural gas by carbon-black manufacturing plants in the Monroe-Ouachita gas fields. A supporter of Parker wrote the Governor in 1924,

> You [Parker] were on record against the smut makers, these wasters and stealers of natural gas . . . you have become silent and inactive while the carbonites have run roughshod over you, your Constitutional Convention, your Legislature, and your conservation law that has nothing in it but soft teeth. . . .
> Governor, you have apparently gone to sleep at the switch and there is very little time left for you to wake up and prevent the awful wreck and destruction of one of Louisiana's greatest natural resources. You should do something for the people of Louisiana by conserving this rich gas field [Monroe] from pillage by foreign corporations that don't give a damn for you, your conservation laws, or the people of Louisiana. . . .[1]

Though Parker ordered his Attorney General to conduct a thorough investigation of the carbon-black problem, the issue was finally re-

[1] O. C. Dawkins to Governor John Parker, April 4, 1924, in Governor's Correspondence, Department of Archives, Louisiana State University.

solved by Huey Long through the imposition of a tax upon the carbon-black industry.

Parker's second failure in this area consisted of not fulfilling his campaign pledge to provide New Orleans with cheap natural gas, an objective which, incidentally, was opposed by the Ring. In response to a letter from a friend who had observed that this remained the major failure of his administration, Parker argued:

> . . . at no time or place have I ever pledged myself to bring gas to New Orleans. My promise was to do all that lay in my power to see whether or not this could be accomplished on practical, common sense lines, and, to that end, exhaustive surveys were made. . . . In my judgment, it is not practical, profitably or financially, to bring gas through the Valley into New Orleans, unless iron-clad contracts can be made for a long time, guaranteeing a minimum consumption at a specified price, which could justify the laying of the pipeline.[2]

These business obstacles, so impressive to a conservative governor, were of little concern to Huey Long in 1928, when he coerced the Ring and the utilities into supplying New Orleans with cheap natural gas.

Of the constitutional provisions in dispute at the 1921 convention, those relating to education and the severance tax, to public roads, and to the income tax highlighted political issues of importance in the period from Parker to Long. Governor Parker's sponsorship of the severance tax was a model of firm and enlightened conservatism. Parker felt strongly that ". . . those who are getting rich from natural resources of the state owe a debt to this and future generations, as they are removing and destroying resources created by the Almighty and were never again to be replaced."[3] Therefore he viewed a tax on the severance of natural resources from the soil as both necessary and just. The revenues received would provide for the expansion of Louisiana State University and Agricultural College without a rise in state property tax rates. Prior to his inauguration, Parker reached a "gentlemen's agreement" with representatives of natural resource industries, an agreement under which the companies agreed to pay a

[2] Governor John Parker to Judge Gilbert Dupre, December 20, 1923, in Governor's Correspondence.

[3] Governor John Parker to R. H. Yancey, March 22, 1922, in Governor's Correspondence.

2 per cent tax on the value of the resources severed without challenging the legality of the tax, while the Governor-elect pledged that his
administration would limit the tax rate to 2 per cent. The 1920 Legislature enacted the agreement as a license law with the understanding
that the severance tax principle would be incorporated in the Constitution of 1921.

By the time of the 1921 convention, other claimants pressed for
shares of the severance tax fund. Out of a tangle of rival proposals
emerged one which received Parker's blessing. At the special session
to be held following the close of the convention, the Legislature
would raise the severance tax on oil to 2.5 per cent. Twenty per cent
of total state severance tax funds were to be returned to those parishes
from which the natural resources were severed, with the maximum
amount returnable to any one parish fixed at $200,000 a year. Louisi-
ana State University would receive up to $6,500,000 from the fund
until 1924, after which time a .5 mill state property tax would be
dedicated to its support. The resource industries agreed not to regard
this as a violation of the gentlemen's agreement. Each of the major
interested parties thus won a point: Parker succeeded in placing the
details of the severance tax in the hands of the Legislature; the oil
companies obtained a "lieu" tax for their graceful acceptance of a
severance tax; and the parishes of production secured a share of
severance tax revenues.[4] In 1922, however, the Legislature increased
the severance tax on oil to 3 per cent, and when the Standard Oil
Company challenged the legality of the tax itself the state courts held
against the company.

Insofar as much of Huey Long's appeal lay in his vast program of
road construction, the convention's provisions on that topic took on
particular significance. Prior to 1921 the parishes were primarily
responsible for the construction and maintenance of roads. Few sections of the state apart from the wealthier parishes of Orleans,
Caddo, and East Baton Rouge had adequate roads. While the 1921
convention was agreed on the need for increased state aid for and
state supervision of public highway construction, conflict was evident
as to the proper methods to achieve those goals. The compromise
finally accepted by the delegates represented the victory of the J. Y.
Sanders pay-as-you-go group over the faction sponsoring the alterna-

    [4] Leslie Moses, "The Growth of Severance Taxation in Louisiana and Its Rela-
tion to the Oil and Gas Industry," *Tulane Law Review*, XVII (1943), 610.

tive fiscal plan of large bond issues. Two new taxes were permitted,
a two-cent gasoline tax and an annual license tax on motor vehicles,
and the revenue from both was allocated to the highway fund.[5] The
Legislature was forbidden to bond any of the new tax revenue for
highway purposes. In the 1921 special session of the Legislature a
highway commission of three appointive members was created; and
by 1926 Louisiana had, at least on paper, 162 "state highway routes."
Nonetheless, the year 1921 was a belated date to tackle the problem
of the deplorable condition of Louisiana roads, and the capacity of
the fiscal program advanced by the convention and by Parker to
satisfy Louisiana's highway needs was questionable.

The convention's dispute over an income tax clearly illustrated the
conservative nature of the Parker administration. Louisiana had
resisted ratification of the federal income tax amendment until
after the amendment had become operative. Apart from the severance tax funds imposed in 1920, the state relied for its revenue almost
exclusively upon a general property tax. A subcommittee of the convention's tax committee, after touring various Northern states, recommended adoption of a graduated income tax. Parker was hostile to
the recommendation, "My personal viewpoint is that a flat income
tax is preferable to the other [graduated income tax] which is cumbersome and often misunderstood."[6] The vehement opposition of the
state's financial and commercial interests led to the inclusion within
the Constitution of a mild permissive clause which fixed the maximum
rate at 3 per cent on the understanding that the income tax either
would be offset by or would serve as a substitute for personal property and license tax levies. In fact, it was not until 1934 that a state
income tax was adopted.

To many present-day Louisianians who bristle at the mention of
the name Long, the Parker administration has become the symbol of
the glory that was pre-Huey Louisiana. There is more irony than
accuracy in that view. For one thing, Parker was as atypical a governor as Huey, though obviously in different respects. Parker, for
example, deliberately minimized his influence in the Legislature and

[5] The minimum annual license for a pleasure car was $15; the license fees
were graded by use and by horsepower. The legislature enacted a one-cent
gasoline tax in 1921, and increased it to two cents in 1924.
[6] Governor John Parker to Sam C. Butterfield, October 30, 1922, in Governor's
Correspondence.

denied himself the opportunity to shape the outcome of various important primary elections during his administration.[7] More important, conservative interests that were later to attack Huey Long and to enshrine John Parker fought Parker in his own day on the issues of severance taxation and larger appropriations to state institutions. From Parker's experiences Huey Long drew lessons which, under the circumstances, were not without logic. Liberal economic policies could be effected only through a concentration of gubernatorial power and through gubernatorial employment of the same kind of tactics customarily used by professional politicians. If political ruthlessness resulted, it could be excused as a precondition for the defeat of Parker's foes, the Choctaws and the unenlightened conservative interests.

The rise of Huey Long, 1920–27

Huey P. Long, Jr., was born in 1893, the eighth of nine children, in the small town of Winnfield, Winn Parish, in north-central Louisiana. His ancestry, as Huey put it, was a mixture of English, French, Scotch, Irish, and Pennsylvania Dutch stock. Huey's father owned 320 acres of poorer soil suitable for subsistence farming, though it was constantly in danger of invasion by second-growth loblolly pine. Typical of the north Louisiana upland country, Winnfield was characterized by large numbers of hogs and children, and by a scarcity of Negroes. Cultural opportunities were limited largely to participation in Baptist revival meetings.

In 1900, the Arkansas Southern Railroad built a small lumber road through Winnfield, bringing the temporary prosperity of the sawmills. By selling some of his land to the railroad, Huey Long, Sr., was able to build a larger house and to send six of his children to college.[8]

---

[7] Typical of Parker's attitude was his response to an inquiry from a friendly editor as to what the Governor's "activity" would be with regard to a forthcoming Court of Appeal primary contest. "I have carefully read your statement," said Parker, " . . . and am going to write you very frankly to say that in my judgment, executive interferences in districts where the Governor does not live are unwarranted and savor too much of the old political dictator plan." Parker to Major George B. Campbell, September 4, 1922, in Governor's Correspondence.

[8] Huey never had to play the log-cabin theme to establish his kinship with lower-class white farmers. In his autobiography, Huey observed, "When I was

Funds ran out, however, by the time Huey was ready for college. For a brief period Huey traveled through north Louisiana selling Cottolene, a lard product for kitchen use. He later held odd jobs in the Southwest. In 1912 he married and, at his wife's insistence and with financial aid from his older brother Julius, set out to better himself. Huey completed the three-year program at the Tulane Law School in less than one year, and, in 1914, passed a special bar examination for which he had petitioned. After a brief law partnership with Julius, Huey struck out on his own as a Shreveport lawyer, specializing largely in industrial compensation cases. During the First World War Huey secured deferment from military service[9] and, in 1918, ran for his first public office.[10]

Huey sought the one state office then open to one of his age and north Louisiana residence: member of the Railway Commission from the Third District.[11] He stumped the uplands, selling himself as he formerly had sold Cottolene, adopting an anti-corporationist program and pledging to reduce utility rates. As a political unknown, Long had few supporters of influence,[12] and competed with three other candidates to unseat the popular incumbent, Burk A. Bridges, who was running for re-election. In spite of these handicaps, Long

born my parents were living in a comfortable, well-built, four-room log house. A year later we moved into a better house which was built on the same premises." *Every Man a King* (New Orleans, 1933), 2.

[9] Deferred because he had a wife and child, Huey tried to secure greater protection by seeking deferment as a public official, i.e., a notary public! Long customarily shrugged off his avoidance of military service with the observation, "I wasn't mad at nobody." Forrest Davis, *Huey Long, A Candid Biography* (New York, 1935), 70.

[10] In 1918, state Senator Harper, a close friend of Huey, ran for the Eighth Congressional District seat on a platform calling for the conscription of wealth as well as of manpower. Long defended Harper in the latter's subsequent trial for violation of the Espionage Act. In the course of his defense, Long had occasion to pen a letter to the New Orleans *Item*, in which he echoed Harper's radicalism on the theme of a minority of the people controlling the bulk of the country's wealth. This was the faint stirring of Huey's later Share-Our-Wealth plan—in fact, the statistics cited by Long in 1918 were repeated rather consistently in his espousal of Share-Our-Wealth from 1933 to 1935.

[11] The Constitution of 1898 prescribed no minimum age qualification for the office.

[12] Oscar K. Allen, of Winn Parish, and John H. Overton, an Alexandria lawyer running for the United States Senate at the same primary, supported Huey. Both backers remained friendly with Huey throughout his lifetime and both were suitably rewarded: Allen with the governorship in 1932; and Overton with a United States Senate seat later in that same year.

secured 5,515 votes to Bridges' 6,979 votes in the first primary, attracting a majority of the vote in eight of the twenty-eight parishes in the
district. In the runoff, Huey won by 635 votes (7,286 to 6,651).

Huey employed his seat on the utility regulatory commission to
settle a personal grudge with Standard Oil and to publicize his con-
demnations of corporation control of state government. Long had
invested in several independent oil companies, and Standard Oil—
in control of the pipelines servicing those companies—had declared
an embargo on all oil shipments but its own. The independents faced
ruin and Huey the loss of his investment.[13] Long countered with an
ingenuity and initiative characteristic of his entire public career.
Shelby M. Taylor, Chairman of the Railway Commission, was persuaded to endorse Huey's view that pipelines were public carriers
and therefore subject to regulation by the commission. Parker secured Huey's backing in the 1920 gubernatorial campaign by agree-
ing to support enactment of legislation confirming that decision of
the commission. But Huey soon broke with Parker over that issue.
Angered by Parker-sanctioned amendments to the pipeline bill
passed by the 1920 Legislature, Long was embittered further by
Standard Oil's failing attempt, in the 1921 convention, to oust him
from his commission seat. Long's public tirade against the Governor
as a tool of New York financial interests, followed by Parker's libel
suit against Huey—in which Huey received a suspended sentence
and a one dollar fine—completed the process of alienation between
the erstwhile allies of the 1920 campaign.

Having secured statewide notoriety through his tilts with Standard
Oil and the Governor, Huey next sought to develop a politically
useful record on the new Public Service Commission, created by the
1921 Constitution in place of the Railway Commission. His golden
opportunity came with the telephone rate controversy of 1920–22.
As a result of hearings held in 1920–21, at which Long usually was
absent, Taylor and John Michel, the other two members of the commission, granted the Cumberland Telephone and Telegraph Company a 20 per cent increase in rates. In 1922, Huey Long, then chairman of the commission,[14] reopened the case. Ultimately the rates
were lowered, and since the reductions were made retroactive to the

[13] Long, *Every Man a King*, 42.
[14] John Michel died in November of 1921, and Francis Williams was elected to
succeed him. Huey became chairman in 1922.

time of the company's application (1920), a large refund was assured
to all telephone users. Huey Long became a state hero overnight.
Long scored on other utility fronts as well, lowering the rates of the
Southwestern Gas and Electric Company, of Shreveport streetcars,
and of all intrastate railroads. Standard Oil, of course, was not overlooked: Long helped persuade the 1922 Legislature to abrogate the
gentlemen's agreement by enactment of a 3 per cent severance tax
on petroleum obtained from Louisiana wells.

By 1923, Huey Long thus was a personal force in state politics, an
ambitious St. George who could not rest content merely with slaying
utility dragons. At the age of thirty, the legal minimum for a gubernatorial candidate, Huey Long made his first bid for the highest
elective state office.

In terms of organized political support Huey placed a poor third
behind his two rivals in the 1924 gubernatorial campaign. Hewitt
Bouanchaud, Parker's Lieutenant-Governor, was supported by the
Governor and the "new regulars," a dissident Choctaw faction
headed by Colonel John Sullivan. Henry L. Fuqua, general manager
of Angola State Penitentiary, was backed by former Governor J. Y.
Sanders and the Choctaws (now also called "old regulars"). Long
had no country parish organization and depended for his Orleans
vote on the *ad hoc* "independent regulars" headed by Gus and
Francis Williams.

Long's hope that the class appeal which he carefully had built up
would compensate for his weakness in organization was shattered
by the emergence of the Ku Klux Klan issue as the foremost concern
in the campaign. The Louisiana Klan had been active sporadically in
recent years and allegedly was connected with several unsolved mur-
ders in Morehouse Parish in 1922 and 1923. Bouanchaud, a south
Louisiana Catholic, was resolutely anti-Klan. Fuqua, a Protestant
from Baton Rouge, was committed in his platform to anti-Klan legislation, though some thought his sincerity on that pledge was questionable. Long, a Protestant from north Louisiana, the section of
greatest Klan influence, did his best to straddle the issue and thereby
earned the judgment of some that he was the Klan candidate.

While his rivals stressed the Klan issue, Huey doggedly stuck to
what he termed "the real issues of the campaign," on which, of
course, he was less vulnerable. Huey likened his opponents to two
eggs from the same corporation basket, as "old Parker strut and

cluck." He breathed fire at Standard Oil, promised New Orleans natural gas from the Monroe fields, and pledged good roads to all. Huey castigated Parker for his concern with the welfare of the University and acidly observed, "our kind don't need college." Specially tailored for "our kind" were Huey's promises of free textbooks for school children, free trapping, and free fishing. Circulars reprinting complimentary press editorials on the telephone rate reductions were distributed by the thousands to people all over the state.

In the tradition of politics, Huey predicted victory barring bad weather, which would decrease the turnout of his backwoods supporters. The results of the first primary held January 15, 1924, are reported in Table 5. In the runoff, held February 19, though Long

TABLE 5. The Louisiana Vote in the 1924 Democratic
Gubernatorial First Primary

	Orleans	Other	State	% State	Parishes Carried by Majority	Parishes Carried by Plurality
Bouanchaud	23,300	60,862	84,162	35.1	22	1
Fuqua	33,194	48,188	81,382	34.0	6	7
Long	12,187	61,798	73,985	30.9	21	7
Total	68,681	170,848	239,529	100.0	49	15

SOURCE: computed from *Compilation of Primary Election Returns of the Democratic Party, State of Louisiana*, held January 15 and February 19, 1924.

refused to commit himself to either candidate, the bulk of his country parish vote went to Fuqua. In spite of Bouanchaud's frantic last-minute endorsement of Huey's free textbook plan, Fuqua was nominated by 57.8 per cent of the total vote cast. He added a 19,334 country parish lead to a 14,540 majority in Orleans to defeat Bouanchaud 125,880 to 92,006 votes.

Although it had rained heavily on the day of the first primary, Huey's defeat was not caused only, or even primarily by, bad weather. Sharp sectional cleavage was evident in the patterns of parish support of the three candidates in the gubernatorial first primary. In essence, south Louisiana went for Bouanchaud, while Long and Fuqua competed for north Louisiana and the Florida parishes. While there were traces of class cleavage—the northeast Delta parishes, for example, opposed Long—for the most part the Louisiana vote of 1924 did not reproduce the pattern of 1896, nor did it neatly predict the fairly consistent pattern that was to come from 1928 on. The essential reasons for Long's defeat thus lay in the dominance of religious, rather than class, issues in the campaign, together with the fact that two Protestants were competing against one Catholic. As Table 5 indicates, it was only because of Fuqua's strength in Orleans that he, rather than Long, had made the runoff.

The lesson of the 1924 campaign was obvious to Huey and to a host of opportunists who came over to his side during the next three years. If he could but maintain his hill parish following and make some inroads in New Orleans and south Louisiana, his election in 1928 would almost be certain. Huey devoted his energies from 1924 to 1927 along the lines of that central strategy.

In September of 1924, Huey was renominated as Third District member of the Public Service Commission. He attracted 83.9 per cent of the total vote cast and carried all twenty-eight north Louisiana parishes in the district. In that same primary, Long supported the renomination of United States Senator Joseph E. Ransdell, a north Louisiana Catholic, who defeated a Shreveport politician, Lee E. Thomas, despised by Long. In the New Orleans mayoralty primary of 1925, Huey aligned himself with Colonel Sullivan's "new regulars" in support of Maloney against Behrman. Some perceptive Behrmanites charged that Maloney was being supported "to make Huey Long governor in 1928."[15]

In the 1926 senatorial campaign, former Governor Sanders, a Protestant dry from the Florida parishes with reputed strength in north Louisiana, entered against the incumbent, Catholic and wet Edwin S. Broussard. Huey seized the opportunity to establish his kinship with south Louisianians by stumping for Broussard in all sections of the state. To avoid alienating his own upland supporters, Long ducked the liquor issue and concentrated his fire on Sanders' advocacy of toll bridges in the New Orleans area. When Broussard won by the narrow margin of 84,041 votes to 80,562, Huey Long promptly claimed credit for the victory. Table 6, however, suggests in specific terms what the significance of Huey Long's support was in this early period of his career. There is no evidence in the table to support the notion that Huey at this time had a deliverable following. Thus, it was largely the narrowness of Broussard's victory, rather than the

[15] Hermann B. Deutsch, "The Kingdom of the Kingfish," New Orleans *Item*, August 6, 1939.

TABLE 6. The Limits of Huey Long's Electoral Influence as of 1924
and 1926: A Comparison of the Vote Cast for Long and for Two
Long-Supported Candidates, for Selected Parishes

Parish	Percentage of Parish Vote Cast for		
	Huey Long Gub., 1924	Ransdell Sen., 1924	Broussard Sen., 1926
Red River	76.4%	37.8%	47.4%
Jackson	75.3	38.1	41.6
Winn	70.0	30.2	39.8
West Carroll	68.0	30.0	29.1
Grant	67.8	30.4	39.5
Caldwell	67.6	34.1	41.8
Union	67.6	24.7	48.2
Vernon	67.5	35.2	39.3
LaSalle	67.3	38.0	33.6
State	30.9	54.9	51.1

SOURCE: computed from *Compilation of Primary Election Returns of the
Democratic Party, State of Louisiana*, held January 15 and February 19, 1924;
ibid., held September 9, 1924; *ibid.*, held September 14, 1926.

high degree of support accorded him by those north Louisiana parishes loyal to Long in 1924, that permitted Huey to stress his contribution to the outcome. In that same primary election, Dudley J.
LeBlanc, an anti-Long candidate, decisively defeated Shelby Taylor
for the Second District Public Service Commission post, which covered the Florida parishes and all of south Louisiana except the
extreme southeast section. Shortly afterwards, Huey was replaced
by Francis Williams as chairman of the Commission.[16]

While Huey mended and extended his political fences, the Fuqua
administration indirectly aided his chances for 1928. The 1924 Legislature, by enacting three anti-Klan measures, wrote an end to the
religious issue which had restricted Long's appeal in 1924 to north
Louisiana. On the other hand, O. H. Simpson, Fuqua's Lieutenant-
Governor, had gubernatorial ambitions which rivaled those of Huey.
When Simpson succeeded to the governorship upon the death of
Fuqua, in late 1926, he promptly set about to create a patronage
machine capable of securing his victory in 1928. The gubernatorial

[16] Williams broke with Long in 1926, when Huey attempted to take credit
for the favorable ruling of the Interstate Commerce Commission in the Galveston
rate case.

campaign, however, witnessed a class revolution in the making which rendered ineffective a primary reliance upon such traditional weapons of politics.

The redneck as reformer, 1928

Huey Long entered the 1928 campaign with considerably greater press and political support than he had enjoyed in 1924. The Sullivan faction backed him in New Orleans[17] and Colonel Ewing, publisher of major newspapers in New Orleans, Shreveport, and Monroe, also supported his candidacy. With the New Orleans *Times-Picayune* and the *Item-Tribune* each behind one of his rivals, it was possible that Huey had the largest press backing, in terms of circulation, of all the candidates.

Neither of his two opponents, by himself, represented very much of a threat to Huey's chances of victory. Governor Simpson, who had been secretary of the state Senate for twenty years, reputedly had a host of friends scattered around the state and had Paul Maloney and the "new regulars" behind him in New Orleans. The Choctaws backed Eighth District Congressman Riley J. Wilson, whose sole claim to fame in fourteen years of Congressional service lay in his contemporary status as official voice of the state in its argument with Coolidge and Hoover over the apportionment of the cost of flood relief measures.[18]

The principal concern to Huey was the likelihood that his oppo-

[17] Major Behrman of New Orleans had died in early 1926, some eight months after taking office again. Sullivan, who had broken with Maloney, and Huey, who had broken with the Williams brothers, worked together in support of Broussard in 1926. Sullivan's known tie-up with racing, gambling, and liquor interests caused Huey's campaign manager to resign after Long accepted an alliance with Sullivan for the state primary. In his autobiography, Long related that he worried over the question of whether to accept Sullivan in order to get Ewing's [the publisher] support, and finally " . . . settled the issue to try to get everybody." *Every Man a King*, 96. Huey subsequently regretted his decision, since his Orleans vote proved to be no better than in 1924.

[18] Hoover, sent by President Coolidge to inspect the flood damage in Louisiana in 1927, had declared the disaster to be a national responsibility. Upon returning to Washington, however, Hoover urged that the affected states should bear the costs equally with the federal government. Wilson, as Chairman of the House flood control committee, was in a strategic position to press the claims of Louisiana.

nents would combine forces against him in the runoff. It was no secret that the Choctaws expected that their strength would place Wilson in the runoff and that Simpson then would throw his support to Wilson. To counter the threat of this alliance Huey employed divide and conquer tactics so effectively prior to the first primary as to make later co-operation between his rivals most unlikely.[19] Huey then subjected each of his opponents to withering attack. Wilson's "flood record" was dismissed with ridicule: "Wilson has been in Congress fourteen years, and this year [1927] the water went fourteen feet higher than ever before, giving him a flood record of one foot of high water a year."[20] Simpson was raked for his padding of the number of employees of the Conservation Commission, "a coonchasin' and possum-watchin' brigade, that does its job cruising around in a fancy boat in the Gulf."[21]

The Orleans bridge controversy provides a useful illustration of the type of pre-Long political shenanigan which permitted Huey to adopt the role of reformer. New Orleans needed an outlet bridge, either over Lake Pontchartrain or across the Mississippi River or both. In 1918 an approved constitutional amendment provided for a toll-free highway outlet by another and longer route across Chef Menteur and the Rigolets. In 1924, however, toll-bridge interests in alliance with the Choctaws persuaded the Legislature to commit the state to a toll-bridge policy in the Orleans area. In spite of Huey's protests and the filing of several law suits, Fuqua let a contract to the Watson-Williams syndicate (whose legal counsel was former Governor Sanders) to build a toll bridge across Lake Pontchartrain along the route authorized by the 1918 law. Preliminary preparations for the bridge had been completed when Fuqua died. Simpson, in an effort to steal Long's thunder, announced a free-bridge policy. But the syndicate, apparently trusting that Choctaw candidate Wilson would win or that the public would lose interest in the issue, went ahead with construction. Huey warned that they were building "the most expensive buzzard roost . . . in the United States." Huey was as good as his word. As Governor, Long ordered construction to be begun on a free bridge via the Chef-Rigolets route, which was completed in mid-1930. In early 1929, the toll-bridge company went into

[19] See Long's own description, *Every Man a King*, 101–103.
[20] Quoted by Davis, *Huey Long*, 91.
[21] Quoted by Harnett T. Kane, *Louisiana Hayride* (New York, 1941), 56.

receivership, and, in 1938, the state purchased the bridge for
$600,000 and converted it into a free bridge.

Long complemented his negative attacks by a variety of substantive pledges similar to those made in 1924: free textbooks; free
bridges;[22] better roads; improved schools; natural gas for Orleans;
repeal of a recently-enacted tobacco tax; enactment of a new occupational tax on Standard Oil; and greater care of the wards of the state.
His criticisms and promises merged in an emotional appeal to the
masses to overthrow the "old gang" and the corporations, in an invitation to lower-class whites to displace the ruling alliance and grasp
political power for themselves. Huey's speech to a Cajun audience,
however melodramatic and overblown the imagery, served to fix
the campaign of 1928 as the culmination of the class struggle in
Louisiana.

> And it is here [at the Evangeline Oak] that Evangeline waited
> for her lover Gabriel who never came. . . . But Evangeline is not
> the only one who has waited here in disappointment. Where are
> the schools that you have waited for your children to have that
> have never come? Where are the roads and the highways that you
> spent your money to build, that are no nearer now than ever
> before? Where are the institutions to care for the sick and the dis-
> abled? Evangeline wept bitter tears in her disappointment. But
> they lasted through only one lifetime. Your tears in this country,
> around this oak, have lasted for generations. Give me the chance
> to dry the tears of those who still weep here.[23]

Table 7 reports the results of the first primary held January 17,
1928.

The New Orleans *Times-Picayune*, backing Simpson but despising
Wilson, was the first major paper to call for Wilson's withdrawal.
Perhaps because professional politicians dislike backing an obvious
loser the Simpsonites announced their support of Huey Long. Perhaps the fact that Simpson later accepted a $5,000 per year state
attorneyship from Governor Long provides the best explanation.

---

[22] Contrary to lore, Huey did not rule out toll bridges entirely. His free-bridge
pledge contained a loophole: " . . . unless in some instances it should be necessary for the State itself temporarily to collect a small toll for the discharge of the
burden in building such structures, but not one cent for profit." Huey Long,
speech at Alexandria, August 3, 1927.

[23] Quoted by Hodding Carter, "Huey Long: American Dictator," in Isabel
Leighton (ed.), *The Aspirin Age* (New York, 1949), 349.

TABLE 7. The Louisiana Vote in the 1928 Democratic
Gubernatorial Primary

	Orleans	Other	State	% State	Parishes Carried by Majority	Plurality
Long	17,819	109,023	126,842	43.9	38	9
Simpson	22,324	58,002	80,326	27.8	6	3
Wilson	38,244	43,503	81,747	28.3	4	4
Total	78,387	210,528	288,915	100.0	48	16

SOURCE: computed from *Compilation of Primary Election Returns of the Democratic Party, State of Louisiana,* held January 17, 1928.

Whatever the case, Simpson's desertion upset the second primary calculations of the Choctaws. Wilson withdrew, obviating the necessity for a runoff, and Long was nominated as the Democratic candidate for governor.

The personal character of Huey's victory was emphasized by the defeat of several members of his state ticket and by the small number of Long-aligned state legislators elected. Long carried with him into office only Lieutenant-Governor Paul Cyr and Treasurer H. B. Conner. In his autobiography, Huey reported that only eighteen members of the House and nine members of the Senate had supported his gubernatorial candidacy.[24]

The distribution of Long's votes (see Figure 3), however, supports the thesis of a continuing class struggle rooted in the history of Louisiana and also serves to fix in broad outline the patterns of electoral allegiance throughout the period of recent state politics. Huey, in 1928, retained the allegiance of the northern uplands and attracted only a slightly higher proportion of the vote in New Orleans than in 1924. The relative increase in his statewide strength thus derived largely from the degree of support offered him by many south Louisiana parishes. The demise of the Klan issue, together with Huey's deliberate actions from 1924 to 1927, had enabled Long's class appeal to undercut sectionalism based on religious differences. The urban electorate, for example, in the north Louisiana parishes of Caddo, Ouachita, and Rapides shifted from the upper half of all parishes in support of Long in 1924 to the lower half in 1928. The north Louisiana Delta areas, as might be expected, maintained anti-Long behavior evident in 1924.

[24] *Every Man a King,* 107.

The data in Table 8 suggest that urbanism generally was associated with a higher degree of anti-Longism.[25] It might be noted
that the parish percentage listed in that table, because it includes
the lower percentage of the ward containing the parish seat, mini-
mizes the difference between the two proportions. Even so, in all
fourteen cases the direction of the difference is consistent, and in
eight cases the difference between the relevant figures is greater than
10 per cent.

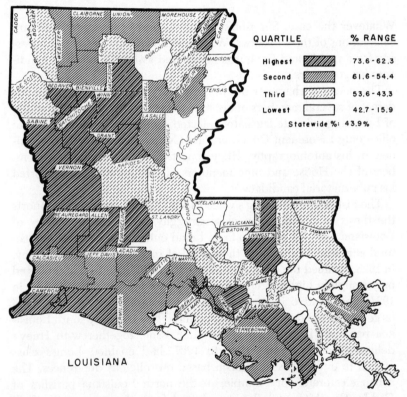

QUARTILE		% RANGE
Highest		73.6 - 62.3
Second		61.6 - 54.4
Third		53.6 - 43.3
Lowest		42.7 - 15.9

Statewide %: 43.9%

FIGURE 3. Quartile map: proportion of parish vote cast for Huey Long,
1928 Democratic gubernatorial primary.

SOURCE: same as that for Table 7.

[25] For an explanation of the conservatism of small urban centers, see Hodding
Carter, *Southern Legacy* (Baton Rouge, 1950), 158–59.

TABLE 8. Anti-Longism in Smaller Cities and Towns: A Comparison of the Vote Cast for Huey Long, by Selected Parishes and by Selected Wards Containing Parish Seats, 1928 Democratic Gubernatorial Primary

Parish	Parish Seat	Ward Containing Parish Seat	Percentage of Vote Cast for Huey Long, 1928, by	
			Ward Containing Parish Seat	Parish, Including Preceding Ward
Natchitoches	Natchitoches	1	44.7%	64.0%
Jackson	Jonesboro	2	47.5	62.7
LaSalle	Jena	4	55.8	60.5
Union	Farmerville	1	49.0	54.4
Webster	Minden	4	45.0	56.8
Lincoln	Ruston	1	32.6	46.8
Caldwell	Columbia	4	43.0	60.0
West Carroll	Oak Grove	4	55.1	65.9
Bienville	Arcadia	1	45.5	59.8
Jefferson Davis	Jennings	2	53.8	55.1
St. Helena	Greensburg	2	52.8	69.3
Vermilion	Abbeville	3	55.1	60.5
Iberville	Plaquemine	2	44.1	52.2
Terrebonne	Houma	3	55.0	58.1

SOURCE: computed from *Compilation of Primary Election Returns of the Democratic Party, State of Louisiana,* held January 17, 1928.

A cleavage between planter and farmer also was evident in the 1928 primary. Strong Long sentiment within the Delta was confined to those sections distant from rich bottom land. In Red River Parish, for example, the three rural eastern wards farthest from the Delta proper each gave Huey more than 70 per cent of the vote, while the two Delta wards each gave only about 40 per cent of its vote to Long.

Huey's 1928 race thus invoked, with more consistency and greater strength, the voting tendencies observed in the 1896 gubernatorial election. The class revolution of 1928 had its tap root in Louisiana history. But the hopes of conservatives that this latest class movement would prove also to be abortive and transitory were illusory. As all Louisianians were to note, Huey Long was, indeed, *sui generis.*

A measure of the class revolution that was Longism was provided by conservative reaction to the Governor's 1928 program. To the outside observer, the policies advocated by Huey in 1928 seemed moderate. Nonetheless, it was only through cajolery and patronage that

Long was able to persuade a majority of the Legislature to go along
with him. Huey met with even less legislative co-operation, however, in his attempts to consolidate control over administrative agencies and state jobs. The conservatives, perhaps alarmed more by the
direction than the actual content of Longite policy, pretended grave
anxiety over Long's tactics. In 1929, the urban-planter alliance translated its fears into near-successful counterattack.

Much of Governor Long's address to the Legislature was devoted
to castigating the economic-political alliance which thus far had
prevented New Orleans from securing inexpensive natural gas. The
situation is worth recounting for the light it shed on the character of
pre-Long politics. In 1921, New Orleans granted New Orleans Public
Service, Inc. (NOPSI) a new franchise which stipulated that the city
could buy the properties of that utility company at a specified evaluation and operate them under municipal ownership. By 1928, NOPSI
still monopolized the supply of power to city consumers, including
artificial gas at the high rate of $1.35 per thousand cubic feet
(MCF). Several interests clamored for the opportunity to sell New
Orleans cheaper natural gas from the Ouachita fields, but NOPSI
had persuaded the Commission Council of New Orleans of the "im-
practicability" of such offers.[26] Governor Long's criticism, unlike that
of Parker, was followed by direct action. Long had Senator Fernandez of Orleans introduce a set of bills authorizing the Commission Council of Orleans to issue bonds to pay for the purchase of
NOPSI's properties. Using those bills as leverage, Huey forced
NOPSI and the Choctaws to agree to allow natural gas to be piped
into Orleans, at a rate to the consumer of $0.90 MCF plus a $0.25
monthly meter charge. Although some charged that the rate fixed
was unnecessarily high, implying a deal between Long and NOPSI,
none could deny that Huey both had fulfilled his campaign pledge
and had beaten the Ring at its own professional political game.[27]

Another of Long's major accomplishments at the 1928 session was
the enactment of a free textbook law. The necessary funds were supplied by changing the base of the severance tax from the value to the

[26] *Report on the Commission Council Hearings into the Question of Natural
Gas*, 1928, Archives of the New Orleans Public Library.
[27] For the details of Huey's maneuverings, see Hermann Deutsch, "The Kingdom of the Kingfish," New Orleans *Item*, August 11, 1939; on the latter charge,
see for example, John K. Fineran, *The Career of a Tinpot Napoleon* (New
Orleans, 1932), 39–44.

quantity of the resource severed, and by allocating severance tax funds to payment of the cost of the textbooks. It should be noted that all elementary- and high-school children—in public, private, and parochial schools—were the beneficiaries of Huey's policy. Huey by-passed the constitutional prohibition on public aid to religious institutions by adoption of the argument that the state was furnishing books to the children directly and was merely using schools as convenient distribution centers. The validity of the free textbook law was upheld by the United States Supreme Court in 1930.[28]

The textbook law, perhaps more than any other act in Huey s career, cemented the loyalty of many Catholic south Louisianians to Longism. Legislative behavior on the measure gave evidence both of sectionalism and factionalism. A Senate amendment to restrict the distribution of free textbooks to public schools was defeated by a vote (16 yes, 21 no). Twelve of the sixteen votes in support of the amendment were cast by senators representing districts in north Louisiana and the Florida parishes. But the senators from the core areas of Longism in north Louisiana (Senate districts 24, 30, 32, 33) opposed the amendment.[29] Another measure of factionalism may be had by noting that four of the six north Louisiana senators who signed the round robin that ended the 1929 impeachment session of Huey Long had voted, in 1928, against the foregoing amendment to the free textbook law.

Passage of a constitutional amendment authorizing the issuance of $30,000,000 of bonds enabled Long to begin to meet his promise of free roads and bridges. The tobacco tax was repealed, but new taxes on malt and on carbon black were enacted. Huey vetoed a moderate tick-eradication bill to placate small upland farmers who were fearful of its cost and effects. While appropriations for state charitable institutions were increased, Long vetoed extra funds for the Public Service Commission because a majority of its members was not of his faction.

In his efforts to extend and consolidate gubernatorial control of patronage, Long met considerable legislative resistance. While he

[28] *Cochran* v. *Louisiana State Board of Education*, 281 U.S. 370 (1930).
[29] *Official Journal of the Proceedings of the Senate of Louisiana*, 1928, 714. Since all of the frequent references in this study to factional alignments of state legislators, on bills and by sessions, are based on an analysis of the pertinent *Official Journal of the Proceedings* of the House or the Senate of Louisiana, repetitious individual citations will be omitted in the rest of this study.

was permitted to reorganize the Orleans Levee Board and the State
Board of Health, the Legislature rejected proposals which, in effect,
would have given Long control of the governing board of New
Orleans Charity Hospital and of the Orleans Courthouse Commission. Another Long bill which sought to replace the elective assessors
of Orleans by one gubernatorial appointee also was defeated. Nonetheless, by a thorough exercise of traditional gubernatorial authority,
Huey Long achieved considerable success by late 1928 in amassing
large numbers of state jobs directly under his control.

The Governor's justification for seeking to enlarge his patronage
powers consisted of the politician's classical plea of self-defense
against the prior aggression of enemies. Long's claim, however, had
some basis in fact. The Choctaws, for example, by challenging the
legality of the revamped severance tax, had threatened to tie up the
free textbook funds for the 1928 fall term. When Huey resorted to
borrowing on authorization of the Board of Liquidation of the State
Debt (an agency controlled by the Governor), bankers were loathe
to make the loan in view of the Choctaw suit. The loan was forthcoming only after the Governor threatened to delay indefinitely the
state's repayment of debts owed to the particular banks in question.
The New Orleans machine, fearful of strengthening Long's power,
also opposed ratification of the constitutional amendment passed by
the 1928 Legislature authorizing the issuance of $30,000,000 of bonds
for highway construction purposes. When every parish but Caddo
endorsed the amendment in the November general election, however, a December special session of the Legislature swiftly enacted
Huey's highway program.

Perhaps made overconfident by his smooth control over the December special session, Huey next committed the blunder of breaking with two allies, Cyr and Sullivan, whose help he could have used
in the dark days of impeachment to come.[30] Lieutenant-Governor
Cyr, had he been loyal to Huey, doubtless could have obstructed the
progress of Long's impeachment trial in the Senate. Similarly, Sullivan's influence in Orleans might have stayed or moderated the drive

[30] Cyr fell out with Huey ostensibly over the latter's refusal to commute the
first death sentence imposed on a murderess in Louisiana. Huey's break with
Sullivan and Ewing supposedly occurred over Sullivan's connection with gambling interests. So deeply did Sullivan come to hate Long that he later returned
to the "old regulars" as a mere co-leader of the Third Ward, with but half a vote
in the Choctaw caucus.

to oust the Governor.

Unaware of his imminent impeachment, Huey Long could look back on his first eight months in office with justifiable pride. Fulfillment of many of his campaign promises had added up to a progressive and free-spending program, doubtless resented by conservatives but one which fell far short of radicalism. His far-ranging quest for patronage constituted no sharp break with Louisiana tradition; even John Parker employed gubernatorial patronage in his battle with the Choctaws.

Why, then, was Huey Long impeached and tried? While the anti-Longs stated their position in the terminology of "honest government," it may be suggested that they were more concerned with the outcome of the game of politics than with how the game was played. Resistance by conservatives to Parker was converted into impeachment of Long essentially because Long sought to root his power in the loyalty of the masses of voters. Inevitably, as the lower classes were made aware of their political strength, there would occur a restructuring of politics disadvantageous to the interests of the upper classes. The anti-Longs resorted to impeachment, then, in order to prevent a distasteful present from becoming an unbearable future.

The anti-Longs counterattack: the impeachment of 1929

Long touched the sensitive nerve of the business-planter alliance by calling a special session of the Legislature in March of 1929 to enact an occupational tax of five cents a barrel on refined crude oil, a measure which had been introduced but later withdrawn in the 1928 regular session. In the belief that he had the pledged support of two-thirds of the legislators, the number required for the suspension of legislative rules, the Governor initially called for a brief six-day session. When it became apparent that his program would meet considerable opposition, Huey issued a supplemental call extending the session for eighteen days, beginning March 20. It was during that period that the drive for his impeachment gathered full steam.

The business elements of the state, under the leadership of Standard Oil, undoubtedly comprised the major force in the anti-Long crusade.[31] To that core were recruited such political enemies of Huey

[31] D. R. Weller, president of Standard Oil of Louisiana, took a suite at the

as the Choctaws, Cyr, Ewing, and Sullivan, and a flood of opportunistic politicians once pro-Long but now deserting what they
believed to be the sinking ship. As the events of March, April, and
May hastened to a climax, Huey wryly commented: ". . . few callers
knocked on my doors. At last I had the peace of quiet and solitude
for which I had so often longed."[32]

On March 20 the House protested Long's personal lobbying on the
floor, and the Governor left the chamber one step ahead of the
sergeant-at-arms. On the 21st of March, Lieutenant-Governor Cyr
accused Huey of approving the leasing of more than $1,500,000
worth of Louisiana land to a Texas oil company on terms grossly
unfair to the state.[33] On that same day, Huey's crude intimidation of
the press in the Manship affair was revealed.[34] On March 22 the
Shreveport *Journal* called for an investigation of the Governor, with
a view toward his impeachment, in an editorial entitled, "Time to
End Tyranny." By March 24 a worried Huey Long was urging legislators to suggest their own tax solutions to satisfy the financial needs
of state charitable institutions and schools. But the tide of anti-Long
charges continued to rise, culminating in a most grave—or a most
absurd—accusation which led to events helpful to the forces in favor
of impeachment.

At the night session of the Legislature on March 25, a date thence-

Hotel Heidelberg in Baton Rouge for the length of the session. When he died
several years later, the obituary columns of the New York press described him as
a prime force in the campaign to oust Long (Davis, *Huey Long*, 105). Standard
Oil was so important to the economy of Baton Rouge that the Manship-owned
Baton Rouge papers reversed their traditional neutrality toward all state administrations and vehemently opposed the Long tax and the Long administration.

[32] Long, *Every Man a King*, 138.

[33] Consult the Baton Rouge *State-Times*, March 27, 1929, for a full review of
Cyr's charge. Long retorted that his approval constituted a routine permission
to drill, and that the lease in question was transferred during the Parker
administration.

[34] Editor Charles Manship detailed the affair in a front-page editorial in the
Baton Rouge *State-Times*, March 21, 1929, entitled, "This, Gentlemen, Is The
Way Your Governor Fights." Huey apparently had warned Manship that if he
persisted in his opposition to the tax, there would be published "a list of names
of the people who are fighting me who have relatives in the insane asylum."
Manship continued by noting that he had a brother, Douglas, who was in the
East Louisiana hospital undergoing psychiatric treatment. "I might say, however," concluded Manship in the editorial, "that my brother Douglas . . . is about
the same age as the Governor. He was in France in 1918, wearing the uniform
of a United States soldier, while Governor Long was campaigning for office."

forth to be known as "Bloody Monday," Representative Morgan of Caddo Parish demanded recognition from Speaker Fournet (a Long-ite) on a point of personal privilege. It was an open secret that Morgan intended to read an affidavit accusing Governor Long of seeking to arrange the murder of anti-Long state Representative J. Y. Sanders, Jr., of Baton Rouge, a son of the former Governor. Speaker Fournet instead recognized a Long stalwart who motioned for immediate adjournment *sine die*. On the roll-call vote on the adjournment motion, the electric tally board behind the Speaker recorded the individual votes every which way. Pandemonium ensued after Fournet declared the House to be adjourned. Order was restored only after it was discovered that the voting machine had locked since the last roll-call. The Speaker's action was declared illegal, and the House remained in session.[35] The next day the House voted its overwhelming opposition to any form of an "occupational tax on industry," and the Senate passed a resolution solemnly warning Huey that it was impervious both to his threats and to his promises.

In its edition of March 27, the conservative New Orleans *Times-Picayune* placed its stamp of approval on the movement to oust Long from office. "The reason for this is that he is temperamentally and otherwise unfit to hold the office. His tactics and methods reveal him to be a cruel political tyrant, willing to resort to almost any expediency to carry out his own wishes and purposes. . . ." Of the two constitutional methods provided for removal of a governor, namely recall and impeachment, the anti-Longs, for obvious reasons, chose the latter. The House thereupon assumed its role as a jury of indictment, weighing the evidence presented on nineteen general articles of impeachment.[36]

---

[35] All but the most extreme anti-Longs accept this version of the story. Even the hostile *Times-Picayune,* March 26, 1929, did, for as Long pointed out, the clerk of the voting machine was a nephew of Senator Ransdell, who was by then a political enemy of Huey.

[36] The nineteen articles charged Huey with the following offenses: use of his appointive power to influence the judiciary, and boasting of that use of power; misuse, misapplication, and misappropriation of state funds; bribery and attempted bribery of state legislators; securing of undated resignations from appointees to the Orleans Levee Board; contracting illegal loans for the state; removal of public school officials for political purposes; unlawful use of the militia to subordinate the civil authority, with reference to early 1929 raids on New Orleans gambling; attempting to force parish officials to follow his dicta-

Although the charges ran the gamut from trivia to matters of import, at the very least the hearings served to publicize some of the less savory aspects of the Long administration.[37] The House processed the charges so slowly, however, that only the Manship press-intimidation item had been voted on favorably by April 6, the adjournment date of the Legislature, as set in Governor Long's call. By its own action the House extended its session, subsequently voted on ten items, seven of them favorably, and sent the latter on to the Senate.

The timing of these actions in the House was seized upon by Huey and his counsel as the basis for his legal defense in the Senate. The Governor's Exception and Demurrer No. 1 argued that House action after the date of adjournment specified in his call was illegal. In effect, Huey recognized the Manship charge as the only legal item of impeachment. On May 15, the Senate rejected Huey's argument by (19 yes–20 no) vote. Long's Exception and Demurrer No. 2 urged that in the Manship affair Huey had acted in a personal rather than official capacity.[38] The Senate, on May 16, sustained Huey's

tion in political litigation as the price of permitting passage of legislation affecting such parishes; habitually carrying concealed weapons; violent abuse of officials and citizens visiting him on public business; gross misconduct in public places; publicly flouting the state and federal constitutions, and usurping the power of the Legislature; purchasing a $20,000 ice-machine for Angola Penitentiary without advertising for bids; intimidating the press in the Manship affair; demolishing the Executive Mansion without express legislative authority and spending $150,000 for a new Mansion; disposing of and destroying furniture in the Executive Mansion without authorization or accounting; unlawfully paroling a convict from the penitentiary; repeatedly appearing within the bar of the House of Representatives in violation of the state Constitution; suborning murder in attempting to hire "Battling" Bozeman to assassinate J. Y. Sanders, Jr. In addition, on April 26, the House voted to send a charge of general incompetence to the Senate.

[37] Sensational high spots of the hearings were Abe Shushan's testimony concerning the proximity of a hula-girl to Long's knee at a party, and Seymour Weiss's stubborn refusal to reveal how several hundred dollars in the Governor's fund to entertain other chief executives had been expended. The former incident caused old Judge Dupre to attack Huey for spending "state money in a whore house . . ." while the latter occasioned a flood of telegrams from governors who had recently visited Louisiana, each protesting the possible inference of immoral entertainment. The *Official Journal of the Proceedings* for the impeachment session (Fifth Extraordinary Session of the Legislature), unlike the usual *Journal*, contains a full record of debate and is immensely valuable for an understanding of the politics of Long's impeachment.

[38] In his defense of Huey on the Manship charge, state Representative Allen J. Ellender admitted, "I really and honestly believe that the charges as prosecuted

point by a 21–18 vote.

The latter vote provided the opportunity for Long's affiliates in the Senate to bring the impeachment trial to an immediate close. Fifteen of the thirty-nine senators, each suitably rewarded by Long at later dates,[39] brought forth the celebrated round robin. "The undersigned, constituting more than one-third of the membership of this Senate, sitting as a court of impeachment, do now officially announce that by reason of the unconstitutionality and invalidity of all impeachment charges against Huey P. Long, Governor, they will not vote to convict thereon. . . ." Since conviction required an absolute two-thirds majority vote in the Senate, the anti-Longs had no choice but to acquiesce in the "round robineers'" motion for immediate adjournment *sine die*. Huey Long thus emerged the victor in the supreme battle of his career.

Anti-Longs have never ceased to belabor the climax of the impeachment trial as a deliberate mockery of justice. That view conveniently overlooked the fact that "justice" was not present, hence could not be mocked. The impeachment was politically inspired from start to finish and, therefore, the round robin was of a piece with the rest of the play. An examination of factional alignments offers convincing proof that most of the legislative cast, Long and anti-Long, knew its lines before the impeachment drama was performed.

The vote on Huey's argument that all items other than the Manship charge were illegal constitutes a useful measure of impeachment attitudes for the members both of the House and the Senate. The House rejected that contention, embodied in a minority report of one of its subcommittees, by a 35–61 vote. The Senate, it will be recalled, defeated Long's Exception and Demurrer No. 1 by a 19–20 vote. The classification of legislators into pro- and anti-impeachment categories in Tables 9 and 10 is based upon the foregoing two roll-call votes.

Table 9 indicates that one could have predicted with fair accuracy

---

might result in a conviction of blackmail . . . ." However, urged Ellender, Long had committed the action in his personal, rather than official, capacity for which he might be punished in the criminal courts if Manship saw fit to sue. Snorted Representative Lavinius Williams, "What a weak, weak defense that is." *Official Journal of the Proceedings, op. cit.*, 279–83.
    [39] Kane, *Louisiana Hayride*, 77.

TABLE 9. The Factional Basis of the Legal Impeachment of Huey
Long: Relation Between Impeachment Vote of Representatives,
1929, and Parish Support of Long in 1928 Democratic
Gubernatorial Primary

| | No. of Parishes in Each Quartile of Support for Huey Long, 1928 | | | |
	High	2nd	3rd	Low
32 parishes, 61 of whose 64 Representatives voted for legality of all eight impeachment items	3	5	13	11
34 parishes, 35 of whose 41 Representatives voted for legality of only the Manship impeachment item*	14	10	5	5

*Totals exceed 64 parishes, 16 parishes per quartile, and 100 Representatives
because split delegations are counted in each category.

SOURCE: Figure 3, and *Official Journal of the Proceedings of the House of
Representatives and the Senate of Louisiana*, Fifth Extraordinary Session, 1929,
85.

the impeachment attitudes of representatives on the basis of relative
parish performance in Huey Long's gubernatorial race in 1928.

Table 10 deals more directly with the factional loyalties of legislators themselves. Of all of Long's major measures enacted in the
1928 regular session, his bill to reorganize the State Board of Health
(HB 315) produced the most opposition votes in both chambers. As
Table 10 indicates, virtually all the legislators opposing that bill in

TABLE 10. The Factional Basis of the Legal Impeachment of Huey
Long: Relation Between Vote of Representatives and Senators
on Key Bill, 1928, and Their Subsequent Vote on Impeachment, 1929

Position on 1928 Bill to Reorganize State Board of Health (HB 315)	Voted for Legality of All Eight Impeachment Items, 1929	Voted for Legality of Only the Manship Impeachment Item, 1929	No Vote 1929
Against Bill:			
40 Representatives	40	0	0
17 Senators	13	4	0
For Bill:			
58 Representatives	21	32	5
21 Senators	7	13	1

SOURCE: *Official Journal of the Proceedings of the House of Representatives
of Louisiana* (June 21), and *of the Senate of Louisiana* (July 4), 1928 Regular
Session; *Official Journal* cited in Table 9, pp. 85 and 243.

1928 turned up in the pro-impeachment camp in 1929, while a clear majority of the legislators in both houses who supported the 1928 bill subsequently opposed impeachment.

The behavior of legislators within the 1929 session itself further testified to the political character of the impeachment proceedings. It will be recalled that the House acted on eleven items of impeachment, passing favorably upon eight of them. Of the sixty-one representatives who voted for the legality of all eight items, fifty-two voted in support of at least nine of those eleven items, including thirty-eight who supported all eleven items. Similarly, thirty-four of the thirty-five representatives who endorsed Huey's argument that only the Manship charge was legal also voted against the Manship item. Thirty-one senators (sixteen of them pro-Huey and fifteen anti-Huey) out of thirty-nine cast their separate votes on Huey's two exceptions and demurrers in the same factional direction. Finally, it is not surprising to learn that the distribution of the votes of the "round robineers" on the key 1928 bill (HB 315) was as follows: thirteen for the bill, one against, and one not voting.

The incredible sloppiness with which the anti-Longs pressed their case against the Governor becomes understandable in the light of the politics of impeachment uncovered above. The items were selected indiscriminately, the hearings were rambling, and effort was diffused. There was no justification for the Manship item to have been the sole charge processed by the original adjournment date of April 6. Had they anticipated a judicial judgment on their case, no body of able conservatives would have relied upon "a farrago of accusations, prepared without intelligence or discretion."[40]

The failure of the great anti-Long counterattack was most costly to their cause. Huey spoke grimly of the future, "I used to try to get things done by saying 'please.' That didn't work and now I am a dynamiter. I dynamite 'em out of my path."[41] The abortive impeachment of Long thus served to intensify his class program and his lust for personal power. The Louisiana hayride had begun in earnest.

[40] Ibid., 73.
[41] Davis, Huey Long, 119.

CHAPTER 3

The Kingfish swallows the pelican

HUEY LONG, 1930–1935

THE STORY OF Long and Louisiana was a tall saga interspersed by Huey's victorious guffaws and by the outraged protests of his opponents. To the enactment of class reforms Long brought to bear a dramatic mixture of arrogance, vindictiveness, and personal ambition. Indeed, the controversy over the evaluation of Long hinges largely on a determination of which of Huey's drives subsumed the others. There can be few doubts, however, about the importance of Longism to the form and content of recent Louisiana politics. Alone of the rude class agitators of the new South, Huey Long created a kingdom and thereby left his indelible mark on the subsequent politics of the Pelican State.

Governor-Senator Huey Long, 1930–33

After shortcircuiting the impeachment drive, Huey turned to laying the groundwork for his control over the 1930 regular session, at which his "good roads measure," a $60,000,000 highway bond bill, was the most controversial item. An understanding was reached with the business interests whereby the Governor promised not to enact any occupational or license tax during his term of office in exchange for business' support of alternative schemes of taxation. The Choctaws were wooed by Long's hands-off attitude in the New Orleans mayoralty contest of January, 1930,[1] and by Long's vague hints that

[1] Long subsequently regretted his decision because Choctaw T. Semmes Walmsley defeated Francis Williams by a margin of less than ten thousand votes. The Governor presumably could have swung five thousand city votes one way or the other had he actively intervened in the election.

additional state revenues usefully could be applied to reduce the $40,000,000 debt of the New Orleans Dock Board, a state agency. In his address to the Legislature, the Governor made no mention of the controversial tick-eradication problem and, in conciliatory fashion, placed the task of securing new revenues in the lap of the legislators. For president pro tempore of the Senate, Huey supported the candidacy of a state senator who had not been one of the "round robineers" and who had supported him on only one of the two impeachment votes.

Huey's concessions reaped a meager reward. Though reduced from its majority proportions of 1929, the anti-Long contingent remained sufficiently numerous and cohesive to produce a stalemated session. The factional alignment of legislators was made evident at the outset of the session. Forty-four legislators supported a motion to reorganize the House which had as its ultimate purpose the ouster of Fournet from the speakership. Forty-three of those legislators had supported Huey's impeachment, while the remaining one was a new member from Iberia Parish who merely continued the anti-Long voting behavior of his predecessor. Seventeen of the sixty-one pro-impeachment representatives, therefore, had gone over to Long's side. In the Senate, seventeen votes were cast against the election of Huey's choice, Alvin King, to the position of president pro tempore. Eleven of those seventeen senators had opposed Huey on both impeachment votes and another was a new member from a Choctaw-controlled district in New Orleans.

Necessarily submitted in the form of a constitutional amendment, Huey's road bond bill never was able to secure the absolute two-thirds majority vote in each chamber required for its passage. The Governor, for his part, easily was able to beat back a host of opposition measures through outright legislative rejection, insertion of weakening amendments, or gubernatorial veto. Typical of his political adroitness was his approval of a legislatively-sponsored measure providing for a tick-eradication program, followed by his veto of a companion appropriation bill which delayed implementation of the program until 1932.[2] When the smoke of political battle was cleared,

[2] In 1932, Governor O. K. Allen levied a special tax on the proceeds of dairy and meat-handling plants to finance the tick-eradication program. Though the doleful prediction of a north Louisiana legislator that the uplands "would run red with blood" never came true, the opposition to the tick-eradication measure

it was apparent that state finances were a major casualty of the session. Appropriations for all state agencies had been reduced and no new revenue-producing measure had been enacted to relieve the situation in the future. By holding Huey to a draw in the legislative arena, however, the anti-Longs inadvertently encouraged him to appeal for support directly to the people. Thus ensued the curious spectacle of a governor running for the United States Senate on the public understanding that he would not leave the governorship for two more years and on a platform pledging a state good-roads program.

On July 17, 1930, the *Louisiana Progress*, Long's personal press organ,[3] announced Huey's senatorial candidacy against that of the incumbent, Ransdell, a veteran of thirty-two years of Congressional office. Huey made it quite clear that if he were elected the hostility of Lieutenant-Governor Cyr required that he complete his gubernatorial term before going to Washington. Louisiana's senatorial representation would not suffer, opined Long, because "with Ransdell as Senator, the seat was vacant anyway." If his bid for the Senate failed, however, Huey pledged himself to resign as Governor.[4]

Ransdell called in vain for issues befitting a senatorial contest. Huey's themes, dramatized by the stalemated session, were good roads and opposition to the Orleans Ring. To beard the "regulars" in their den, Huey formed the Louisiana Democratic Association, with Robert Maestri, Conservation Commissioner and financial angel to Huey during the 1929 impeachment, as its Orleans chief and Dr. Joseph O'Hara, head of the State Board of Health, as its state president. Both sides wallowed in vilification. While Huey scathingly referred to the goateed Ransdell as "old Feather Duster," the Governor was roasted as a caesar, braggart, thief, liar, non-family man, and character assassin. Major Roland B. Howell, a past commander of the state American Legion, informed an anti-Long rally that the "sole and only issue in this campaign is decency versus degradation" and closed his address with an appeal in the name of the Louisiana

in the 1930 session did come from the poorer north Louisiana and Florida parish areas.
[3] The first issue of Long's paper was published March 27, 1930, was intended to be a weekly paper, and always featured the acid cartoons of Trist Wood. The irregular publication dates of the *Progress* provide a rough index of the vicissitudes of Huey's political career.
[4] Long, *Every Man a King*, 224.

dead of the First World War. "I am giving you the message you would hear from their lips if they had not lost their lives in the service which Huey Long hid to evade."[5] So bitter grew the campaign that even the race issue, dormant since 1920, reappeared.[6]

Table 11 reports the results of the senatorial primary held September 9, 1930. In other primaries held the same day, pro-Long candidates Fernandez and Maloney defeated Choctaw entrants for the First and Second Congressional District seats respectively, while

TABLE 11. The Louisiana Vote in the 1930 Democratic Senatorial Primary

	Orleans	Other	State	% State	Parishes Carried by Majority
Long	38,682	110,958	149,640	57.3	53
Ransdell	43,373	68,078	111,451	42.7	11
Total	82,055	179,036	261,091	100.0	64

SOURCE: computed from *Compilation of Primary Election Returns of the Democratic Party, State of Louisiana,* held September 9 and October 14, 1930.

Longite Harvey G. Fields won nomination as Third District Public Service Commissioner in the runoff primary.

Figure 4 ranks the parishes within quartiles of support for Long. It would be appropriate at this juncture, to avoid confusion, to remind the reader that the use of quartile rankings in the maps in this study facilitates the analysis of *relative* parish response to Long candidates. In other words, parishes of high Long and anti-Long strength are determined purely by reference to a ranking of all parishes, by the proportion of the parish vote each casts for the Long

[5] New Orleans *Morning-Tribune*, September 4, 1930.

[6] Senator Ransdell had supported the appointment of Judge Parker, of North Carolina, to the United States Supreme Court. To organized labor, Parker symbolized the "yellow dog contract," and the Louisiana Federation of Labor rejected Ransdell accordingly. Defending his support of Parker, Ransdell asserted that the National Association for the Advancement of Colored People had opposed Parker, and therefore his pro-Parker stand had been conditioned by racial, not anti-labor, considerations. Hence, argued Ransdell, returning to the offensive, Long's assault on his support of Parker indicated that Huey favored the equality of Negroes with whites. The *Progress* of September 4, 1930, retaliated by reprinting a letter Ransdell had written to Walter L. Cohen, the Negro secretary of the Republican State Committee of Louisiana, in which the latter was addressed as "Mr. Cohen" and "Dear Mr. Cohen" (in the customary headings), and in which Ransdell requested Cohen's endorsement of a Negro applicant for a civil service position.

candidate, within four quartiles of sixteen parishes each. For purposes of studying *absolute* parish performance in one or a series of primaries through inspection of these maps, the most the reader can do is to pay close attention to the percentage ranges represented by each quartile and to the table preceding each map which reports the actual vote in the primary. Inspection of Figure 4, for example, reveals that Huey carried, by majority vote, at least forty-nine parishes and identifies forty-eight of them, namely all those in the highest, second, and third quartile of support. Table 11 provides the

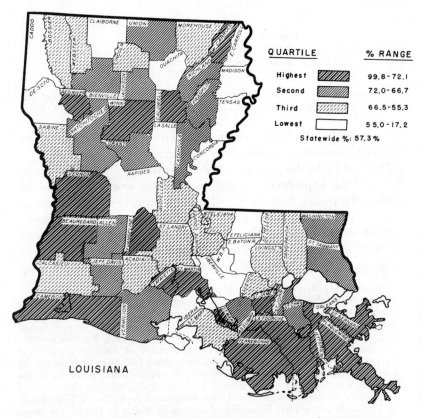

FIGURE 4. Quartile map: proportion of parish vote cast for Huey Long, 1930 Democratic senatorial primary.

SOURCE: same as that for Table 11.

more precise count of fifty-three parishes without providing information on the absolute performance of any parish except Orleans. The
reader is cautioned, however, that shifts in the quartile position of a
parish from one primary to another permit no conclusion as to
whether the Long candidate's percentage of that parish's vote declined or increased unless, by happy accident, the percentage ranges
assigned to each of the quartiles in question happen to provide that
information.

Comparison of Tables 7 and 11 reveals that Huey increased his
proportion of the state vote from 43.9 per cent in 1928 to 57.3 per
cent in 1930, while the total vote cast in 1930 declined 27,824 from
that of 1928. Although most of the decreased turnout came from
parishes other than Orleans, Huey was supported by roughly the
same number of voters outside Orleans in 1930 (110,958) as in
1928 (109,023). At the same time, Long doubled his share of the
Orleans vote (23 per cent in 1928, 47 per cent in 1930). While both
factors, of course, were important to his victory, perhaps Huey's performance in Orleans deserves special emphasis. If Ransdell had
attracted the same proportion of the 1930 Orleans vote as that secured
by Simpson and Wilson in 1928 (77 per cent), Huey would have won
office by only 50.1 per cent of the total state vote.

On the question of relative parish performance in 1930, as compared to 1928, Table 12 provides a basis for evaluating the shifts in

TABLE 12. Continuity and Change in the Centers of Long Strength
and Opposition, 1928–30

	No. of Parishes in Each Quartile of Support for Huey Long, 1928 Gub.			
Sixteen Parishes in	High	2nd	3rd	Low
High quartile for Long, 1930 Sen.	8	5	1	2
Low quartile for Long, 1930 Sen.	0	3	4	9
	Quartile of Support for Huey Long, 1930 Sen.			
	High	2nd	3rd	Low
High quartile for Long, 1928 Gub.	8	5	3	0
Low quartile for Long, 1928 Gub.	2	2	3	9

SOURCE: Figures 3 and 4.

parish position evident from comparative inspection of Figures 3
and 4. The behavior of the parishes in each of the extreme quartiles
examined in Table 12 confirms the conclusion that changes in the

quartile position of parishes in 1928–30 were numerous, but suggests that the changes did not constitute a sharp deviation from past factional patterns. Three-fourths of the parishes in each extreme quartile examined, for example, appeared in the factionally appropriate upper or lower half of all parishes in the other election.

Comparison of the 1930 and 1928 primaries thus leads to the conclusion that elements of continuity overshadowed those of change. With regard to the latter, perhaps worthy of special comment was the heightened support given Huey by the south Louisiana parishes of St. Bernard, Plaquemines, and Jefferson, explainable in each case by the existence of a tightly knit parish organization under the control of a boss. In general, though, in 1930 as in 1928, Long was relatively stronger in sections other than the urban areas, the cotton Delta, and the Sugar Bowl.

The reaction of anti-Longs to Huey's triumph in the senatorial primary broke the factional deadlock in the state. It was generally agreed that the Legislature should pass favorably on any measure implementing Long's pledges of good roads. There were, of course, some honest die-hards, such as venerable Judge Gilbert Dupre of Opelousas, who stubbornly maintained:

> A man's conscience should govern him, provided it is not corrupted. . . . The election just held was for a senatorship. No amount of cant can resolve otherwise. . . . He [Long] won the senatorship. Now I am requested to recant, to surrender, apologize, and eat up what I have spoken, what I have written. Others may do this. I will not. . . . On the contrary, I adhere to all I have written and spoken. . . . The legislature may ratify what they [Long] propose, the people confirm it, but I am not going to be included in the bargain. I am going to vote NO, even if I am the only member of the house to do this.[7]

The trend, however, was away from Judge Dupre's zealous opposition. The Constitutional League, an anti-Long organization which

[7] Baton Rouge *State-Times*, September 17, 1930. A story, doubtless apocryphal, constitutes a sort of epilogue. Upon entering the House chamber during the 1930 special session, the Governor was called upon by Dupre to notice the leaking roof. Dupre urged Huey, as custodian of the House, to have the roof repaired. In response to the nearly-deaf Dupre, Huey wrote upon a pad the question, "Are you in favor of the new state capitol bill?" "Hell, no," Dupre snorted. Huey then moved Dupre's chair to a spot directly under that part of the roof which was leaking, and wrote on Dupre's pad, "Die, then, damn it, in the faith."

Huey derisively had dubbed "the constipational league," disbanded the day after the senatorial primary. The Choctaws struck a deal with the Governor which committed them to support a $75,000,000 highway bond bill, a one-cent increase in the gasoline tax to the level of five cents, a bond issue for the construction of a new state capitol, and the withdrawal of the 1929 impeachment charges.[8] In return, Long agreed to dedicate .45 of the new one-cent gasoline tax to payment of the debt of the Port of New Orleans, to make an annual appropriation of $700,000 for the paving and repair of the city's streets, to reserve $7,000,000 of the road bond issue for construction of a free bridge across the Mississippi River at New Orleans, and to support a refinancing plan for the city.

Within one week after the date of the senatorial primary the Legislature, in special session, was in the process of enacting the Long-Choctaw agreement. The easy passage of Huey's program, however, should not obscure the fact that Judge Dupre was far from alone in his opposition to the Governor. In spite of the outcome of the senatorial primary and the defection of the Choctaw delegation, a high total of twenty-one representatives opposed Ellender's motion to expunge the impeachment charges. The persistence of anti-Long voting behavior by many legislators on a wide range of measures emphasized the ongoing development of a durable bifactionalism which was Long's most significant contribution to the structure of Louisiana politics. The story of recent Louisiana politics deals, in essence, with the rivalry of these two major factions, Long and anti-Long, in primary after primary and in legislative session after session.

By the close of 1930, the dominance of the Huey Long faction was quite evident. As good a measure as any was the fact that the *Louisiana Progress,* a weekly since its inception, converted in November to a monthly publication. The *Times-Picayune,* in an editorial of November 5, 1930, solemnly warned that Long had been given greater control of the state than any predecessor and, therefore, that he should be held responsible for the product of politics in the future. But Huey Long soon was to show, through an ingenious and ruthless exercise of increasingly centralized power and through the distribution of material benefits, how easily the forms of political accountability could be stripped of substantive value.

[8] Another secret condition was fulfilled by the Choctaws in March, 1931, when Sullivan was ousted from his ward leadership.

A suggestive prediction of dictatorial things to come was provided by Huey's handling of the problem of Lieutenant-Governor Cyr. Cyr, backed by some anti-Longs, had never ceased to insist upon the illegality of Huey's dual position as Governor and Senator-elect. In October of 1930, Cyr made his move and had himself sworn in as governor by a Shreveport notary. Huey promptly responded by having Alvin King, president pro tempore of the Senate, take the oath as governor. Long then blandly informed Cyr that his gubernatorial oath was illegal and that he had forfeited his position as Lieutenant-Governor by virtue of his illegal assumption of the governorship![9] In January, 1932, the Louisiana Supreme Court, in a 4–3 decision, held that it lacked jurisdiction over Cyr's suit and urged that the United States Senate was the proper body to determine the date on which Long had qualified as a Senator. Thus Alvin King finished out Huey's term as Governor, and Huey rid himself of a troublesome political enemy.

By making his bid for the Senate, Huey Long had no intention of relinquishing his grip on state politics. Indeed his ability to engage in free-wheeling tactics within the Senate rested in good part on the solidity of his political foundations in Louisiana. Hence, it surprised no one when Long unfurled a full ticket of nine candidates for the January, 1932, state office primary. For governor, Huey offered Oscar K. Allen of Winn Parish, one of his original 1924 supporters, whom Huey had made chairman of the Highway Commission; for lieutenant-governor, House Speaker Fournet, anathema to the anti-Longs because of "Bloody Monday" back in the 1929 impeachment session.[10] The designation of the slate as the "Complete the Work" ticket set the traditional Longite campaign theme of promises of material benefits on a grand scale. Huey's alliance with the Choctaws, however, resulted in the unusual spectacle of his defending the Ring against attacks leveled by other candidates.

[9] A reasonable commentator, looking back on the Cyr affair, holds it to be " . . . one of the most bizarre decisions in American judicial history. . . . The decision merely reveals how completely the Long machine dominated Louisiana politics." Cortez A. M. Ewing, "Southern Governors," *Journal of Politics*, x (May, 1948), 400–401.

[10] Huey, firm in his belief that one Long in politics was ample, assigned Fournet the post over the protests of Earl Long, his younger brother, who wanted the office for himself. Earl ran on the Guion ticket for lieutenant governor, and all of the immediate Long family supported Earl over Fournet.

Dudley J. LeBlanc, a Catholic south Louisiana politician and a Public Service Commissioner, headed a bob-tailed state ticket and provided the major anti-Allen force in the campaign.[11] George S. Guion led another incomplete anti-Long state ticket and had the support of the disgruntled Cyr. Two non-serious gubernatorial candidates also entered.[12] The campaign was a bitter one. Guion attacked the Long administration for catering to the "power trust" and for blocking tick eradication. LeBlanc tried to outdo Long's promises by pledging the enactment of $30-a-month old-age pensions to those over sixty years of age. In view of the later myth that Huey Long fathered old-age pensions in Louisiana, it should be noted carefully that Huey opposed LeBlanc's plank with the observation that the cost of the program would exceed $60,000,000 a year and that at least $20,000,000 of that amount would be going to Negroes.[13] Throughout much of the campaign, Long and LeBlanc remained sidetracked over the spurious issue of loyalty to the white race of Louisiana.[14]

The outcome of the 1932 primary, as reported in Table 13, was a victory for Longism by roughly the same proportion of the state vote as Huey secured in 1930 (Table 11). Allen's entire ticket won office with him. But the pattern of relative parish behavior in 1932 (Figure

---

[11] A bob-tailed or incomplete state ticket was one that failed to offer candidates for each of the nine state offices at stake. LeBlanc, for example, had a ticket candidate only for the posts of lieutenant-governor, secretary of state, and superintendent of education.

[12] The two minor gubernatorial candidates were William C. Boone and William L. Clark, Jr. They secured a combined total of 1,346 votes in the primary.

[13] Baton Rouge *State-Times*, November 30, 1931.

[14] LeBlanc was head of the Thibodeaux Benevolent Association, a mutual aid association catering to the very poor people, black and white, in the state, with apparent financial success for the officials of the organization. Typical of Huey's vitriolic attacks on LeBlanc and his organization was the following speech at Colfax in Grant Parish. "Then that other candidate, LeBlanc, he operates a nigger burial lodge and shroud and coffin club. He charges for a coffin and he charges $7.50 for a shroud. I am informed that the nigger is laid out, and after the mourners have left, LeBlanc takes the body into a back room, takes off the shroud, nails them up into a pine box, and buries them at a total cost of $3.67 and ½ cents" (New Orleans *Times-Picayune*, December 6, 1931). Issue after issue of the *Progress* prominently displayed LeBlanc's picture framed by those of his Negro fellow-officers of the Association. LeBlanc retaliated by charging on his campaign circulars that "Huey Long and Allen were nigger-lovers, and gave preference to blacks over whites," illustrating that theme by showing Long passing out textbooks, paid for by the taxpayer, to Negro children (Conway Collection of Huey P. Long Materials, v, 73, in Louisiana State Library, Baton Rouge).

5) was somewhat different from that uncovered for 1930 (Figure 4). While LeBlanc's "friends and neighbors" influence accounted for the

TABLE 13. The Louisiana Vote in the 1932 Democratic Gubernatorial Primary

	Orleans	Other	State	% State	Parishes Carried by Majority	Plurality
Allen	69,849	144,850	214,699	56.5	43	11
LeBlanc	17,545	92,503	110,048	29.0	6	4
Guion	11,244	42,512	53,756	14.1	0	0
Other	198	1,148	1,346	.4	0	0
Total	98,836	281,013	379,849	100.0	49	15

SOURCE: computed from *Compilation of Primary Election Returns of the Democratic Party, State of Louisiana,* held January 19, 1932.

shifts in quartile position of several south Louisiana parishes, two other major deviations from the 1930 pattern occurred in north Louisiana. Relative to the performance of all parishes, the pro-Longism of the cut-over, subsistence-farming parishes of Allen, Catahoula, Grant, LaSalle, Natchitoches, Sabine, and Vernon decreased. The pro-Longism of the northeast Delta parishes, by the same measure, increased.

Likely reactions to the strange new alliance between Huey and the Orleans machine provide a plausible explanation for the foregoing deviations from the 1930 pattern. Both Delta planters and some of the pro-Longs may have interpreted the Long-Choctaw entente as the death knell of Long as reformer. The injection of the racial issue into the campaign also may have increased Delta antipathy to LeBlanc as a possible alternative to Allen. In the Delta parishes, Guion was runner-up to Allen, and LeBlanc's vote was negligible. In the former Long strongholds in the upland parishes cited above, however, LeBlanc consistently was runner-up to Allen, and in the case of Grant Parish was stronger than Allen. This suggests that an active defection from Longism had occurred in the upland parishes, particularly in view of the fact that LeBlanc's candidacy may have had racial and religious connotations distasteful to white Protestants.

If the foregoing explanation be accurate, then the upland and Delta interpretation of the meaning of Huey's alliance with the Ring could not have been farther from the mark. With Allen as his puppet in the Executive Mansion, Long set out on the distinct, but related, tasks of solidifying his personal power and effectuating his class program. Huey's partnership with the Choctaws, far from having been a "sell-out," continued only as long as it contributed to Long's accomplishment of those two tasks.

Choctaw support of the state administration provided the basis for the endorsement of Long's heavy taxation program by the 1932 regular session of the Legislature. Anti-Longism in the House seldom attracted more than thirty to thirty-five legislators, a number insufficient to prevent the Long forces from enacting new taxes on tobacco, soft drinks, electricity, kerosene, beef and dairy products, and cor-

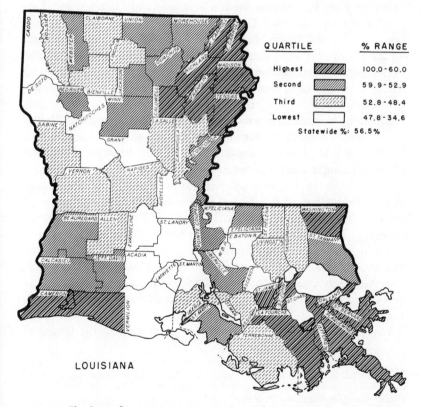

FIGURE 5. Quartile map: proportion of parish vote cast for Allen, 1932 Democratic gubernatorial primary.

SOURCE: same as that for Table 13.

poration capital, the combined annual yield of which was estimated
at $5,000,000. Other things remaining equal, if the Choctaws had
joined with the anti-Longs the Longites would have been outnumbered in the Legislature. That simple arithmetical calculation is
fallacious, however, in the degree to which the anti-Long attitudes
of the legislators from the parishes of Sabine, Vernon, Natchitoches,
Red River, and Winn—and possibly others—derived from the fact
of the Long-Choctaw alliance itself.

Of proven value in the legislative session, Long's entente with the
Ring was extended through the Congressional primaries of September, 1932. Huey and the Choctaws jointly backed the winning candidacies of John H. Overton for the Senate,[15] and Maloney and Fernandez for Orleans' two Congressional seats. In addition, Huey's
candidate, Sheriff Wade Martin of St. Martin Parish, defeated Dudley LeBlanc, the incumbent, for Second District member of the
Public Service Commission. The primaries were marked by so much
fraud, however, as to render any interpretation of the results questionable.

Electoral irregularities were revealed as a consequence of United
States Senate committee hearings into the fitness of Overton to take
his Senate seat. Though instituted technically because of charges
of fraud brought against Overton by his defeated opponent, Senator
Broussard, the investigation actually resulted from Huey's incurrence
of the displeasure of the Roosevelt administration. Hearings were
held in New Orleans in October, 1932, and in February and November, 1933. The unusual conclusion reached by the investigating subcommittee was that fraud had been proven on the part of the
organization backing Overton, but not on the part of Overton himself. Although Overton was permitted to take his Senate seat, the
subcommittee hearings did air the less creditable aspects of Long's
Louisiana.[16]

Particularly useful for the insights it provided into the tactics of

[15] In 1918 Overton ran unsuccessfully for the Senate, at the same time backing
Huey's winning race for the Railway Commission. In 1929, Overton was one of
Huey's legal counselors at the impeachment and, in 1931, he was elected to the
Eighth Congressional District seat.
[16] The testimony may be found in United States Senate *Hearings of the Special
Committee on the Investigation of Campaign Expenditures,* 72nd Congress, 2nd
Session (1932), and *Report No. 191,* 73rd Congress, 2nd session (1934). A
resume of the main charges, together with extensive quotations of testimony,

the Kingfish was the testimony extracted at subcommittee hearings on "deducts" and on "dummy candidates." It was revealed that the campaign costs of the Long faction were met in part by deductions from the paychecks of employees of the Highway Commission, the Dock Board, and the Conservation Commission. State Senator Harvey Peltier of Lafourche Parish, a Long supporter, expressed his belief that all public jobs down to that of the lowest-paid day laborer were political in Louisiana.[17] Other aspects of Long's campaign finances were doomed to secrecy by the uncommunicativeness of the Long faction's treasurer, Seymour Weiss.[18]

Other testimony revealed Long's heavy use of "dummy candidates" to enhance Overton's chances of securing friendly commissioners at the precinct polls.[19] Dummy candidates blanketed five of the eight Congressional districts, leaving only the traditional Long stronghold of north Louisiana untouched. The effect of such spurious candidacies in the Orleans area left Broussard with 200 precinct commissioners to counter 1,100 for the Long-Choctaw-Overton forces.[20] Huey justified his actions by noting the traditional use of dummy candidates in state politics and by urging that the only practical defense against one side's use of that tactic was its even greater use by the other side.[21] Conveniently ignored by Long in his veiled

may be found in Hilda P. Hammond, *Let Freedom Ring* (New York, 1936). It was inevitable, in view of the seat of political power in Louisiana, that the committee hearings would investigate the career and tactics of Huey Long. Huey was not inaccurate when he snarled that "you [the committee] have undertaken to try the public and private life of Huey P. Long for fourteen years back."

[17] Hammond, *Let Freedom Ring*, 65.

[18] Weiss insisted that he kept no bank or written records as treasurer for the Long faction. Committee counsel Ansell thus was forced to probe into Weiss's personal finances in the hope of uncovering some clues, but to each of his questions along such lines Weiss arrogantly responded, "None of your business." The Broussard forces, with some justification, expected Weiss to be cited for contempt of Congress, but no such action was forthcoming. *Hearings of the Special Committee*, 1047–60.

[19] For a discussion of the problem of factional abuse of primary machinery, see above, pp. 36–38.

[20] *Hearings of the Special Committee*, 654–55.

[21] Long traced the use of dummy candidates back to 1920, when Sullivan used them to aid Parker. Anti-Long Francis Williams admitted that Sullivan used dummies to further Williams' race for the Public Service Commission in 1922. Ellender and Peltier testified that Huey used dummy candidates in the 1930 Senate primary, though ostensibly to counter prior Choctaw use of the device. *Hearings of the Special Committee*, 227, 275, 692–93.

plea of self-defense was the fact that his smoothly-working organization gave his faction a distinct edge in such matters.[22]

The margin of Overton's victory is reported in Table 14. When to
that data is added the fact that relative parish response to Overton
closely approximated the 1930 Long pattern, with the exception of

TABLE 14. The Louisiana Vote in the 1932 Democratic Senatorial
Primary

	Orleans	Other	State	% State	Parishes Carried by Majority
Overton	56,970	124,494	181,464	59.2	48
Broussard	31,093	93,842	124,935	40.8	16
Total	88,063	218,336	306,399	100.0	64

SOURCE: computed from *Compilation of Primary Election Returns of the
Democratic Party, State of Louisiana,* held September 13 and October 18, 1932.

Overton's greater relative strength in south Louisiana, it may be suggested that Longite fraud undoubtedly swelled Overton's majority
but probably did not determine the outcome. In the south Louisiana
contest for a Public Service Commission seat, however, since LeBlanc
lost to Martin by 3,739 votes out of 115,831 votes cast, the use of
dummy candidates may have been crucial.

By mid-1933, relations between Huey and the Choctaws had
cooled. In point of fact, Long's activities in the Senate ran counter
to the Ring's traditional alliance with the national Democratic administration and to the loyalties of Long's supporters to New Deal
measures. To further his national ambitions, which apparently compelled him to work against the best interests of his own state, Huey

[22] The following series of events suggests the smoothness with which the various parts of the Long machine functioned. Dummy candidates were used with
effectiveness in the Third Congressional District (south Louisiana), wherein
LeBlanc and Broussard had considerable strength. Anti-Long Judge B. F. Pavy
enjoined the Democratic Executive Committee of St. Landry and Evangeline
parishes from accepting the names of poll commissioners designated by those
dummy candidates. Attorney General Porterie instructed the committee chairmen
to certify the names. Pavy ordered five members of the Evangeline Parish committee to jail for disobeying his injunction. Governor Allen issued telegraphic re-
prieves suspending the sentences until November 10, and Supreme Court Justice
St. Paul, recently renominated as a Longite candidate, delayed the sentences
still further until January. By that time, the matter was dropped. Deutsch, "Kingdom of the Kingfish," New Orleans *Item,* August 29, 1939.

Long had to develop a base of unchallengeable state power independent of any deals with the city machine. The events of Long's Senate career thus deserve brief examination since they intimately affected the development of Longism in Louisiana from 1933 to 1935.

Tomorrow the nation? Long vies with Roosevelt, 1932–35

Like the national press, the Senate at first was inclined to dismiss Huey as a rustic clown, a Southern oddity in the tradition of Dixie demagogues. It was easy to caricature a man who caricatured himself, for ever since the Green Pajamas incident Huey had taken to the path of political buffoonery.[23] Most writers thus were misled into viewing Long as a combination vaudevillian and Peck's bad boy. They should have known better. Huey, alone of the rude, plain-spoken agitators of the new South, was founding a personal dictatorship. They soon were to know better.

Although Long worked valiantly for Roosevelt's nomination at the 1932 national convention,[24] very early in his Senate career he voiced national aspirations that were a portent of his future rivalry with the President. By March of 1932, the freshman Senator already had unveiled his Share-Our-Wealth program, whereby "Every man was a king, but no man wore the crown," a phrase adapted by Huey from Bryan's Cross of Gold speech. Share-Our-Wealth was the class program for America's economic salvation and the vehicle for Huey's national ambitions. Though its terms were made flexible to meet competition from rival depression-medicine organizations, the main outlines of the program were as follows:

[23] In February, 1930, Governor Long, clothed in a pair of bright green pajamas, received the visit of a German high naval dignitary. The press had a gay time with the affair and showered Huey with laughing praise. Huey later made amends to the Admiral by calling upon him in proper dress and offering a tongue-in-cheek apology to the effect that a Louisiana farm-boy could not be expected to know about such matters of diplomacy.

[24] A seasoned politician close to Roosevelt has observed of Long's efforts: " . . . there is no question in my mind but that without Long's work Roosevelt might not have been nominated." Edward J. Flynn, *You're the Boss* (New York, 1947), 101. For a reporter's confirmation of Long's herculean labors to secure Roosevelt's nomination, see Thomas L. Stokes, *Chip Off My Shoulder* (Princeton, 1940), 321–22.

1. All personal fortunes over $3,000,000 would be liquidated, yielding $170,000,000,000 to be turned over to the United States Treasury.

2. From this fund, every family in the United States was to receive about $4,000 (or $5,000?) to purchase a home, an automobile, and a radio. The estimated government expenditure for these services was $100,000,000,000.

3. All persons over sixty-five (or sixty?) years of age were to receive pensions of $30 per month (or at an adequate rate?).[25]

4. The minimum wage would be adjusted to provide a floor of $2,500 a year per worker, resulting in, among other things, a permanent increase in the purchasing power of the benefited group.

5. Hours of labor would be limited to balance industrial production with consumption and enable the worker to enjoy some of the conveniences of life.

6. The government would purchase and store agricultural surpluses in order to balance agricultural production with demand, "according to the laws of God."

7. Cash payment of veterans' bonuses would begin immediately.

8. From the remainder of the Treasury fund, boys of proven ability, as determined by intelligence tests, were to receive a college education at governmental expense.

Share-Our-Wealth properly should be viewed as a product of political craftsmanship by a skilled artisan who had been intermittently at work on his masterpiece since 1918.[26] Its main plank may have been nothing but expropriatory socialism, but in the absence of an elaborate theoretical structure and of a special concern for the working class, it could be advocated as part of the native tradition of naïve, direct-action progressivism. In a word, "soak the rich!" There was something in it for everybody: farmers; urbanites; the aged; poorly paid workers; all workers; veterans; and high-school graduates. General Hugh S. Johnson, unleashed by Roosevelt to ridicule Long and Father Coughlin, the two major irritants to the national administration, inadvertently testified to the political potency of Huey's economic nostrum. "Who is going to attempt to tell

---

[25] Huey began with a $30 monthly pension, then shifted to an "adequate" pension, since other groups were offering more, particularly the Townsendites, who were promising $200 a month. Gerald L. K. Smith, Huey's right-hand organizer, observed that by this method many Townsendites were attracted to Share-Our-Wealth. Carleton Beals, *The Story of Huey P. Long* (Philadelphia, 1935), 314.

[26] See above, Chap. 2, n. 10.

any man he ought not to have $5,000 a year, if Huey can get it for him—or even why he shouldn't be a King? The fact is that nobody is answering Huey in language anybody can understand. He is getting away with it without a contest."[27]

Local S-O-W clubs, requiring no dues of its members, mushroomed in the depressed rural areas of the nation. Members received, without charge, copies of Huey's autobiography, which he had published in mid-1933, and the editions of Long's re-activated paper, appropriately re-titled *American Progress*.[28] Although there was at least one club in every state, membership in 1935 was concentrated in the South and the far north-central states. Long claimed a total of 27,431 clubs as of February, 1935, while his staff claimed to possess the names and addresses of over 7,500,000 persons on file.[29] Commentators who attributed to Huey a hankering for fascistic control of the nation saw the proliferation of these local clubs as far more "than a glorified mailing list." It was, rather, "the nucleus of a nation-wide political machine."[30]

Democratic party leaders were somewhat less than enthusiastic over Long's panacea. To remind his colleagues, particularly party wheelhorse Senator Robinson of Arkansas, that his influence was not confined to Louisiana, Huey invaded Arkansas in a successful whirlwind campaign to elect Hattie Caraway to a full Senate term in mid-1932. As a gesture of protest against Senate Democratic leadership he resigned his committee memberships. Under Robinson's prodding, the Senate retaliated by voting to conduct an inquiry into the election of Overton to the Senate, an investigation which necessarily aimed at discrediting the Long organization itself. The Administration jumped on the bandwagon by instructing the Bureau of Internal Revenue to examine the income tax returns of Long and his chief lieutenants.

[27] *Congressional Record*, LXXIX (March 5, 1935), 74th Congress, 1st Session, 2943.
[28] The first issue of the *American Progress* appeared on August 24, 1933, as a weekly, with the hope of a national subscription. Until February, 1934, at which time it began to beat the drums for a national Share-Our-Wealth movement, the *Progress* was essentially a Louisiana organ. In April of 1934, it converted to monthly issues and claimed a circulation of nearly 150,000.
[29] Unofficial Observer (John F. Carter), *American Messiahs* (New York, 1935), 22.
[30] Raymond Gram Swing, *Forerunners of American Fascism* (New York, 1935), 98.

While Huey endured the Senate's probe into the manner in which he controlled Louisiana, he could not submit to Roosevelt's attempt to undermine that control. At the same time that the Choctaws were revolting against the Allen administration, Postmaster General James Farley was channeling federal patronage to the anti-Longs. In the ensuing battle for political supremacy, which raged through 1934, Long emerged as the uncontested King of Louisiana. In April of 1934, when the outcome of the battle was evident, Senator Long loudly proclaimed his divorce from the White House on all farm, banking, and economy phases of New Deal policy. While, doubtless, Long's temperament and his ideological commitments contributed to his decision to make war on Roosevelt, the factor of political ambition should not be minimized. The Kingfish apparently hoped to attract a number of underprivileged voters sufficient to hold the balance of power for the 1936 Democratic presidential nomination or, failing in that objective, to amass gradually a loyal following that would sweep him to victory in the presidential campaign of 1940.[31]

Huey roared into national prominence as the bitterest critic of Roosevelt and the New Deal. His acid tongue coined nicknames for several Administration stalwarts: Lord Corn Wallace; Ickes, the Chicago Chinch Bug; Sitting Bull Hugh Johnson. In reference to the President's fondness for vacationing aboard Vincent Astor's yacht, Huey dubbed him, "Prince Franklin, Knight of the Nourmahal." Within the Senate, Long earned for himself the rating of "its most tempestuous filibusterer."[32] Lashing back, Roosevelt, through Ickes, curtailed over $10,000,000 of PWA projects in Louisiana. Seymour Weiss and Abe Shushan, prominent Long aides, were indicted for income tax evasion as part of an intensive investigation which ultimately helped to break up the Long dictatorship in 1939–40.

There can be little doubt that Long's growing appeal worried top Democratic officials in 1935. Referring to Huey's strength, as revealed in a secret national poll, Farley noted in dismay, "It was easy to conceive a situation whereby Long . . . might have the balance of

[31] In an interview shortly after Long's death, Ellender stated that the legal obstacles confronting any third party movement had persuaded Huey to concentrate on securing control of a bloc of convention votes to prevent the renomination of Roosevelt in 1936. If necessary, Ellender stated, Long would have supported a progressive Republican in 1936. United Press dispatch, September 13, 1935.

[32] Franklin L. Burdette, *Filibustering in the Senate* (Princeton, 1940), 3.

power in the 1936 election."[33] Raymond Moley reported that Roosevelt spoke of the need of doing something to "steal Long's thunder."[34] Liberals in particular expressed concern over the possibility of a Huey-led fascist revolt or of the even more alarming situation of a smashing endorsement of Long via the ballot box.[35] But the threat of the Kingfish was destined to be ended by the bullet of an assassin. Huey Long paid with his life for creating a personal statewide dictatorship reflective of his overweening national ambitions. The structure of this tyranny on American soil next deserves careful attention.

From Kingfish to crawfish and back: the Louisiana events of 1933–35

The Roosevelt administration's attacks on Huey in 1933–34 coincided with a series of setbacks for the Kingfish in Louisiana. When Sixth District Congressman, Bolivar Kemp, died in mid-1933, the Long-controlled Democratic district committee declared Kemp's widow the party nominee instead of calling a primary, as required by state law. Anti-Longs in the affected parishes boycotted the general election and, on the basis of a special election of their own, sent J. Y. Sanders, Jr., to challenge Mrs. Kemp in Congress. Neither was given the seat, and in the ensuing legitimate primary Sanders secured the nomination. The second setback developed from Long's dissolution of his partnership with the Ring. In the January, 1934, New Orleans mayoralty primary, Choctaw Walmsley and his slate easily defeated a rival city ticket sponsored by Long. The third setback was the most serious, involving public humiliation rather than temporary political defeat. The Kingfish, quite drunk, insulted a lady at a private party in Sands Point, Long Island; her escort promptly

[33] James A. Farley, *Behind the Ballots* (New York, 1938), 250.

[34] Raymond Moley, *After Seven Years* (New York, 1939), 305. In a recent work, *Twenty-Seven Masters of Politics* (New York, 1949), 229–30, Moley, a New Dealer turned conservative, argued that some of Roosevelt's 1935 proposals were aimed in part to forestall Long. Even after Huey's death, Moley averred, Roosevelt, Hopkins, Wallace, and others had become disciples of the Kingfish to a degree they probably never suspected. Moley divides the New Deal era into two periods, the first to rejuvenate capitalism as an accepted system, and the second, from 1935 on, to seek " . . . political power by a simple process of redistributing existing wealth under the guise of social justice and uplift by law."

[35] For a typical expression of this liberal neurosis, see Swing, *Forerunners of American Fascism*, Chapter 1.

knocked the Senator down in the privacy of the gentlemen's room. The discomfited Huey helped turn chuckles to guffaws when the press discovered that he had written to the imprisoned Al Capone, offering him his freedom if the Chicago racketeer would confess that he had arranged the fracas at the behest of the moneyed interests![36]

Reaction adverse to the Kingfish was not confined to those gleeful anti-Longs who chanted:

> So I sing the song of muskellonge,
> The lobster, eel, and crab,
> The bullfrog in his puddle
> With his gift of gall and gab.
>
> I lift a glass of legal booze
> And toast the happy guy
> Who sent the fish back to his mud
> With a beefsteak on his eye.[37]

Jeering audiences in Donaldsonville and Monroe taunted the Senator on the whereabouts of his numerous bodyguards during the late, great Wall Street plot; crowds pelted him with eggs in Alexandria. The Kingfish had become a crawfish, and the nation's press echoed each other in their solemn mourning of the political death of the Senate's stormy petrel.

The obituary was most premature. Huey reinvigorated his waning political strength by having the 1934 Louisiana Legislature enact measures favorable to lower-class interests, by declaring war on the Choctaws, and by erecting, through laws, the most thorough state dictatorship known to twentieth-century America.

Longite majorities in the 1934 regular session of the Legislature were ample for enactment of ordinary legislation and, in most cases, for the passage of constitutional amendments as well. Even the resumed alliance of Choctaws with the anti-Longs brought no solid bloc of city legislators to the side of the opposition, for six representatives and four senators from Orleans aligned themselves with the Long-Allen forces. Factional lines usually held firm in both chambers on a wide variety of tax proposals, of punitive measures against New Orleans, and of factional power-concentration bills.

Two constitutional amendments were passed which aimed at rein-

[36] Davis, *Huey Long*, 195–202.
[37] *Ibid.*, 207.

forcing the allegiance of Huey's supporters. The first exempted, from state, parish, and special district taxation, the first $2,000 of assessment on dwellings occupied by the owners. Municipal residents, except in New Orleans—which was both a parish and a municipality —were not granted that homestead exemption on the municipal property tax. Two comments should be noted. The law permitted the homestead exemption to be lowered to the first $800 of assessed valuation, and it was not until the Leche administration that the state exemption reached the $2,000 figure. Second, the tax savings to the homeowner easily could be nullified by an increase in the assessed valuation of his home—and the controls over assessment rested ultimately with two Huey-controlled agencies, the State Tax Commission and the State Board of Equalization. The second measure lowered license-plate fees for automobiles and small trucks, excluded autos from the list of assessable property, and provided for additional highway and bridge construction. The drop in state revenues occasioned by the reduced auto-license fees was more than made up by repeal of the annual $700,000 payment to New Orleans for repair and paving of city streets.[38]

To balance the estimated loss of $7,000,000 in state revenues resulting from homestead exemption a Property Tax Relief Fund was created, which was the depository of the revenues from newly levied taxes on income, liquor, public utilities, and the cotton exchange. Tobacco and corporation franchise taxes were increased, but the soft-drinks levy was repealed. The fixing of a new severance tax rate on sulphur could be interpreted in terms of Long's alliance with the political leaders of Plaquemines Parish,[39] while the imposition of a

---

[38] Since the reduction in licenses for cheaper cars was estimated to cost the state $300,000 a year, in effect New Orleans was made to bear twice that loss of revenue itself, while the other sixty-three parishes shared in the loss of $300,000. Long's action flagrantly violated his earlier agreement with the Ring, under which the Choctaws had supported the highway bond constitutional amendment at the special session and the general election of 1930. The Kingfish also had failed to redeem his 1930 promise to the farmers of $28,000,000 of secondary road construction; even by 1934, the highway bill provided only $7,000,000 for such purposes. For an eloquent protest against Huey's actions, see state Senator Boudreaux's explanation of his vote against the highway bill, *Official Journal of the Proceedings of the Senate of Louisiana*, 1934 regular session, 803–805.

[39] Though a severance tax rate of $1.25 per long ton of sulphur had been urged to make the tax on sulphur comparable to that on oil, Huey personally had the rate set at $0.60 per long ton. The political leaders of Plaquemines

90 THE KINGFISH

2 per cent tax on the gross advertising receipts of the larger Louisiana newspapers permitted but one interpretation in view of the anti-
Longism of the urban press.[40]

Lower-class whites presumably would be most appreciative of
Long's tax efforts on their behalf. To encourage maximum turnout of
that group, Long had a constitutional amendment enacted abolishing the payment of a poll tax as a qualification for suffrage. Another
likely motivation was the desire to undermine the influence of the
Ring and of those anti-Long sheriffs who paid the poll taxes of large
numbers of voters and then "persuaded" them to vote against Long.[41]
Certainly Huey had no intention, as some absurdly charged, of increasing Negro voting in Louisiana.[42] In the November general election, at which 83 per cent of the vote cast on the amendment was
favorable, relative parish performance suggested the anticipated
effects of the repeal of the poll tax.[43] Fourteen of the sixteen parishes
in the lowest quartile of support for repeal had been in the lower two
quartiles of support for Long in 1930.

Power that rested on the fickle stuff of human loyalty and grati-
tude was hardly, in Long's view, secure power. What if lower-class
voters failed to come to the polls in sufficient numbers to assure con-
tinuous Long dominance in politics? Huey's answer to that question,
which consisted of rigging the election machinery in his favor, took
on added insolence by the manner in which the legislation was
enacted. The Long forces amended anti-Long bills to reverse their

Parish, in which nearly all Louisiana sulphur was mined, allegedly had agreed
to forego the severance tax refund to the parish if the severance tax rate was kept
low. In 1935, however, Huey-sanctioned legislation allowed Plaquemines to
collect one-third of the state revenues derived from the severance tax on sulphur
mined in that parish.

[40] The United States Supreme Court later unanimously invalidated Huey's tax.
Justice Sutherland observed, " . . . [the tax has] the plain purpose of penalizing
the publishers and curtailing the circulation of a selected group of newspapers."
Grosjean v. American Press Co., 297 U.S. 233, at 251 (1936).

[41] Key, Southern Politics, 603.

[42] Huey countered the accusation by indicating the effective mechanism of
Negro disfranchisement in Louisiana: " . . . the poll tax will not affect the
status of the Negro at all. Negroes can pay and do pay their poll taxes now, but
that doesn't give them any better chance to vote. It is the registration law and
the white primary that keeps the Negro out of our elections." Quoted by Sender
Garlin, The Real Huey P. Long (New York, 1935), 24–25.

[43] Key estimates that repeal of the poll tax in Louisiana was responsible for the
additional turnout of at most 10 per cent of the adult whites. Southern Politics,
605.

meaning, denied the authors permission to withdraw their amended bills, and then acted favorably on those bills. In one case a measure providing that no voting registration records could be removed from a registrar's office except by court order was amended to read that no court had the authority to order the registration records out of the custody of a registrar. Another bill sought to end the practice of dummy candidates but emerged as a law concentrating the power to select poll commissioners in the hands of the state administration faction. Parish boards of election supervisors, two of whose three members were gubernatorial appointees, were authorized to select all poll commissioners. As amended in 1935, this procedure was applied to all primary and general elections in the state until the law was declared unconstitutional in 1937.[44]

On the heels of the adjournment of the Legislature, Huey declared total war on the Ring. Long's public motive was moral: New Orleans must be cleansed of vice and sin. Virtue, of course, was its own reward, but if Huey also could gain control of the city's voting registration records and could begin to lay siege to the Choctaw Club, the odds were that such additional rewards would not be turned down. On Governor Allen's orders, but without a proper warrant, the invitation of the civil authorities, or a proclamation of full martial law, the National Guard invaded the city and seized the registration offices. "I warn you," Mayor Walmsley shouted, "Huey Long, you cringing coward, that if a life is spent in the defense of this city and its right of self-government, you shall pay the penalty as other carpetbaggers have done before you."[45] After supervising the nomination of his candidates for Congress, Public Service Commission, and state Supreme Court from the Orleans area in the September primary, Long retired the Guard from the city. As arrogant as Long's actions were, they represented nothing more than a minor sortie in comparison with events to come.

From August, 1934, through September, 1935, seven special sessions of the Legislature enacted measures which, in their combined effect, reduced the citizenry of Louisiana to political vassalage to the Kingfish and his faction. The cohesion of anti-Long legislators was

[44] In March, 1937, in *State ex rel. Ward* v. *Board of Supervisors of Elections, Parish of Rapides*, 186 La. 949, the state Supreme Court, by six to one vote, held the latter act unconstitutional.

[45] Davis, *Huey Long*, 218.

high, but their numbers, abouty thirty in the House and ten in the
Senate, were too few. For the first time in recent history, each chamber permitted its procedures to be changed or suspended by simple
majority vote rather than by the customary two-thirds majority
vote.[46] The Long forces could meet that modest requirement even in
the face of considerable absenteeism in their ranks. At each of the
special sessions bills were referred to a single committee, hearings
were perfunctory, and frequently Senator Long was the sole witness
on a bill.[47] Columnist Westbrook Pegler acidly observed of the Legislature, "They do not permit a house of prostitution to operate within
a prescribed distance of the state university, but exempt the state
Capitol from the meaning of the act."[48]

Personally riding herd on his followers at each session, Senator
Long conducted an all-out assault on New Orleans. Many of the
powers of the Commission Council and of other parish offices, including the issuance of business licenses, the regulation of utilities, and
the assessment of property, were transferred either to existing state
agencies or to new state-appointed authorities. Huey did not cease
his usurpation of city powers until "the New Orleans city administration did not have enough patronage . . . left to support the government of an unincorporated village."[49] The state administration then
used its new powers to impair the fiscal solvency of the city. On the
one hand, the total assessed valuation of city property was reduced
and city license fees were retained by the state. On the other, the
Legislature raised minimum city appropriations for firemen and
policemen, and depression-induced demands for greater public assistance became more insistent. In terms of the 1935 city budget, the
Ring had to make $2,300,000 of revenues meet $4,100,000 of expenses.[50] When, through court action, Huey prevented New Orleans
from borrowing in anticipation of its 1935 taxes, the last escape-hatch

[46] In the 1 E.S. 1934 session, the House so changed its rules by 53–35 vote
and the Senate by 21–7 vote.
[47] Swing characterized Long's performance at the 3 E.S. 1934 session as
follows, "Huey stood there [on the floor of the House] the entire time, the chairman's only function being to call for a vote, bring down his gavel, announce that
the measure was approved . . . ." *Forerunners of American Fascism*, 68.
[48] Quoted by Kane, *Louisiana Hayride*, 114.
[49] Thomas O. Harris, *The Kingfish: Huey P. Long, Dictator* (New Orleans,
1938), 219.
[50] New Orleans Bureau of Governmental Research, "A Travesty in Finance,"
City Problems Series, No. 29, July 18, 1935.

was battened down. Under legislation enacted at the 2 E.S. 1935 session, the state, in effect, took over supervisory control of the city's finances. By the time of Huey's death in September, the Choctaws were waving the white flag of surrender.

Local governmental units generally suffered a diminution of authority. Through ripper bills, the city officials of Baton Rouge, Shreveport, and Alexandria were replaced by Allen appointees. The Public Service Commission was given control over municipal utilities. The governor was empowered to fill vacancies, regardless of the length of the unexpired term, in public offices at all governmental levels. The reviewing authority of the State Tax Commission could nullify the power of the parish assessor. A State Bond and Tax Board was created, allegedly to curtail unwise bond and tax policies of local governmental units, but actually designed to function as supreme controller of municipal fiscal affairs.

By a misnamed state civil service law, the governor was granted an appointing authority over nonelective municipal fire and police chiefs, which was later extended to cover nearly every appointive municipal and parish employee in the state.[51] Establishment of a State Budget Committee, composed of the governor, the state superintendent of education, and the state treasurer, permitted centralized control of parish school boards and of the educational workforce, including teachers, school-bus drivers, and janitors.[52] Not even Huey's own legal profession was spared from attack. When the Louisiana Bar Association sought to bring disbarment proceedings against Attorney General Porterie because of his attempts to stifle vote-fraud prosecutions in New Orleans, Huey retaliated by creating a State Bar of Louisiana, headed by the Attorney General. Lashing out against an old enemy by a measure later held unconstitutional, Long had the Public Service Commission empowered to charge utility

[51] Long's first action under the civil service law was to fire the police chief of Alexandria, who had failed to apprehend those who showered Huey with rotten eggs in 1933. In August, 1938, by a 4–2 decision, the state Supreme Court upheld the act as a legitimate interpretation of the constitutional clause in question. When Maestri became mayor of Orleans in 1936, control over city employees was shifted to his office.

[52] The State Budget Committee was authorized to control the appointment of teachers and the finances of school boards. State Superintendent T. H. Harris was opposed to the measure and succeeded in securing its moderate enforcement during Huey's time and its repeal by the Leche Legislature in 1936.

companies for expenses incurred by the commission in conducting
rate investigations. For purposes of personal enrichment and political
harassment, Long had himself appointed as attorney to the Public
Service Commission, and as roving prosecutor for the State Tax Commission to ferret out delinquencies and evasions for a fee of 33 per
cent of the sums recovered.

A variety of techniques was used to neutralize strategic public
officials or to dragoon them into Long's service. The superintendent
of state police was authorized to appoint all the deputies of the
Baton Rouge sheriff and all in excess of five deputies in all other
parishes. An over-conscientious district attorney could be super-
seded, in any criminal or misdemeanor case, by the attorney general
at the latter's discretion, which could not be questioned or inquired
into by any court. In New Orleans the method was more direct:
District Attorney Eugene Stanley resigned in protest when the state
assumed power to appoint his legal staff. A persistently troublesome
district judge, if the situation permitted, could be gerrymandered
out of office.[53] The state Supreme Court offered no problem because
electoral successes of the Long forces since 1928 had given them
majority control of the seven-man court. The factional alignment
within the highest state court—and it can be called little else—
remained firm during this period when Long adhered to the forms
of constitutionalism while perverting its substance.

A well-ordered dictatorship must take force into account. The
governor, therefore, was authorized to call out the militia at his
pleasure without challenge from the courts. Long had Allen utilize
this open-end grant of power in connection with the Baton Rouge
Square Deal incident of early 1935, to be discussed shortly. The governor also was empowered to increase, without stated limit, the personnel of the State Bureau of Identification, more familiarly known
in Louisiana as Huey's Cossacks.

By late December of 1934, Long's estimate of his strengthened
position persuaded him to do battle with Standard Oil at the same
time he was besieging the Choctaws. The Legislature enacted Huey's
pet proposal of a tax on refined oil of five cents a barrel. Standard
Oil, employing 3,800 workers of the total Baton Rouge labor force of

---

[53] One bill gerrymandered the Evangeline-St. Landry judicial district so as to
assure the defeat of incumbent B. F. Pavy. One of Pavy's daughters was married
to Dr. Carl A. Weiss, Jr., the man who assassinated the Kingfish.

30,000, promptly replied by dismissing nearly 1,000 workers. Some of the latter, together with some disgruntled discharged state employees, banded together in the Square Deal organization and spoke grimly of violence. In January, 1935, the state militia was called out to deal with a "revolt" by an armed group of Square Dealers. At the famous "Battle of the Airport" in Baton Rouge, the dissident anti-Longs were routed easily with a minimum of violence. The economic power of Standard Oil proved more durable, however, and Long shortly afterwards agreed to come to terms with the company. Standard Oil consented to increase its production and refining of Louisiana crude oil, in return for which Huey had the Legislature empower the governor to suspend all or part of the tax for any period of time through late July, 1936. Governor Allen reduced the tax by 80 per cent, but the flexible authority retained by the governor enabled Huey to maintain the threat of raising the tax at will.

Since the measure had sparked Huey's impeachment a brief six years earlier, passage of the Standard Oil tax provided an apt commentary on the kingdom erected by the Kingfish. Long had taken advantage of every inadequacy of the state Constitution and every exigency of the depression to centralize power and to suppress opposition. In terms of the controls he possessed, the Kingfish had swallowed the Pelican State. *L'état, c'est Huey*. However, by making ineffective the expression of opposition through legitimate channels of action, Huey exposed his regime to extra-legal attacks by the anti-Longs. The Square Deal protest doubtless was a fiasco, but it was instructive as to the degree of desperation and proneness to violence to which Huey had reduced his opponents. At the peril of his personal safety, Long had chosen to ignore the prediction of Mason Spencer, a Delta legislator, who had commented as follows on Long's measure to place the selection of poll commissioners in the hands of a parish board controlled by the state faction: "When this ugly thing is boiled down in its own juices, it disenfranchises the white people of Louisiana. I am not gifted with second sight. Nor did I see a spot of blood on the moon last night. But I can see blood on the polished floor of this Capitol. For if you ride this thing through, you will travel with the white horse of death. White men have ever made poor slaves."[54]

[54] Quoted by Hodding Carter, in Leighton (ed.), *The Aspirin Age*, 343.

The murder of the Kingfish

In September, 1935, Huey hurried back to Baton Rouge from
Washington for the opening of the year's fourth special session of the
Legislature and to decide upon a successor to O. K. Allen in the coming gubernatorial primaries. At the Sunday night session of the Legislature, September 8, Huey left the Governor's room on the main floor
of the Capitol at a brisk pace, well ahead of his bodyguards. A tall,
bespectacled young man walked across the corridor toward Huey,
who extended his hand to him in a politician's greeting. A few
moments of conversation ensued. Suddenly, the visitor fired one
shot. Long staggered away, clutching his stomach. The bodyguards
opened fire and the assassin crumpled, sixty-one bullets in his chest,
back, and head.[55] Huey struggled for his life for several days. The
entire Long family, forgiving old enmities in the face of tragedy, was
gathered with the Senator at the last.

Long's assailant was Dr. Carl A. Weiss, Jr., a medical specialist
who previously neither had met Long nor taken any direct part in
politics. Members of his family, however, were prominent anti-
Longs. His father had been head of the State Medical Association
and was a vocal opponent of the Kingfish's attempts to regiment the
faculty of the Tulane University Medical School. His father-in-law
was District Judge B. F. Pavy, an Opelousas anti-Long about to be
gerrymandered out of office. Some Longites sought to label the
murder as political, recalling the New Orleans meeting of anti-Long
Louisiana congressmen in July and Huey's talk, in August, of an
assassination plot.[56] The standard text of the plot version had Weiss
picking the short straw at a murder-meeting of the anti-Longs. While
no supporting evidence was offered,[57] the subsequent behavior of
Long's lieutenants indicated that the unproven plot version was

[55] No assassin or would-be assassin of a president, except in the attempt on
President Truman's life, has ever been killed; all were disarmed, or captured
later, and stood trial.
[56] On July 24, 1935, a group of pro-Roosevelt and anti-Huey leaders gathered
at the DeSoto Hotel in New Orleans. One result of the meeting was the issuance
of a statement by the five anti-Long congressmen affirming their allegiance to
the national administration. The signers were Sandlin (Fourth District), Wilson
(Fifth), Sanders (Sixth), Dear (Eighth), and Montet (Third).
[57] Two anti-Long commentators maintain that Washington had advance knowledge of the assassination. Allan A. Michie and Frank Ryhlick, *Dixie Demagogues*
(New York, 1939), 116.

preferred to whatever might be uncovered by a thorough investigation into the assassination. Some anti-Longs, for their part, consoled themselves with the thought that perhaps one of Huey's bodyguards accidentally—perhaps even purposely, some mused—had shot his chieftain.[58]

The generally-accepted version of the murder rejects the foregoing partisan accounts and runs about as follows. In harassing Pavy, Weiss's father-in-law, Long had implied that there was Negro blood in the Pavy family. Weiss had brooded about that insult. On that fateful Sunday, Weiss had conducted himself quite normally. After attending church, he went over to south Baton Rouge to engage in what apparently was the local sport of shooting snakes. He appeared that night at the State Capitol, and accosted Huey, perhaps with a view toward demanding an apology. Whatever the conversation, Weiss scuffled with Long, then drew his gun and fired a single shot. If this version be substantially correct, Huey fell victim in the deepest sense to the Southern tradition of personal honor and personal violence.[59]

It would not distort the foregoing version, however, to suggest that a link nonetheless remains between the murder of Huey Long and his development of a tyranny. The insult of Pavy and the erection of a dictatorship had a common source in Long's ruthless nature, his vindictiveness, his arrogance, his inability to forget a grudge or forgive an enemy. At bottom, then, the very traits which underlay Huey's rise to power contributed much to bringing about his own death.

[58] See the column by C. P. Liter in the Baton Rouge *Morning Advocate*, September 9, 1945, for a citation of this version.

[59] Weiss was a "practical Catholic," that is, one to whom religious tenets were deeply held and to whom killing was abhorrent. Archbishop Rummel of New Orleans, accepting the view that only a temporary mental aberration explained Weiss's action, sanctioned a Catholic burial for the assassin.

CHAPTER 4

One man wore the crown

AN APPRAISAL OF HUEY LONG

TO GREAT NUMBERS of Louisianians, Huey Long was either the salvation or the ruination of Louisiana. It is not surprising, therefore, that most judgments of the Kingfish, whether derived from adulation or detestation, are essentially one-dimensional. A more accurate view of Huey must stress the mixture of types he actually was and the many-sided impact of his reign on succeeding state politics. The importance of a full understanding of Long scarcely can be exaggerated, for to him must be attributed much of the form and content of recent Louisiana politics through 1952.

Temperament and tactics

Even those who deplored his actions and objectives recognized in the Kingfish a man of unusual talents. Raymond Moley has written that his feeling, on Long's death, ". . . was a sense of tragedy—a tragedy of wasted talent. . . . He had, combined with a remarkable capacity for hard, intellectual labor, an extraordinarily powerful, resourceful, clear and retentive mind, an instrument such as is given to very few men. No one can tell what services he could have rendered his state and nation had he chosen to use that mind well."[1] Will Percy, the vigorous Mississippi planter spokesman, put the same thought less elegantly, "[Huey Long] was . . . a moral idiot of genius."[2]

Too much of the daringness and imaginativeness which Huey

[1] Moley, *Twenty-Seven Masters of Politics,* 221.
[2] William A. Percy, *Lanterns on the Levee* (New York, 1941), 144.

brought to his career was devoted to devising ways to punish his political foes. Long understated the streak of vengefulness in his nature when he observed in his autobiography, "Once disappointed over a political undertaking, I could never cast it from my mind."[3] His rudeness and his predilection for engaging in personal abuse, both stemming from his egocentricity, merited the observation that ". . . Huey P. Long . . . would not have been allowed to live a week if the code duello had still been in force."[4]

Yet the vilification and occasional crucifixion of his political adversaries were part of that intense personalization of politics by which Huey was able to erect and maintain a highly personal dictatorship. Many Louisianians idolized Long: some of the Kingfish's devoted Catholic followers, for example, unofficially canonized him.[5] The state presented a statue of Huey as one of its two great sons entitled to recognition in Statuary Hall in Washington, purchased Long's New Orleans home for a museum, and made his birthday a legal holiday. By capitalizing on the political potency of Long's name, his successors in 1936 were able to retain the loyalty of his following while at the same time to mock his memory by enacting a state sales tax and by burying Share-Our-Wealth. In his campaigns for office following Huey's death, brother Earl always has had to explain away the accusations he had made against Huey in the 1932 Senate investigation of Overton's election.

The emotional loyalties which Huey Long aroused, in Louisiana and in the nation, reflected the fact that, at his oratorical best, Huey expressed the yearnings of the "have-nots" for a material level of living consonant with the equality of citizens proclaimed in the Constitution. In the midst of the depression, here was a homely philosopher who applied, in the vernacular of the uneducated man, the verities of the Bible and the American Constitution to the terrifying and bewildering economic problems of the day.[6] Here was a dedicated leader for the "forgotten men." From their viewpoint, it was a man of courage and sincerity, not a petty, vindictive tyrant, who informed his colleagues in the Senate on March 5, 1935,

[3] Long, *Every Man a King*, 31.
[4] W. A. Roberts, *Lake Pontchartrain* (New York, 1946), 331.
[5] The personal columns of the New Orleans *Times-Picayune* for several years after Long's death frequently included such items as "thanks to St. Peter, St. Joseph, . . . St. Huey . . . ."
[6] Swing, *Forerunners of American Fascism*, 95; Kane, *Louisiana Hayride*, 80.

Mr. President, I am not undertaking to answer the charge that I am ignorant. It is true. I am an ignorant man. I have had no college education. I have not even had a high-school education. But the thing that takes me far in politics is that I do not have to color what comes into my mind and into my heart. I say it unvarnished. I say it without veneer. I know the hearts of the people because I have not colored my own. I know when I am right in my own conscience. I do not talk one way in the cloakroom and another way out here. I do not talk one way back there in the hills of Louisiana and another way here in the Senate. I have one language. Ignorant as it is, it is the universal language of the sphere in which I operate. Its simplicity gains pardon for my lack of letters and education.

Nonetheless my voice will be the same as it has been. Patronage will not change it. Fear will not change it. Persecution will not change it. It cannot be changed while people suffer. The only way it can be changed is to make the lives of these people decent and respectable. No one will ever hear political opposition out of me when that is done.[7]

That Huey could alternate between vindictiveness and disarming rusticity testified to his capacity to adapt skillfully his tactics to his objective and his audience. Particularly noteworthy was his deliberate exploitation of a comic role through which he sought favorable press attention to enhance his class leadership and to obscure the uglier aspects of his regime. Huey observed of his sobriquet, "Kingfish," derived from "Kingfish of the Mystic Knights of the Sea" from the "Amos and Andy" radio show, that "it has served to substitute gaiety for some of the tragedy of politics."[8] Outrageous burlesque, however, also was a most useful disguise for grim purpose.[9] The Sands Point incident marred an otherwise consistent pattern of the Kingfish basking in the warmth of friendly national laughter, his antics successful in disarming, not repelling, most people.

Back home in Louisiana, however, in view of the events of state politics, Long's pose of comic relief was a bit difficult to sustain. The press in Louisiana, therefore, was raped rather than seduced. By ridiculing the urban press as biased spokesmen for "the interests," Long not only minimized the impact of their anti-Longism but also made them suspect as prejudiced reporters of the political news of

---

[7] Excerpts from this speech have been inscribed on the statue of Huey Long standing on the lawn of the State Capitol in Baton Rouge.

[8] Long, *Every Man a King*, 278.

[9] Burdette, *Filibustering in the Senate*, 4.

the day. The country parish weekly press supported the Long faction, either willingly or because they were in too precarious a financial position to withstand intimidation by the state administration.[10] Not content with undermining the influence of the daily newspapers and with controlling the weekly press, Long spread the gospel through his own organ, the *Progress*, "the most cheerfully venomous regular publication in the nation."[11] For those special occasions when Long's viewpoint had to be communicated swiftly to all parts of the state, Huey perfected an efficient system of direct distribution of circulars which involved the use of state printing equipment, the state highway police, and factional leaders in the parishes. Long's treatment of the Louisiana press helped explain his creation of a dictatorship based upon mass loyalty to his person. As Huey liked to boast, "When I lie from the stump, I lie big, because no matter what the newspapers say, 90 per cent of the people will believe me."[12]

Long applied a similar heavy hand, for the most part, in solving the troublesome problem of political finances. Huey's power and magnetism attracted the backing of some wealthy adventurers and businessmen, most prominent of whom was Robert S. Maestri, appointed by Huey as Commissioner of Conservation and by Huey's heirs as Mayor of New Orleans. Financial contributions also were forthcoming from the usual groups anxious to do business with the state, particularly since Huey's bent for power assured the partisan administration of many functions of government. Another important source of funds was suggested by the admission of Seymour Weiss that commissions from Louisiana highway surety bonds were held for the benefit of the Long political machine.[13] The public boast of the Long forces that theirs was a people's movement applied quite clearly to the raising of campaign funds. Salary deductions and forced subscriptions to the *Progress* were imposed upon public employees and justified as "a legitimate and honorable way of raising funds from people who owe their jobs to the administration and who

[10] A State Printing Board controlled the selection of official parish journals, and to many of the smaller newspapers the revenues so obtained represented the difference between survival and failure. Hodding Carter has written of his difficulties in maintaining an anti-Long paper in Hammond, Louisiana, in Leighton (ed.), *The Aspirin Age*, 341, 356–57.

[11] Kane, *Louisiana Hayride*, 78.

[12] Baton Rouge *State-Times*, September 4, 1930.

[13] Harris, *The Kingfish*, 239.

would have nothing otherwise. . . ."[14] Besides, averred the Longites, was it preferable to rely upon big business for the money necessary to win elections?

On balance, it was the brazenness of Long's tactics more than any other feature of his dictatorship which distinguished his rule from the practices of other American political bosses. The following comment, accurate so far as it goes, misses entirely the significance of Huey's rather unique combination of retention of mass appeal while in open pursuit of a concentration of personal power. "His [Long's] political methods, as developed in Louisiana, are the methods of orthodox American politics of the machine school, plus a little gaudy drama. When he takes personal command of the Louisiana Legislature and of its committee hearings, shouts down opposition, drives through bills that nobody has read, and plays the legislature like a pack of cards, he is only doing a little more openly what many another political boss has done more quietly over his office-telephone."[15] It would have been better for Louisiana if Long had been either the old-fashioned despot who dispensed with the Legislature, the courts, and the ballot box or the hidden boss who pulled the strings via his office telephone. Either way would have been less demoralizing to Louisianians than Long's version of absolute power, which was lawlessness, not merely legally entrenched but highly visible and candid in its operation and enjoying continued popular endorsement. These circumstances suggest the pertinence of the story of Huey P. Long to those who are concerned about the capacity of constitutional democracy to endure.

A spotty record of performance

An objective evaluation of Huey's record of highway expansion, doubtless his most publicized achievement, must entertain some doubts which would be of little concern to adulatory Longites. Governor Sanders deserves some credit for fathering the good-roads movement in the state through education of the public before Huey

---

[14] From a speech by Earl Long, New Orleans *Times-Picayune*, December 11, 1935.

[15] Unofficial Observer, *American Messiahs*, 6, quoted approvingly by P. Odegard and E. A. Helms, *American Politics* (New York, 1938), 438.

Long entered the scene, however inadequate Sanders' financial program was in meeting his own objective. Second, unpublicized testimony in connection with the Senate subcommittee's investigation into Overton's election suggests that Huey was an inconstant proponent of free bridges. Dudley L. Guilbeau, a former member of the Louisiana Highway Commission, testified that Overton had urged Long to support a program of seven toll bridges to be constructed by the Nashville Bridge Company, Overton's client. Governor Allen admitted that Huey had asked him to approve that program, but in the face of opposition from Allen and the Highway Commission, Huey had withdrawn his support.[16] Third, the magnitude of Huey's road expenditures should be noted: from 1928 to 1936, about one hundred million dollars were collected by the state and some ninety-six million dollars of road bonds issued. In 1936, four cents of the five-cent gasoline tax were allocated to the payment of the highway debt, of which only eight million dollars had been retired by that year.[17] Finally, Huey's concentration, intentionally or otherwise, on highway construction as distinct from road maintenance yielded him a maximum of political benefit and his successors a maximum of highway repair bills.

To the Louisiana citizen familiar with road conditions in the state before Long, the foregoing qualifications may appear as mere quibbles. Perhaps they are. In 1928, with a two-cent state gas tax, road district property tax funds, and federal aid, Louisiana had 296 miles of concrete roads, 35 miles of asphalt roads, and 5,728 miles of gravel roads. Only three major bridges were included within the state highway system. By the close of 1935, after a total expenditure of $133,000,000, based on a five-cent gas tax of which four cents was bonded, Louisiana had 2,446 miles of concrete roads, 1,308 miles of asphalt, and 9,629 miles of gravel roads under state maintenance. Over forty major bridges were within the state highway system. Even the hostile New Orleans press admitted in 1936, "The hard-surfaced roads reach sixty-one of the sixty-four parish seats . . . and good gravel and shell roads connect with the missing three pending the

[16] *Hearings of the Special Committee*, 935–42, 1087; see also 797–802, 860, 876, 620–23, 1085–89.

[17] Louisiana road construction has some costly features worthy of note, e.g., lack of raw materials, large areas of swampland, frequent stream and river crossings. On the other hand, state purchase of rights-of-way are less dear in Louisiana than in the more urbanized and industrialized states.

completion of hard-surfacing to them. Nearly every community in the state which is not on a hard-surfaced road is on a graveled road, and the farmers' road program, being carried out with state and federal funds, is bringing all-weather roads to the comparatively small number now without them."[18] It was on the basis of his record, then, that Long snarled in reply to a query about graft in Louisiana, "We got the roads in Louisiana, haven't we? In some states they only have the graft."[19]

Huey turned in a contradictory performance in his other major publicized accomplishment, public education. In the field of higher education, credit for arousing public interest in an expanded state university must be assigned again to predecessors of Long, namely Governor Parker and Colonel Boyd, President of Louisiana State University.[20] Long, on the other hand, deserves exclusive recognition for his drive on adult illiteracy and for his free textbook program. However, while state expenditures for education climbed to more than 50 per cent of total school revenues by 1936, the proportion of total state expenses allocated to education declined from 14.4 per cent under Simpson to 9.7 per cent under Long and 12.2 per cent under Allen.[21] Teachers' salaries in Louisiana remained low, and only long-time State Superintendent of Education Harris prevented Huey from intimidating teachers through the State Budget Committee.[22] Huey showered material benefits on "his" State University, but some students were placed on the state payroll or on political scholarships, and although apparently a high degree of academic freedom existed, its maintenance was conditional upon the whimsical good humor of the Kingfish.[23]

[18] New Orleans *Times-Picayune and States*, May 10, 1936. The preceding data comparing 1928 and 1935 highway conditions are drawn from this source.

[19] Quoted by George E. Sokolsky, "Huey Long," *Atlantic Monthly*, CLVI (November, 1935), 526.

[20] Consult Marcus M. Wilkerson, *Thomas Duckett Boyd* (Baton Rouge, 1935), for the full story of the battle for a better state university.

[21] New Orleans *States*, editorial, October 28, 1935.

[22] The documented story of Harris' opposition to Huey on this matter is contained in Guy C. Mitchell, "The Growth of State Control of Public Education in Louisiana," unpublished doctoral thesis, University of Michigan (Ann Arbor, 1942), 400–406.

[23] One non-Longite observer has concluded, "But Huey is discussed frankly— and criticized frequently—on the campus and in the faculty rooms of Louisiana State University, where, according to an imposing array of investigators, broad social and economic problems are discussed more freely than in most American

Other significant gaps in Huey's record are worth noting briefly. Share-Our-Wealth notwithstanding, Long's consumer taxes on gasoline and cigarettes were high, and his 1934 income tax law provided for only a small spread in the tax rates for lower and upper income brackets. Huey's sorry labor record typed him, at best, a rural liberal. Long enacted no pro-labor law of note, not even relative to a strengthened workmen's compensation system which he had urged when a young lawyer in 1917. Shrimp cannery supporters of the Kingfish killed a bill setting maximum hours for female workers. Long is on record as having said to a labor delegation, "The prevailing wage is as low as we can get men to take it,"[24] and in 1930 he revived the practice of farming out state prisoners at Angola to private contractors.[25] Long's coolness toward the idea of old-age pensions has been discussed earlier; he also weakened the mothers' pension law and refused to appropriate funds for its operations during the depression.[26] In his control of patronage Long spared not even the welfare institutions, which were so sacred to him as a candidate in 1924 and 1928.[27] And, while Huey enforced the anti-gambling laws in the selective manner of most Louisiana governors, he had the dubious distinction of having invited Frank Costello to set up slot machine operations in the state.[28] As a final point, it might

universities" (Unofficial Observer, *American Messiahs*, 15). Yet there is the fact of Huey's appointment of James M. Smith as President of L.S.U. because he had "a hide as thick as an elephant," a most unique educational qualification. And there was the time that the Kingfish had the University suspend the publication of the undergraduate newspaper when that publication attacked Long. Explained Huey, "I like students, but this *State* is puttin' up the money for that college and *I* ain't payin' nobody to criticize me" (emphasis added). Quoted by Davis, *Huey Long*, 227.

[24] Kane, *Louisiana Hayride*, 117.

[25] Carleton Beals and A. Plenn, "Louisiana's Black Utopia," *The Nation*, CXLI (October 30, 1935), 504.

[26] For a full account, see Worth Dinwiddie, "A History of Mothers' Pensions in Louisiana," unpublished master's thesis, the Tulane University (New Orleans, 1935).

[27] The cynical conversion of New Orleans Charity Hospital into a satrapy of the state administration is documented in Stella O'Conner, "The Charity Hospital of Louisiana at New Orleans: An Administrative and Financial History, 1736–1941," *Louisiana Historical Quarterly*, XXXI (January, 1948), 86–94.

[28] Testifying before a New York grand jury, Costello asserted that Long forgot to legalize the operation of slot machines and therefore failed to levy an annual tax of $30 per machine. Concerning New Orleans operations, Costello stated he believed that the "mayor got $30 for the city instead of the state, whereas Mr. Long intended to get it for the state." New Orleans *Times-Picayune*, May 9, 1940.

be noted that Long's benefits were costly: in 1935, state revenues from some forty-five taxes, many of them burdensome nuisance levies, were $38,000,000, an increase of 75 per cent over 1927 revenues, and Louisiana had the second highest per capita state debt in the nation.

The validity of the many charges of personal corruption leveled against Long, while highly relevant to a judgment of his record, for obvious reasons is impossible to determine on the basis of public information. Among the more authoritative accusations is that of Elmer Irey, who labeled Long, on the basis of his information as head of the Internal Revenue, as the "greatest 'confidence' man in the century," and stated that the federal government was on the eve of a tax prosecution case against Huey when he was assassinated.[29] Irey made no mention of the source of Huey's money, but two of Huey's brothers publicly charged him with selling out to the business interests he attacked from the stump. Brother Earl alleged that Huey personally had accepted a $10,000 bribe from a utilities executive in late 1927.[30] Brother Julius testified at the Overton hearings, "As a candidate for Governor the first time [1924], Huey Long received his principal financial support from the Southwestern Gas and Electric Company and their allied interests. . . ." All in all, sadly concluded Julius, "the trust could not have a better agent than Huey Long. . . . They could not get a man that would stand hitched better."[31] While such sell-outs by Southern lower-class leaders have not been uncommon, Huey's blanket denial rang true to his egocentric temperament. "Only stupid politicians take bribes. I'm my own boss. If I take a bribe, I accept a boss. There's no man living can tell me I must do this or that because some time in the past I put myself under peculiar obligations to him."[32] Perhaps more to the point, the Kingfish's pursuit of money, as well as most of his other tactics, should be understood and evaluated in the larger terms of

[29] Elmer L. Irey, *The Tax Dodgers* (New York, 1948), 88–117. Huey's will revealed an estate of $115,000, largely derived from his fees for collecting back-taxes as the state's roving attorney in 1935. It might be noted that Governor Allen's will revealed an estate of $296,000, mostly in property and mineral leases.

[30] *Hearings of the Special Committee*, 817–18.

[31] *Ibid.*, 953, 963.

[32] Interview of Huey by William K. Hutchinson, St. Louis *Post-Dispatch*, September 11, 1935.

his ambitious quest for power.

What may be said of this uneven record of Long as class reformer? To some observers, Huey's policies stamped him as a precursor of the New Deal. Longite state Senator Ernest Clements asserted, "I believe Louisiana under the leadership of the late Huey P. Long pioneered America in social legislation. I believe the national pattern was taken from the social legislation enacted in the State of Louisiana."[33] A case might be made that Long's espousal of Share-Our-Wealth caused Roosevelt to swerve to the left, but surely there was nothing in Huey's Louisiana program, except perhaps its remarkable political results, of which the New Deal was not already aware. Whether measured, then, against the New Deal or against his capacity to have the Legislature enact his policies, Long's achievements were less than spectacular.

In particular, Long's performance revealed an undue concentration on tangible and showy benefits at the expense of civic education and perhaps in ignorance of the deeper economic and social problems of his state and nation. One of Huey's stump speeches is instructive as to what "Longism" meant to its leader,

> They tell you that you got to tear up Longism in Loozyanna. . . . All right, my friends; go get you a bomb or some dynamite and blow up that building yonder. Go out and tear up the concrete roads. Get yourself some spades and shovels and scrape the gravel off them roads we've graveled and let a rain come on them. That'll put 'em back like they was before I come. Tear down the buildings I've built at the University. Take the money away from the school boards that I've give them to run your schools. And when your child starts out to school tomorrow morning, call him back and snatch the free school books out of his hand that Huey Long gave him. . . . Then you'll be rid of Longism in this State and not till then."[34]

A thorough program was carried through by Long in only one particular: the erection of a dictatorship. The rejoinder by the Long partisan that Huey's life was snuffed out before the class fruits of the dictatorship could be harvested will not stand examination. The simple and damning answer is that no dictatorship would have been required to effectuate an even more coherent and penetrating class

[33] *Proceedings of the 36th Annual Convention of the Louisiana State Federation of Labor* (1948), 128.
[34] Davis, *Huey Long,* 171.

program than that which Long did perform. The guidestar of the Kingfish was politics, not service.

A three-dimensional judgment of Huey Long

What may be termed the classic defense of the Kingfish was rendered by Senator Overton in his Memorial Address for Huey Long delivered on the floor of the United States Senate on January 22, 1936. In that speech, Overton candidly recognized that "it has been repeatedly contended by many of his critics that Senator Long rose to political power by ruthless and unscrupulous methods." Overton chose not to attempt denial of the truth of the charge but to blunt its force by asserting that Long's methods had to be understood in the context of "both the modern political history of Louisiana and the political career of the man. . . ." The crux of the ensuing argument was that the "ruthless warfare against Governor Long" conducted by the discredited "political aristocracy" he had displaced, culminating in the 1929 impeachment effort, compelled Long, "in order to save himself [and] his friends and associates from political annihilation . . . to build and maintain an organization as ruthless perhaps, as was the opposition." In short, Overton's defense was made largely on relative grounds, with the "better elements" and the Choctaws used as constant foils.

There was much of persuasive substance in Overton's hymn to the memory of Huey. If, as has been argued here, the class reforms of Long were limited both in scope and content, then the popular inflation of his reputation for liberalism commented strikingly on the inadequacies of prior state administrations. That a majority of the citizenry acquiesced in tyranny because of the benefits it yielded them condemned the conservative predecessors of Huey far more than it did the Kingfish. As Long liked to say, Louisiana had been suffering from a Tweedledum-Tweedledee administration: "one of 'em skinned you from the ankles up, the other from the neck down."[35] Compared with past governors, Huey gave more to the people, and few of his followers looked, or apparently even cared, to see if he also took more for himself.

Perhaps that indifference of Louisiana citizens reflected their long

[35] Kane, *Louisiana Hayride,* 62.

acquaintance with malodorous political tactics. There were solid precedents for a Huey Long in the looting of Reconstructionists, the immorality of the Louisiana Lottery Company, and the maneuvers of the Choctaws. Shifting and cynical alliances among governors, the Ring, blocs of legislators, and courthouse groupings were traditional in state politics. And the urban press, roasted by Huey as partisan, indeed often was thoroughly partisan. Yet, whatever the similarities of some of Long's tactics to those of preceding governors, the fact remains that only Long erected a ruthless dictatorship. If his autocracy was not justified by reference to past politics or to his current commitment to realize a class program, then it could be justified only, as Overton had urged, by the strength and tactics of the anti-Longs. The kingdom of the Kingfish, however, failed to pass that test.

The impeachment session of 1929 and the deadlocked session of 1930 were the high-water mark of anti-Long strength. From late 1930 on, Huey's torch flared ever brighter, while that of his opposition feebly flickered. A strange alliance of conservatives, malcontents, and those primarily disturbed by the increasing power of the Kingfish vainly sought to oppose effectively the kingdom that Huey built. "[Their] combined cries for good government made a dissonant chorus,"[36] and their continued unity was a function not of aggression but of survival. A minority to begin with, anti-Longs further limited their appeal by opposing indiscriminately any and all Longite measures, by harshly applying that extreme stand to determine friend from foe, and by refusing to offer reasonable alternatives to the class policies of Longism.[37] In such post-1930 circumstances, political enemies of the Kingfish posed no real threat to his leadership and compelled no resort to dictatorship. It was Huey who chose not to be a democratic leader, to substitute compulsion for persuasion and to adopt domination in place of the give and take of constitutional politics. In a democracy, a minority faction without constructive

[36] Carter, in Leighton (ed.), *The Aspirin Age*, 360.
[37] Hodding Carter has observed, "Looking back, I know now that part of our failure arose from an unwillingness to approve any Long-sponsored proposal for change, regardless of its merits." *Ibid.*, 360–61. In 1934, state Representative Pegues of DeSoto Parish broke with the anti-Longs. He charged them with a reckless and blind opposition and castigated them for their insistence upon a pristine purity of complete hostility to all Long bills. As Pegues put his case, he stated that the Orleans press had labeled him "a tool of the dictator" because he had supported one measure backed by the Kingfish. *Official Journal of the Proceedings of the House of Representatives of Louisiana*, 1 E.S. 1934, 101–104.

program, popular appeal, or much access to the policy-making centers of government deserves compassion, not extirpation.

The fact of Huey's ruthless bossdom, admitted even by Overton,
became virtually the single datum in the confirmed anti-Long's judgment of the Kingfish. Long, according to this view, was nothing but
a neurotic seeker of power, a political racketeer who would have
slashed his way to autocracy in any state. The inferences followed
that the substance of Huey's policies did not necessarily reveal anything about the true nature of his class sympathies and that a meaningful analysis of Long should confine itself to the dissection of the
techniques by which he achieved and wielded power.

To date there is not available, and perhaps there never will be
available, the kinds of materials and data which would permit an
assessment of the validity of the foregoing anti-Long judgment. In
the opinion of this writer—and it remains only an opinion—it is highly
likely that Long was possessed of deep proletarian sympathies. Those
sympathies, however, became so enmeshed with a lust for power
and with a determination to avenge every real or fancied personal
grievance as to make futile any attempt to gauge the sincerity of his
policies. It seems likely also that, far from being born with a scepter
on his mind, Long did not plan much in advance, if at all, either the
fact or the details of his dictatorship. Indeed, the Kingfish probably
was not possessed of overweening ambition until late 1932, after
Allen's and Roosevelt's elections, and coincident with the full impact
of the national depression. Less speculatively, the anti-Long judgment under discussion was defective in that it adopted an "evil great
man" approach to politics which conveniently divorced Huey from
his Louisiana setting and thereby exonerated the anti-Longs from
having contributed in any measure to the character of his regime.

The popular view of Huey Long dismisses him as little else but a
highly successful member of the family of post-bellum Southern
poor-white leaders loosely termed demagogues. What, then, is a
demagogue? The term usually refers to a rider of discontent, one
who propounds quack remedies insincerely for personal or political
gain. To uncover a demagogue, the observer is supposed to pay particular attention to irrational appeals, attempts to sway emotions,
attention-getting stunts and so forth. Such criteria, it may be suggested, are inadequate and misleading and have made of the term a
subjective epithet to be used with abandon against the politicians

one dislikes.

Irrationality, or emotionality, is a constant factor in all mass appeals. The simplification and dramatization of complex issues are essential to a democratic politics which strives to secure a continuing consent to governmental decisions through popular participation in or understanding of public actions. The restriction of demagogy to "insincere" advocates likewise provides no firm measurement. Few will deny that most politicians, indeed, most human beings, possess and act upon personal ambition in addition to principles. And what of the zealous bigot who holds to undemocratic beliefs with the tenacity of a fanatic? An unbiased application of these popularized standards of demagogy, then, would lead to the conclusion that demagogy is an inherent part of all political appeals and a tactic of most politicians.

There is a more useful standard by which to distinguish between types of political leadership. "The politician says: 'I will give you what you want.' The statesman says: 'What you think you want is this. What it is possible for you to get is that. What you really want, therefore, is the following.' . . . The politician, in brief, accepts unregenerate desire at its face value and either fulfills it or perpetrates a fraud; the statesman re-educates desire by confronting it with the reality, and so makes possible an enduring adjustment of interests within the community."[38] From the perspective of the political leader, the difference lies in the desire to be a leader of the people in contrast to the desire to lead the people somewhere. Every politician must have some broader cause to serve if his action is to have inner strength.

Within this broader category of demagogy as distinguished from statesmanship, emotionalism in politics has a neutral value. Since irrationality is a universal theme of politics it is morally neutral, and must be judged in terms of its consequences, by the kinds of emotional responses elicited. Assume the initial irrationality of a complaint. It is a longing, a feeling, an unconscious grievance or felt tension, an aggressive frustration. To some extent the reformer, the revolutionary or the leader sublimates and socializes the complaint, to some degree he intellectualizes the complaint to a higher plane of awareness, and calls for a revision of some part of the social, economic, or political framework as the necessary solution. The dema-

[38] Walter Lippmann, *A Preface to Morals* (New York, 1929), 281–82.

gogue personifies the complaint, intensifies the original irrational elements or merely relieves tension by expressing feeling. By so doing, he seduces his followers into an emotional attachment to his person which effectively blocks any group awareness of either the real sources of their discontents or the real areas of solution.

There was much in Huey Long's career which qualified him for inclusion within the category of "demagogue" as here redefined. But there were other aspects of Long's record and impact which suggest that, if the judgment of demagogue is retained, Long should be credited with having been one of the most useful and effective demagogues produced by the new South.

Unlike Mississippi's Bilbo and South Carolina's Ben Tillman, Georgia's Tom Watson and Eugene Talmadge, Huey Long eschewed "nigger-baiting," the most common tactic of Southern demagogues. While Long was no active friend of the Negro in terms of helpful legislation,[39] he did not echo Tillman's call for repeal of the Fourteenth Amendment nor Bilbo's plan for the mass emigration of Negroes to Liberia. His Share-Our-Wealth movement erected no racial barriers, not even in Louisiana,[40] and his stump speeches customarily made no reference to the race issue. Indeed, Long himself was on occasion the victim of racial alarums inspired by the opposition, as in the case of poll tax repeal in 1934. In similar fashion, Long did not follow the lead of Tom-Tom Heflin of Alabama in his baiting of the Pope, though the bi-religious setting of Louisiana gave the Kingfish little choice on the matter.[41]

In company with other poor-white leaders, though, Huey did bait corporations and urbanites, the "better elements" and the professional politicians, marking him as a legitimate heir of the suppressed

[39] For a full account of Long's record toward Louisiana Negroes, see Beals, *The Story of Huey P. Long,* 349–63.

[40] In connection with his sociological investigations into "Southerntown," John Dollard noted that some anti-Long elements stressed that thousands of Negroes in the state belonged to S-O-W clubs, seeking to raise the issue that Long was disloyal to Southern custom. *Caste and Class in a Southern Town* (New Haven, 1937), 214.

[41] In view of the foregoing, Manning J. Dauer, "Recent Southern Political Thought," *Journal of Politics,* x (May, 1948), 334, distorts Long's record when he observes, "Under him [Long], Gerald L. K. Smith learned the program which he has been advocating ever since. Since the death of Huey Long, Smith has emphasized even more the ideas of so-called one hundred per cent Americanism, racial supremacy, and related programs and has sought to transfer the movements to a national scale."

dirt-farmer movements of the nineteenth century. Indeed, as one astute student of Southern history has argued: ". . . perhaps these despised 'upstarts' [rural demagogues], as spokesmen of the agrarian interests, more nearly represented a continuation of the political and economic ideas of the ante-bellum South than did the 'developers of resources,' who were engaged in forming a New South."[42] Crushed as Populists and untouched by the urban progressivism of Wilson,[43] lower-class rural whites in Louisiana found themselves voiceless until the entry of Huey Long into state politics.

The mere presence in office of the vitriolic Kingfish gave an outlet to the accumulated resentments of the dirt-farmer community. Long's castigation, for example, of "Turkey-Head" Walmsley, "Feather-Duster" Ransdell, "Donny-boy" Ewing, and "Prince" Franklin Roosevelt fulfilled beyond the wildest of expectations the symbolic role required of him by his class leadership. His supporters could applaud vicariously as the Kingfish guffawed and "cut the Big Boys down to size," for "it was as if they themselves had crashed the headlines."[44]

It was the fact that Huey went beyond serving only or primarily as a catharsis for his following that distinguished him from many another Southern demagogue. Pappy O'Daniel and Eugene Talmadge also claimed to be neo-Populist rebels, only to effectuate opposite policies. Talmadge jettisoned the New Deal because it went too far;[45] Long ostensibly because it did not go far enough. Long may have been, as his bitter foe Sanders characterized him, "a pigmy disciple of radicalism," but his free-spending and heavy-taxing ways strongly contrasted with political leadership elsewhere in the South. The brazen dictatorship which Huey constructed and ran should not hide his substantial accomplishment of redeeming some of his promises of lower-class benefits.

By keeping at least partial faith with his supporters when in office,

[42] Daniel M. Robison, "From Tillman to Long: Some Striking Leaders of the Rural South," *Journal of Southern History*, III (August, 1937), 310.

[43] "The Wilson movement was in charge of . . . citified progressives, and Wilson's smooth, academic shibboleths of progressivism found less lodgment in the rural than in the urban mind." C. Vann Woodward, *Origins of the New South, 1877–1913* (Baton Rouge, 1951), 477.

[44] Percy, *Lanterns on the Levee*, referring to Bilbo and his rural appeal, 148.

[45] Stated Georgia's Eugene Talmadge, "I don't believe in its [Share-Our-Wealth] full program of the government doing everything. . . . I believe in small government and small taxes and getting the government out of business." Macon *News*, September 12, 1935.

Long provoked a rural lower-class protest which exceeded that of Populism in intensity and durability. The fury and substance of Longism stimulated the interest and participation of masses of whites,[46] and made them aware of the relevance of state politics to the settlement of their demands. Huey captured in his state the hitherto nonvoting elements which the New Deal had attracted on a national scale. Such a change in the composition of the electorate by itself heralded a different content of politics than in the pre-Long days.

More crucially, Longism itself set both the form and content of subsequent politics. The distracting appeals of localism and personality common to multifactionalism were reduced to minimal proportions as the bulk of voters affiliated themselves, in a close approximation to a two-party system, with the two major factions, Long and anti-Long. Candidates for state offices and many of the candidates for Congress and for parish and local offices publicly proclaimed their loyalty to one or the other faction. Factional lines within the state Legislature became firmly drawn; when combined with the customary majority support for the incumbent administration, this gave to Louisiana governors a control over legislation unequalled in most other Southern states. Huey's heavy-handed injection of realism into the content of state politics was carried forward by brother Earl so that the Long forces gained a continuity of headship normally denied to personal factions.

Longism thus was no flashing meteor of Populism, brilliant but transient. It aroused the politically quiescent have-nots and showed them unforgettably the total victory that was theirs for the balloting. It unified the fragments of politics—expectations, candidates, institutions—by means of one deeply felt adherence, pro- or anti-Longism. It came closer to the salient issues of the day than had a raft of "good government" predecessors of Huey. The policy impact of Longism was strikingly attested to in the state office campaign of 1940, when the anti-Longs, despite the involvement of the Longites in the corruption of the "Scandals," saw fit to pledge liberal measures which, in toto, made Huey's performance eight years earlier appear conservative. The persistence of the factional loyalties and the issues created by the Kingfish thus accounted in large part for the content

---

[46] Consult Key, *Southern Politics*, 523–24, for statistical verification of increased turnout of voters under Long.

and form of post-Huey politics in Louisiana.

It is no small entry on the credit side of Huey's ledger to conclude that the pervasiveness, durability, and substantive meaning of recent Louisiana bifactionalism owe much to his charismatic demagogy. In terms of total judgment, however, the immorality of his regime, neither deniable nor justifiable, tips the scales in the opposite direction. By his wholesale bribery of some communities and his ruthless raping of others, Long promoted cynicism in all as to the legitimacy of constitutionalism and its values. The anti-Longs were provoked to violence, the Longites to a countenancing of corruption and dictatorship. As defiantly phrased by Longite disciple Ellender, "I repeat, we had neither a dictator nor a dictatorship in Louisiana. If dictatorship in Louisiana, such as was charged to Huey Long, will give to the people of our nation what it gave to the people of my native state, then I am for such a dictatorship."[47] Widespread popular acceptance of the principle that the ends justify all means thus was Huey Long's morally enervating legacy.[48]

Ironically, then, in the final analysis the overriding factor in the judgment of Long becomes the hollow anti-Long battle-cry of "decency versus degradation." Yet surely the moral cost of pre-Huey state government also had been too high. Big business, the planters, and the Choctaws also had looked upon the forms and processes of government as manipulatable means to a desired selfish end. Neither pro- or anti-Longs, in truth, had a high regard for the value of constitutional machinery. The Kingfish's abuse of democratic forms was

[47] Harris, *The Kingfish*, 283.
[48] In a Gallup poll taken in late 1939, *after* the Scandals had broken in the press, the following results were obtained in response to the question: "Taking everything into consideration, do you think that Huey P. Long was a bad or a good influence in Louisiana?"

	Good Influence	Bad Influence	Both Good and Bad	No Opinion
Total state	55%	22%	14%	9%
Upper Class	33	39	20	8
Middle Class	53	23	15	9
Lower Class	65	14	12	9

While the differences in class evaluations conform to expectations, noteworthy is the high class-consciousness of the lower classes and the deep inroads into the middle and upper classes made by Long. The "total state" data may be found in Gallup and Rae, *The Pulse of Democracy* (New York, 1940), 157–58; the class breakdown was secured through the courtesy of Robert D. Coursen of the American Institute of Public Opinion.

but the more dramatic and conspicuous, since aggressive changes in the status quo required a greater co-ordination of state institutions than did conservative inaction. A plague on both their houses then. Neither upper-class rule before Huey nor one-man rule by Huey in the name of the lower classes can be adjudged satisfactory substitutes for vigorous democracy.

CHAPTER 5

The spoilsmen

THEY SHARE THE PEOPLE'S WEALTH, 1935–1940

DRAWING UPON HIS CLASS SUPPORT, the heirs of the Kingfish could have continued to wage war upon Louisiana conservatives and the New Deal administration. But, reversing Long, his successors pursued power as a means to the accumulation of money. They chose to placate the anti-Longs and to come to terms with Roosevelt, thereby achieving a broader-based political power than that possessed by their late chieftain. But they betrayed that support by an orgy of corruption and graft. They overlooked the fact that Huey's ruthless exploitation of government had been coated to some degree with the advocacy of a "cause," with the espousal of a class mission. Failing to provide a plausible justification for lining their own pockets, the Longite leaders, as an aftermath of the Scandals of 1939, lost their control of state government.

All the king's men scramble for the crown

The highly personal dictatorship of the Kingfish had arranged for no known line of succession. As a Texas legislator once observed, "Long stands politically like a mule—without pride of ancestry or hope of posterity."[1] But the hold of Long upon the loyalties of his following was so intensified by the manner of his death that it was a foregone conclusion that whichever Longite faction could snare the mantle of "my fallen leader" (as G. L. K. Smith put it) would carry the 1936 state primary with ease. The inner meaning of the

[1] Quoted by Davis, *Huey Long*, 147. The occasion was the acrimonious exchange between Huey and several Texas state legislators hostile to Long's Drop-A-Crop cotton plan of 1931.

assassination of the Kingfish was expounded by a red-eyed Governor Allen, who exhorted the loyal supporters of Huey to carry on his program "by perpetuating ourselves in office."[2] For a brief period subsequent to the death of Huey, however, Long's lieutenants jockeyed for position as the legitimate heirs of the Kingfish.

Two rival groupings of Longites, with some overlapping in composition, were evident. The Share-Our-Wealthers, headed by G. L. K. Smith, Earle J. Christenberry, secretary to the Kingfish, and James A. Noe, state Senator and acting Lieutenant-Governor, espoused a continuation of the master's economic nostrums and anti-New Deal strategy and held considerable attraction among the rural supporters of Longism. The more conservative and frankly political rival coterie was headed by Robert Maestri, Seymour Weiss, Abe Shushan, state legislators Jules Fisher and Allen Ellender, Public Service Commissioner Wade Martin, Sr., and John Fournet, by then a member of the state Supreme Court. This group, particularly since Weiss, Fisher, and Shushan were under federal income tax indictments, was anxious to restore harmony with the national administration and to condemn Share-Our-Wealth to a silent death as soon as possible. Governor Allen, though ostensibly affiliated with the latter group, tended to shift allegiances until his own political place was secured.[3]

Seeking to capitalize upon the confusion attendant on Huey's death, G. L. K. Smith announced that both Long and Allen had given support to the candidacies of Noe for governor and Martin for senator.[4] Allen retorted that no disposition of the candidacies had been concluded, and shortly afterwards announced the "official" slate: Richard W. Leche for governor; Earl Long for lieutenant-governor; and Allen and Ellender for the short- and long-term Senate seat respectively.[5]

[2] Quoted by Kane, Louisiana Hayride, 136.

[3] Since the Louisiana Constitution prohibited two successive terms for its governors, Allen could only work for the nomination to the office of United States senator.

[4] Noe was a wealthy oil producer from Monroe who had been state senator in 1932, president pro tempore in 1934, and acting lieutenant governor in 1935 after Fournet had been elected to the state Supreme Court. It was Smith's intention to become secretary to Martin, and to conduct the Share-Our-Wealth crusade with the aid of the franking privileges accorded a United States senator. Kane, Louisiana Hayride, 153.

[5] The date of the Congressional primaries of 1936 had been shifted from September back to January to coincide with the state-office primary, in order to permit Huey to run for president in 1936, if he so desired, without having to forfeit his re-election to the Senate. Since the 1938 Legislature restored the

The name of the Kingfish was invoked to bless the relatively obscure Leche.[6] Allen opined, "Fortunately, . . . there was no doubt in the mind of Senator Long as to who his candidate for Governor would be."[7] Klorer of the *Progress* stated that Huey had been trying for months before his death to persuade the reluctant Leche to run for governor.[8] The headlines of the *American Progress* of September, 1935, trumpeted: "Followers of Senator name Allen Leader, then Select the Real Huey Long Ticket. Huey Long's Wishes Carried Out in Selecting Leche for Governor. Leaders from Each of the Sixty-Four Parishes Meet and Unanimously Put Forth Ticket that had been Agreed Upon Before Assassination of the Senator, a 100 Per Cent Huey Long Ticket." Even Noe, angered when Gerald L. K. Smith announced his support of the Allen ticket, lent backing to the publicized notion that the Kingfish personally had selected Leche. Noe alleged that Huey had agreed to put Noe in as lieutenant-governor under Leche, on the understanding that Leche would run for the state Supreme Court in 1938, thereby delivering the governorship over to Noe.[9]

Disaffected rural Longites, however, denied that Huey had designated his succession prior to his murder. Harvey G. Fields of Union Parish, for example, stated categorically, "It is definitely true that Huey Long had not finally made out a ticket or selected Leche as his candidate."[10] The pressures upon Longite candidates in the 1940 state-office primaries brought forward significant revelations. If Earl Long was, as he averred, in the line of legitimate succession to Huey,

September date, the 1936 race was the only one in recent Louisiana politics in which gubernatorial and senatorial candidates ran for nomination at the same time.

[6] Leche was born in 1898, in New Orleans, the son of a Catholic father and a Protestant mother. A practicing New Orleans attorney when he entered politics in 1927, he allied with Governor Long after losing his race for state senator as a Simpson affiliate. By 1930, Leche was Huey's campaign manager in the Second Congressional District and also supervised the New Orleans mayoralty race of Huey's candidate in late 1933. Leche became secretary to Governor Allen and in 1934 was appointed to the Orleans Parish Court of Appeal to fill the vacancy caused by Justice Higgins' election to the state Supreme Court. Though known to some extent around the state, Leche hardly was to be considered as a member of the top echelon of Long leaders.

[7] New Orleans *Times-Picayune and States*, September 22, 1935.

[8] John Klorer (ed.), *The New Louisiana: 1936 Inaugural Publication*, 202.

[9] Kane, *Louisiana Hayride*, 155.

[10] Harvey G. Fields, *A True History of the Life, Works, Assassination and Death of Huey P. Long* (Farmerville, La., 1944), 56.

and Leche was the hand-picked candidate of the Kingfish, how could the Leche Scandals of 1939 be disassociated from either Huey or Earl Long? The answer to this problem in the 1940 campaign was simple: Huey Long had never selected Leche as his candidate. In February of 1940, G. L. K. Smith stated, "We took poor Oscar's [Allen] advice and presented his [Leche's] name to the people."[11] In a campaign speech in January, 1940, Earl Long informed a rural crowd, "I begged O. K. Allen not to make Leche the candidate. I knew that Leche was a city man, who knew nothing about the problems of the people in the country. . . . But Allen would not listen to me. They made Leche the candidate and I went along with them. . . ."[12]

A fair judgment would seem to be that the Maestri-Weiss faction, through the medium of Allen, dictated the priority of succession among Huey's heirs. Rural Longite distrust of the ascendant power of Maestri, Weiss, Leche, and other New Orleansites was indicated in the short-lived October, 1935, candidacies of Lewis Morgan for governor and Allen for the full-term Senate seat allocated to Ellender. By November, however, full accord had been reached by the Long forces: Leche and Earl Long headed the state ticket, Allen was assigned to the short-term Senate seat of Huey, Ellender to the Kingfish's full-term Senate seat, and Noe contented himself with re-election to the state Senate. It was with a reasonable degree of unity, then, that the Longites waged their campaign.

In view of the heterogeneous nature of the anti-Longs—remnants of the Square Dealers and of the Walmsley minority of resisting "old regulars," the five Louisiana congressmen to whom federal patronage was being channeled, and the Orleans contingents of the Women's Committee of Louisiana, the Honest Election League, and the Jackson Democratic Clubs of Francis Williams—their aggressive platform and tactics during the 1936 campaign must be commended.

Congressman John Sandlin, of the Fourth District, entered against Ellender; Frank Looney of Caddo contested Allen's candidacy; while Congressman Cleveland Dear, of the Eighth District, headed a full state ticket composed of nonincumbents in opposition to the Leche slate. Styling themselves as Home Rulers, Dear, Sandlin, and Looney exploited the themes of dictatorship and corruption in a joint effort

[11] New Orleans *Times-Picayune*, February 13, 1940.
[12] *Ibid.*, January 13, 1940.

to arouse the citizenry and sow discord among the Longite leaders. Rural antipathies were catered to by the (accurate) accusation that Maestri was the *de facto* head of the Long organization and would be made mayor of New Orleans. In an attempt to shift the onus of assassination upon Huey's heirs, the anti-Longs pledged a Congressional investigation into the circumstances of Huey's murder and castigated Allen for his conspicuous failure to probe the matter. The deprivations forced upon Louisiana because of Huey's vendetta with the national administration were depicted in graphic detail, and the anti-Longs pledged a resumption of friendly relations with the federal government. Dear promised repeal of coercive laws which gave the Long faction control over teachers, public employees, sheriff's deputies, and polling booth personnel.

The anti-Longs also recognized to some extent the core appeal of Longism by pledging themselves to the enactment of a liberal program which included the reduction of automobile licenses to three dollars, the discontinuance of the gasoline tax upon fuel used by fishermen, the creation of a state department of social welfare to supervise social security and old-age pension payments, and the continuation of good roads, free textbooks, and homestead exemptions.[13] But the weapons at the disposal of the anti-Longs were limited. Their only significant control over votes stemmed from the federal patronage of WPA work orders, which the five anti-Long congressmen distributed to thousands of the unemployed. But, as one observer noted, "they didn't help much. The poor jobless devils took the work orders readily enough, but they didn't vote WPA."[14]

The campaign requirements of the Long forces were far simpler than those of their opposition. The Leche-Long full state ticket, composed largely of incumbents,[15] had only to maintain factional unity, to wax wrathful over the murder of the Kingfish, to promise to complete his work, and to bring to the polls a sufficiently high proportion of the majority of voters who were attached to Longism. As G. L. K. Smith phrased the dominant Longite theme of assassina-

[13] See New Orleans *Item-Tribune*, September 22, 1935; New Orleans *Times-Picayune and States*, October 27, 1935; and Kane, *Louisiana Hayride*, 161.

[14] Carter, in Leighton (ed.), *The Aspirin Age*, 357.

[15] The exceptions included Leche for governor, Earl Long for lieutenant-governor, and Pat Tugwell, recent head of the Louisiana Highway Commission, for state treasurer.

tion, "The martyr's blood is the seed of victory."[16] The acceptance of
brother Earl on the ticket symbolized, despite the rift in 1932 between Earl and Huey, the continuing devotion of Huey's successors
to his memory, a devotion further proved by the pledge of a thorough investigation into Huey's death. Leche guaranteed that no sales
tax would be enacted during his administration and, together with
Superintendent of Education T. H. Harris, promised to repeal the
laws politicizing teachers and to enact a teacher tenure law.[17] New
Orleans, restored portions of its legitimate revenue through special
session action in September, was promised a new era of plenty, contingent upon the ousting of Walmsley and Ring co-operation with
Maestri.

Despite Leche's dedication to furthering "the advances of the
Long-Allen administrations," the observant citizen could detect significant differences between Dick Leche and the Kingfish. Though
not committing himself to any sweeping repudiation of dictatorial
laws, Leche gave evidence of his intent to use them for different
ends. Not even campaign lip-service was accorded Share-Our-
Wealth, and the known desires of the Maestri-Weiss group assured a
peace with Washington in the event of Longite victory. Of equal
significance was the passage, in the September, 1935, special session
(4 E.S. 1935), under the direction of Huey's heirs, of a concurrent
resolution which pledged no new or increased taxes upon the oil
industry for a ten-year period. Finally, Leche's grudging espousal of
old-age pensions, occasioned by the necessity of matching anti-Long
promises, clearly forewarned of the restricted liberalism to be expected of his administration.[18]

[16] Report of H. O. Thompson, United Press staff writer, September 13, 1935.
[17] Louisiana educational institutions already had run afoul of accrediting asso-
ciations because of undue politicization. In December of 1935, the Southern
Association placed Louisiana Normal College on probation, and the Council of
Legal Education of the American Bar Association placed Louisiana State University Law School on probation.
[18] Midway in the campaign, Longite Wade Martin attacked the federal old-age
pension law as a "joke." "You got to be so old as even not to be able to dream,
and you have got to sign affidavits that are not worth a damn before you can get
the old age pension. The federal government set aside $49,000,000 for all the
states, and after you take out the administrative expenses, you haven't got enough
left to pay 30 cents a month pension" (Baton Rouge *State-Times*, November 25,
1935). In early January, Leche finally agreed to support old-age pensions and to
work with the federal government on the rest of the welfare programs available
with federal aid. The February, 1936, issue of the *American Progress*, appearing

The immediate consequences of Leche's modifications of Longism were gratifying to his faction. The results of the primary election of January 21, reported in Table 15, were noteworthy for the high proportion of the state vote secured by the Long faction and for the high number of parishes carried by them. Since all Congressional

TABLE 15. The Louisiana Vote in the 1936 Democratic Gubernatorial and Senatorial Primaries

Office and Candidates	Orleans	Other	State	% State	Parishes Carried by Majority
Governor					
Leche	103,666	258,836	362,502	67.1	61
Dear	40,052	136,098	176,150	32.6	3
Other	216	1,502	1,718	.3	0
Total	143,934	396,436	540,370	100.0	64
Senate (short-term)					
Allen	103,074	265,041	368,115	68.7	62
Looney	38,910	121,656	160,566	30.0	2
Other	863	6,163	7,026	1.3	0
Total	142,847	392,860	535,707	100.0	64
Senate (full-term)					
Ellender	103,517	261,414	364,931	68.0	61
Sandlin	39,052	128,419	167,471	31.2	3
Other	587	3,590	4,177	.8	0
Total	143,156	393,423	536,579	100.0	64

SOURCE: computed from *Compilation of Primary Election Returns of the Democratic Party, State of Louisiana,* election held January 21, 1936, issued by the Secretary of State, for the Senate primaries; adapted from Alexander Heard and Donald S. Strong, *Southern Primaries and Elections,* 70–71, for gubernatorial primary.

posts were at stake along with the usual state legislative and parish offices, the 1936 victory was more sweeping in scope than Huey had ever enjoyed. Administration-backed candidates captured all eight Congressional seats, the contested seat for the state Supreme Court, and that for the Public Service Commission. Only a handful of anti-administrationists was returned to the Louisiana House,[19] and but few anti-Long sheriffs survived.

before the primary election, urged a vote for the Leche ticket as the only way to get old-age pensions for Louisiana. "A vote for Cleveland Dear will be a vote *against* such pensions, and will mean a continuation of the bulldozing political methods of the W.P.A. dole."

[19] The anti-Long legislators hailed from East Feliciana, West Baton Rouge, DeSoto, and St. Mary parishes. Noe's later opposition to Leche also caused state Representative Fink of Ouachita to deny support to the state administration.

Table 15 reveals the striking similarity in the vote for each of the three Long candidates, on the one hand, and for each of the three anti-Long candidates on the other. An examination of the relationship between the vote for governor and that for the members of his state ticket yields the same finding. For example, the total vote of each of the candidates for minor state office on Leche's ticket ranged between 360,000 and 370,000. Although several of those candidates were veteran officials reputedly possessed of personal followings, a parish by parish statistical breakdown of the vote provides no signifi-

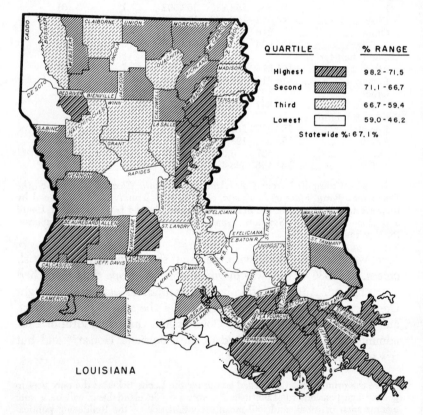

FIGURE 6. Quartile map: proportion of parish vote cast for Leche, 1936 Democratic gubernatorial primary.

SOURCE: same as that for Table 15.

cant evidence of deviation by those candidates from Leche's voting pattern. The inference of a disciplined vote for factional tickets is further borne out by noting the pattern of relative parish response. Fifty-three of Louisiana's sixty-four parishes ranked in the same quartile of support for Longism (and for anti-Longism) in each of the three races considered in Table 15. The remaining eleven parishes shifted no more than one quartile of support from one contest to another. Figure 6, which deals with Leche's race, would serve almost equally well for Allen or Ellender.

The January, 1936, primary thus demonstrated in almost pure form the cohesive and disciplined bifactionalism which has characterized recent Louisiana politics since the days of the Kingfish.[20] Catholic Ellender, from Terrebonne, Protestant Allen, from Winn, and Leche, of mixed religious background from Orleans, drew upon the same sources of electoral support in about the same degree of strength. Relative parish performance on Longism (Figure 6) continued the basic pattern earlier uncovered with the exceptions of the cluster of high-quartile parishes in southeast Louisiana, largely a function of Choctaw backing of the state administration, and of the third-quartile position of some of the northern upland parishes. Since Natchitoches, Winn, Grant, and LaSalle each supported Leche by nearly a two-to-one vote, they were, however, among the highest of the third-quartile parishes.

The ascendancy of Leche and the forces behind him was threatened briefly in the few months between the primary election and inauguration by the death of Oscar Allen, Governor and Senator-elect for the unexpired term of the Kingfish.[21] State Senator James A. Noe succeeded to the office of governor, and proceeded to exercise

---

[20] Harold F. Gosnell, *Grass Roots Politics* ([Washington, D. C., 1942], 120–21), concluded that "the 1936 primary elections in Louisiana offer an example of machine and factional cohesion that is unparalleled in existing studies of American voting behavior."

[21] Of mediocre talents and able to take orders, O. K. Allen was typical of Long's lieutenants. A poor boy from Winn Parish, Allen had been a part-time teacher and sawmill operator before his entry into local politics. He became clerk of the Winn Parish police jury in 1912, and parish assessor in 1916. Allen backed Huey in the latter's 1918 Railway Commission race and was Long's Fifth District campaign manager in 1924. Following his 1928 election to the state Senate, Allen was made Longite floor leader and then resigned to accept appointment to be chairman of the Highway Commission. For his proven loyalty, Allen was rewarded by Huey with the governorship in 1932.

its powers to bolster his own intended candidacy for the governorship in 1940. Seeking to establish himself as *the* true follower of the Kingfish, Noe revived Share-Our-Wealth and had the Democratic State Central Committee affirm his gallant suggestion to appoint Huey's widow to complete Long's Senate term. But Noe, not then the unrelenting critic of the Leche administration that he was to become, soon made peace with the Long forces. Had he used the full power of his office against the Leche faction, the history of the next four years of Louisiana politics might well have been different. As it happened, the Louisiana hayride went on uninterrupted and, under Leche, moved into high gear.

The Second and Third Louisiana Purchases

Scarcely had the Kingfish been interred when his lieutenants sought to strike an alliance with Huey's arch rival, the national administration. It was rumored as early as September, 1935, that Congressman Paul Maloney had been sent as an emissary to Washington to pledge support for Roosevelt, in both the Congress and the national party convention, in exchange for a cessation of federal income tax indictments and for Louisiana's receipt of PWA construction funds.[22] Events buttressed rumors as Leche, in the 1936 regular session, had repealed Huey's anti-Roosevelt laws, and the President appointed a Leche-endorsed candidate as customs collector for the port of New Orleans. In late May, the Justice Department announced its abandonment of criminal tax proceedings against Longite leaders in Louisiana. Although federal officers vigorously defended that action, many observers interpreted it as conclusive proof of the existence of a deal between state and national leaders.[23]

[22] New Orleans *Item*, September 13, 1935.
[23] In April, 1935, state Representative Joseph Fisher was convicted of income tax evasion and sentenced to eighteen months in prison. Fisher had taken kickbacks from contractors supplying the Highway Commission with coral shells at inflated prices. In October, 1935, Abe Shushan, then president of the Orleans Levee Board, was indicted for income tax fraud in connection with the alleged receipt of more than $500,000 in bribes but was acquitted by a federal jury. On May 30, 1936, United States Attorney Rene Viosca, asserting that the Shushan case had been the government's strongest, dismissed criminal proceedings in income tax fraud cases against Weiss, Jules Fisher, Mike Moss, Joseph Haspel, and others. In mid-June, nine of the twenty-three members of the

Both sides lived up to what the press and hostile critics dubbed "the Second Louisiana Purchase." In mid-June, 1936, the Louisiana Legislature recessed to sojourn to Texas to applaud the President's visit to the Texas centennial celebration. Later that month Seymour Weiss headed the state's delegation to the Democratic National Convention, at which Louisiana seconded the nomination of and gave its twenty votes to Roosevelt, and supported the abrogation of the two-thirds rule for nominations, thereby minimizing future Southern influence over the selection of presidential candidates. By late 1936, Gerald L. K. Smith and other Share-Our-Wealthers were *persona non grata* in Louisiana. Leche leaders, cognizant of the political impact of the shower of federal gold, wasted no time in elaborate defense of their reversal of the policies of the Kingfish. Federal moneys were used to expand the physical plant of Louisiana State University, New Orleans Charity Hospital, and of other state institutions and to construct free bridges.

Except for the occasional defection of Overton,[24] the Leche forces went right down the line in support of Roosevelt. The grave issues presented by the President's court-packing plan were easily resolved by Leche who observed, "To oppose this plan of the president is like breaking up a ball game with the winning run on the third base."[25] In April, 1937, the President and the First Lady visited New Orleans,[26] and in May, Jim Farley appeared as commencement speaker at Louisiana State University. In 1938, on orders from Leche, all Louisiana congressmen backed the wages and hours bill, and in 1939, Leche announced his support of a third term for Roosevelt. Longite relations with Roosevelt seemed secure enough by 1938 for the Louisiana Senate to urge the President to pardon former state

Orleans grand jury which had indicted Huey's aides protested Viosca's decision, but United States Attorney General Homer Cummings reiterated his full confidence in Viosca and termed the dismissal of the indictments as "purely routine." The federal government did institute civil suits and collected over two million dollars in the next few years.

[24] Overton opposed the 1937 court-packing plan and a third term for Roosevelt.

[25] New Orleans *Times-Picayune and States,* February 14, 1937.

[26] Roosevelt's visit gave Mayor Maestri his day in the national press. After the President had been served a dish of New Orleans' famed Oysters Rockefeller, Maestri blurted, "How ya like dem ersters, huh?" (quoted by Michie and Ryhlick, *Dixie Demagogues,* 124). The celebrated Antoine's Restaurant in New Orleans displays an interesting set of photographs of the President and the entourage of Louisiana politicos taken on that occasion.

Representative Joseph Fisher, convicted of income tax evasion in
1935. And throughout 1938 and early 1939 there persisted the rumor
that Governor Leche was considering acceptance of an appointment
to the federal judiciary.

The outbreak of the Scandals put the quietus on the latter rumor
and signalled the end of the cynical arrangement between the state
and national Democratic parties. Though productive of great material benefit to the citizens of Louisiana, the Second Louisiana
Purchase reflected credit to neither contracting party. Roosevelt's
political manipulation of relief and construction funds for Louisiana
echoed Huey's amoral tactics in his selfish war with the federal
government. Moreover, the uninhibited looting of public funds by
the Leche administration as revealed in the Scandals probably should
be understood in terms of the entente with Roosevelt. Since the Long
forces controlled the state courts, the establishment of "friendly"
relations with Washington could be interpreted as a guarantee
against legal punishment for malfeasance in office, an open invitation, as it were, to rob with impunity. But in their reckless exploitation of all avenues of governmental graft, the Leche faction forgot the
prophetic words of the Kingfish, "If those fellows ever try to use the
powers I've given them without me to hold them down, they'll all
land in the penitentiary."[27]

In view of Huey Long's furious attack upon the national administration, the Second Louisiana Purchase was unconcealable and was
fully revealed by press coverage. But the Leche forces engaged in
another and more subtle purchase which escaped the attention of
the press, one which sapped the political morality of voters in a more
invidious manner than had the tactics of the Kingfish. Leche's success in that effort may be termed the Third Louisiana Purchase,
which consisted of confirming the belief of the Longite partisan that
liberal government necessarily meant buccaneer government and
that of the anti-Long which sanctioned buccaneer government so
long as the product of politics was reasonably conservative.

Continued Longite support of Leche was not surprising because
the Long followers had never rejected the kingdom of the Kingfish
nor insisted upon a more systematic liberal program. But the acceptance—nay, praise—of the Leche regime by the anti-Longs revealed

[27] Quoted by Michie and Ryhlick, *Dixie Demagogues,* 138.

the heart of the Third Louisiana Purchase. Leche's retention of Huey's gross powers was condoned by anti-Long spokesmen because the Governor's policies hewed closer to conservatism than any had dared predict possible for a successor of the Kingfish. The intensity of the anti-Long's adherence to their principles of good government thus varied once again in relation to the policy content of politics. That the anti-Longs were aroused by the Scandals to a greater degree than the Longite rank and file should not obscure the crucial observation that both sides apparently were willing to accept corrupt government for a price. In the Leche days of extensive governmental action, this fundamental immorality of the Louisiana electorate invited that perversion of public office into private advantage known as the Scandals.

Factional opposition to and criticism of Leche's actions were minimal. In both the 1936 and 1938 regular sessions only a handful of representatives opposed the state administration, and then not consistently, while Noe of Ouachita and Sweeney of Calcasieu were the sole persistent opponents in the upper house. For his efforts, the Longites shunted Noe to unimportant committee assignments, made his defeated state senatorial opponent Commissioner of Highways, rigged the city elections of Monroe against his candidate, and brusquely condemned him in the *American Progress* as "Monroe's Millionaire Senator."[28] In 1936 and 1938, all constitutional amendments were endorsed by the voters.[29] In 1938 all incumbent congressmen were returned and Senator Overton was renominated without opposition.[30]

On several occasions when Leche sought to repeal one of Huey's pet laws or to abandon one of the Kingfish's favored tactics, some of his legislative following defected. For example, in the 1936 session, twenty-two House votes were cast against repeal of the adjustable occupational license tax on Standard Oil, and thirty-seven House votes were cast against repeal of Huey's restrictions on the establish-

[28] *American Progress*, July 20, 1936.
[29] Amendment No. 15 on the 1936 ballot was defeated, but Leche desired its defeat. New Orleans *Times-Picayune*, June 22, 1937.
[30] Earl Long, for some unexplained reason, broke with Congressman Newt Mills of the Fifth District and opposed his re-election in 1938, inducing Leche to oppose Mills late in the campaign. Though Mills was returned to Congress, the conflict was more in the nature of an intra-factional tiff than a significant defeat for the Leche administration.

ment of trust estates. A bill to create an additional assistant district
attorneyship for the (anti-Long) parish of East Baton Rouge was
opposed by seventeen representatives, while forty-four negative
votes defeated a measure providing back pay for one-time Public
Service commissioners Harvey Fields and Dudley LeBlanc. In the
1938 session, some Share-Our-Wealthers, among them representatives
Peters of Winn, Beckcom of Bossier, and James of Caldwell, opposed
Leche's support of salary raises for sundry officials in view of his
insistence upon levying a sales tax to secure needed state revenues.
On the whole, however, Leche faced less legislative opposition than
had Huey or any other recent chief executive.

Inheritance of Huey's laws which inflated executive power combined with absence of factional opposition to give Leche an impreg-
nable base for political action. The anti-Long press, rather than urge
Leche to divest himself of some of those inherited powers, contented
itself by piously hoping that the Governor would use his extraordinary political strength wisely, that is, conservatively.[31] In the main,
Leche satisfied the anti-Longs, though he did reinforce the allegiance
of his Longite following in ways more significant than declaring
Huey's birthday to be a legal holiday. The free textbook law, for
example, with Leche's addition of free basic school supplies, was
imbedded in the Constitution. The homestead tax exemption law
was liberalized in amount and coverage, debt moratoriums were
continued through 1939, and an additional $35,000,000 of highway
bonds were issued.

Other important measures enacted policies objectionable to no
reasonable faction. Social security and unemployment compensation
systems were launched in co-operation with the federal government.
A state hospital board was created, and Leche undertook some
reorganization of the structure of state administration. The terms
under which public lands could be leased for mineral exploitation
were tightened. As the first act of his administration, Leche issued
lifetime commissions to city police and firemen. As pledged, Huey's
law creating a state budget committee was amended to establish a
tenure law for teachers, and, in addition, a retirement system for
teachers was begun.

Unlike Huey, however, the public policy orientation of Leche was

[31] See, for example, the editorial of the New Orleans *Times-Picayune*, May 11,
1936.

basically favorable to business. The Governor was in line both with Louisiana conservatives and some Southern leaders elsewhere in seeking salvation in industry for the economic backwardness of the region. As part of a program to attract industry, Leche insisted upon the repeal, over strong Longite protests, of Huey's prohibitions on trust estates, his "roving attorney" law, and his occupational tax on Standard Oil.[32] Brazen political harassment of business ceased. A new program of ten-year tax exemptions for new industries or additions to existing industry was established, to be administered by a new State Board of Commerce and Industry. Governor Leche was granted an appropriation of $100,000 to "advertise Louisiana." The state administration's attitude toward labor was conditioned by its industrial bias.[33] The following event of December 6, 1938, inconceivable under Huey, testified to the new directions of Leche's Longism: A. B. Paterson, president of New Orleans Public Service, Inc., presented a $13,000, 40-foot cruiser yacht to Leche as a gift, on behalf of a number of New Orleans businessmen, "in recognition of his efforts in increasing employment and industry in Louisiana."[34]

Tax measures reflected the confusion of public policy occasioned by the modification of traditional Longism by Leche. Although the severance and corporation franchise taxes were increased, so also was the liquor tax, while new taxes on lubricating oils and on soft drinks were levied. Most revealing of all was the enactment of a

[32] Earl Long and the Share-Our-Wealth contingent narrowly averted repeal of Huey's restrictions upon trust estates in 1936 when the Senate refused to accept House amendments to the repeal measure. The 1938 Legislature passed the repeal measure unanimously and also repealed the roving-attorney law after Hugh Wilkinson had sought unsuccessfully to compel Standard Oil to pay alleged back taxes and accrued penalties for a seven-year period. Leche additionally had enacted a bill prescribing a three-year period for proscription of tax cases. The 1936 session, amid cries that Leche was surrendering to Standard Oil, fixed the occupational tax at one cent a barrel and eliminated the provisions giving the Governor discretion to set the tax anywhere under the maximum of five cents a barrel.

[33] Leche opposed a 1936 bill to create a commission to draft an improved workmen's compensation law and a 1938 bill to establish a workmen's compensation commission in place of the courts for the handling of such cases. He vetoed a maximum hours bill for women in 1936, though allowing its passage in 1938. An anti-sitdown-strike bill was pushed, and Maestri's record against labor in New Orleans was notorious. Though hardly pro-labor, Leche did not go to the extreme of attempting to suppress labor organization and depress wages as inducements for outside industries to settle in Louisiana.

[34] New Orleans *Times-Picayune*, December 7, 1938.

sales tax, a form of taxation condemned by Huey,[35] and repudiated by candidate Leche in 1935.[36] In the 1936 session, Leche had
enacted a 2 per cent "luxury tax," significantly supported by the
urban press and business organizations and opposed by labor groups,
Noe, and other extreme Longites. In defense of the measure, Leche
pleaded the necessity of meeting the costs of social welfare programs[37] together with a description of the tax as "impos[ing] no
levy on anything a poor man eats, wears, or uses in pursuit of his
occupation."[38] In 1938, pointing to inadequate welfare funds, Leche
converted the "luxury tax" to a straight one per cent sales tax.[39] The
bill passed the House by 93-4 vote, with only representatives Jewell
and Peters feeling it necessary to explain their support for a policy
Huey abhorred.[40] Leche did violence to still another of his campaign
pledges by insisting successfully on the abandonment of an investigation into the circumstances of Huey's assassination.[41]

The ability of the Leche organization to face two directions at
once and not provoke legislative dissension was due in part to its
retention of many of Huey's coercive powers. Although some of
Huey's laws had been repealed by the Legislature or overturned by
the courts, the foundations of his dictatorship remained intact under
Leche. The Governor additionally relied heavily upon patronage and
the "bribery" of legislators through dual job-holding. Legislative

[35] In his *Every Man a King*, 289, speaking of the sales tax fight in Congress,
Long observed, "I regarded the sales tax as a disaster . . . ."
[36] *American Progress*, October, 1935.
[37] Leche was quoted as asserting that a 5 per cent sales tax would be enacted
if that were necessary to support a legitimate social welfare program. Baton
Rouge *State-Times*, October 16, 1936.
[38] *American Progress*, June 20, 1936.
[39] The straight sales tax made use of tokens. The search for an appropriate
slogan to sugar-coat the tax may be traced through the 1938 issues of *Public
Welfare*, official monthly publication of that Louisiana state department. The
July and August issues suggested, "The token really isn't this big—a penny is ten
times as large." From September on the catch phrase, with authorship credited
to Leche himself, was, "A tax so small a penny is too big to pay it with."
[40] For their explanation, consult *Official Journal of the Proceedings of the
House of Representatives of Louisiana*, 1938 regular session, 358.
[41] Leche took personal responsibility for killing state Representative Simpson's
(Caddo) bill providing for a six-man commission, with $100,000 appropriations,
to investigate the facts of Huey's death. The Governor argued that the known
assassin was dead and that the primary responsibility for investigation lay with
Mrs. Rose Long, his widow, who had served for a brief period as a United States
Senator.

defeat, in 1938, of a limited civil service measure half-heartedly backed by Leche insured the availability of state jobs for spoils politics.[42] A Leche-sponsored constitutional amendment removed the disqualifications of state legislators for offices created, or for offices the salaries of which were increased, during their term of legislative office. When the books of the Debt Moratorium Commission were opened under the succeeding Jones administration, it was revealed that thirty-seven of the legislators elected in 1936 and seven of the legislators elected in 1940 had received a total of nearly $300,000 in salaries and fees from the agency in the period from January 1, 1936, to May 31, 1940.[43] Thirteen of the twenty-eight Orleans legislators in the House and Senate were on the city payroll for various periods of time from 1936 to 1940.

Funds for the Long faction continued to be drawn in part from the imposition of deductions. The director of New Orleans Charity Hospital, in an inadvertently crude manner, extracted two dollars from every pay envelope for subscriptions to the *Progress*. When the *Times-Picayune* exposed the practice, he lamely termed his action "a mistake."[44] An auditor in the Highway Department, later fired, asserted that the state administration exacted a 5 per cent deduction on the salaries of public employees and required, in addition, that each worker sell (or pay for) from five to ten subscriptions to the *Progress* annually.[45] Public agencies contributed to the faction's coffers and doubtless to the pockets of factional leaders by contracting for advertising in the *Progress*, the advertisements frequently being little else than endorsements of the Leche administration.[46]

[42] In 1938, Leche supported civil service for employees of the welfare and labor departments, the State Hospital Board, and the charity hospitals of New Orleans and Shreveport. The House passed the bill after excluding the Department of Labor and the two hospitals from its coverage. The Senate then defeated the measure, making civil service one of the few Leche measures which failed of passage. For a similar performance by Earl Long in 1950, again on civil service, see below, p. 228.

[43] Baton Rouge *State-Times*, May 31, 1940.

[44] New Orleans *Times-Picayune*, May 15, 1938.

[45] Baton Rouge *State-Times*, May 19, 1938. In mid-1940, two of Leche's department heads were indicted for violation of a federal statute prohibiting the solicitation of political funds from employees whose salaries were paid in part or in full by federal funds. The department heads had attempted to sell the employees subscriptions to the *Progress*, which the indictment accurately termed a "political paper." Baton Rouge *State-Times*, June 29, 1940.

[46] The *Progress* of May 14, 1937, commemorating the first anniversary of Leche's inauguration, contained much advertising of this type. Westbrook Pegler,

From the evidence available to the public, even early in the Leche administration, it required no great stretch of the imagination to conclude that spoils politics, together with some of its uglier consequences, was widespread. Leche purchased an estate of two hundred acres in St. Tammany Parish in late 1936 and admitted to an income of $90,000 his first year in office.[47] In 1936, Noe accused the state administration of levying salary deductions, and, in 1938, he introduced a series of reform bills in the Senate designed to expose the machine tactics relied upon by Leche.[48] A publicized incident in the 1938 legislative session dramatized the Governor's tight control of the Legislature. Coleman Lindsey, Leche's floor leader in the Senate, offered an amendment to the sales tax bill which was represented as having the support of Leche. The amendment passed, 24-9. Lindsey revealed the next day that Leche, in fact, was opposed to the amendment. The Senate promptly reversed its action, 35-2. The reversal was quite complete, for the two supporters of the amendment on the second vote were not among the twenty-four who had voted favorably the first time—they were the persistent critics, Noe and Sweeney, who had been absent on the first vote on the amendment.

In view of the rather obvious existence of machine and spoils politics under Leche from 1936 on, the question arises as to why it was not until 1938 that the urban (anti-Huey) press began to oppose Leche aggressively. It may be suggested that, once again, the anti-Longs were more concerned with the product than the methods of politics. The patronage, waste, and graft of the Leche administration helped increase the state budget which approached, as the *Times-Picayune* observed in alarm in mid-1938, "$100,000,000 [a year]."[49] Under such circumstances, that newspaper could not countenance the substitution of a general sales tax for the luxury tax it had supported two years before,[50] and editorialized against the "policies of

in receipt of a copy, cited the *Progress* as Leche's personal organ and quipped, "Chum, that is no organ. That is the massed bands of all the official departments, state and municipal, in all Louisiana." Syndicated column of Pegler, in Hammond, La., *Vindicator*, April 15, 1938.

[47] Alva Johnston, "They Sent a Letter," *The Saturday Evening Post*, CCXII (June 22, 1940), 29.

[48] See Senate bills Nos. 28, 29, 31–33, 35–38, 40–43, and 45 of the 1938 regular session. All the bills were called up and indefinitely postponed, by 33–3 vote, when Noe was absent from the Senate.

[49] New Orleans *Times-Picayune*, editorial, May 26, 1938.

[50] *Ibid.*, May 28, 1938.

SHARE THE PEOPLE'S WEALTH 135

recent Legislatures to vote new taxes and deny the possibility of
their repeal by funding the proceeds into bonds. . . ."[51] In short, the
conservatives became aroused in the manner of Representative
Brownell's (St. Mary Parish) acid query of his fellow-legislators in
1938, "Our present policy seems to be to raise salaries, add taxes,
increase appropriations, entertain endowments and memorials and
buy real estate. Let's ride high, wide and handsome—on with the
dance. Who pays?"[52]

That the initial moderate policies of the Leche administration
should have gratified the anti-Longs is quite understandable. But a
passionate espousal of good government should not await a fiscal
accounting at the close of the first biennium. An acid test of the sincerity of anti-Long advocacy of proper political tactics occurred at
the outset of the Leche term, and in New Orleans, the home of the
Times-Picayune and other leaders of state conservatism. Anti-Long
conservatives failed that test badly.

As a result of the pressures exerted upon the city through the
punitive actions of the Kingfish, the Choctaws capitulated shortly
after Huey's assassination. Some financial aid from the state was
forthcoming, and control over taxes, revenues, and city departments
was returned to the Ring.[53] The Choctaws and New Orleans paid
dearly for this measure of fiscal solvency and self-government. Mayor
Walmsley committed himself to resigning in the middle of his term,
on the understanding that Robert Maestri would succeed him without opposition in a special election. Maestri secured the Democratic
nomination without challenge in July, 1936, and upon the withdrawal of a Republican candidate, was declared Mayor without a
general election on August 17, 1936. In anticipation of Maestri's
mayoralty, the Leche Legislature of 1936 revamped the city's charter, without submitting its revisions to the electorate for approval,
to give the mayor almost complete authority over the commission
council and the city government and control over patronage which

[51] *Ibid.*, June 2, 1938.
[52] New Orleans *Times-Picayune,* June 1, 1938.
[53] With Leche's aid, New Orleans secured a loan of $4,000,000, issued bonds
for New Orleans Charity Hospital and for street paving, once again received
$700,000 annually from the state for the maintenance of city streets, and garn-
ered millions of dollars worth of PWA contracts. The city was empowered to
collect its taxes at the beginning of the year, thereby eliminating the necessity of
borrowing at high interest rates to meet its obligations.

enabled Maestri to take over the leadership of the Choctaws. Not content with arbitrarily tailoring the structure of city government to accommodate a partisan affiliate, the Leche forces enacted a constitutional amendment postponing (i.e., eliminating) the mayoralty election scheduled for 1938. The voters of New Orleans would have to wait until 1942 to pass judgment upon a mayor "elected" without opposition in 1936.

Anti-Long reaction to these high-handed political maneuvers was one of co-operation, if not praise. The constant themes in the judgment of the New Orleans press were the wisdom of Walmsley's self-sacrifice, dislike of the Ring, and the friendship with the city pledged by Leche and Maestri.[54] Those themes evaded the basic point that the city government had been raped and its voters scorned. No amount of editorializing could gloss over the fact that Huey's heirs had abused power in a manner as flagrant as any punitive action of Huey Long. Yet the anti-Longs, shrill advocates of "clean government," wished Leche and Maestri well.

The brazen, jeering Kingfish conducted his tyranny openly, with the blare of trumpets and the crash of cymbals which, in view of his class program, left the conservatives little choice but opposition. The silent Maestri and the jovial Leche ran their dictatorship quietly and were amenable to the businessman's point of view. These circumstances made reaction to the Leche administration a fairer test of the sincerity of the anti-Longs' position than did their attitudes toward Huey or the Scandals. It was most revealing, therefore, that a measure of restored conservatism wedded many anti-Longs to the Leche administration in the same manner as Huey's bludgeoning liberalism had attracted lower-class loyalties.[55] Fortunately for the moral fiber of the anti-Longs and other Louisiana citizens, the Leche faction itself broke the spell of the Third Louisiana Purchase by overstepping the fuzzy limits of allowable graft. By indulging in wholesale corruption in high and low places, the Leche forces aroused in large

---

[54] See, for example, Walmsley's farewell speech as reprinted in the New Orleans *Item*, June 30, 1936; the editorial in the *Item* of the same date; and the editorial in the New Orleans *Times-Picayune*, July 1, 1936.

[55] For example, see the editorial in the Baton Rouge *State-Times*, June 22, 1939, written before the full extent of the Scandals was suspected. Grateful for the increase in industry in Baton Rouge since 1935, the paper lavishly praised Leche for the accomplishments of his term of office, avoiding a hint of dissatisfaction on any count.

segments of the voters an appreciation of the value of morality in politics. When tested by that standard, Longism was found wanting —but by only a bare majority of the people.

The Scandals

During 1938 and early 1939, bickerings among the Longites and the disillusionment of the urban press with Leche combined to heighten the tempo of accusations of irregularities made against the state administration. Disgruntled former supporters of Leche added their charges to those made by Noe ever since the outset of Leche's term,[56] while the Shreveport papers and the *Times-Picayune* and *States,* of New Orleans, pressed members of their staff into quasi-detective service. Their efforts were amply rewarded on June 9, 1939. Noe and a photographer from the *States* disclosed that a supporter of Leche was using materials and men from the State University in the construction of his private home. From such pedestrian graft the Scandals were uncovered.[57]

When the WPA announced its interest in University policies, Leche, aware that a full-scale investigation would bare extensive irregularities, announced his intended resignation for reasons of "ill health." On the 25th of June, University President James M. Smith resigned and disappeared in the wake of revelations that he had embezzled over $500,000 of public funds. On June 26, Leche resigned, and the following day Earl Long assumed the governorship, adopting as his motto, "Better a little with righteousness, than a great revenue without right." Long pledged a full investigation into all abuses, and "let the chips fall where they may."[58]

Earl Long, as a product of the state factional machine who was

[56] For example, Hugh Wilkinson, a law partner of Huey Long, was angered by Leche's repeal of Huey's "roving attorney" law, an action which was directed against a repetition of Wilkinson's harassment of Standard Oil. In March, 1939, Wilkinson charged that several lawyers were engaged in a racket of reducing assessments in Orleans. Again, Dr. Vidrine, demoted from his directorship of Charity Hospital since Huey's death, urged the federal authorities to investigate University President Smith for alleged financial irregularities.

[57] The thoroughness of Harnett T. Kane's account of the Scandals in his *Louisiana Hayride* (New York, 1941), permits the writer to concentrate here on a few essential themes of interpretation.

[58] Quoted by Kane, *Louisiana Hayride,* 275.

dependent upon its strength for his gubernatorial candidacy in 1940, had no genuine desire to annihilate the Long-Leche organization. More indicative than his inaugural promises were his stubborn refusal to order the opening of the books of the Conservation Commission and his hampering of the operation of the Orleans Parish grand jury. As part of the same pattern, Longite district attorneys, district judges, and local officials sought to block parish prosecutions of uncovered graft. Apart from East Baton Rouge, the effective role of Louisiana grand juries in this period was less to promote local prosecution than to acquaint voters with the shocking scope of fraud and to facilitate federal grand jury action. The urban press proved a valuable ally of grand juries in accomplishing those objectives.[59]

The indictment and prosecution of the Leche forces were handled largely by the federal government, now freed of the commitments of the Second Louisiana Purchase. The brunt of the task of prosecution fell to O. John Rogge, new head of the criminal division of the Department of Justice, an idealistic reformer who never ceased to be morally dismayed as the evidence of corruption mounted. The obstacles to federal prosecution were considerable. Since the success of federal income tax civil suits in 1935–36, the Longites had learned to share their illicit booty with the Internal Revenue Bureau. Many offenses, such as bribes and kickbacks among state personnel, were not within federal jurisdiction. A few of Leche's chieftains, however, were vulnerable to "hot oil" charges. For the rest, Rogge hit upon an ingenious charge: use of the mails to defraud. To the outraged cries of Longites he sharply retorted: "Major criminals should not commit minor crimes."[60]

The magnitude of official malfeasance under the Leche administration may be indicated by a selective review of major federal indictments and convictions. Leche, Weiss, Commissioner of Conservation Rankin, and F. W. Burford were indicted for violations of

[59] From June, 1939, through the primary election of January, 1940, the *Times-Picayune* and the *States* (both owned by the same company) prominently displayed on their front pages a "Chronology of Events," a list of "Resignations of Parish Officials to Date," and a boxed column containing the "Pertinent Questions" asked daily of Governor Long. For a discussion of the role of the urban press, particularly in New Orleans, consult George E. Simmons, "Crusading Newspapers in Louisiana," *Journalism Quarterly*, xvi (December, 1939), 328–33.

[60] Quoted by Kane, *Louisiana Hayride*, 337.

the Connally "hot oil" Act. Income tax liens totaling nearly $100,000 were filed against the former Governor. Leche also was indicted for mail fraud in connection with padding landscaping contracts at the University, and was convicted for mail fraud and sentenced to ten years in prison on the charge of defrauding the highway department of $31,000 of excess profits on a truck purchasing agreement.[61] Weiss, "Doc" Smith of the University, and Smith's nephew, J. Emory Adams, were convicted of using the mails to defraud in connection with the double purchase of the furnishings of the Bienville Hotel by the University. Weiss and Smith were sentenced to thirty months, Adams to twelve months. Investment brokers Newman and Harris were convicted on the same charge for their part in a 1936 refunding contract for the Orleans Levee Board. The business manager and some other personnel of the University were convicted of engaging in a construction racket and of "double-dipping." The sole major successful state prosecution, however, was limited to the conviction of Doc Smith for his University embezzlement.

The seeds of Huey Long thus bore bitter fruit in the Scandals of Dick Leche. The heirs of the Kingfish, inheriting his power and class support, solidified factional control by making peace with federal and state opposition, and then proceeded to conduct the affairs of government as a plunderbund. Yet the Scandals were, in reality, not a betrayal of Huey but a natural and logical fulfillment of the mass acceptance of amoral politics induced by the kingdom of the Kingfish. In the Louisiana of 1939, however, no serious political aspirant would dare connect the Scandals with the sacrosanct memory of Huey Long. Quite the contrary. Earl Long and Jimmy Noe, each claiming exclusive kinship with the Kingfish, belabored Leche as the betrayer of Huey. Sam Jones, the anti-Long reform candidate, avowed often and vociferously that "my pappy was for Huey." In the deepest sense, then, regardless of the outcome of the 1940 primary election, Longism was triumphant in Louisiana.

[61] Many Louisianians believed that the sentence was too severe, particularly since Leche's codefendants only were fined. It should be noted, however, that the federal government did not press the other cases pending against Leche in view of his conviction and sentence on the foregoing indictment. Leche subsequently removed his name from the list of practicing attorneys (in the face of certain disbarment), was paroled in mid-1945, and was given a full pardon by President Truman in December, 1952. Leche since has been readmitted to the Louisiana bar.

The gubernatorial primary of 1940

The financial cost of the Scandals to the state, frequently estimated at $100,000,000, perhaps was offset by the citizen spirit
aroused by the exposures of governmental corruption. Many voters,
morally flabby under the assaults of the Kingfish and Leche, participated in a kind of popular uprising for clean government, for a
breath of political fresh air. The white hope of these crusaders was
Sam Houston Jones of Lake Charles, who announced his candidacy
for the governorship in late July, 1939.

Although he was the candidate of the anti-Longs, Jones had assets
calculated to appeal to all varieties of voters. Forty-two years of age,
Jones was born of poor parents in rural Beauregard Parish. A World
War I veteran and a past state commander of the American Legion,
he was a successful lawyer in southwest Louisiana, untainted by
close connections with New Orleans corporations. Though committed to clean government, Jones had never been identified among
the prominent anti-Longs. His public officeholding had been limited
to a delegateship at the constitutional convention in 1921 and to an
assistant district attorneyship in the Fourteenth Judicial District, in
southwest Louisiana. Jones's candidacy, therefore, gave the Longites
no opportunity to divert the issues of the campaign from responsibility for the Scandals to a plebescite on the continued popularity of
Huey Long. Jones recognized the danger and countered it directly.
"Now I am not running against a dead man. I am running against a
gang of rascals as live as any gang that ever lived, and I'm running
to clean out every one of them."[62] As part of his theme of political
reform, Jones pledged the installation of civil service, fiscal and
administrative reorganization, reduction of gubernatorial power,
abolition of deductions and "deadheadism," and a revamping of the
election laws.

Promises of good government did not exhaust the armory of the
anti-Longs. Indeed, Jones's attempts to answer the "why a Huey
Long" question bespoke a new enlightenment of the conservatives.
In his opening campaign speech Jones admitted,

   The present regime, at its inception, was ushered in because of
   the sins and faults and defects of pre-existing groups. Many thousands of Louisianians were ready for a change which would dig

[62] Baton Rouge *State-Times*, October 26, 1939.

up by the roots the powers then entrenched and give to the people the benefits to which they were justly entitled. Among these were many thousands as honest, sincere, and conscientious as can be found in the state of Louisiana. Among these was my own father, who hated with holy fervor, all that smacked of corrupt politics.[63]

Later, in his first message to the Legislature on May 20, 1940, Jones again commented:

I occupy a unique position in Louisiana political life. I am a liberal who had consistently opposed the outgoing political regime . . . because of its tendency toward dictatorship; because of the many flagrant vices evident in the system used by it. To me these were paramount issues because the methods used were destructive of democracy itself. But I believe in benefits and services to the people on a safe and sane basis. I have had the audacity to say that the regime which commenced in 1928 came about as a result of the faults, defects and omissions of the administrations which preceded it. . . .[64]

In line with his version of anti-Longism, liberal policies were promised by Jones during the campaign: reduction of auto license fees to three dollars; abolition of the sales tax; increased educational appropriations and welfare payments; and $30 monthly pensions to those sixty-five years of age and older in need of state assistance.

Anti-Long campaign tactics also testified to their political astuteness. Following Cleveland Dear's technique in 1936, Jones urged his rural audiences to reflect on the proposition that a vote for Long meant a vote "for a man like Bob Maestri."[65] Anticipating the need for Noe's support in the runoff primary, Jones studiously avoided attacking him during the campaign. He similarly ignored the candidacies of rivals Henry Vincent Moseley and James H. Morrison in order to press his own claim as the major anti-Long entrant. The

[63] New Orleans *Times-Picayune*, September 22, 1939.

[64] *Ibid.*, May 21, 1940.

[65] In a speech at Ringgold, in north Louisiana, Jones argued that under Leche and Long the state had been returned into the hands of New Orleans. "The government of the state today consists of only one man, Bob Maestri, the Mayor of New Orleans, who rules through his puppet, Earl Long . . . " (Baton Rouge *State-Times*, December 1, 1939). On the other hand, Jones occasionally hinted that Earl Long was compelling Maestri's support by threatening to order the opening of the books of the Conservation Commission, an agency headed by Maestri before becoming mayor. *Ibid.*, December 30, 1939.

latter objective was achieved: the urban press, for example, endorsed
Jones and his ticket[66] as the one most likely to defeat Long.[67]

The gubernatorial candidacy of an Opelousas attorney, Vincent
Moseley, delightfully caricatured an unregenerated anti-Long campaign. Opposing all professionalism in politics, Moseley styled himself as the only true "independent" in the race, refused campaign
contributions, and scorned the formation of a state ticket. He doggedly called a spade a spade and laid the blame for the Scandals on
the doorstep of the Kingfish. "I for one can never defend Huey
Long," Moseley frankly stated. "I do not believe that either you or
I can ever condone his methods or elect a candidate who does, a
candidate who announced that 'Huey Long was betrayed,' when he
well knew that his was the master mind and he the master evil."[68]
As the campaign progressed it became difficult for the observer to
ascertain whether Moseley was running against Earl Long or Sam
Jones. For the latter was concocted a Moseleyism of startling meta-
phor, "His [Jones] is the voice of Jacob but the hand of Esau presented to the electorate as a corporate lamb over which has been
thrown the hide of a wolf that he may run with the political pack.
Beware of this Trojan horse. . . ."[69] Treated with patronizing respect
by the urban press, Moseley was ignored uniformly by all other
candidates.

Of a more serious nature was the candidacy of state Senator James
A. Noe, wealthy Monroe oil and gas entrepreneur, whose rising
Longite career had been halted by the hostility of the Leche forces
in 1935–36. Noe legitimately claimed that he had forewarned of
corruption before any other, had fought Leche since 1936, and had
participated directly in the uncovering of the Scandals. His espousal
of Share-Our-Wealth doctrines further attracted the support of
Longites dismayed by the graft of the Leche regime. Heading a bob-
tailed state ticket,[70] Noe endorsed measures of political reform and

---

[66] Jones had a candidate on his ticket for every state post except register of the
land office. All were nonincumbents except Treasurer Tugwell, who had broken
with Leche and Long.

[67] The *Times-Picayune* and the Shreveport *Times* early backed Jones, and even
the New Orleans *Item*, sometime ally of Leche, finally endorsed Jones in early
January, 1940.

[68] Baton Rouge *State-Times*, November 30, 1939.

[69] *Ibid.*, December 1, 1939.

[70] Noe supported no candidates for secretary of state, auditor, or superintendent

SHARE THE PEOPLE'S WEALTH

economic liberalism similar to those of Jones,[71] although he frequently attacked Jones as a corporation lawyer who lacked governmental experience. Veteran anti-Longs, however, who feared that Noe intended to control the Leche machine, rather than to dismember it, had their doubts intensified by press-reported allegations linking Noe personally to the Scandals.[72] Noe's appeal, consequently, was restricted largely to disaffected supporters of Huey Long.

The sincerity of the last anti-Long candidate, James H. Morrison, was the most open to doubt. A descendant of an upper-class family and a graduate of the Tulane Law School, Jimmie Morrison achieved a local reputation by his organization of the strawberry farmers of Tangipahoa Parish over the mild opposition of Leche. His attempt to ride that success into capturing the Sixth District Congressional seat failed in 1938, but Morrison received statewide notoriety by his claim that he had been assaulted and shot on orders of Leche.[73] The conduct of his 1940 campaign evidenced his belief that showmanship was half the battle. Heading a state ticket of relative unknowns,[74] and rarely committing himself to policies, Morrison stumped the state heaping abuse upon Leche and Long. He took with him a leashed monkey called "Earl Long," for which name Morrison frequently apologized to the simian, to the delight of the crowds. The capstone of Morrison's vaudeville was his "convict parade" through New Orleans and most of southern Louisiana, featuring major figures of the Leche faction, each garbed in prison clothes. Despite such

of public education, endorsed incumbents Grace and Wilson and Jones-backed candidates for treasurer and attorney general, and entered a candidate for lieutenant-governor exclusively on his own ticket.

[71] Noe's liberality was slightly more promising than that of Jones, e.g., $30 monthly pensions to those over sixty years of age, and an increase in homestead exemptions to $5,000. For a resume of Noe's platform, see New Orleans *Times-Picayune*, December 26, 1939, or Baton Rouge *State-Times*, January 11, 1940.

[72] In July and August of 1939, Noe was charged with "hot oil" profiteering and with bribing personnel of the Louisiana Department of Conservation.

[73] Two days before the Congressional primary in 1938, Morrison reported that he had been shot in the shoulder while driving on a lonely road. The state administration tartly replied to Morrison's claim that he had been shot on orders of Leche that he had shot himself for publicity. What actually happened has never been determined.

[74] Morrison's state ticket lacked only a candidate for treasurer. On January 1, 1940, Joseph P. Dixson, Morrison's running-mate for lieutenant-governor, withdrew his candidacy and announced his support of Noe. Sighed Morrison, "General Washington had his Benedict Arnold, Caesar had his Brutus, and I suppose I had to have my Dixson." Baton Rouge *State-Times*, January 1, 1940.

antics, Morrison's appeal was localized to the Sixth Congressional District, and his suspected Longite sympathies were revealed prior to the runoff primary.

The common target of the foregoing candidates was Earl Kemp Long,[75] a younger brother of the Kingfish who finally had realized his political ambitions. Appointed by Huey to a patronage attorneyship in 1928, Earl later attacked his brother in his failing bid for the lieutenant-governorship in 1932. After his rift with Huey had been healed prior to the assassination, the Leche group tapped him for a place on their state ticket to symbolize tangibly the link between Longite heirs and their deceased martyr-leader. Earl was self-admittedly dumber than Huey: "I've got to go slower than my brother." But he was every inch a masterful spoils politician.

Earl's central strategy was to disassociate both Huey and himself from the Leche administration and then to associate himself and his policies with the class appeal of Huey Longism. Since Earl had been characterized by Leche, in mid-1938, as ". . . a man who stood four-square for two years without deviating one single iota from the course we chartered,"[76] his task was not without difficulty. The Earl of 1939 appealed to the voters to develop a sense of selectivity, not to condemn the barrel because of a few rotten apples. "Smith [president of the University] is only one man," cried Long. "Don't blame everybody. Look at Jesus Christ. He picked twelve. And one of 'em was a sonofagun."[77] Earl admitted to having heard of some questionable activities under Leche but, commented Earl, with a delightful candor characteristic of the Long family at its political best, "The office of Lieutenant Governor is a part-time job paying $200 a month. While I was Lieutenant Governor I spent twenty per cent of my time in Baton Rouge. The rest of my time I spent on a pea patch farm in Winnfield or practicing law in New Orleans."[78] While Earl was not involved in any federal indictment, many voters, nonetheless, remained convinced of the justice of the anti-Longs' retort that a high official under the Leche regime who disclaimed a knowledge

[75] Several important candidates withdrew from the gubernatorial race before the first primary, including Sam Caldwell, Mayor of Shreveport, Treasurer A. P. Tugwell, and Cajun politician Dudley LeBlanc. All three supported Jones, although Tugwell also ran on the Noe ticket for renomination as treasurer.

[76] New Orleans *Times-Picayune*, May 10, 1938.

[77] Quoted by Kane, *Louisiana Hayride*, 288.

[78] Baton Rouge *State-Times*, December 30, 1939.

of graft was either a guilty participant or too stupid to be governor.[79]

On the relationship between the brothers Long, Earl countered the urban press's recitation of his 1932 attacks against Huey by disarmingly noting, "God knows I'm sorry Huey and I fell out. What more can I say?"[80] He promptly proceeded to say more by placing Earle Christenberry, Huey's secretary, on his ticket as candidate for treasurer, by filling the rest of the ticket with incumbents and Longites, by having Huey's widow make occasional speeches on his behalf, and by importing Gerald L. K. Smith for campaign stumping before the runoff primary. Liberal policies were pledged to clinch the identification between Earl and Huey: a minimum $2,000 homestead exemption; a doubling of old-age pensions;[81] and free school lunches to all children, regardless of need.[82] To Long's credit, he did not accompany promises of increased benefits by a pledge to repeal the sales tax. Asserting his neutrality on the issue, Earl promised only to have the Legislature submit to the people a constitutional amendment abolishing the tax.

Though Earl had ended some abuses after taking gubernatorial office,[83] his endeavors on the good-government front were far from reassuring. Deductions were continued under the guise of "voluntary contributions," the Conservation Commission kept its records hidden, and Earl made no commitment to repeal any of Huey's dictatorial laws. In fact, despite protestations to the contrary, Earl Long made full use of the power of the political machine which had been

[79] It probably was true that Long had been elbowed away from the trough. Leche had not intended to support Earl for the governorship in 1940, and Earl stood no chance of victory without the backing of Maestri or Leche. It was this dependency upon the machine organization, rather than personal involvement in corruption, which stilled Long's tongue from 1936 to 1939—as well as the fact that his own sense of governmental ethics was not highly developed.

[80] Baton Rouge State-Times, January 10, 1940.

[81] Since the average old-age pension payment in mid-1939 was $12.70, Earl's pledge of a doubled payment placed him a poor third behind the promises of Jones and Noe. In point of fact, Earl Long was quite careful about the relation between tax income and benefits pledged in his 1940 campaign, a trait he was to abandon after his defeat.

[82] Under authority of the Board of Liquidation of the State Debt, Earl secured legislative consent to borrow $250,000 to begin the school lunch program before the first primary.

[83] For example, the American Progress, which Earl acquired from Leche, ceased to compel advertising from state agencies. Department heads were ordered to stop buying supplies from companies in which they had a financial interest, and the Highway Commission was persuaded to purchase only at wholesale rates.

created since 1928. State and New Orleans agencies were padded systematically with deadhead employees.[84] In New Orleans, and probably elsewhere in the state, public employees were intimidated by threats of dismissal, demotion, or less pleasant working conditions.[85] But factional manipulation of the election machinery, a mainstay of the Ring and the Kingfish, doubtless was limited by the pre-primary warnings of O. John Rogge, who threatened to prosecute primary-election irregularities under mail fraud charges or under the civil rights section of the Federal Criminal Code.

With reference to his major opponents, Earl castigated Noe as "a crook and an oil-chiseler," and Jones as not one "of our rural kind." "He's High Hat Sam, the High Society Kid, the High-Kicking, High and Mighty Snide Sam, the guy that pumps perfume under his arms."[86] During the closing months of the campaign Earl urged, "If you're going to vote against Earl Long, vote for Sam Jones, because you'll be throwing away your votes if you give them to Noe and Morrison."[87] Such counsel probably reflected Earl's preference for Jones rather than Noe as a runoff-primary opponent.

The results of the January 16 primary, reported in Table 16, provided cause for worry in the Long camp. Maestri had been unable to deliver more than a bare majority to Long in New Orleans, while Earl's non-Orleans strength lagged behind the usual Longite performance. Jones, on the other hand, in spite of the multiplicity of anti-Long candidates, had done almost as well as Cleveland Dear had against Leche in 1936 (see Table 15). Long trailed Jones not only in several urban and plantation parishes traditionally anti-Long

[84] The total number of state and local public employees in New Orleans rose from 10,600 in January, 1939 to 15,800 in February, 1940. For a documentation of payroll padding, consult New Orleans Bureau of Governmental Research, "Public Employment in New Orleans, 1939–1942," *City Problems Series*, No. 82 (October 1, 1943).

[85] Accessible original source material on the Longs or their methods of operation is virtually nonexistent to date. Information in several letters in the Wisdom Collection of Long Materials, the Tulane University, New Orleans, while too limited for generalization, provides a hint of the tactics relied upon by the Ring and the Longites, at least in the 1940 campaign. See especially the correspondence between First District Congressman J. O. Fernandez and Long's campaign manager in New Orleans, John R. Land, Jr., and that between Land and a William J. Fischer, in December, 1939. The correspondence concerns the political intimidation of firemen and policemen in the Ninth Ward of New Orleans.

[86] Quoted by Kane, *Louisiana Hayride*, 434.

[87] Baton Rouge *State-Times*, January 9, 1940.

TABLE 16. The Louisiana Vote in the 1940 Democratic Gubernatorial First Primary

	Orleans	Other	State	% State	Parishes Carried by Majority	Plurality
Long	70,899	155,486	226,385	40.9	8	33
Jones	35,720	119,216	154,936	28.0	1	10
Noe	27,732	88,832	116,564	21.1	1	4
Morrison	6,685	41,558	48,243	8.7	0	7
Moseley	623	6,972	7,595	1.3	0	0
Total	141,659	412,064	553,723	100.0	10	54

SOURCE: adapted from Alexander Heard and Donald S. Strong, *Southern Primaries and Elections*, 70–71.

but in some south Louisiana parishes as well. Moreover, Noe cut heavily into the north Louisiana vote and Morrison into that of the Florida parishes. If most of the votes for Noe and Morrison signified anti-Long behavior which would redound to Jones's benefit in the runoff, then the Long faction indeed had cause for alarm.

In the five weeks between primaries, Noe endorsed Jones and actively campaigned for him. Morrison, however, in a neutrality tinged with pro-Longism, declared he would "go off fishing" on election day, and his state ticket candidates divided in their endorsements for the runoff.[88] Defending himself against Earl's charges of fiscal demagogy, Jones maintained that spoils politics had cost the state $25,000,000 a year, a sum adequate to finance increased old-age pensions and to offset reduced license fees.[89] Passing over to the offensive, Jones charged that Earl was straddling the issue of sales tax repeal so that he could throw the weight of the Long faction against repeal in a constitutional amendments election.[90] Less than one week before the February 20 primary, Jones received the active aid of Rogge and the Roosevelt administration in the form of a Department of Interior charge that Maestri, when Conservation Commissioner, had profited in "hot oil" in a New Iberia field in which he held half-interest.[91]

Earl, for his part, fanned the ruralite's antipathy toward the city

[88] Morrison observed, "It is better to carry on as we have, with the present state administration . . . " (Baton Rouge *State-Times*, January 25, 1940). Four of his ticket affiliates announced for Jones, three for Long.

[89] Baton Rouge *State-Times*, February 1, 1940.

[90] *Ibid.*, January 27, 1940.

[91] *Ibid.*, February 15, 1940.

by shouting, "You vote for one of your own kind. Don't you vote for that high-hat sweet-smelling little thing from Lake Charles. You vote for a good old country boy from over here in Winn parish that thinks and smells like you on Saturday."[92] Spellbinder G. L. K. Smith was hired to evoke pleasing memories of Share-Our-Wealth and the glory that was Huey. Appealing to the poorer (and richer) owners of live-stock, Earl pledged his opposition to any state stock-fencing law. In a speech in Grant Parish, Earl pointedly reminded his audience that the liberalism of Longism made the urban areas underwrite most of the costs of highways, education, and welfare in the poorer rural sections of the state.[93]

Long exploited fully his dual position as gubernatorial candidate and Governor. After Noe declared for Jones, Earl called a six-day special session of the Legislature, the first and only lame-duck special session called in recent Louisiana politics. Twenty Long bills were passed in near-unanimous fashion, while all opposition measures were throttled. Anti-Long tempers ran high: Brownell of St. Mary Parish, for example, expressed his sympathy to the Orleans delegation for their having to obey the dictates of "a pot-bellied Dago."[94]

The product of the special session represented Long's down-payments on the benefits and reforms he had pledged. One million dollars were appropriated for an increase in old-age pensions, and a like sum for the free school lunch program. Constitutional amendments repealing the sales tax and exempting farm machinery fuel from the gasoline tax were enacted. Earl had repealed those of Huey's laws that gave the state faction control over the selection of sheriff's deputies,[95] that closed the records of the State Bond and Tax Board to public inspection, that enabled the state to control the local government of Baton Rouge, and that permitted the state faction to intimidate the country press by authorizing the state to designate official parish journals. In addition, restrictions were placed on advertising in newspapers by state agencies and on dual officeholding and

[92] New Orleans *Times-Picayune*, February 11, 1940.
[93] *Ibid.*, February 10, 1940.
[94] Baton Rouge *State-Times*, January 23, 1940. *Il Messaggero*, an Italian-language New Orleans weekly which supported Long, prominently reprinted Brownell's abuse of Maestri in its issues of February 10 and 17, 1940.
[95] About forty sheriffs pledged their support of Earl in the interim between primaries, no doubt in part because of his repeal of Huey's law.

nepotism on the part of legislators.

The Legislature's liberalism was quite deceiving, for the funds to pay the added appropriations were not specified, an action not unrelated to the fact that the General Fund was overdrawn and the Board of Liquidation of the State Debt was in debt to the extent of $4,000,000.[96] The introduction by Noe of a host of alternative bills similarly revealed the shallowness of Earl's reform measures. The special session, nonetheless, was a successful maneuver, at least in the sense that legislators found it inexpedient to oppose state handouts. Thus even Noe, while he decried Long's bills as bait for the voters, supported the passage of most measures.

Although the special session had earmarked severance tax receipts exclusively for public education,[97] the teachers' lobby remained dissatisfied with Earl's handling of the issue of a twelve-months salary for teachers. In a most impolitic manner, Earl retorted that he was "not ready to turn the affairs of the state over to the teachers—not by a devil of a lot,"[98] and defended the priority given to school lunches and to old-age pensions over salary increases for educational personnel. In a letter to the New Orleans Teachers' Federation, Long hinted that the teachers had better think twice before actively opposing him. Though taking credit for the enactment of the teacher tenure law in 1936, Earl recalled and endorsed an earlier statement of his. "I further said that I understood that a few teachers in this state had failed to cooperate with the hot lunch program and they tried to give the impression that it was just a temporary vote-getting scheme, and that I expected to make an investigation after the election and if these charges are proven true, I wanted them removed from the teacher's profession as they are unworthy of being in it." Earl concluded his letter: "To be brief, no one can put a pistol to my head because the election is a few days off and make me commit myself to something just because they are taking advantage of cir-

[96] See the New Orleans *Times-Picayune,* January 30; February 1, editorial; and March 1, 1940.

[97] In writing free school supplies into the Constitution, the 1936 Legislature eliminated a provision restricting legislative appropriations from the severance tax fund to school purposes. In 1938, the Legislature appropriated over $1,500,000 from that fund for non-school purposes, bringing about a shortage of educational moneys which was met only by borrowing $1,000,000. Baton Rouge *State-Times,* August 10, 1939.

[98] New Orleans *Times-Picayune,* February 11, 1940.

cumstances. I may be defeated—but I do not think so."[99]

At the February 20 primary, however, the results of which are reported in Table 17, Jones won the governorship by a narrow mar-

TABLE 17. The Louisiana Vote in the 1940 Democratic Gubernatorial Second Primary

	Orleans	Other	State	% State	Parishes Carried by Majority
Jones	63,389	221,048	284,437	51.8	41
Long	78,534	186,869	265,403	48.2	23
Total	141,923	407,917	549,840	100.0	64

SOURCE: adapted from Alexander Heard and Donald S. Strong, *Southern Primaries and Elections*, 71.

gin. The trends indicated in the first primary were borne out in the second. The bulk of the vote for Noe and Morrison had gone to Jones so that Long's showing in the runoff was not much stronger than his first-primary performance. For the first time in recent politics, a Long received a majority of the New Orleans vote but a minority of the vote cast outside of New Orleans. Those members of Long's state ticket entering the runoff were defeated also, including the veteran State Superintendent of Public Education, T. H. Harris. On the legislative front, taking both primaries into account, thirty-nine Longites were elected to the House and fifteen Long-aligned candidates to the Senate, the remainder being either anti-Longs, Jonesites, or "independents."[100]

Notwithstanding the reduced proportion of the state vote going to Earl, the pattern of relative parish support (Figure 7) continued essentially in the Long tradition. The more pro-Long sections again comprised the second or western tier of upper Mississippi Delta parishes, several of the Florida parishes, and the west-central and northern uplands of cut-over land and subsistence farming. The high Longite support of St. Bernard, Plaquemines, and Orleans should be understood in terms of boss control. Correspondingly, the more pro-Jones sections were the urban areas, Madison and Tensas in the Delta, and the large sweep of south Louisiana parishes, whose inhabitants, apparently, had become morally aroused over the Scandals.

[99] Baton Rouge *State-Times*, February 14, 1940.
[100] New Orleans *Item*, February 25, 1940.

Analysis of ward behavior in the 1940 gubernatorial primaries uncovers pockets of high Longite strength in the Mississippi Delta parishes. Those wards provide a striking commentary on the rural-class basis of Longism, for the shift in their voting behavior since 1928 reflected a change in population composition. Hundreds of poor white farmers and their families had migrated from Mississippi and Arkansas to new farm settlements in the less desirable lands in the Delta.[101] Their proletarian attitudes effectively challenged, within

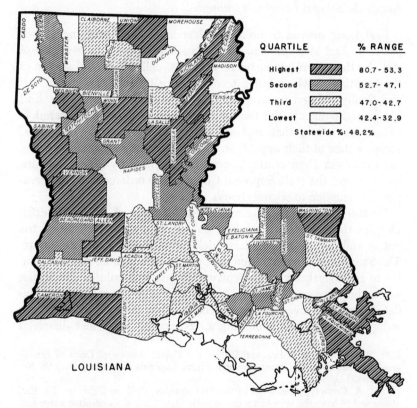

FIGURE 7. Quartile map: proportion of parish vote cast for Earl Long, 1940 Democratic gubernatorial second primary.

SOURCE: same as that for Table 17.

[101] The New Ground settlement of white farmers in the upper Mississippi Delta region of Louisiana has received considerable study. See, for example, Homer L.

certain wards, the traditional political hegemony of the Delta planters. In Ward 2 of Tensas Parish, for example, to which large numbers
of dirt farmers had come, 32.7 per cent of the ward vote had gone to
Huey Long in 1928, but 62.2 per cent went to Earl Long in the 1940
runoff. The respective figures for Ward 3 of Tensas, which included
the parish seat, were 7.4 per cent and 34.1 per cent.

Long's defeat and Longism's triumph

Earl Long proved to be a graceless loser. Following the second
primary, Earl attempted to have himself confirmed as secretary of
state by the governing party committee,[102] called a special session of
the Legislature which failed to materialize for lack of a quorum,[103]
and finally refused to attend Jones's inauguration. But while Earl
Long might dispute the fact of defeat, none of his allies cared to
follow him along that reckless path. Maestri and the "regulars"
served notice of their opposition to the calling of any special session,
the Louisiana Democratic Association, founded by Huey, was disbanded, and the state Supreme Court finally ordered the Conservation Commission to open its books.

On the other hand, Longism had no intention of going into exile.
Despite the Scandals, Earl had polled close to a majority of the
voters and had returned a large delegation to the state Legislature.
The Sam Jones administration thus entered office in no manner similar to the overthrow of the corrupt Republican rule of the 1870's,
when the *Picayune* boasted, "So ends the Kellogg regime. Big, inflated, insolent, overbearing, it collapsed at one touch of honest
indignation and gallant onslaught. Its boasted armament dissolved

Hitt, "Recent Migration Into and Within the Upper Mississippi Delta of Louisiana," Louisiana State University Agricultural Experiment Station, *Bulletin* No.
364 (1943), 1–53.

[102] E. A. Conway, nominated in the first primary, died on February 19. Earl
attempted to have the lame-duck Democratic State Central Committee name him
for the post, but under Jones's pressure, both old and new committees selected
Jones's ticket candidate, Gremillion.

[103] In addition to proposing several benefits, Earl intended to penalize sheriffs
who had not supported him in the runoff and to hamper the new attorney general
in his prosecution of governmental irregularities. Only forty-eight House and thirteen Senate members appeared in response to his call. New Orleans *Times-
Picayune*, March 2, 3, 1940.

before the furious rush of our citizens; its thieving, sneering unscrupulous chieftains hid like moles, and its mercenaries fled like stampeded cattle."[104] Anti-Longs in the 1940's, therefore, had to adjust to the realization that their durability as the dominant faction depended in considerable measure on their reaffirmation of the economic liberalism symbolized by Huey Long. The apparent incapacity of anti-Long leaders to make that adjustment resulted in the triumphant return of Earl Long to the governor's chair in 1948.

[104] New Orleans *Picayune*, September 15, 1874, as quoted by Ella Lonn, *Reconstruction in Louisiana (After 1868)* (New York, 1918), 273.

CHAPTER 6

Anti-Longism has its chance

SAM JONES, 1940–1944

SAM JONES'S TASK of charting a "safe and sane liberalism" was no easy chore. Commitments obligated him, with regard to the making of policy and the distribution of jobs, to factions other than the veteran anti-Longs. The precarious legislative support accorded him throughout his term of office also cautioned him against treading a dogmatic path of anti-Longism. Furthermore, unlike the Kingfish, Jones remained largely a symbol who never attained the flesh-and-blood dimensions of a charismatic leader. An informed judgment of Jones's performance in office, therefore, must be based on the recognition that he possessed neither the factional strength of Leche nor the emotional hold of Huey and was denied, by the tenets of good government, the use of those methods by which Longites forged subservient majorities in the Legislature.

*The 1940 legislative session:
good government tinged with liberalism*

The 1940 legislative session fixed the direction and most of the content of the Jones administration. Although compromise was necessary, particularly with the New Orleans machine, Maestri's refusal to ally his city forces wholeheartedly with the country Longites enabled the Governor to achieve much of his program. While the reform forces made no attempt to turn back the clock in connection with the economic content of Longism, their primary concern with the honesty and efficiency of state government was seized upon by the Longites as the pretext for a sustained assault upon the "do-gooders" in state office.

154

Without ever relinquishing an active legislative role, Jones encouraged a new conception of an uncontrolled Legislature, one illustrated by the counsel to his colleagues of Speaker of the House Norman Bauer. "There is a vast distinction," noted Bauer, "between receiving the recommendations of the governor with an open mind, even to the extent of giving him the benefit of every doubt, and servilely accepting, without due consideration, a legislative program inimical to the interests of a free people we are sworn to serve. . . . There is a sensible middle course that the people of Louisiana expect us to follow."[1]

Laws which buttressed the kingdom of the Kingfish were repealed, including those granting the state administration power to arrest and hold citizens without bond, to place the National Guard above the civil courts, and to control the legal profession. Measures were enacted restrictive of deductions, deadheadism, payroll padding, double-dipping, dual jobholding, and nepotism, all favored tactics of the Leche-Long regime. The debt moratorium commission, a past avenue of dual jobs for legislators, was abolished. Grand juries were freed of the hamperings of tyrannical judges, though not of partisan district attorneys.[2] All public records, apart from the necessary exceptions, were declared available for public inspection.

As a consequence of past factional abuses, reformers clamored to "take key functions of government out of politics," an objective which spurred drastic reorganization of the governing boards of Louisiana State University and the Port of New Orleans.[3] Improved bidding and leasing policies were made mandatory for the State Mineral Board to protect the state from the private exploitation of natural resources. The naming of state public property after living persons was pro-

---

[1] Baton Rouge *State-Times,* May 13, 1940.

[2] Representative deLesseps Morrison and other supporters of Jones in the New Orleans area pressed for a bill allowing grand juries to bypass hostile district attorneys through employment of special counsel. Attorney General Stanley, former district attorney of New Orleans, opposed the measure, which failed to pass.

[3] In the reorganization of the Dock Board, Jones appointed a full new governing board of five members for staggered terms ranging from four to eight years; future vacancies were to be filled by the governor from lists of candidates submitted by New Orleans trade organizations. The term of appointive members to the Board of Supervisors of Louisiana State University was set at fourteen years. In both reorganizations, the appointees were protected against arbitrary removal by a governor.

hibited, and the oil portrait of Governor Leche hanging in the State Capitol was ordered removed. Two of Huey's weapons, however, were retained deliberately by Jones: the authority of the attorney general to supersede district attorneys solely at his or the governor's discretion was maintained in order to prosecute the Scandals with dispatch; and the extraordinary powers of the Board of Liquidation of the State Debt were applied by Jones to meet the major financial difficulties of his administration.

The registration and primary-election laws underwent rather extensive revision, the details of which reflected awareness of the various ways the Long faction had manipulated election machinery to its advantage during the 1930's. In 1939, for example, the Orleans registrar of voters in effect had kept his registration books hidden by insisting that an examination of them would interfere with the orderly conduct of his duties. In 1940, provision was made for parish registrars to make their books available for public inspection for several hours after the close of work each day. Another facet of the reform drive against false registration was an improvement of the purging procedure, under the terms of which reporting to the parish registrar of voters was regularized and made mandatory on the part of clerks of courts, boards of health, and the heads of state institutions.

A beginning step, one not very effective, was taken to deal with the troublesome problem of dummy candidates.[4] The authority to select poll commissioners for the state-office first primary was lodged with candidates for local office, while the two gubernatorial candidates controlled their selection for the runoff. To solve another recurring problem Jones advocated the end of poll commissioner assistance to illiterate voters, but he had to accept a milder provision which permitted commissioners to extend assistance to those voters who had affidavits attesting to their illiteracy. Another law made mandatory the installation of voting machines in every precinct in New Orleans before the Senate primary of 1942, the cost of the program to be borne equally by the city and the state.

---

[4] No local candidate could withdraw from a primary contest after election commissioners had been chosen without forfeiting his filing fee and paying an additional penalty of $100. In addition, if a local candidate polled less than one per cent of the total vote cast for the office sought he could not be appointed to any public office at any governmental level for a period of one year following the election.

Except to intervene in the compromises made necessary because of factional opposition, the Governor gave a free hand to the Louisiana Civil Service League, a private civic organization, to eradicate the spoils system in state and New Orleans politics. In order to placate the Choctaws, Jones and the League decided, as a matter of tactics, not to attempt to imbed civil service itself in the Constitution but to secure a constitutional amendment which required that subsequent changes in the city and state civil service laws be passed by a two-thirds vote in each chamber of the Legislature. The latter method, in other words, omitted the requirement of popular ratification contained in the former. While the gravity of that omission was made clear in 1948 when a Legislature obedient to Governor Earl Long repealed the merit system, there was little else that Jones could do, given the factional circumstances in the 1940 session. In the absence of some such concession by the Governor, Maestri's Choctaws would have opposed the constitutional amendment not only in the general election but in the Legislature as well, and the size of a united Ring-country Longite bloc threatened legislative defeat of any measure submitted in the form of a constitutional amendment.

It was quite understandable, in view of the rich heritage of spoils politics in Louisiana, that civil service was viewed less as the personnel arm of the governor and of the New Orleans mayor than as an independent agency dedicated to the permanent depoliticization of state and city employees. Accordingly, the civil service commissions were to be "kept out of politics" through the same sorts of devices employed for the revamped Dock Board. The five members of the State Civil Service Commission were to be appointed by the governor from a list of eligibles submitted by the presidents of five colleges in the state. The terms of office of the commissioners were overlapping, and their tenure protected against arbitrary removal. The State Commission was to choose a state director of personnel through competitive examination and to appoint two of the three members of the City Civil Service Commission, the Orleans Commission Council selecting the remaining member.

Other features of the civil service measures, as finally enacted, reflected the effectiveness of political pressures, factional and otherwise, in securing concessions from the reformers. The League sought to secure civil service for all parochial employees, though, in view of the small numbers of employees in country parish offices, its real interest in the matter lay with the urban parishes. When, however, many of the sheriffs who recently had been returned their authority to select their own deputies expressed their opposition, and the urban parishes refused to be singled out for special coverage, Jones and the League abandoned the attempt to extend the scope of civil service to parochial employees. On the matter of restricting the political activities of civil servants, Maestri's opposition forced adoption of moderate bans in place of more stringent provisions modeled on the federal Hatch Act, originally advocated by Jones.

The effective date of state and city merit systems was set at July 1, 1942, a date which followed the mayoralty primary in New Orleans and preceded the senatorial primary. State employees as of that effective date were to be blanketed in under the merit system after passing a noncompetitive qualifying examination, while subsequent recruitment and promotion were to be based upon competitive examinations. Longites frequently were to accuse Jones of protecting the employees his faction appointed in place of Longite workers ousted during 1940–41, but when New Orleans employees (Maestri and Choctaw followers) were blanketed in on July 1, 1942, without any qualifying or competitive examination at all, Jones's accusers were conspicuous by their silence. No tenet of good government, after all, required Jones to give tenure to the political appointees of Leche and Allen. The Longites, moreover, were not unaware of the fact that state employees would have voted against the civil service constitutional amendment if they had to undergo competitive examinations in mid-1942 in order to retain their jobs under civil service.

Still another major theme in Jones's reform movement was "the business efficiency of governmental operations," with particular reference to the long overdue reorganization of the executive branch. Since 1921, the Legislature had declined to act on its constitutional authority to reorganize administrative departments; and the Constitution itself multiplied the number of executive offices not under the control of the governor. By 1940, there were at least 122 state agencies under varying degrees of gubernatorial control, the governing authorities of which were selected by various elective, appointive, and qualified-appointive methods.[5] The chief executive's control over

---

[5] The Topsy-like growth of state agencies may be traced in Melvin Evans, *A Study in the State Government of Louisiana* (Baton Rouge, 1931); Roderick L. Carleton, *The Reorganization and Consolidation of State Administration in*

his rambling bureaucracy depended in considerable measure on his *de facto* political power.

Jones's proposals for an administrative and a fiscal code, prepared by a commercial management firm, Griffenhagen and Associates, adhered to the "orthodox" view of state reorganization, which sought an integrated administrative structure and centralized controls for the handling of public moneys under the direction of the governor. State agencies and offices were regrouped functionally under twenty departments, with the addition of four independent agencies. Each of the departments was headed by an executive officer responsible to the governor. Political pressures, as might be expected, brought about some changes from the original proposals. Thirteen departments, for example, were assigned "departmental boards" in order to curb arbitrary action by the department head. Those offices which had been elective remained elective, while the new Department of Local Government was prohibited from auditing municipal finances. The fiscal code, of greater durability than administrative reorganization, for the first time provided Louisiana with an executive budget, pre- and post-audit controls, centralized purchasing, quarterly allotments, unified accounting, and departmental control of investigations. The director of finance became the most important state official after the governor.

Despite Jones's assertion that "this re-organization bill does not give the governor one bit more power than he already has,"[6] the Griffenhagen program, in common with orthodox reorganization in other states, enhanced the power of the governor by providing him with formal structural authority in place of informal influence. It may be suggested that Jones perhaps was insufficiently aware of the consequences of administrative reorganization in terms other than the business notion of efficiency and the purist concept of political reform. In any event, the Louisiana situation was an apt illustration of a generalization advanced by one student of public administration, "[the orthodox reorganizationists] have failed to warn their clients ... of the enormous risk involved in creating a powerful chief executive in a state which has no responsible legislature and in many

Louisiana (Baton Rouge, 1937); F. J. Mechlin and Charles S. Hyneman, *The Administrative System of the State of Louisiana,* Louisiana State University Bureau of Government Research (1940).
[6] New Orleans *States,* June 14, 1940.

instances no effective opposition party."[7] The impact of Jones's reorganizations on Louisiana will never be known, however, because
a furious Longite counterattack in the courts overturned those laws
shortly after they were enacted.

Jones's attempt to complement his political reforms by a rounded
economic program was complicated by the Longite legacies of popular expectations of ever-expanding governmental largesse, on the one
hand, and a heightened state debt on the other. Maestri's alliance
with Jones enabled the latter to enter upon his term of office without
additional financial burdens when Earl's constitutional amendments
repealing the sales tax, dedicating all severance tax funds to public
education, and exempting fishing boats and farm equipment from
gasoline taxes were rejected by the voters. Nevertheless, as the situation was described by Jones, the anti-Longs were faced with an
inherited deficit of $10,000,000 and a future loss of another $16,000,-
000 after the sales tax was ended and auto license fees reduced. After
making allowance for the economies stemming from the efficient
operation of good government, the Jones forces estimated their needs
at $10,000,000 of new revenues to underwrite a biennial appro-
priation of $154,000,000, one roughly equal to that of the Leche
administration in 1938.

The Governor suggested five new taxes to offset the anticipated
deficit: a privilege tax on the gathering of natural gas; an extension
of severance taxes to other natural resources; an increase in corporate
and individual income tax rates in the middle and upper income
brackets; a doubling of the tax on liquor and wines; and an elimination of the permissive 3 per cent deduction on gasoline taxes for oil
refineries. The benefits pledged, contingent upon the adoption of
that tax program, included an increase in old-age pensions to $30
monthly, continuance of the school lunch program, expansion of the
network of trade schools over the parishes, progress toward a twelve-
month salary for teachers, and elimination of the gasoline tax on
fuel used by motor boats of fishermen and trappers.

The tax program actually enacted bore some resemblance to what

[7] Charles S. Hyneman, "Administrative Reorganization: An Adventure into
Science and Theology," *Journal of Politics*, i (1939), 75. For a thoughtful analysis of Jones's proposals, see Robert H. Weaver, *Administrative Reorganization in
Louisiana*, Louisiana State University Bureau of Government Research (1951),
16–70.

Jones had urged but provided for less state revenues than he had suggested. The tax rate on natural gas was considerably lower than that proposed by Jones, and income tax rates were revised only after several industry-sponsored amendments had been accepted.[8] The Legislature repealed Huey's taxes on bank surpluses and on the New Orleans Cotton Exchange, reduced auto license fees, and provided for repeal of the sales tax at the close of the year. A gift tax was instituted and a higher tobacco tax enacted. In addition, the Legislature sanctioned for submission to the electorate Jones's measures for the issuance of $17,000,000 of bonds to balance current highway and other deficits.

Extreme conservatives were disgruntled by the Governor's sponsorship of additional taxes, while Longites attacked the late date at which sales tax repeal was to become effective, the inadequacy of state aid for education, and the failure to obtain $30 old-age pensions as violations of Jones's campaign pledges. A notation of several important bills which attracted significant cross-factional support serves to highlight legislative discontent with Jones's performance in this area of public policy. Against the background of Jones's failure to secure the dedication of all severance tax funds to public schools and to redeem fully his promises on teachers' salaries, forty representatives from anti- and pro-Long factions voted against the Jones-sponsored amendment fixing state educational payments at $17 per educable child rather than at the $20 figure stated by Jones in his gubernatorial campaign. Forty-nine members of the House sought without success to have Jones duplicate Earl's generosity by supporting a constitutional amendment exempting from the state tax gasoline used in fishermen's boats and in farmers' equipment. The appropriation of $1,000,000 that Jones requested, following his reduction of state aid to education, for the operation of a State Crime Commission designed to uncover and prosecute the wrongdoings of the Scandals, was reduced by half in the Legislature.

Such legislative behavior helped confirm the appraisal of Jones's 1940 performance as good government tinged with liberalism, a judgment inadvertently echoed by the Governor himself. After

[8] Standard Oil executives threatened not to locate a new butane plant in Louisiana and to "liquidate and dismember itself" and move to another state unless two amendments to the income tax law were adopted. The amendments were adopted. Baton Rouge *State-Times*, June 12, 20, 1940.

asserting that "there can be no doubt that the legislation which has been passed was the most humanitarian, economical, and liberal that has ever been passed by any legislature," Jones characterized it as ". . . legislation which has knocked the professional politician into a 'cocked hat' and has placed the ordinary citizen in control of his state."[9] As a consequence of the limitations of their economic policies, relative both to their campaign pledges and to the alternatives put forward by the Longites, the anti-Longs were on the defensive for the remainder of Jones's term.

The complete counterattack: Longism in opposition, 1940–42

In their new role as the opposition, the Long faction exhibited a fury and a vindictiveness which did credit to its martyred leader, the Kingfish. Jones was challenged, more often successfully than not, at legislative sessions, constitutional amendments elections, Congressional primaries, and at the New Orleans mayoralty contest. Longite opposition was characterized by a ruthless obstructionism which aimed at discrediting and hobbling the reform program. Although Sam Jones upheld the new political order by refusing to retaliate in kind, his failure to meet the test of state government always met by Huey Long exposed his administration to adverse judgment. In terms of the product of politics, Jones neglected to prove to the mass electorate that broad class benefits and anti-Longism were not strange bedfellows. The significance of that failing may be gauged from the fact that the anti-Longs, within one year after the outbreak of the Scandals, were on the defensive in state politics.

Aware of the pcwer of a united Longite faction, Jones sought, in the 1940 session, to continue the working agreement with Maestri, which was struck subsequent to the gubernatorial runoff primary in February. Although the alliance dismayed some reformers, others hoped that in the long run the effects of the reform program would prohibit state and New Orleans bossism. Mayor Maestri, whose domination of city politics derived in large part from state legislation enacted in 1936, was willing to accept a temporary truce. Both sides

---

[9] Baton Rouge *State-Times,* July 12, 1940.

profited from the agreement. At the 1940 session, in spite of the many anti-Ring bills introduced by the few reform legislators from New Orleans, the Choctaws were visited with no worse treatment than a slight reduction of their patronage and a prohibition upon New Orleans from levying a city sales tax. In return for such gentle handling, the Choctaw contingent supported many of Jones's key measures, often securing additional concessions, as in the case of civil service, as the price of their bloc support. Because of this alliance, House opposition to Jones was limited to about twenty or thirty members, largely from north Louisiana, while Senate opposition numbered about twelve or fifteen legislators, more evenly divided between south and north Louisiana.[10]

Believing that the reform forces had profited more from the truce than the Choctaws, the Governor continued the arrangement for the Congressional primary in September, 1940. Jones supported challengers against incumbent Longites in the First, Second, Third, Sixth, and Eighth districts, backed an unopposed reform candidate in the Seventh, and called for the repudiation of Longite congressmen in the Fourth and Fifth districts. In the Orleans area, the Choctaws agreed to support Jones-Noe candidates for Congress, for the Public Service Commission, and for certain local offices in return for Jones's neutrality toward the renomination of incumbent city judges.[11] All jointly-endorsed candidates in the Orleans area won,[12] but Jones was disregarded in the Fourth, Fifth, and Eighth Congressional districts.

Maintenance of the state-reform—city machine entente was essential to Jones for the November, 1940, constitutional amendments election, at which the fate of some major economic and reform legislation was to be determined. The importance of the Ring vote was magnified at general elections because the level of voter turnout declined less sharply in New Orleans than in the rest of the state. In the Novem-

[10] The reader is reminded again that all references to factional alignments and roll-call votes on bills within the state Legislature contained in this study are based upon an analysis of the pertinent *Official Journal of the Proceedings* of the respective chambers for the respective sessions, regular and extraordinary.

[11] Details of the deal were revealed in the New Orleans *Times-Picayune*, July 18, 1940.

[12] Choctaw backing embarrassed the Jones forces in the Second Congressional District, where fraud was employed to aid T. Hale Boggs, Jones-endorsed candidate for Congress. In the federal prosecutions which followed, important legal precedents ultimately were established by the United States Supreme Court. See *United States* v. *Classic*, 313 U.S. 299 (1941).

ber, 1940, election, for example, more than one-third of the total state vote came from New Orleans. Jones and Maestri agreed to support all twenty-eight amendments, but considerable Choctaw hostility was evident in the case of several, particularly those dealing with civil service, administrative reorganization, and the forbidding of cities to levy a sales tax. In the country parishes, Earl Long, Jimmie Morrison, and state Senator Ernest Clements, of Allen Parish, urged that the amendments be defeated because they gave dictatorial power to Jones comparable to that possessed by Hitler, forbearing to allude to the more relevant model of the Kingfish in that regard. Even the pro-Jones urban press urged defeat of certain of the amendments. Jones's October campaigning for endorsement of the amendments reflected a belated realization of the magnitude of the opposition, an understandable error in that most constitutional amendment elections in the past had gone the way the state administration of the day had desired.

The November election resulted in the first of many serious setbacks for the Jones faction. Nine amendments were rejected, including the income tax, an extension of tax exemptions for industry, and a single measure which bound together the quite different matters of an increase in the salaries of legislators with restrictions on nepotism and dual jobholding by legislators. By and large, the customary factional pattern prevailed on the important amendments. The northern upland parishes and the west-central parishes of Vernon and Allen, for example, voted against the amendments dealing with the income tax, civil service, and $10,000,000 of highway bonds. The proportion of the Orleans vote favoring each of those three amendments was less than that of the non-Orleans vote, indicating that the "regulars" had not been faithful to the bargain struck with the Governor.

The defeat of the income tax amendment, the most important victory of the Long faction at the election, in fairness could not be laid entirely at the feet of the Choctaws and the "out" faction. On the basis of some 270,000 votes cast in the state, the conversion of a majority of 19,356 votes in favor of civil service to a slim majority of 7,069 votes against the income tax also reflected the defection of urbanites who were otherwise pro-Jones. In the urban parish of Caddo, for example, 62.4 per cent of the vote cast on civil service was favorable, compared to 51.1 per cent on the income tax. A similar

pattern occurred in Jefferson Parish, where the corresponding figures
were 59.1 per cent and 48.6 per cent. If, as Jones reiterated frequently
during his term, the defeat of the income tax amendment critically
undermined the financial resources of the reform forces, then the
anti-Longs must bear as much blame as the Long partisans. It was a
most costly pursuit of unenlightened self-interest that led some supporters of good government to define their faction's objectives in
terms inclusive of civil service but exclusive of more equitable taxation. At the same time, the negative obstructionism of the Long faction was clearly revealed by their opposition to Jones's revision of
income tax rates.

In the face of unrelenting opposition from the Long forces and of
increasing unrest within his own factional ranks, Jones increased his
political problems by breaking with Noe. The cause of the split
ostensibly was patronage difficulties, either the inability or the
unwillingness of Jones to meet what Noe termed ". . . an understanding with the governor . . . that my people would get 50 per cent of
the jobs."[13] The satisfaction of purist reformers with the rupture of
this alliance was heightened when Noe was indicted, in late 1940,
for income tax evasion.[14]

However comforting Jones's abandonment of Noe (or Noe of
Jones) was to the clean-government element, it foredoomed any
possibility of state administration victory in the New Orleans mayoralty contest of January, 1942. So bleak were the Governor's prospects
that he toyed for weeks with the idea of supporting Longite ex-
Congressman Paul Maloney for mayor in order to split the Choctaw
ranks. Reform leaders rejected that tactic, and Jones ultimately
backed Herve Racivich, a young lawyer identified with the good-
government forces. Noe supported the Choctaw slate as an "ally and
partner" of the Ring. Maestri began a perfunctory campaign shortly
before the primary, extolled his "business performance" and his ad-
mittedly substantial accomplishments since 1936, and pledged himself to co-operate with the major state reforms recently enacted. At

[13] Baton Rouge *State-Times*, July 24, 1940.
[14] Noe and Seymour Weiss were indicted by a federal grand jury for evasion of
$32,000 income and excess profits taxes on the 1935 income of the Win-Or-Lose
oil corporation. Weiss pleaded guilty. Noe fought the charge and was acquitted
in April, 1942, on the defense that he had affixed his signature to the corporation's income tax statement without any understanding of its contents, and
hence was innocent of any intent to defraud the government.

the January primary, which was distinguished by the use of voting machines in every precinct, Maestri amassed a majority of nearly 15,000 votes over the combined vote of three rivals.

Governor Jones pretended to take solace from the fact that ". . . the more significant thing is that the machine found it advisable to declare itself in favor of all the governmental reforms enacted by the 1940 Legislature. This was the outstanding accomplishment of the campaign so far as the welfare of the people is concerned."[15] Maestri, who had not infrequently referred to "the hypocrite Sam Jones" during the conduct of his city campaign,[16] soon proved that the Governor was whistling in the dark. The New Orleans machine added its full weight to the movement of country parish Longites to cripple the state administration, and together they achieved that objective in the 1942 regular session of the Legislature.

From 1940 to 1942, the Jones forces could have embarked upon a factional offensive, one that doubtless would have seriously challenged the Longite hold upon the state, by vigorously uncovering and prosecuting the miscreants of the Scandals. And that was the goal of the reform faction, as Jones himself pledged in his inaugural address. "I said that I intended to destroy the state machine—and I meant it. I propose to uproot it, rip it limb from limb, branch from trunk and leaf from twig. . . ."[17] But, once again, in this area as in state finances, Jones performed in a hesitant manner which alienated friends and multiplied enemies.

In his address to the 1940 Legislature, Jones urged the creation of a Crime Commission, to be composed of the governor, his executive counsel, and the attorney general, to facilitate state action in the wake of federal revelations and prosecutions. Legislative reaction to Jones's request and to other programs of state investigations revealed initial misgivings which were to grow in time. Only four senators, for example, opposed Jones's partisan ouster of State Bank Commissioner Brock; but eleven opposed an appropriation of $100,-000 for an auditing and reorganization study of the operations of state, parish, and municipal agencies. Legislative resistance eliminated a provision of the administrative reorganization act empowering the Department of Local Government to audit municipal finances

[15] New Orleans *Times-Picayune*, January 29, 1942.
[16] Baton Rouge *Morning Advocate*, January 13, 1942.
[17] Baton Rouge *State-Times*, May 14, 1940.

and led to amendment of a reform bill requiring the publication of parish records. The fears of some legislators that state investigation and supervision of local government would be converted, in the manner of the Kingfish, into a factional dragooning of local communities, were fanned by the reckless conduct of Senator LeBlanc in proposing investigations obviously motivated by personal ambition.[18] Suspicion of the Governor's intentions combined with resentment against the moderacy of his program of benefits to persuade a majority of legislators to slash by 50 per cent Jones's request for a biennial appropriation of $1,000,000 for the Crime Commission.

The civil and criminal prosecutions undertaken by the commission, in general, were far from spectacularly successful. Reporting to the Senate in June, 1942, the commission disclosed that it had recovered state funds totaling $212,000 at a total cost of $121,000. Roughly two-thirds of the commission's expenditures, however, represented transfers to allied state agencies, and the grand total of funds recovered was considerably higher.[19] Investigations by the commission and by Supervisor of Public Funds Hayes charged gross mismanagement on the part of the Highway and Conservation commissions, the Orleans Levee Board, and the State Board of Health.[20] The treasurer of Livingston Parish and Longite sheriffs or former sheriffs of St. Landry, Evangeline, Jefferson, Iberville, and Rapides were accused of malfeasance in office. A 1941 civil suit against Maestri for his "hot oil" activity was unsuccessful, and a suit filed in 1940 against Earl Long for embezzlement and extortion in connection with deadhead-

---

[18] LeBlanc's insistence upon a legislative investigation of the Public Service Commission was accurately characterized by Longite Clements as an effort to discredit Wade Martin, Sr., a commission member, as part of the running battle between them as to who was "King of the Cajuns" (Baton Rouge State-Times, June 3, 1940). The Senate sanctioned an investigation only after barring LeBlanc from membership on the investigating committee and extending the scope of the committee's inquiry to cover the period of LeBlanc's own membership on the Public Service Commission. LeBlanc next demanded an investigation of state leasing of trapping lands, but it was discovered that LeBlanc himself had attempted to secure a lease for a friend without competitive bidding. Despite an eloquent defense by a Cajun colleague, the Senate voted down a motion of confidence in LeBlanc. By the 1942 session, LeBlanc, who had supported Jones before the 1940 runoff, had transferred his allegiance to the Long faction.

[19] How much higher is not known because the books of the commission were closed to public view after the state courts held the commission to be illegal.

[20] Baton Rouge State-Times, December 28, 1940; New Orleans Times-Picayune, June 8, 1941.

ism on the Dock Board proved abortive.[21]

The urban press during 1941 and 1942 voiced the dissatisfaction of the anti-Longs with the progress of state investigations into the Scandals. The Shreveport *Times* of September 1, 1941, editorialized, for example, that ". . . the *Times* regrets that while the administration of Governor Sam Jones has done well in re-establishing honesty in state affairs, there has been a lamentable delay on the part of the attorney general's office in lodging civil suits against large-scale marauders who made away with funds rightfully belonging to the state." The title of the editorial in the New Orleans *States* of May 19, 1942, read as follows: "Promises made people during campaign to prosecute all thieves are not being kept."

Yet if the inadequacy of state prosecutions nettled the anti-Longs, the fact of state investigations aroused the Longites. Since the Jones program fell short of a policy of "thorough," the determination of which parishes were to be investigated inevitably led to the counter-charge of partisanship. Jones, therefore, convinced few Louisianians of either the sincerity or adequacy of his drive against the Scandals participants.

In explanation of the setbacks which befell the reformers during 1940–42, Jones could point, with considerable justification, to the obstructionist tactics of a harsh opposition faction. Weakened by Maestri's temporary alliance with the state administration, country Longites worked through the judiciary, politicized under Huey and Leche, as the vulnerable chink in the armor of the anti-Long forces. They launched a bewildering attack against the reforms of civil service, reorganization, voting machines, and state investigations and sought to hamstring the attempts of the anti-Longs to meet their fiscal commitments. Although the Legislature could have rebuffed the assault by enactment of corrective legislation, the 1942 session saw the anti-Jones forces in virtual control of the Senate. Playing the role of the irresponsible opposition, then, the Long faction succeeded in humbling the "in" state faction, a reversal of political power unparalleled in recent Louisiana politics.

[21] New Orleans *Times-Picayune*, July 24, October 3, December 12, 1940. A 1941 state prosecution of Maestri failed because of the courts' narrow interpretation of Act 127 of 1912, under which it was held that the Commissioner of Conservation was not covered in the Act's prohibitions upon employees of the Department of Conservation from becoming actively interested in the exploitation of the natural resources of the state.

With the aid of Longite Judge Womack, ensconced strategically in the district court at Baton Rouge, and of Longite partisans on the high court, the anti-Jones faction exploited the judicial process for factional gain. It constitutes no violation of fundamental Anglo-Saxon concepts to attach a partisan significance to the fact that the same "professional" taxpayers brought suit after suit against Jones's legislation, and that counsel for the various plaintiffs included such Longite luminaries as Wade Martin, Jr., Jimmie Morrison, Leander Perez, George Wallace, and state Senator Joe Cawthorn. Litigation filed by the Longites failed to prevent the installation of voting machines in the precincts of New Orleans prior to the mayoralty contest of 1942 and to block the establishment of state and city civil service systems, but otherwise it was successful.

Throughout 1941, anti-Jones litigants and even parish grand juries beholden to partisan parish and district officials attempted to block the joint efforts of Hayes and Stanley to prosecute the Scandals sinners. In Tangipahoa, for example, the grand jury rewarded Hayes's efforts to indict the sheriff by giving the latter a clean bill of health and indicting Hayes on charges of libel. In August, 1941, Womack effectively tied up Hayes's funds, and in December the Supreme Court unanimously held the Crime Commission unconstitutional on technical grounds.[22] Earlier in the year, by a 5–2 decision, the high court determined that the reorganization constitutional amendment, although ratified by the people, was illegal.[23]

The Longite judicial attacks of greatest threat to Jones were aimed at increasing his fiscal difficulties. In the face of an estimated biennial deficit of $14,000,000,[24] the Governor turned to the questionable

[22] The reasons were the multiplicity of objects contained in the title of the legislative act, and improperly made appropriations for the Commission.

[23] Twin defects recognized by the court were the omission from the amendment passed by the Legislature of the date of submission to the electorate and the inclusion, within a single measure, of some forty-five amendments to the Constitution, amending nearly that number of different sections.

[24] Consult New Orleans Bureau of Governmental Research, "Memo on Impending State Deficit," December 13, 1940. The Bureau, a private nonpartisan organization, took strong issue with Jones's version of the causes of the deficit and claimed that Leche's debts and the defeat of the income tax revision accounted for considerably less than 50 per cent of the problem. The Bureau stressed overappropriations by the 1940 Legislature, Board of Liquidation borrowings, and the lack of effective executive and fiscal controls as the prime causes of financial troubles.

borrowing and fund-transferring authority of the Board of Liquidation of the State Debt, an agency whose powers he had pledged to
restrict during the campaign.[25] Longites retaliated by securing an
injunction from Judge Womack restraining the board from shifting
$150,000 to Hayes's office and $750,000 to the Department of Finance. Jones avoided financial paralysis only by securing legislative
consent to additional board loans for welfare payments, New Orleans
Charity Hospital, and for the Department of Finance. Even so, the
financial straits of the Jones forces were such that Charity Hospital
had to discontinue 479 beds in February, 1941.[26]

The Longites had set the stage carefully for the legislative events
of 1942. Through propaganda and the courts they had made a sham-
bles of state prosecutions of the participants in the Scandals and of
fiscal and administrative reorganization. Maneuvering the reform
administration into an unenviable financial position, they then berated Jones all the more for his limited program of benefits. They not
only had survived as the "out" faction but soon were to be a cohesive
near-majority force seeking to wrest control of the Legislature from
Jones. The ability of the defeated Longites to make the winning faction run the gauntlet was in part a function of the new political
freedom, but it rested at bottom, as has been argued earlier, on the
inability of the reform forces to take to heart why Sam Jones's "pappy
was for Huey."

Stalemate, compromise, and continued bifactionalism, 1942–43

Strengthened by resumption of the alliance with Maestri, the Long
faction blocked passage of Jones's fiscal measures at the 1942 regular
session of the Legislature. The Governor, in turn, prevented enactment of Longite proposals. The people of Louisiana suffered while
both sides exchanged heated words of blame. A factional stalemate
to which the funds necessary for hospitals, education, and welfare
fell victim was intolerable to supporters in both camps. Compromise

[25] See New Orleans Bureau of Governmental Research, *Louisiana's 'Little
Legislature': A Study of the Board of Liquidation of the State Debt,* Monograph
No. 1 (1945), for a thorough analysis of that agency and of the growth of its
inflated powers.
[26] New Orleans *States,* February 20, 1941.

between Maestri and Jones was concluded in the special session of August, 1942. The remainder of Jones's term was devoted to "holding the line," while Longites intensified their harrying of the state administration. Both sides, in fact, had reached an uneasy balance of power that could be broken only by the outcome of the 1944 gubernatorial primary.

Factional lines remained firm in the Senate and only slightly less firm in the House through the 1942 regular session. In the Senate, early skirmishes over the selection of various aides revealed a maximum of nineteen confirmed Longites, the hard core of which were the ten who voted against a motion to recess the Senate for the purpose of hearing the Governor's address.[27] Most of the senators who opposed Jones hailed from southeast Louisiana (Orleans and environs) and north Louisiana. The occasional defection from the Jones forces of senators Aucoin, Dolby, and Ellis[28] gave the Long faction a one- or two-vote margin of victory on some issues. House opposition to Jones, although drawn from roughly the same areas of the state as that in the Senate, never approached majority proportions. It was of sufficient size, however, to block passage of constitutional amendments and to permit only minimal absenteeism in reform ranks.

The factional alignment prohibited passage of bills advanced by either camp. Thus Jones successfully resisted attempts to repeal basic parts of the re-enacted fiscal and administrative codes and the dual officeholding law, to curb the governor's powers in the much-abused name of home rule, and to create a roving legislative commission of investigation into the executive department. By the same token, Longites were assured of enough reform antipathy toward "spite" legislation to ward off the bills of Jones's New Orleans supporters that were designed to end the commanding position of Mayor Maestri in city politics. The anti-Jones legislators, in fact, played both ends against the middle, interrupting their own partisan per-

[27] In its editorial of May 13, 1942, the New Orleans *States* cried, "CONTEMPTIBLE," and scored the action of the ten senators as a blow to our state and national governments and as a boon to Hitler and Tojo.

[28] As president pro tempore of the Senate, Ellis displayed a curious tendency to stray from the Jones fold. In the 1942 sessions, for example, he voted against the sales tax and for postponement of civil service. A partial explanation might have been that Ellis perhaps was seeking cross-factional support for his possible gubernatorial candidacy in 1944.

formance to cry that "reprisal measures were not in line with Jones's pledge of harmony." Politics, in their view, was a one-way street.

Secure against reprisals, the Longites fought the Governor's legislative program, obtaining a mild concession on civil service and achieving greater victory on state finances. Though unable to force a postponement of the application of the merit system to a date after the 1944 state primaries, they were successful in delaying the effective date of civil service for six months, that is, until January, 1943.[29] With regard to state finances, Jones urged an increase in revenues to underwrite extended benefits and proposed a 2 per cent retail sales tax as his central tax measure. When reminded of his campaign pledge to end the sales tax, which had been ended belatedly in December, 1940, Jones retorted, "I would rather defend my support of a sales tax than explain closed hospitals and hungry old people and bankrupt local governments and unbalanced budgets and underpaid teachers and impassable roads."[30] The measure passed the House, 52–43, but in the Senate, with Ellis and Gay reversing their usual pro-Jones behavior, the sales tax bill was indefinitely postponed by a 21–17 vote.

As in the 1940 session, those proposals which attracted cross-factional support highlighted public policies on which there was broad discontent with the actions of the Governor. Jones's failure to meet his old-age pension promises led the Legislature to return the proceeds of one cent of the gasoline tax to the welfare department, reversing their 1940 endorsement of Jones's transfer of those proceeds to the highway department. The Senate, by a 20–18 vote, also adopted LeBlanc's amendment to the general appropriation bill which provided for an additional $2,500,000 allocation for old-age assistance. Forty-six representatives supported Longite Dodd's failing attempt to increase state educational aid to the level of $20 per educable person, and thirty-six supported a nonadministration bill to increase teachers' salaries. The Senate slashed the appropriations

[29] The Civil Service League was willing to grant the extension because preparations for installing the city civil service system were not yet complete. For reasons of equity and to avoid arousing factional suspicions, the same extension of time was granted the state civil service system.

[30] Baton Rouge *Morning Advocate*, June 16, 1942. Jones frequently alleged, without any apparent justification, that the defeat of the income tax constitutional amendment in November, 1940, implied popular support for a reimposed sales tax.

for Hayes's office, and the Crime Commission law was repealed by unanimous vote with no attempt made by the Jones forces to establish another investigatory body in its place. Huey's law which enlarged the discretionary authority of the attorney general to supersede district attorneys was repealed, and thirty-nine votes were cast in support of a constitutional amendment which would have virtually eliminated the attorney general's power in this area.

For the first time since the regular session of 1930, the Governor and the Legislature were deadlocked. Jones had something to show for his efforts: most of his revamped reorganization program had been enacted; the power of district judges to enjoin the operation of state agencies was restricted; and Huey's once-controversial tax on the refining of oil was repealed in order to encourage the industrial growth of Lake Charles. The resolution of larger issues had been doomed by factionalism, however, so that few could agree with Jones that the legislators had made "a very creditable showing."[31]

As in the 1930 session, state finances were the major casualty of the bifactional stalemate. Jones's legislative leaders, preferring to rely upon his veto rather than upon the selectivity of the Senate, had encouraged the passage of inflated appropriations. The unhappy consequences of that scheme became apparent when it was realized that since the Governor had only an item veto and more than half of the state's revenues were allocated by law, 80 per cent of all items that could be vetoed fell in the humanitarian field of welfare, schools, and hospitals. Defending his actions in terms of constitutional necessity and Longite obstructionism, Governor Jones reluctantly vetoed $9,000,000 in relief and welfare funds, $5,000,000 of school funds, and the entire $8,000,000 appropriation for New Orleans Charity Hospital.

The latter action was a calculated risk which, while exposing Jones to the charge of abandoning the sick, maintained the operation of country parish hospitals around the state, dramatized the factional conflict, and forced Maestri to pursue alternatives to a continuation of the stalemate.[32] Nonetheless, in spite of continued urban press support, Jones's position was deteriorating, for the Louisiana citizen was too unused to uncontrolled legislatures to depart from the tra-

[31] New Orleans *Times-Picayune,* July 9, 1942.
[32] Jones secured legislative consent for the Board of Liquidation of the State Debt to borrow $600,000 to finance the hospital until September 1, 1942.

ditional mode of fixing political accountability on the governor. Symptomatic of this attitude were the vague statements of civic leaders of New Orleans blaming "politicians" in general for the imminent shutdown of Charity Hospital.

Within one month after the close of the regular session, Jones and Maestri came to an understanding, and the Governor called a special session to meet for twelve days beginning August 12 ". . . to prevent people from dying . . . to prevent the old from starving . . . to save the schools of this state . . . to keep country roads from going to pieces. . . ."[33] Jones urged passage of a 1.5 per cent sales tax,[34] a reduction from his previously defeated proposal. After noting that he had lost two more votes in the Senate,[35] Jones candidly admitted, "I, therefore, know, and you know, that without support from opposing political groups, we cannot succeed. I plead especially for support from the Orleans delegation . . . to rise to the occasion and save your people—not by being little politicians, but by being big men. . . ."[36]

The House passed Jones's sales tax, the Choctaws remaining in opposition, by a 53–33 vote. As the condition of Senate passage, however, Maestri forced a compromise which resulted in the opposition only of eleven country-parish Longites to enactment of a one per cent retail sales tax, the proceeds of which were dedicated to a War Emergency Revenue Fund for welfare, hospital, education, and highway purposes. It is instructive to note that of the eight senators who voted on the sales tax in 1938 and in 1942, all eight had supported Leche's sales tax and opposed Jones's in the regular session of 1942. Those five of the eight who were Choctaws supported Jones in the 1942 special session as a result of the compromise described above; the remaining three continued to oppose Jones's one per cent sales tax, notwithstanding their earlier support of Leche on the same measure. It might be noted also that Maestri's insistence upon a low state sales tax stemmed from the fact that New Orleans had levied a 2 per cent city sales tax shortly after the constitutional amendment

[33] Baton Rouge *Morning Advocate*, August 20, 1942.
[34] It might be noted, in view of the outcome, that Jones continued, "With the strictest economy, this might be able to provide the required revenues. Nothing less than this amount [1.5 per cent sales tax] would, in my opinion, be sufficient." Baton Rouge *Morning Advocate*, August 21, 1942.
[35] Senator Cotton was serving in the Army and Senator Brown had been appointed head of the State Board of Health.
[36] Baton Rouge *Morning Advocate*, August 21, 1942.

prohibiting city sales taxes was defeated in the November, 1940, general election.

Rejoicing over the outcome of the session, Jones chortled that "this crowd [Longites] has taken a political shellacking and they know it."[37] Maestri retorted that the Governor had "us[ed] the great Charity Hospital of New Orleans as a weapon to force the enactment of excessive taxes."[38] There was some truth in each appraisal. The fiscal position of the reformers was now secure, the Director of Finance estimating, in March of 1944, that the state would have a $12,500,000 surplus at the close of the fiscal year.[39] On the other hand, so large a surplus subsequent to passage of an allegedly inadequate one per cent sales tax strongly implied that the Jones administration had been guilty of unintentional, perhaps deliberate, financial deceit.[40]

Events during the remainder of Jones's term yielded few clues as to the likely outcome of the 1944 state contest. The Congressional primaries which followed closely upon the heels of the special session in 1942 witnessed the easy renomination of Senator Ellender, who attracted 68.0 per cent of the state's vote, losing only in the parishes of St. Bernard and St. Landry, against a reform candidate not openly backed by Jones.[41] Choctaw Congressional candidates captured the First and Second districts, Longites the Fourth, Sixth, Seventh, and Eighth districts, and Jones's endorsees the remaining Third and Fifth districts. Shreveport's Jimmie Davis defeated Longite Patton for the north Louisiana Public Service Commission seat,

[37] *Ibid.*, August 30, 1942.
[38] *Loc. cit.*
[39] Shreveport *Journal*, March 30, 1944.
[40] Jones's budget-makers had miscalculated the impact of the war upon Louisiana taxes, in which increased income and consumer tax revenues counterbalanced the decline in gasoline and severance tax collections. There still remained the fact, for which Jones made no explanation, that while Jones had asserted a 1.5 per cent sales tax was necessary to produce the very minimum of funds needed, enactment of a one per cent sales tax produced a $12,500,000 surplus by the end of his administration. Issues of the *Plaquemines Gazette*, the organ of Leander Perez, should be consulted for Longite interpretations of state finances under Jones.
[41] E. A. Stephens, a wealthy Jones backer and his Commissioner of Conservation, entered the race early and without Jones's endorsement, eliminating Jones himself, so the rumor went, as a candidate for Ellender's seat. Although Stephens attacked Ellender as a "front man" for Longism, bifactional voting behavior was not much in evidence at the primary. This illustrates the thesis that Louisiana's bifactionalism becomes fuzzy in primary elections other than state office contests.

a Long candidate for the Supreme Court was defeated in north
Louisiana, and Judge Womack of Baton Rouge failed to be re-
elected. As a whole, the Congressional primaries yielded no certain
factional conclusions other than that Jones had surprising strength
in north Louisiana, that the Third District apparently still remembered the Scandals, and that Longites had not been alienated by the
anti-Jones tactics of their country leaders and Maestri.

Two challenges to the power of the state government highlighted
the last year of the Jones administration. One was a "friendly" suit
brought by reformers which succeeded in restricting the powers of
the Board of Liquidation of the State Debt, a move with which Jones
co-operated in view of the new financial stability of his administration. The other was a brazen defiance of state authority reminiscent
of the savage days of the Kingfish, involving Leander Perez, boss
of Plaquemines and St. Bernard parishes.[42] Perez, a veteran Longite,
disputed the Governor's right to name a new sheriff of Plaquemines
subsequent to the death of the elected sheriff on June 1, 1943.[43] In
defiance of judicial rulings, Perez blockaded the courthouse at
Pointe-a-la-Hache, thereby persuading Jones of the necessity of
proclaiming martial law in order to install his new sheriff. The battle
of grand juries and judges ensued, with Perez and the state administration filing charges and countercharges not excluding kidnaping
and murder. In April, 1944, a district court held illegal Jones's declaration of martial law, and shortly afterwards the state Supreme
Court refused review in all cases arising from the conflict because
the issue had become moot. In the primary of January 18, 1944,
Perez' candidate had been elected for the full four-year term as
sheriff. The reform forces could sadly agree with the expressive judgment of a south Louisianian: "La Politique . . . She Stink, She
Stink!"[44]

[42] During the 1940's, Sheriff "Dutch" Rowley of St. Bernard at times disputed
Perez' control, so that, while each always delivered lop-sided majorities to a
candidate, they sometimes worked opposite factional sides of the street.

[43] The legal dispute hinged upon a determination of the length of the unexpired term of the deceased sheriff: if less than one year, the governor appointed
a successor; if more than one year, the governor had to call a special primary.
Since the end of the sheriff's term was determined to be May 19, 1944, Jones was
advised of his right and obligation to name a successor to finish the term.

[44] Chapter 16 of Harnett T. Kane, *Deep Delta Country* (New York, 1944), is
so entitled.

An appraisal of Sam Houston Jones, "The Liberator of Louisiana"

Political developments under Jones could not be ascribed automatically to his wishes; the Governor had to deal, to improvise, and to compromise. Yet he was also supposed to be the voice of reform anti-Longism. Fancy clashed with fact, his assigned role with political reality. The resulting compromises of the Jones administration dismayed many anti-Longs and converted few Longites. Still, few could deny that Louisiana had not been exposed to a full education in the value of clean, or at least cleaner, government. Furthermore, despite obvious failings, Jones's economic policies were reflective of the fact that Huey Long had stridden through the Louisiana scene. That degree of anti-Long enlightenment was no small gain in itself, although whether the voters would be satisfied with small, rather than giant, steps forward was another matter.

Temperamentally, Jones was not a politician; his was a brusque, incisive manner which said what it had to say, and little else. The Governor admitted his limitations in reply to a query as to whether Louisiana would be content to diet on economy and sound legislation instead of bread-and-circuses. "Whether it can or not, it is the best I can do. I'm not in this job to make myself a popular hero. . . . I'm not Governor because I want hooray and applause. I'm Governor because someone had to clean up the mess that Huey and his successors left . . . ."[45]

On the other hand, Jones could take credit for enlarging and holding together his legislative following despite unrelenting Longite attacks. To those critics, friend and foe alike, who charged that the Governor was no politician, Jones retorted in effect that he was, at the very least, an astute political tactician.

"I have been some sort of politician," bragged Jones in a radio talk, ". . . [to have gotten] the most far-reaching program in Louisiana's history enacted into law. . . . When you go a step farther and remind yourself that this program [1940] was enacted with a legislature overwhelmingly against me you might pick up a bit of respect for my political ability. When you dig deeper and find that I had to get, and did get, twenty-six votes out of a Senate in which I had but fifteen friends that respect commences to in-

[45] Robert Van Gelder, "Mopping Up Louisiana," *New York Times Magazine* (September 15, 1940), 18.

crease. And then when you find that I had to get, and did get, sixty-seven votes in the House where but thirty-five members were elected on my ticket, I became pretty well fixed in your mind as a rather good politician. . . . And what was once your criticism, I say candidly [sic], is bound to turn to admiration."[46]

Though Sam Jones was fond of asserting that he had fulfilled forty-three of forty-five campaign promises,[47] many of his actions alienated segments of the voters. Some in the reform wing—anticipating in Jones another Parker committed to a holy war against the evils of machine politics, corruption, and extravagant taxation—were shocked to see "Louisiana's Liberator" engage in deals with Noe, Maestri, and the Choctaws, impose more taxes than needed, and abandon the "leaf from twig" approach to Scandals prosecutions.[48] And the late effective date of civil service, although explainable on other grounds, nonetheless allowed Jones to continue in the spoils politics tradition for the first half of his term. The *Times-Picayune* estimated, for example, that about 35 per cent of the employees of the New Orleans Charity Hospital had been fired partisanly by Jones.[49]

More to the central failing of the Jones administration were the dissatisfactions stemming from the limited liberalism of the four-year record. Organized labor viewed the reformers as less sympathetic than previous administrations,[50] and teachers and old-age pension recipients were far from pleased with reform performance. Parish police juries resented their inability to procure state funds for the building of farm-to-market roads. Finally, the Governor's insistence upon a sales tax to provide necessary state revenues followed in the steps of Leche's sharp reversal of Huey Long's class-taxing program.

Sam Jones was not, however, a "do-nothing" illiberal governor. Far

[46] Baton Rouge *Morning Advocate*, December 23, 1943.
[47] The two broken pledges admitted to were the abolition of the sales tax and the guarantee of $30 monthly old-age pensions, and both were attributed to the obstructionism of the Long faction.
[48] For a typical expression of reformer disillusionment with Jones, see W. V. Holloway, "The Crash of the Long Machine and Its Aftermath," *Journal of Politics*, iii (August, 1941), 348–62.
[49] New Orleans *Times-Picayune*, August 12, 1952.
[50] See *Louisiana Labor Leader*, February 25, 1943, the official voice of the State Federation of Labor. Two qualifications should be noted: use of the phrase "organized labor's view" implies a cohesiveness to Louisiana unions in politics which in fact does not exist; and, second, Lige Williams, veteran president of the State Federation, always retained close personal ties with Longite leaders.

from it. Twenty-eight per cent of the increased state budget was allocated to education, 17 per cent to charities and welfare, 15 per cent to highways. State aid for education reached $20 per educable person by the close of Jones's term, the school lunch program was extended, old-age pensions increased to $21 monthly, and homestead exemptions were pegged at $2,000. Auto license fees were reduced, the sales tax abolished for a short period, and despite the war, reasonable highway programs were maintained. In Mississippi, Jones might have been adjudged radical. In Louisiana, what was essentially a retention of the Longite class program contrasted sharply with his feverish activity in the field of good government.

Compared to past administrations, then, the strength of Jones lay in the broad area of honest government. Civil service, despite its defects, had been instituted, and reorganization of the diffused bureaucracy undertaken. Some of the dictatorial laws of the Kingfish were repealed and provision made for honest elections. Safeguards were adopted against the venality of public officials and for the handling of public funds. The Legislature was freed from gubernatorial shackles, and the courts gradually were losing their intense factional coloration. For all the carping about minor phases of the clean-politics program by reformers and Longites, there can be no doubt that Jones's accomplishments were very real and very vital, and in view of factional hostility, very remarkable.

Throughout his term, Sam Jones used the "good politics" argument to induce new business to locate in Louisiana. On several occasions, Jones toured the Midwestern states, preaching the virtues of the Mississippi River and the Gulf of Mexico as arteries of trade with Latin America. He became, in effect, a regional spokesman, a role unthinkable for Earl Long and one embraced for personal advantage by Huey Long. To hasten and prepare for the millenium of a Louisiana "fairyland of industries," the Governor established an Economic Development Committee to deal with postwar problems, advocated the use of federal and state funds to drain more than ten million acres of Delta and prairie land soils, and persuaded the Legislature to adopt a resolution opposing the piping of Louisiana natural gas to Eastern states possessed of a ready supply of coal. Jones also spoke out against the freight-rate structure disadvantageous to the South and went so far as to talk ominously of a third-party movement unless the national government ceased to regard the South, in effect, as a conquered province.[51]

Much of the dissatisfaction with Jones should be understood in terms of the growing pains of a struggling democracy. As the Governor observed on one occasion, "Some of the very people who suffered most at the hands of the tinhorn dictators now fidget and frown in the strangeness of being free again. . . . The poison lives in the body long after the symptoms are cured . . . ."[52] At the same time, the directions of Longite attack were clearly indicated: the innovations of good government were to be belittled; the Governor to be accused of partisan motives; and the product of reform politics to be dismissed as "do-nothing." As Representative Dodd of Allen Parish, a Longite and head of the teachers' lobby, put it: "No one accuses him (Jones) of stealing or grafting, but he is making the people a poorer, honest governor than some of those whom he called thieves and crooks."[53]

Perhaps so, but to the best of his ability Sam Jones, as he himself stated, "kept faith with the people." His program of enlightened conservatism, despite factionalism and war, refuted dire Longite predictions and disappointed perhaps over-idealistic reform hopes. His administration permanently revised the concept of government from that of an avenue for personal gain to one of public service. He had sought, with but moderate success, to revamp the tone of anti-Longism from tax consciousness to one dedicated to enlarging the areas of self-help and opportunity for the bulk of citizens. "Louisianians would no longer," proudly proclaimed the Governor, "have to hide their heads in shame." Although Jones was but narrowly vindicated in the 1944 primaries and was overwhelmingly repudiated in the 1948 primaries, the moral and governmental principles of his brand of progressive conservatism became impressed upon large numbers of voters—and upon more than a few candidates—as a reasonable alternative to the buccaneering liberalism of the Longs.

[51] Sam H. Jones, as told to James Aswell, "Will Dixie Bolt the New Deal?" *The Saturday Evening Post*, ccxv (March 6, 1943), 20ff.

[52] New Orleans *Item*, June 5, 1941.

[53] Baton Rouge *Morning Advocate*, June 4, 1942.

CHAPTER 7

The lull that caused the storm?

THE CAMPAIGN AND ADMINISTRATION of Jimmie Davis was a strange interlude in the intense bifactionalism of Louisiana politics which perhaps satisfied a populace weary of global war and local political bitterness. An era of peace and harmony settled upon the state, with the Governor happily presiding over the distribution of ever-increasing state revenues in a manner calculated neither to enlarge reform prestige nor to arouse factional animosities. This progressive dulling of customary bifactionalism was shattered by the state campaign of 1948, in which the reform forces sought to re-create the good fight of 1940. Unfortunately for their purposes, the Scandals no longer fed the flames of an incensed morality, and the reforms so dear to the heart of Jones appeared to many voters to have less value than the welfare-state pledges of Earl Long. Good government, as defined by the actions of Sam Jones and Jimmie Davis, had failed to win the allegiance of a majority of voters.

The gubernatorial primary of 1944

On the surface, the 1944 state primaries were marked by seemingly contradictory and confused actions. Although Governor Jones endorsed no candidate openly and Earl Long ran for lieutenant-governor, those rivals of 1940 and the issues they raised provided the meaning of the campaign. The major reform candidate offered "peace and harmony" in lieu of specific planks and preached soft words even unto the Longites. The Choctaws, for their part, publicly violated the Ring rule, often privately flouted in the past, by hand-picking a gubernatorial candidate whose country parish popularity was unproven. Both major factions suffered from a multiplicity of

competing candidacies. But these contradictions were resolved by a
Louisiana electorate which apparently had the good sense to per-
ceive the underlying realities of the campaign.

Attempts by the reformers to broaden their electoral support revealed their unexpressed conviction that the gubernatorial candidacy
of a known anti-Long stood little chance of success. In April, 1943,
Jones appointed George Wallace, a veteran Longite who had been
the architect of several of the court suits against good government
in 1941–1942, as director of the State Department of Commerce
and Industry. Shortly afterwards, Jones tentatively endorsed A. P.
Tugwell for governor in the forthcoming primaries. Tugwell, who
had broken with Leche in 1939, was the Jones-Noe winning candidate for state treasurer in 1940 and had been state treasurer under
Leche and Highway Commission chairman under Allen. Reformers
had to look elsewhere, however, when the incidental revelations of a
mid-1943 federal income tax trial of Lake Charles oil man W. T.
Burton indicated that Tugwell had been the recipient of an unethical
gift of $5,000 back in 1936.[1] Reform support of yet another guber-
natorial candidate was undertaken but, significantly, never publicly
announced, in deference to the supported candidate's fear that an
open endorsement by Jones might, on balance, be detrimental to
his victory.

The choice of the reform faction was Jimmie H. Davis, former
teacher, court clerk, and city commissioner of Shreveport, and recent
victor over a Longite candidate for the north Louisiana seat on the
Public Service Commission. Doubtless more widely known as "Singing Jimmie" Davis, composer of the popular song "You Are My Sunshine," he conducted a disarmingly apolitical campaign, complete
with cowboy bands and song-fests, rejecting the traditional Louisiana technique of hellfire from the stump.[2] Davis, however, was no
urban buffoon imitating Texas' Pappy O'Daniel. Simply put, Davis
sought cross-factional support from a relatively disciplined bifactional electorate. By being *sui generis*, at least in terms of campaign
tactics, Davis attracted a sufficient number of voters in addition to
the anti-Longs to defeat his Longite rivals. Who would condemn

[1] New Orleans *Times-Picayune*, July 18, 1943. Tugwell withdrew his gubernatorial candidacy and ran for renomination as treasurer.
[2] Consult the Shreveport *Journal*, October 25, 1943, for a detailed description
of one of Davis' campaign talks.

tactics so successful?

Davis' campaign made good sense, therefore, when fitted into his strategic objective. His proud claim of independence was supported by the absence of Jones's public endorsement and by the moderacy of his comments on his rival candidates.[3] Although heading a state ticket, Davis asserted that he had chosen like-minded independents without regard to the niceties of a sectionally balanced slate, and that he deliberately had not created a network of parish candidates in support of his state ticket.[4] His most important specific pledges— and they were few—included maintenance of civil service, protection of the state's natural gas resources,[5] no further taxation, and enact- ment of state and city employee retirement systems. All the good legislation of past administrations would be retained, and "progress" would be made for the benefit of farmers, workers, recreationists, the aged, motorists, the infirm, the plain citizen. The governor and the people would be "just good friends."

Davis' unusual campaign, however superior tactically to one that would have been waged by an unrelenting anti-Long, gave the urban press difficulty in justifying their support of him in the heady terms of principle.[6] The New Orleans *Item* consequently explained its approval of Davis in realistic terms of expediency. "He is the most likely independent candidate to lead the field against the candidates put forward by the old machine."[7] In the accuracy of that judgment lay the answer to the otherwise astonishing action of the reform forces in backing a "song-and-dance man" for the highest state office.

Reformers had to support Davis because none of the three more vociferous anti-Long candidates had any chance of victory. Most significant of the three candidacies was that of Sam Caldwell, three- term mayor of Shreveport, who persuaded popular Frank Ellis of

[3] While it was an open secret that Jones supported Davis, there was no public endorsement—the political difference between the two is considerable.

[4] Baton Rouge *State-Times*, October 29, 1943. However, Davis' claimed dis- dain for sectional balance was somewhat dubious in that the four members of his bobtailed state ticket did hail from different sections of the state.

[5] In view of the later importance of the natural gas issue, it would be useful to note Davis' specific pledge to " . . . oppose with all the force at my command the exploitation of natural gas reserves and other natural resources which are known to be limited." Baton Rouge *State-Times*, December 11, 1943.

[6] See, for example, the New Orleans *States*, editorial, December 6, 1943, for a laughable exposition of its "reasons" for supporting Davis.

[7] New Orleans *Item*, editorial, January 8, 1944.

St. Tammany Parish, Jones's president pro tempore of the Senate, to run for lieutenant-governor on his ticket.[8] Supported by the Ewing papers in Shreveport and Monroe, they appealed to voters disaffected with any and all organized factions, and sought to become the major rivals to Longism by frequently attacking Jimmie Davis. Lee Lanier, anti-Jones editor of the *Amite News-Digest* of Tangipahoa, a former Longite apparently on the outs with that faction, headed a bob-tailed state ticket composed mostly of candidates endorsed by other rivals. Lanier pledged a $5 minimum daily wage for highway workers, a five-year public works program of $50,000,000 annually, $30 monthly old-age pensions, and, with doubtful sincerity, committed himself to support of civil service.[9] Finally, there was Vincent Moseley, ticket-less as usual, who berated Jones for fulfilling only three of Moseley's twenty planks in 1940, ridiculed "Sinatra" Davis and "wheel chair" Morgan (the major Longite candidate), and solemnly warned the voters that his defeat would ensure the enthronement of machine politics.

On the other side of the factional fence, Longites were displaying little of the solidarity which had marked their resistance to the Jones administration. In March, 1943, country parish Longites formed the Louisiana Democratic Organization in an effort to counterbalance Maestri's influence over the naming of the Longite ticket. There was no dearth of willing candidates: by May, Noe, state Senator Ernest Clements, and Earl Long had announced for the governorship, and Jimmie Morrison, Dudley LeBlanc, and Senator Ellender were yet to be heard from.[10] Earl Long did most of the Longite speechmaking in the summer of 1943, and was rewarded by the endorsement of the Louisiana Democratic Organization in early September. In addition to stressing the themes of his innocence of the Scandals and Jones's demagogy, Earl affirmed his intention never to be deficient in the

[8] Ellis had announced his own bid for the governorship, but later withdrew to join up with Caldwell.

[9] See the September 23, 1938, issue of the *Amite News Digest* for Lanier's earlier views on the merits of the spoils system. Late in the 1944 campaign, the Louisiana Civil Service League reported that Lanier had withdrawn his civil service pledge.

[10] According to press reports, Ellender was willing to run if all Longites would unite behind him and if his Senate seat were not traded to Jones in return for reform faction support. Quite apart from the inner squabbling of Longite leaders, organized labor would have nothing to do with the conservative Senator. Baton Rouge *Morning Advocate*, September 22, 1943.

promises of politics. Advocating a decrease in revenues by repeal of the state property tax, Long pledged extensive benefits, including a widening and fencing of all main highways, an increase in the salaries of schoolteachers and school bus drivers, $30 monthly old-age pensions, and the establishment of a trade school in every parish.[11]

Maestri, however, had no intention of backing Long,[12] and in mid-October selected his own candidate, Lewis Morgan of St. Tammany Parish, over sixty years of age, a former Sixth District congressman, state representative, and district attorney, a minor Longite who had held several attorneyships to state agencies under Huey and Leche. That the city machine had hand-picked Morgan was undeniable, for he first had qualified for the office of attorney general, only to withdraw and qualify for governor shortly before the official announcement of Ring support. Earl Long, always a political realist, accepted the post of lieutenant-governor on the Morgan ticket, while other Longites completed the ticket.[13] Ironically, the Morgan-Long ticket frequently had to defend itself against a charge of conspiracy to the effect that Morgan intended to resign shortly after taking office and allow Earl Long to claim the governorship. The accusation failed to appreciate the degree of Choctaw antipathy to Long.

Morgan's platform embraced Earl Long's pledges as further liberalized by promises of old-age pensions to those over sixty years of age and of gasoline tax exemption to both fishermen and farmers in the use of their machinery. Longite attitudes on civil service varied: Morgan endorsed the principle; but Long and Cawthorn (the ticket candidate for attorney general) opposed it. Concentrating upon Davis as his only serious rival, Earl frequently alluded to that "banjo-picking song-and-dance man" whose "say-nothing" stump speeches were rewritten into policy statements by a partisan urban press, and he attempted to hammer home the theme that Jimmie Davis was nothing but the candidate of the Jones administration. Rival Longite candidacies were ignored, although the intra-factional

[11] New Orleans *Times-Picayune*, March 28, 1943.
[12] Believing that Earl had booted the 1940 primaries because of his erratic temperament, Maestri had no wish to expose himself to that risk again. Before deciding upon Morgan, the Choctaws vainly had attempted to secure combined support for Ellender.
[13] The Morgan-Long state ticket included veteran incumbents Wilson and Grace, state Senator Joe T. Cawthorn, an original Noe ally, for attorney general, and Wade O. Martin, Jr., for secretary of state.

competition, together with Senator Overton's rupture with the Choc-taws,[14] threatened the success of the Morgan-Long ticket.

Two opportunistic Longites allegedly possessed of personal fol-lowings entered the gubernatorial contest. One was Jimmie Mor-rison, Sixth District Congressman since 1942, who adopted most of Morgan's planks, added a pledge to repeal Orleans and state sales taxes, and berated Davis, Morgan, and the Choctaws with fine im-partiality. The other was Dudley LeBlanc, who endorsed candidates on other slates to construct his own state ticket and munificently guaranteed veterans' bonuses, a free college education to all, subsidies to farmers, state assumption of all public educational costs, and—not to be outdone by any—$40 monthly old-age pensions.

A third Longite completed the bewildering array of candidates. State Senator Ernest Clements of Allen Parish, former Conservation

TABLE 18. The Louisiana Vote in the 1944 Democratic First Primary for Governor and Lieutenant-Governor

Office and Candidates	Orleans	Other	State	% State	Parishes Carried by Majority	Parishes Carried by Plurality
Governor						
Davis	36,910	130,524	167,434	34.9	5	28
Morgan	52,944	78,738	131,682	27.5	3	9
Morrison	7,887	68,194	76,081	15.9	4	7
LeBlanc	535	39,857	40,392	8.4	2	4
Caldwell	4,345	29,990	34,335	7.2	0	0
Clements	1,056	19,348	20,404	4.3	2	0
Moseley	391	6,994	7,385	1.5	0	0
Lanier	408	1,233	1,641	.3	0	0
Total	104,476	374,878	479,354	100.0	16	48
Lt. Governor						
Long (Morgan)	50,778	143,477	194,255	41.9	18	26
Verret (Davis)	27,331	100,901	128,232	27.6	2	9
Ellis (Caldwell)	15,859	88,274	104,133	22.4	1	7
Other	5,860	31,567	37,427	8.1	0	1
Total	99,828	364,219	464,047	100.0	21	43

SOURCE: computed from *Compilation of Primary Election Returns of the Democratic Party, State of Louisiana*, elections held January 18 and February 29, 1944, issued by Secretary of State; Alexander Heard and Donald S. Strong, *Southern Primaries and Elections*, 71–72.

[14] Overton charged that the Choctaws had persuaded Noe to support the hand-picked Morgan-Long ticket by offering to back Noe against Overton in the Senate primary of 1944. Though denying the charge, the Ring conspicuously re-frained from committing themselves in support of Overton's renomination.

Commissioner under Leche and fierce legislative foe of Jones, identified himself as the only true disciple of Huey Long, espoused planks
roughly identical with those put forward by Morgan, and flayed
civil service as a reform ruse. Noe's withdrawal from the race in
September and his announced support of the Morgan-Long ticket
eliminated a fourth aspirant in the Longite free-for-all.

The outcome of the January 18 primary, reported in Table 18, at
first glance seemed to predict a certain victory for the reform forces
in the runoff. Davis exhibited great statewide strength, polling 25 per
cent or more of the vote in fifty-seven of the sixty-four parishes. That
support was garnered largely at the expense of Morgan, for LeBlanc,
Clements, and Morrison each attracted a localized following respectively in south Louisiana, west-central Louisiana, and in the Florida
parishes. Thousands had not voted straight factional tickets, as
judged by the voting data on gubernatorial and affiliated lieutenant-
gubernatorial candidates. The urban press, supporting Davis, chose
to interpret the results as proof of the existence of many "independent" voters, whose freedom from bifactional and ticket-voting habits
assured Davis' nomination in the second primary.

A close look, however, at the results of the race for lieutenant-
governor (Table 18 and Figure 8), in which only three major candidates competed, suggested another interpretation. Earl Long did as
well, in New Orleans and in the rest of the state, in the 1944 first
primary as he had done as a gubernatorial candidate in the 1940 first
primary (see Table 16). The pattern of relative parish support for
Earl reflected customary bifactionalism and gave evidence of returning Long strength in some south Louisiana parishes. Nor was there
evidence to support the reformers' hope that Maestri's selection of
the Longite ticket would alienate many Longites. On the contrary,
since country Longite Clements logically would have been the recipient of such protest votes, the restriction of his support mainly to
his native area of Allen and Beauregard parishes attested to the
insignificance of that factor in Longite voting behavior.

It was, therefore, the multiplicity of Longite gubernatorial candidates which misled the partisans of Davis in their interpretation of
the first primary. That multiplicity necessarily resulted in deviations
from straight-ticket voting and gave the impression that bifactionalism had been displaced by a new and different multifactionalism.
On the basis of Earl Long's performance, however, the runoff pri-

mary gave every indication of being as close as the 1940 runoff had
been.

Bifactionalism made its indisputably clear appearance in the six
weeks between primaries. Clements, Morrison, and senators Ellender
and Overton declared for Morgan.[15] Opportunistic LeBlanc announced for Davis; Caldwell and Ellis maintained neutrality; and
Moseley, ever in character, endorsed a split ticket of Morgan and
Verret. Davis' state ticket took on Coxe and Tugwell for superin-

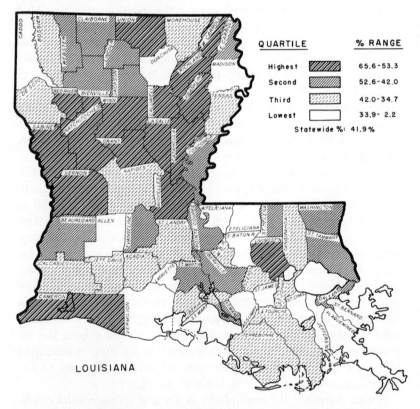

QUARTILE		% RANGE
Highest		65.6 - 53.3
Second		52.6 - 42.0
Third		42.0 - 34.7
Lowest		33.9 - 2.2

Statewide %: 41.9%

LOUISIANA

FIGURE 8. Quartile map: proportion of parish vote cast for Earl Long,
1944 Democratic lieutenant-gubernatorial first primary.

SOURCE: *Compilation* cited for Table 18.

[15] Overton stated that he had received written assurance from the Ring that no
treachery was intended with reference to the senatorial primary later in the year.

tendent of education and treasurer respectively, while Baynard linked up with Morgan as his ticket candidate for auditor.[16]

Two incidents, both casting discredit on the Longites, marked the pre-runoff period. The first was the withdrawal of James Gremillion, incumbent Secretary of State running for renomination on the Davis ticket, which enabled Longite Wade O. Martin, Jr., to claim the office without a second primary.[17] The second involved the attempt of Long and Cawthorn to persuade the Choctaws to withdraw their support from Morgan, thereby forcing him to quit the race, so that they too might win the nomination to the lieutenant-governorship and the attorney generalship respectively without a second primary.[18] Maestri, however, opposed the scheme, thus frustrating one of Earl's most brazen political maneuvers.

The results of the February 29 primary are reported in Table 19.

TABLE 19. The Louisiana Vote in the 1944 Democratic Second Primary for Governor and Lieutenant-Governor

Office and Candidates	Orleans	Other	State	% State	Parishes Carried by Majority
Governor					
Davis	50,856	200,372	251,228	53.6	44
Morgan	59,218	158,697	217,915	46.4	20
Total	110,074	359,069	469,143	100.0	64
Lt.-Governor					
Verret (Davis)	52,882	184,570	237,452	51.2	33
Long (Morgan)	55,829	170,820	226,649	48.8	31
Total	108,711	355,390	464,101	100.0	64

SOURCE: computed from *Compilation of Primary Election Returns of the Democratic Party, State of Louisiana*, elections held January 18 and February 29, 1944, issued by the Secretary of State; Alexander Heard and Donald S. Strong, *Southern Primaries and Elections*, 72.

It was obvious that Long had run ahead of Morgan in the state outside of Orleans, a fact which bolstered Long's pre-runoff assertions that Morgan hindered the success of the ticket. Relative parish re-

[16] Subsequently E. J. Bourg, Choctaw candidate for auditor, withdrew, making L. B. Baynard the nominee.

[17] In the first primary, Gremillion had 172,500 votes, Martin 198,293. Had he remained in the race most probably he, like the rest of the Davis ticket, would have been nominated. Gremillion offered no reason for his withdrawal. He was an attorney on Martin's staff from 1944 until his death in 1951.

[18] For a discussion of the law which Long and Cawthorn sought to exploit, see above, pp. 37–38.

sponse to Morgan, however, was quite similar to that for Earl, and both closely resembled Earl's first-primary pattern (Figure 8). The only parishes which shifted by more than one quartile of support for Long, from the first to the second primaries, were Plaquemines and Allen. Ticket voting was restored, with Fred LeBlanc, Tugwell, and Coxe gaining their nominations to state offices as affiliates of the Davis ticket. What appeared to some observers of the first primary as a fuzzy sort of factionalism thus emerged in the runoff as the same bifactionalism evident in Earl's first-primary race for lieutenant-governor. "You Are My Sunshine" had not displaced the Kingfish.

The major events of the Davis administration

Sam Jones held high hopes at the outset of the Davis administration. "This is a great victory for clean government—even greater than that of 1940. The 1940 campaign was won by the flame of spontaneous revolt against shocking scandal. This triumph [1944] was brought about by the unspectacular, but deliberate determination of the people to continue clean, independent government. It marks the first time in forty years that an independent governor has been succeeded in office by an independent governor."[19] But after the 1948 state primaries, at which Earl Long secured the governorship, reform forces tended to blame Jimmie Davis for the decline in popularity of the good-government movement. There seemed to be considerable evidence for that judgment. Davis was frequently absent from the state,[20] to the extent of making a Hollywood movie on state time. Administration leadership was woefully inept, and gubernatorial guidance of the Legislature often was lacking. Yet there were elements of strength in the Davis performance never clearly realized by the reformers and completely obscured by Sam Jones's campaign in 1948. For all of his tendencies toward indecision, fiscal circumstances made Davis anything but a "do-nothing" governor. That mistaken verdict was stamped in the minds of a majority of Louisiana voters by the ineptitude of anti-Long campaigning in 1948, together with

[19] Baton Rouge *Morning Advocate*, March 2, 1944.
[20] Davis was absent from the state 44 days in the fiscal year 1944–45, 68 days in 1945–46, and 108 days in 1946–47. Appropriations for the contingent fund to pay the Lieutenant-Governor when acting as Governor were twice exhausted.

the personal unpopularity of Jones, rather than by the actions of the Davis administration itself.

Gubernatorial leadership was vacillating in the field of state finances. The administration's budgetary miscalculations were so gross as to warrant a judgment of intentional deceit, although the tactic failed in the objective of stampeding legislators to the support of increased taxes. On the other hand, the persistent appearance of surpluses attracted raids upon the state treasury by well-organized pressure groups, particularly the education lobby. Direction of financial policy thus became, under Davis, more of a legislative free-for-all with less executive control than ever before in recent Louisiana politics.

Unlike his predecessors, Davis entered office with an inherited surplus of $12,000,000 instead of a thumping deficit. Nonetheless, in his submission of a $197,500,000 biennial budget, some $16,000,000 more than Jones's 1942–44 budget, Davis argued that a deficit of $43,000,000 loomed. The revision of erroneous administration estimates, however, ended the contradiction and easily realized a balanced budget.[21] The accuracy of the revised estimates was ensured by swift re-enactment of the sales and natural gas gathering taxes.[22]

Anticipating that current taxes would yield increased revenues in the postwar years, Davis endorsed a proposal to freeze most of the state surplus he had inherited in the form of an untouchable trust fund.[23] Essentially a sound conservative plan backed by the urban press, Davis clumsily sought to disguise the bill as a measure for the benefit of returning war veterans. The lean years of the war proved too much for legislators, however, and the bill was defeated in the House, 45–46. The Legislature appeared to be firmly committed to

[21] Initial estimates omitted receipt of revenues from several taxes, such as the sales tax and the gas gathering tax, which were due to expire at the close of fiscal 1943–44 but were almost certain to be re-enacted by the 1944 Legislature, and the estimates also overlooked the inherited surplus from the Jones administration.

[22] In exchange for the administration's endorsement of the current rate of the gas gathering levy, gas interests agreed not to challenge the legality of the tax—an agreement identical to that employed by Governor Parker in his initiation of severance tax legislation in 1920.

[23] About one-sixth of the surplus already had been allocated for an increase in teachers' pay, an amount which Jones had sanctioned and which would have been distributed earlier except for the reform suit against the Board of Liquidation of the State Debt. The remainder of the surplus, about $10,000,000, was the amount in question.

a policy of heavier spending, but Davis' attempt to read into the defeat of the postwar trust fund an implicit endorsement of additional taxation met with failure. Treasurer Tugwell proposed a doubling of the sales tax to provide capital outlay for public educational facilities and other state institutions, and for agricultural and drainage purposes, though once again the measure was touted as legislation for veterans. The Governor initially endorsed the proposal only if enacted as a constitutional amendment, which would require popular ratification. In view of Choctaw opposition to the bill, however, he later sanctioned its passage as ordinary legislation. The urban press opposed the bill and the House, by a 47–48 vote, rejected it.

Without the Governor's tutoring in the facts of fiscal life, the Legislature evidenced an unrestrained largesse in matters of finance. By vetoing $15,000,000 of appropriations in 1944, largely at the expense of a statewide drainage program and of highway construction, Davis maintained both a balanced budget and a wide distribution of benefits. Teachers' salaries were increased and state payments to education advanced to the level of $22.50 per educable person. State mental institutions at long last were granted appreciably increased appropriations. Funds were allocated to all parishes for highway aid and to poorer parishes to supplement their own meager revenues. Salary raises for various public offices were enacted. Only on the matter of old-age pensions was a go-slow policy adhered to, and there because of anxiety not over state finances but over the fact that mandatory state payments of $30 a month, regardless of need, might jeopardize federal support of the program. Fiscal surpluses nonetheless continued to mount, persuading the legislators assembled in special session in October, 1945, to appropriate $17,000,000 for new highways and for a statewide drainage program. Like the bottomless well, however, the General Fund surplus at the outset of the 1946 regular session was estimated at $19,000,000.

Legislative irresponsibility apparently increased in direct proportion to the availability of surplus funds. Davis had to veto $14,000,000 of appropriations in order to balance the budget at the close of the 1946 session. An additional $35,000,000 of bonds were issued for the construction of roads and of a new Shreveport Charity Hospital. Although resisting the teachers' lobby's pressure for either (or both) a doubled sales tax or an increased gas gathering tax, the Legislature did increase state aid to education to $27.50 per educable person and authorized the expenditure of $6,400,000 for raising the salaries of teachers. A state employment retirement system was established, and the salaries of state legislators and elective state officials were increased. Municipalities, in recognition of their financial plight, were allocated a greater share of chain store taxes and were permitted to levy an additional tax on beer. State property tax exemptions for new industry, discontinued since 1941, again became official state policy. The anticipated revenues from the development of tidelands oil were dedicated to the retirement of the state debt, in effect releasing highway revenues that were being applied to the retirement of the highway bonded debt.

The 1946 session appropriated $76,000,000 for all educational purposes, a sum which represented one-third of tax revenues and an increase in educational appropriations of 46 per cent since 1944. Nevertheless, a special session called in March, 1947, allocated another $17,000,000 to increase teachers' salaries, to advance state payments close to $40 per educable person, and to provide capital outlay for public educational institutions. In such fashion was the windfall of state revenues disposed of, with hardly a thought given to a reduction in taxes or to the swifter retirement of the state debt. By the time Earl Long claimed the governor's office in 1948, he was heir to a $45,000,000 state surplus and to a legislative appetite for increased appropriations which helped to explain the intensified liberalism of the 1948–52 period.

Davis' record on the good-government front consisted essentially of his retention of Jones's reforms. There was a flurry of reform opposition in 1946, with reference to a Davis-sponsored bill excluding from civil service coverage the superintendents and business managers of state institutions and to the Governor's insistence on re-creating a State Printing Board to handle state agency contracts, a method used under Leche and ended by Jones. Both actions, however, were defensible in their own right and neither heralded any abandonment by Davis, as some reformers had feared, of the tenets of good government. A useful contribution of Davis to the structure of state administration was his decision to separate the administration of penal institutions from that of health institutions within the single Department of Institutions, established under Jones.

The anti-labor sentiment which swept the Southern states in the

immediate postwar period was productive of controversy in Louisiana during the Davis administration. Several bills restrictive of
labor's powers were introduced in the 1946 session with the backing
of an *ad hoc* Louisiana Citizens' Committee. Representative Cleveland of Acadia Parish urged the outlawing of the closed shop in two
bills, one in the form of ordinary legislation, the other a constitutional amendment. Senator Goff of northeast Louisiana introduced
a measure, modeled on the federal Case bill which was later passed
by Congress but vetoed by Truman, which prohibited unions from
coercing employers, from employing violence in strikes, and the like.
The Goff bill was amended in committee to provide for the regulation of management practices as well, and subsequently was described by its author as a "mutual responsibility" measure. A fourth
bill denied state unemployment benefits to strikers.

Davis' determination of his position on the various anti-labor measures was complicated by the fact that the labor attitudes of legislators did not coincide with the bifactionalism of state politics. The
fifty-four House members who supported passage of the Cleveland
bill came from rural and urban parishes, from Long and anti-Long
strongholds. The House subsequently rejected the Cleveland constitutional amendment, 65Y–33N,[24] while the Senate passed both the
Cleveland (22–16) and Goff (25–14) bills. The Governor finally
resolved the conflicting pressures on him first by vetoing the Cleveland bill as "an interference with the right of collective bargaining,"
and then by endorsing passage of the Goff bill and of the measure
forbidding strikers from drawing unemployment benefits.[25] Prior to
enacting the latter bills, the House, in a rare show of strength,
mustered forty votes in a failing effort to override Davis' veto of the
Cleveland bill. For his actions Davis was hailed by labor leaders,
though not until after the 1948 primaries, as "the best governor
Louisiana labor ever had."[26]

[24] Cleveland's proposal to ban the closed shop received more votes as a constitutional amendment (65) than as an ordinary act (54). This illustrates the
tendency of some Louisiana legislators to seek to escape the responsibility assigned to them by the Constitution of screening proposed constitutional amendments by hiding behind the "democratic" slogan, "let the people decide."

[25] Although Davis was only an honorary member of the American Federation
of Musicians, he never could give the lie to the delightful rumor that he had
vetoed the bill less as Governor than as trade-union member.

[26] Davis was introduced to delegates at the 1952 annual convention of the State

The controversy which enveloped the state's natural gas policy under Davis offered an insight into the vulnerability of Sam Jones's gubernatorial candidacy in 1948. It will be recalled that Governor Jones, stressing Louisiana's lack of coal and hydroelectric power and the limited extent of its known natural gas reserves, persuaded the Legislature, in 1942, to pass a concurrent resolution which declared the public policy of the state to be against any new exportation of Louisiana natural gas to Eastern states in which coal was readily available. Although Davis adhered to Jones's conservationist views in the 1944 campaign, he gradually shifted to a neutral position as legislative opposition to the policy mounted.

In 1945 came the first official complaint against state policy, from Congressman Charles McKenzie of the Fifth District, speaking on behalf of the royalty landowners of north Louisiana. In the 1946 session, the state's natural gas policy frequently was a center of controversy. Conservationists succeeded in extending the jurisdiction of the Public Service Commission to cover intra-state pipelines, a move which permitted a measure of governmental control over rates as part of the larger problem of increasing the well-head price of natural gas.[27] But the tide clearly was turning in favor of the anti-conservationists. Their charge that their opposition was allied with Eastern coal interests gained credence when Sam Jones admitted that he was legal counsel for a major Eastern coal firm. They defeated (43–43) a conservationist proposal to increase sharply the gas gathering tax rate despite the entry of the education lobby in support of the measure. They defeated another bill empowering the conservation commissioner to fix the well-head price of gas, mustered thirty-one House votes in a failing effort to repeal the 1942 conservationist policy, and failed by one vote in the Senate to delete the appropriation of $70,000 for the State Gas Conservation Commission.

The pro-conservationist *Times-Picayune* attributed the failure of their side to the power of a "gas lobby" desirous of preventing an

Federation of Labor with those words by Lige Williams, president of the Federation. Baton Rouge *State-Times,* April 9, 1952.

[27] While the Public Service Commission had the authority to regulate the rates charged by distributing companies in their sale of gas to cities, this bill enabled the commission to control the prices charged the distributing companies by the pipeline companies. This was an indirect attempt to deal with the grave problem of the discrepancy between the low price of well-head gas and the high price of gas as paid for by industrial and domestic consumers.

increase in the taxation or price of well-head gas and of reversing the 1942 gas policy of the state.[28] The political influence of the gas industry, however, reflected its ability to enlist the greed of landowners, particularly in north Louisiana, whose royalties would increase if all the Louisiana natural gas that out-of-state companies were willing to buy could be exported. Almost all north Louisiana legislators, including those from Caddo, Ouachita, Rapides, and the Delta parishes, voted against an increase in the gas gathering tax or for a repeal of conservationist policy in the 1946 session. A survey of police-jury sentiment held in early 1947 also revealed the same sectional antipathy to the Jones-Davis natural gas program.[29] In the March, 1947, special session, anti-conservationists succeeded easily in repealing the 1942 policy and in abolishing the office of executive director of natural gas conservation. Since Sam Jones had been, and continued to be, the chief proponent of conservationist policy, its legislative repudiation warned of sectional hostility to his candidacy in 1948.

The foregoing brief review of the major events of the Davis administration suggests that the intense bifactionalism under Jones, Allen, and Huey was considerably subdued under Davis. Entering office with few specific pledges, Davis refused to stake his prestige on any subsequent policies. Most important, state revenues were so plentiful as to blunt bifactional alignments and, since no new taxes were enacted, to arouse few special-interest groups to opposition. Davis' inadequate legislative leadership both reflected a dulled factionalism and, in turn, permitted shifting combinations of legislators, pro-Long and anti-Long, to control the direction of state policy. In the 1944 session, for example, the Davis administration urged a freezing of the state surplus, a doubling of the state sales tax, and the defeat of a measure decreasing income tax rates. The House legislators who supported Davis on all three measures came from ten parishes, seven of which had placed in the upper half of all parishes in support of Earl Long in the 1944 runoff primary. Perhaps the most telling evidence of the decline of legislative bifactionalism under

[28] Article by B. L. Krebs, New Orleans *Times-Picayune*, July 3, 1946.

[29] Several south Louisiana parishes—for example, St. John, St. Charles, and St. James—held the same views as the northern parishes. The survey referred to may be found in *Louisiana Police Jury Review*, xi (April, 1947), 21.

Davis would be to take scholarly notice of the high jinks at the close of the 1944 session. The Governor led the House in a rendition of "You Are My Sunshine," Representative Santos of the Choctaws released two pigeons dubbed "Peace" and "Harmony," and Davis left the chamber amid cheers that he was the best-liked governor ever.[30]

With one exception, factional lines were not drawn sharply in the major primary contests during the Davis administration. In the primaries held in the fall of 1944, all eight Congressional incumbents were returned, while Wade Martin, Sr., defeated Dudley LeBlanc for the Second District seat on the Public Service Commission. In 1946, only two Congressional seats changed hands, Boggs winning in the Second District and Passman in the Fifth, while the reform candidate won the First District Public Service Commission seat. All important constitutional amendments supported by Davis were ratified by the voters in 1944 and in 1946. In the Senate primary of September, 1944, Overton ran for renomination against E. A. Stephens, who had been defeated by Ellender two years earlier. Stephens claimed the backing of Davis, but the Governor never openly endorsed him. Overton secured 61.6 per cent of the vote, carrying fifty-seven parishes by majority vote and scoring heavily in nearly all the parishes bordering the Mississippi River, where voters apparently appreciated Overton's flood control record in the Senate.[31] As had been the case with Ellender in 1942, Overton was viewed by many voters in terms other than traditional bifactionalism.

The most important, and surprising, upset to be credited to bifactionalism occurred in the New Orleans mayoralty of January 22, 1946. Supported by Jones and Davis, city reform forces organized into an Independent Citizens Committee. The committee at first backed J. O. Fernandez, Collector of Internal Revenue for New Orleans and Longite Congressman from 1930 to 1940, in an effort to cut into the Ring vote. The absurdity of such action was underlined in early December, when Fernandez withdrew from the race and announced

[30] Baton Rouge *State-Times*, July 6, 1944.
[31] Overton met serious opposition only in East Baton Rouge and St. Bernard parishes; several southwest parishes gave majorities to native son Griffin T. Hawkins of Lake Charles. A fourth minor candidate was Charles S. Gerth, a New Orleans businessman.

his endorsement of Maestri and the "regulars." At the last minute deLesseps S. Morrison, a former anti-Long legislator, newly-returned from the war as a colonel, was persuaded to run against the Choctaws.

The issues of the city campaign were mostly local ones, such as vice and gambling, the inadequacy of garbage collections, the lack of street repairs, and the maintenance of a political machine.[32] Over-confidence on the part of the Choctaws contributed to the unexpected outcome, in which Morrison defeated Maestri by 4,372 votes out of a total vote of 133,708.[33] For the first time since the Parker-McShane administrations in 1920, reform forces had captured Orleans and state governments at the same time. And New Orleans, unlike the state, was to get a taste of progressive reformism under its dynamic young mayor of which it has yet to tire.[34]

By the close of Davis' administration it was understandable that reform forces were somewhat disappointed with the performance of Jones's successor. Some reformers of high principle never became reconciled to the notion of "Singing Jimmie Davis" as the flag-bearer of good government. Others more tax conscious resented Davis' inability to direct overflowing state revenues into channels increasing the basic productivity of the state. In contrasting the spirited headship of Jones with the vacillating leadership of Davis, few ardent reformers dared conclude that the latter was the more popular. To this group, therefore, Jones's disastrous candidacy in 1948 was explainable only in terms of the handicaps to reformism growing out of the Davis administration.

The reform appraisal of Davis as "the lull that caused the storm" of Earl Long runs up, however, against the contradictory fact that bifactionalism became fuzzier, not sharper, under Davis. The product

[32] As one reform informant gleefully related to the author, the good-government forces employed the same fallacious argument against Maestri that the Longites had used against the Jones administration, namely, that the public officials were to blame for shortages and inadequacies actually caused by the war.

[33] Morrison's amazed reaction to the news was, "If I am elected, you can put me down as the most astonished and happiest mayor this city ever had" (New Orleans *Item,* January 23, 1946). Maestri began campaigning in early January of 1946.

[34] In addition to revamping the structure of city government and curbing organized gambling and vice, Morrison stressed Orleans' role as the port of Latin American trade and encouraged a large-scale construction program for the city. His city leadership, it would appear fair to judge, comprised a blend of practical politics, liberalism, good government, and aggressive leadership which neither Jones nor Davis gave to the state.

of politics under Davis, when judged by the voting behavior of Choctaw and Longite legislators, seemed much more satisfactory than had been the case with Jones. At the very least, then, Davis, whether through accident or design, had brought about a measure of Longite support of reformism which was conspicuously lacking in the case of Jones. Hence it may be suggested that Jones's tactics in his 1948 campaign did more than anything else to fasten the label of "do-nothing" on the Davis administration. In that campaign, Jones refused to benefit from any of the accomplishments of Governor Davis and then blindly insisted upon treating the Davis period as an appendage to his own term of office. Jones became his own greatest obstacle to victory by converting the election of 1948 into a plebescite on the wisdom of the outcome of the 1940 primaries. By so doing, he helped confirm the Longite charge, made for obvious campaign reasons, that the Davis administration was barren of achievements.

The 1948 gubernatorial primary

The 1948 state-office campaign witnessed a curious blend of the tactics of 1940 and 1944. Apparently convinced that Jones had won in 1940 by outpromising him, Earl Long pledged a sweeping program of 'do-everythingism" which no sincere candidate could hope to match. Sam Jones, for his part, made a number of mistaken assumptions in his conduct of the campaign. He essayed the vague Davis platform of 1944 while reviving the factional bitterness of 1940, a combination fraught with danger to the tenure of reformism. Jones viewed the contest as 1940 come again, overlooking the not minor point that the Scandals had broken in 1939, not 1947. Thus the reform forces foolishly banked their hopes on equating Longism with sinfulness, on preaching (in lieu of liberalism) the moral doctrine that virtue was its own reward. By dressing in holy robes and challenging Lucifer the Long on moral grounds, Louisiana reformers were to ʹdiscover that virtue was their only reward.

There was some inner jockeying for Longite leadership in 1947 reminiscent of the pre-primary maneuvers in the 1944 campaign. Wade Martin, Jr., Secretary of State by virtue of Gremillion's withdrawal in 1944, announced in March, 1947, for the governorship only to withdraw in October to file for renomination on the Earl Long ticket. Ellender again coyly expressed his gubernatorial ambitions, but never took the decisive step. Clements and LeBlanc supported Long, and Noe and Cawthorn were eliminated by running afoul of the law.[35] Jimmie Morrison, however, remained a rival to Earl.

The dual tactics of Earl Long's campaign were to condemn the Jones-Davis administrations as "do-nothing" and alien to Louisiana traditions, on the one hand, and, on the other, to pledge pie in the sky for all. Remaining discreetly silent on the question of increased taxation, Earl promised to widen all main highways in the state, to complete all farm-to-market roads and all school-bus and mail routes, and to fence all the rights of way on hard-surfaced roads where live-stock was permitted to roam at large.[36] Old-age pensions of $50 a month and homestead tax exemptions of $5,000 were pledged. Earl guaranteed a minimum teacher's salary of $2,400 a year, a twelve-month salary for school-bus drivers, and reiterated his 1944 pledge of a trade school for every parish. World War II veterans would be granted a state bonus. The mental, penal, and hospital institutions of the state would be improved.[37] Restrictions on the export of natural gas would be ended, and the drivers' license law, enacted over the protests of rural areas, would be repealed. The Port of New Orleans would be investigated with a view toward improving the efficiency of its operations. Finally, to assure the voters that the extensive bene-fits he planned excluded his own pocketbook, Long urged passage of a law requiring the governor to file a statement of his financial con-dition before and after his term of office.[38]

[35] In January of 1946, Noe, Cawthorn, and two others were indicted for seek-ing to influence jurors in the income tax trials of William T. Burton. In late 1947, Noe was acquitted, but Burton and Cawthorn were found guilty and sentenced to two years imprisonment.

[36] The latter plank attempted to compromise the urban-rural feud over restric-tions upon cattle wandering on highways. In many areas, wealthy livestock owners used open ranges for feeding their cattle, but whenever the Legislature was considering a compulsory fencing law, small livestock raisers would be pre-sented to plead that adoption of such a law would threaten their livelihood. The best that urbanites had been able to secure was a system of local option, on a ward basis, for ending or retaining open-range practices.

[37] The total cost of the fulfillment of Long's pledges was estimated by the reform faction to be $892,000,000 a year. Sam Jones argued that if half of Earl's pledges were enacted, taxes would have to be doubled. Taxes were increased by 50 per cent under Earl Long.

[38] Earl finally got around to having that proposal enacted in 1950, but he never filed a financial statement upon leaving office in 1952.

At the outset of the campaign the Long ticket was not considered the leading slate. A typical prediction was that of the political reporter of the New Orleans *Item*, who observed in mid-April, "Both [Long and Robert F. Kennon] are reported to have a strong following in north Louisiana. They can play an important role in a second primary, assuming both try for the governorship in the first primary."[89] At a later date, Earl himself commented, "When I started out as a candidate for governor, practically every politician in this state gave me a cold shoulder . . . ."[40] By intense campaigning and by building up a thorough grass-roots organization, Earl emerged at the close of 1947 as the leading gubernatorial entrant. Influential support helped: Huey's son, Russell, actively stumped for Uncle Earl; Huey's widow announced her support of his candidacy; Clements, LeBlanc, and Perez backed Long; Maestri and many of the Choctaws, refusing to endorse Morrison openly, aligned with Earl; and wealthy oil-and-gas man William Feazel met some of the high costs of statewide campaigning.

Jimmie Morrison, trying for the governorship for the third time, was the other Longite in the race. The desperate Choctaws, now deprived of city and state patronage, endorsed his candidacy as early as April, causing the resignation of more than a few Ring leaders, including Maestri, who preferred to support Earl Long. Urging that the twin issues of the campaign were the domination of the state by the *Times-Picayune* and the deteriorated condition of the highways, Morrison pledged a liberal program only slightly less exuberant than that of Long, clumsily sought to conceal his hostility to civil service, and constantly magnified the importance of Ring backing in an effort to displace Earl as the major Longite candidate.

The lesser known of the two anti-Long candidates was Circuit Judge Robert F. Kennon of Webster Parish, whose entry and campaign helped to divide the reform forces.[41] Kennon attacked his three rivals as machine candidates, branding Jones in particular "a wolf in sheep's clothing." He pledged an end to industrial tax exemptions together with a decrease in taxes on industry and an abolition of the state property tax, and promised to maintain civil service. His attacks

[89] Column by Edward Stagg, New Orleans *Item*, April 14, 1947.
[40] Baton Rouge *State-Times*, May 11, 1948.
[41] So said the Jones forces. In view of the outcome, however, perhaps the shoe was on the other foot.

against Jones, coming from the same side of the factional fence, probably helped to persuade many voters that Jones's professions of virtue were more claimed than real.

Sam Jones cast his candidacy in the moral terms of "good" versus "evil" and spent most of his campaign reviewing the events of 1939–44. The question was "proud progress or depravity."[42] The excessively moral cast of his campaign was all the more difficult to understand since in the heyday of the Scandals Jones had seen fit to stress the intended liberalism of his administration. There was but a whisper of concrete benefits in the Jones of 1948. Jones put in an exaggerated claim for credit for the state's wartime gains, predicted a reforested, drained, and industrialized Louisiana, heralded a richer South no longer the "hod-carriers of the nation," and welcomed 1948 electoral judgment on the basis of the reforms of 1940. While going so far as to pledge elimination of the gas tax for commercial fishermen and farmers (which he had opposed in 1940) and to engage in a strategic retreat on the natural gas issue,[43] Sam Jones was content largely to rest his case on the "obvious" superiority of his character and intentions as compared to Longites Earl and Morrison and the obscure Kennon. When, however, late in the campaign, Jonesite Congressman Domengeaux of the Third District accused Earl Long of a federal income tax liability in excess of $100,000 for 1938–39, and could not back up his charge with public evidence, the moral distinction between Longite and anti-Long tactics may have become too fine for many citizens.

The Jones ticket did not suffer in the 1948 campaign for lack of influential backing. Senator Overton, stressing his opposition to Jimmie Morrison, declared for Jones. Governor Davis, in the first flat endorsement of his official career, backed Jones late in the campaign. Reform Mayor Morrison of New Orleans, engaged in creating his own durable organization, announced support of Jones, and the New Orleans press followed suit.[44] Jones's repudiation in the 1948 election, therefore, was not explainable in terms of the reluctance of important political leaders to proffer active support.

---

[42] New Orleans *Times-Picayune,* January 30, 1948.

[43] Jones now argued that after seventy-five Louisiana towns were supplied with natural gas, state export restrictions on gas should be abandoned.

[44] Symptomatic, perhaps, of the antipathy to Jones's natural gas program, the Ewing papers and the Shreveport *Journal* remained neutral.

The results of the first primary of January 20, reported in Table 20, spelled disaster for the reform faction.[45] Earl carried the Longite upland and cut-over regions of north Louisiana together with scat-

TABLE 20. The Louisiana Vote in the 1948 Democratic Gubernatorial First Primary

	Orleans	Other	State	% State	Parishes Carried by Majority	Plurality
Long	48,071	219,182	267,253	41.5	28	22
Jones	51,227	96,102	147,329	22.9	0	3
Kennon	14,548	113,021	127,569	19.8	0	2
Morrison	33,252	68,502	101,754	15.8	2	7
Total	147,098	496,807	643,905	100.0	30	34

SOURCE: adapted from Alexander Heard and Donald S. Strong, *Southern Primaries and Elections*, 72–73.

tered parishes in south Louisiana. Morrison's influence was localized to the Florida parishes and to several south Louisiana parishes bordering his Sixth Congressional District. Kennon edged out Jones in most rural parishes, and in Caddo and Calcasieu as well. Jones's main strength came from East Baton Rouge and Orleans; his combined vote in those two parishes comprised about 40 per cent of his total vote. In fifty-two parishes, Jones secured less than 25 per cent of the parish vote. While Earl's proportion of the state vote was no better than it had been in the 1940 first primary, the Morrison of 1948 was Choctaw-backed and pro-Long, and the aroused anti-Longism which attached to Noe's vote in 1940 certainly did not characterize Kennon's vote in 1948. There was no basis, in short, for the hope that Jones could come from behind to win in 1948 as he had in 1940.

To some extent, Jones's defeat was explainable in terms of his personal unpopularity, his campaign tactics, and the resentments created by his Crime Commission investigations and his natural gas policy. But the root of the matter lay in his reckless forgetfulness of why his pappy had been for Huey. Faced by an adversary possessed of the magic name of "Long," who pledged enactment of a sweeping liberal program, Sam Jones could do no better than to attempt to

[45] For an analysis of the 1948 state primaries, employing special cartographic techniques, see Rudolf Heberle and Alvin L. Bertrand, "Factors Motivating Voting Behavior in a One-Party State," *Social Forces*, XXVII (May, 1949), 343–50.

link Earl with the fading bitterness toward the Scandals. The reform faction paid a class price for its class oversight. In a study of Baton Rouge precincts in the 1948 first primary, it was found that "generally Morrison carried the 'worker' areas and Jones the 'middle class' areas. . . . In fact, where Jones had pluralities Kennon was a strong second choice, whereas in the precincts carried by Morrison . . . both Jones and Kennon [were] somewhat further behind."[46] In short, Jones restricted his appeal largely to the "better elements," while Morrison and Long monopolized the masses of lower-class voters.

Desperation moved the reform forces to sorry actions in the period before the runoff primary. Jones implied fraudulent voting in the first primary,[47] surrendered abjectly on his natural gas position,[48] and revealed his income tax statements for years past, challenging Earl to do likewise.[49] A new liberal program was unveiled, embracing doubled old-age pensions, labor benefits, and farm-to-market roads. Resort was had even to Earl's favorite tactic: Jones announced that Davis had agreed to call a special session in the event that Jones was nominated in the runoff, to consider the questions of a bonus for veterans, welfare legislation, and the like. Perhaps the most suspect

[46] Perry H. Howard, "An Analysis of Voting Behavior in Baton Rouge," *The Proceedings of the Louisiana Academy of Sciences,* xv (August, 1952), 92. Similar class patterns of voting behavior exist for New Orleans, where census tracts coincide exactly with precinct boundaries (see Rudolf Heberle, "On Political Ecology," *Social Forces,* xxxi [October, 1952], 8). Because the following manuscript is under preparation, the analysis in this book has made no attempt to deal with voting behavior in the Orleans area: Carmelo Graffagnini, "A Case Study in Political Sociography: The Relationship Between Socio-Economic Status and Political Consensus as Evidenced by Voting Behavior and the Significance of this Relationship for Delineating Areas of Common Values in New Orleans," Pilot Study for the Institution of Population Research, Department of Sociology, Louisiana State University.

[47] After having made the traditional pleas for maximum turnout, Jones professed to see skullduggery in the fact that 100,000 more votes were cast in 1948 than in 1944. Conveniently ignoring, among other things, that the 1944 primary had been held in wartime, Jones asserted, "I say that there were between 75,000 and 100,000 votes tabulated that weren't cast." Shreveport *Journal,* January 29, 1948.

[48] Jones now suggested that the parties involved develop their own policy on natural gas.

[49] Jones revealed an income of about $9,000 a year from 1936 to 1939, and about $23,000 a year after his gubernatorial term, from 1944 to 1947. Replying to the challenge, Earl indicated that his declared taxable annual income from 1928 to 1936 ranged from $5,000 to $9,000, increased to about $14,000 for the 1937–39 period, and subsided to $3,600 to $7,000 from 1940 to 1947.

of all these maneuvers was Jimmie Morrison's declaration of support for Jones. The Choctaws, with greater consistency, announced for Long, while Kennon maintained neutrality after the first primary.

Earl Long was given the largest absolute majority of any gubernatorial candidate in recent Louisiana politics in the runoff primary of February 24, 1948, the results of which are given in Table 21. All of Earl's state ticket went into office with him, and ". . . some 75 per cent of the candidates elected to the State Legislature were supported by him and he by them. Many local officials rode into office on his coattails."[50]

TABLE 21. The Louisiana Vote in the 1948 Democratic Gubernatorial Second Primary

	Orleans	Other	State	% State	Parishes Carried by Majority
Long	94,316	338,212	432,528	65.9	62
Jones	56,146	167,825	223,971	34.1	2
Total	150,462	506,037	656,499	100.0	64

SOURCE: adapted from Alexander Heard and Donald S. Strong, *Southern Primaries and Elections,* 72–73.

Figure 9 ranks the parish performance for Long in the runoff primary. The conformity of the pattern there depicted with that of customary bifactionalism is all the more striking when the magnitude of Earl's victory is recalled: Long carried, by majority vote, all but East Baton Rouge and West Feliciana parishes,[51] and all but 33 of the state's 539 wards. Some minor exceptions to the pattern should be noted. South Louisiana support for Long appeared relatively weaker than usual, although Jones's Calcasieu residence might occount for the relative decline in the southwest Louisiana section. The stronger support accorded Long by the parishes of Bossier and Ouachita probably reflected reaction to the natural gas controversy. In general, however, the centers of Long and anti-Long strength, defined in relative terms, remained fairly constant in Earl's defeat of 1940 and his smashing victory of 1948.

[50] "Earl Long Makes Remarkable Comeback," *Louisiana Police Jury Review,* XII (April, 1948), 89.
[51] West Feliciana's performance was explainable in terms of the local anti-Long leadership, or bossdom, of Sheriff Theodore H. Martin.

Earl Long, the reformers' best friend

The overwhelming defeat of the reform forces in 1948 reflected more than the personal failings of Jones or Davis or the defects in their liberal policies. A reform administration, by its elimination of waste, boodle, and extraneous jobs, made enemies; even reformers were human enough to want good government applied to all sections of state government except the bailiwicks of their particular concern. Perhaps most basically, compromise government lacked the spectacular flavor by which Huey Long was able to command the loyal-

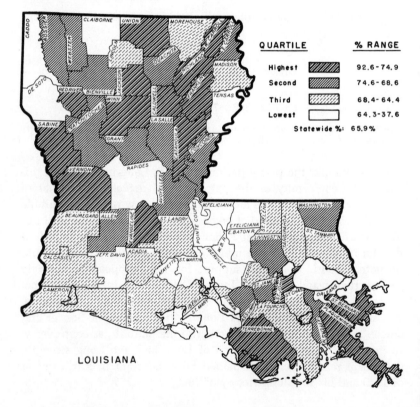

FIGURE 9. Quartile map: proportion of parish vote cast for Earl Long, 1948 Democratic gubernatorial second primary.

SOURCE: same as that for Table 21.

ties of thousands of citizens. The reform forces had not learned fully how to make good government attractive to the masses of voters.

Earl Long's administration from 1948 to 1952 taught the voters to appreciate good government in a manner more dramatic than could a dozen Jones-Davis administrations. The uglier manifestations of Longism reappeared, including a controlled Legislature, a war against New Orleans, and tendencies toward dictatorial power. Most shocking of all, taxes kept pace with expanding benefits, which undermined Longism's persuasive propaganda that its liberalism was somehow "free of charge." But Earl Long was to discover, as Jones had before him, that factional victory was not a mandate to turn back the clock. The curious spectacle of Earl Long's candidate affirming his loyalty to civil service in 1952 thus must be understood in terms of the Long-induced popular comprehension of the vital importance of certain reform principles, notwithstanding popular repudiation of Jones in 1948.

CHAPTER 8

Buccaneering liberalism
is returned but not enthroned

EARL LONG, 1948–1952

SAM JONES greeted the news of Earl Long's victory in the runoff primary with the observation that ". . . for the sake of Louisiana, I hope that the new governor will rise above the past." On state taxation and expenditure Earl Long rose well above the past, and on spoils politics he returned happily to the past, though scrupulously avoiding any repetition of the Scandals. But apparently the Long formula of benefits and bossism had lost its magic; the reform era of Jones and Davis had left its imprint on the Louisiana electorate. By the time of the state-office primaries of 1952 the Long faction was rent by inner dissension, and the hand-picked candidate of Earl Long was repudiated at the polls. The political career of only one major Longite was on the ascent at the close of Earl's administration: Russell B. Long, son of Huey and nephew of Earl, who became Louisiana's junior Senator in 1948 and was renominated for a full term in 1950. And as the mark, perhaps, of a coming political era in Louisiana politics, young Russell sought to make his political way by employing cross-factional appeals designed to hasten the end of the class bitterness bequeathed to the state by his father.

Tax, spend, politicize—and voter reaction: the events of 1948

Earl Long, before he took office, listed the order in which he would fulfill his pledges of benefits: old-age pensions; road improvements; hospital construction; veterans' bonuses; fencing the highways; and building trade schools.[1] Most of that program was enacted in the 1948 regular session, but it necessitated a resort to increased taxation on a scale which for the first time in Longite history starkly revealed the non-free nature of state benefits lavished upon selected segments of the community. Further, Earl affirmed anew the apparent incompatability between Longism and good government by returning to the well-blazed paths of spoils politics and hostility to New Orleans. Legislative resistance to these programs was confined to a handful of legislators from the parishes of Caddo, East Baton Rouge, Calcasieu, and some of the wards of New Orleans, but electoral hostility was quite evident in the senatorial primary and in the constitutional amendments election after the close of the 1948 session. Huey Long's tax-spend-politicize formula no longer guaranteed, in 1948, a product like the kingdom of the Kingfish, rooted in popular support.

Current state revenues, together with Davis' surplus of $45,000,000, were quite inadequate for Earl to carry out his campaign pledges. The Governor proposed to an acquiescent Legislature new levies, many of which were direct consumer taxes, which were conservatively estimated to yield $80,000,000 of new revenue for the biennium.[2] The gasoline tax was increased by two cents a gallon; the tax on bottled beer multiplied fivefold to the level of two and one-half cents a bottle; and the sales tax doubled in rate and broadened in coverage. The increased revenues were allocated respectively to highways, veterans' bonuses, and public welfare. A 50 per cent reduction in the rate of tax on soft drinks was more than balanced by an increase in the cigarette tax of three cents a package, the proceeds of which were shared by municipalities and the State University.[3] Long's proposal to quadruple gas gathering taxes was compromised at double the old rate, that is, at one cent MCF. Severance tax rates were almost tripled on oil and were doubled on all other natural resources except sulphur, and the yield was allocated to education. So far did Earl wander in search of revenue that his final levy taxed

[1] New Orleans *Times-Picayune and States*, February 29, 1948.

[2] Whether deliberate or not, Long's underestimation of tax yields was firmly in the tradition of politics. The four major consumer taxes alone produced $80,000,000 in the next two years.

[3] The increase in the tobacco tax placed the purchase of a package of cigarettes in the beginning bracket for sales tax collections, and thereby helped swell sales tax proceeds as well.

slot machines, the ownership and operation of which were illegal under state laws.

While some urban legislators and newspapers opposed the new taxes, most resignedly echoed the New Orleans *Item*'s observation: "It's what they voted for."[4] Governor Long straight-facedly informed a statewide radio audience, "If you look these taxes over carefully you'll find that they won't hurt anybody."[5] In the distribution of biennial appropriations totaling over $400,000,000 Earl did his best to counterbalance the painful politics of industry and consumer tax hikes.

The payment of fifty-dollar old-age pensions to those over sixty-five years of age was begun by Earl within seventy days of taking office.[6] Free ambulance service to the state's charity hospitals and free dental trailer service were enlarged. Charity beds in private hospitals were provided for under a contract system, and an expansion program was scheduled for mental hospitals. Appropriations were quadrupled for an expanded school lunch program. Education came in for its customary healthy share: state payments per educable person were increased to well over $40; $8,000,000 were appropriated for a minimum teacher salary program and for a racial equalization of teacher salaries; capital outlay funds were provided for state colleges; and five new trade schools established. Veterans gained a $5,000 homestead exemption until 1954 and received a state bonus through bond issues secured by the beer tax in one of Earl's fancier fiscal maneuvers.[7] Of particular benefit to rural areas were increased state payments to each parish of $30,000 of unrestricted funds and $10,000 of gravel for road maintenance, while municipalities were assigned per-capita shares in the proceeds of the increased tobacco

[4] New Orleans *Item*, editorial, May 19, 1948.
[5] New Orleans *Times-Picayune*, May 31, 1948.
[6] Earl slightly stinted on his pledge: two old-age pensioners living in the same household were allocated a maximum of $90 monthly. On the other hand, through a relaxation of the Other's Assistance category, needy individuals over sixty years of age were assisted for a time by state payments within the limits of the lower budget used in Other's Assistance.
[7] The payment of veterans' bonuses required the issuance of bonds, the security for which was the tax on bottled beer. The effective date of the beer tax, however, was immediately after the Governor signed the measure rather than a date which would follow popular ratification of the constitutional amendment on veterans' bonuses in November, 1948. In the customary manner, payment on the bond principal was to be deferred for four years. Earl thus secured $35,000,000 of beer tax revenues for his expenditure on other matters.

tax. Labor, too, gained, with the repeal of the Goff "mutual responsibility" law and an increase in workmen's compensation payments.

Had Earl Long been content, in accord with his view of his mandate, to distribute new tax burdens and new governmental benefits, ultimate popular reaction might well have been favorable. At the very least, the anti-Longs would have been restricted to a defensive tax-conscious strategy. But Longism, as interpreted by both Huey and Earl, apparently required the worship of spoils politics and the extirpation of the enemy. Earl had learned part of his 1939 lesson—there was no hint of neo-Scandals during his administration nor of wholesale firings from public jobs—but he had failed to understand that the reformers in their eight years of office had molded public expectations. It was the buccaneering quality of Longite liberalism which combined with Earl's tax programs to arouse majority sentiment against his faction by 1952.

In the 1948 regular session, some of Earl's spoils measures were enacted as ordinary legislation and others necessarily in the form of constitutional amendments. Among the more important of the latter were those which became factional issues in the November general election. These included Long's selective advocacy of administrative reorganization simply to secure control of the governing boards of the State University and the Port of New Orleans, his reinvigoration of the powers of the Board of Liquidation of the State Debt, and an amendment which linked the creation of a retirement system for the state judiciary with a provision prohibiting state judges (Kennon in particular) from running for other than judicial office without first resigning their judgeship. Other Longite measures required no amendment of the Constitution. For patronage purposes, separate boards were created for several state hospitals,[8] and the Highway Commission was reorganized to institutionalize representation from the state's eight Congressional districts. Reform fiscal reorganization was repealed and replaced by a centralized Division of Administration in the office of the Governor. The state parole system was re-

---

[8] Presumably Long had hoped that a board of "good citizens" in the local area would govern an institution more effectively than could a centralized Department of Institutions and would relieve the Governor of the necessity of making policy decisions with reference to hospitals servicing a local community. Unhappily for Earl, the arrangement turned out otherwise. Board members tended to interfere with the superintendent in the details of administration, creating local conflicts which eventually had to be resolved by the Governor himself.

turned to its pre-1942 form.[9] An Alcoholic Beverage Control Board was created with broad powers to regulate the liquor industry and to fix the retailers' minimum selling price.[10]

Patronage politics reached its climax with the crippling of civil service in the regular session of 1948 and its repeal in the following September special session. The immorality of such action may be gauged by noting that on the one hand all gubernatorial candidates (Earl included), sixty-three representatives, and twenty-four senators had pledged themselves in support of civil service, while on the other, a two-thirds majority in each chamber was necessary to enact changes in the established merit system. Longite deceit was evident at the outset of the session, when a resolution pledging the legislators to continued support of the merit principle was tabled by a 63–27 vote. Later in the regular session the Madden bill, politicizing civil service, was enacted by 72–23 and 28–9 votes, with the help of fifty legislators who violated their pre-election pledges on civil service.[11] In the September special session, Longite Representative Anzalone of Tangipahoa set the tone for repeal of civil service: "Let's feed the horse that brought in the feed and the fodder during the campaign."[12] State civil service was repealed by 70–20 and 28–10 votes, but since the reformers controlled New Orleans, Long retained city civil service. In addition, the standard merit system was maintained for the six state agencies operating in part with federal funds.

[9] Under Jones, the Board of Parole was composed of the Welfare Department director, the Attorney General, and the judge of the court wherein the prisoner was convicted, and the Welfare Department was responsible for investigation and supervision of parolees. Under the 1948 act, the Governor appointed a three-member state parole board and a state parole officer who headed a staff which assumed the duties formerly held by the Department of Welfare in this field.

[10] The price-fixing provisions of the liquor control law were held unconstitutional in late 1949. The agency did so little throughout Long's administration that legislative sentiment for its abolition overrode Governor Kennon's desire to reconstruct it to useful purposes in 1952.

[11] Under the terms of the Madden bill, the members of the State Civil Service Commission were chosen by the Governor, and the director of personnel by the commission, with no restrictions upon either appointing authority imposed. The state commission appointed a majority of the membership of the City Civil Service Commission. The director of personnel was empowered to hear all appeals from ousted employees. Finally, all employees who had been blanketed in without taking competitive examinations, i.e., Jones's people, ceased to be regular employees as of July 28, 1948, and had to compete against all applicants for their former jobs. For a review of civil service under Earl Long, consult the New Orleans *Times-Picayune*, September 25, 1951.

[12] New Orleans *Times-Picayune*, September 25, 1948.

The suspicion of some observers that Earl was trying to play by ear some of Huey's favorite melodies was strengthened when the Legislature, under his direction, launched an assault against New Orleans. In contrast to 1934, Earl enlisted the support of the Ring, now an officeless group dependent upon the Governor for patronage, humiliated by Morrison's showing in the 1948 primary, and cynically anxious to betray their city's welfare for a chance to displace the reform faction. Thus, of the legislators from Orleans, none but the handful of Mayor Chep Morrison's adherents opposed the attacks upon the city's finances and governmental structure.

The city's share of tobacco tax revenues was fixed arbitrarily at the low maximum of $650,000 a year, and the city sales tax was slashed in half to one per cent, with a consequent annual loss of $4,500,000 to New Orleans. In a transparent gesture of home rule, Long had the September special session enact a constitutional amendment which permitted New Orleans to have a referendum on the question of imposing an additional one per cent city sales tax. The charter of New Orleans was amended, without provision for a city referendum, so as to restrict the power of the mayor and to pave the way to Choctaw victory in the 1950 mayoralty primary. The Commission Council was enlarged from five to eight members each of whom, except for the mayor, was to be elected from one of the city's seven assessment districts. Each council member, including the mayor, was to head a city department. Apart from the glaring administrative defects of such a system,[13] the obvious Longite intent was to permit a faction to concentrate its activities in four assessment districts containing only 35 per cent of the voters, and thereby to control the Commission Council which now had greater power than the mayor. A final punitive measure created a partisan commission, headed by Francis Williams and armed with a $50,000 appropriation, to investigate the affairs of the Port of New Orleans.

To the veteran anti-Long, Earl's program of 1948 must have seemed like the Kingfish born anew. To many of both major factions, Long's measures were a shock, for benefits obscured taxes in Earl's

---

[13] A fractionalized council was inevitable, with each department head given incentive to offer disproportionate service to the single district to which he was electorally accountable, and with the power of the Mayor, the sole city-wide elective official, curbed. Finally, the use of municipal assessment districts as electoral units produced grave inequities in representation.

campaign oratory. The total of state taxes was increased about 50 per cent and included the imposition of direct consumer taxes whose impact was felt daily, while the state debt was increased by 33 per cent. Simply put, the political impact of Long's program depended upon whether large spending would counteract tax resentments and adverse reaction to spoils and punitive legislation. As judged by the Senate primary in August and the constitutional amendments election in November, Earl Long no longer commanded the sure loyalty of a majority of Louisiana voters.

The circumstances which enabled a senatorial contest to act as a barometer of state bifactional sentiment began with the death of Senator Overton, in May of 1948. Governor Long selected his wealthy backer, William C. Feazel, as an interim appointee with the understanding that Huey's son, Russell, upon reaching thirty years of age, would qualify in the fall primary to complete the remaining two years of Overton's term. Robert Kennon, the Minden judge who ran a surprisingly strong race in the 1948 gubernatorial primary, entered against Russell with the backing of the anti-Longs and of Mayor Morrison. At that same primary of August 31, Allen J. Ellender ran for renomination, opposed by former Third District Congressman Jimmie Domengeaux and by Charles S. Gerth, the New Orleans businessman who had run a poor race against Overton in 1944.

Having no record other than identification with the recent programs of Earl, young Russell conducted his campaign exclusively in terms of state issues—and Kennon was only too happy to second that tactic. The Long-Kennon race, therefore, provided a measurement of electoral reaction to Earl's legislative record. Ellender's bid for renomination failed to offer a similar test because he ran on the basis of a Senate record far broader than his constant attachment to state Longism. The *Times-Picayune* and the *Item*, for example, strongly urged Kennon's nomination at the same time that they maintained neutrality in the regular Senate contest,[14] while Mayor Morrison entered into a deal with Maestri whereby the former's organization, the Crescent City Democratic Association, would not actively oppose the renomination of Ellender.

The results of the August 31 primary are reported in Table 22, while Figure 10 maps the parish performance for Russell Long in

[14] New Orleans *Item*, editorial, August 26, 1948; New Orleans *Times-Picayune*, editorial, August 22, 1948, and August 30, 1948.

the accustomed manner. In spite of Ellender's considerably higher proportion of the state vote, his pattern of relative parish support was not markedly different from that of Russell Long. Fourteen of

TABLE 22. The Louisiana Vote in the 1948 Democratic Senatorial Primaries

Office and Candidates	Orleans	Other	State	% State	Parishes Carried by Majority	Plurality
Short-Term						
R. Long	52,329	211,814	264,143	51.0	44	--
Kennon	78,071	175,597	253,668	49.0	20	--
Total	130,400	387,411	517,811	100.0	64	--
Full-Term						
Ellender	55,221	229,072	284,293	61.7	59	4
Domengeaux	25,418	94,041	119,459	25.9	0	1
Gerth	11,012	46,035	57,047	12.4	0	0
Total	91,651	369,148	460,799	100.0	59	5

SOURCE: Long-Kennon race: adapted from Alexander Heard and Donald S. Strong, *Southern Primaries and Elections*, 75–76; Ellender-Domengeaux-Gerth race: *Report of Secretary of State to the Governor of Louisiana*, 1947–48, 23–24.

the sixteen parishes in the highest quartile of support for Ellender were in the upper half of all parishes in support of Russell; fifteen parishes in Ellender's lowest quartile were in the lower half of Long's parishes. Only eleven parishes shifted position by more than one quartile from one race to the other. The evidence suggests, therefore, that Ellender's candidacy was linked somewhat more closely to state bifactionalism than had been intended or anticipated by either state faction. A major distinction between the candidacies of Ellender and Long is apparent, however, in the data in Table 22. The difference in the proportion of the state vote for each lay less in Ellender's greater number of votes than in the difference in total vote cast in the two contests. A plausible guess would be that most of the 57,012 extra votes cast in Long's race were cast against him. Moreover, since New Orleans accounted for two-thirds of the difference in total vote in the two races, Mayor Morrison doubtless had kept his word to oppose Long but not Ellender.

Relative parish response for Russell (Figure 10) was basically similar to that for Earl six months earlier (Figure 9), notwithstanding the sharp difference in the percentage of the state vote garnered by each. Of Russell's highest quartile parishes, eleven had been in

Earl's highest quartile and another three in his second quartile. Ten of the sixteen parishes in Russell's lowest quartile had been in Earl's lowest quartile, four others in Earl's third quartile. The return of Ouachita and Bossier to a stronger anti-Longism probably reflected the demise of the natural gas issue, while the relatively greater Russell Long support in southwest Louisiana perhaps was due to the efforts of local leaders Dudley LeBlanc and Lieutenant-Governor Bill Dodd.

The narrowness of Russell's victory, in spite of the fact that he carried forty-four parishes by majority vote, suggests a high degree

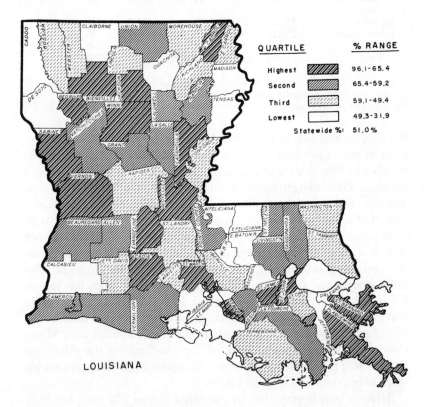

FIGURE 10. Quartile map: proportion of parish vote cast for Russell Long, 1948 Democratic senatorial primary.

SOURCE: same as that for Table 22.

of urban anti-Longism, which further investigation verifies. A reading of Table 23 illuminates Russell Long's difficulties in 1948. Of the candidates and primaries treated in that table, Russell attracted the lowest proportion of the urban-parish vote in a primary in which the proportion of the total vote cast by the urban parishes was highest. Comparison with either or both Earl Long and Ellender emphasizes Russell Long's reduced support both in urban and nonurban groupings, and that the greater decline occurred in the former. In a post-

TABLE 23. Urban Anti-Longism: Vote for Long Candidate of the Most-Urban Parishes and of the Rest of the State, for Selected Democratic Primaries, 1944 and 1948

Primary and Long Candidate	% of State Vote Cast by Six Parishes	% of Total Long Vote Derived from Six Parishes	% of Vote for Long Candidate in		
			Six Parishes	Rest of State	State
1944 Gub.-2nd, Morgan___	40.5	40.0	46.0	46.7	46.4
1948 Gub.-2nd, E. Long___	40.7	37.4	60.5	69.8	65.9
1948 Sen., R. Long_____	44.2	34.8	40.2	59.6	51.0
1948 Sen., Ellender_____	40.0	36.0	55.6	65.8	61.7

SOURCE: computed for the parishes of East Baton Rouge, Caddo, Calcasieu, Orleans, Ouachita, and Rapides from the sources indicated in Tables 19, 21, 22. The foregoing parishes represent urban areas not dominated by agriculturally oriented industry; see above, p. 29.

election statement, Russell Long noted with accuracy, "I want to thank all my friends and supporters, especially those good boys who laid down their cotton sacks, plows and hoes and went to the polls to elect Russell Long U. S. Senator. I never would have made it without a heavy country vote. But I am most thankful also for my faithful city workers who kept me from being badly snowed under in the cities."[15]

Urban anti-Longism triumphed at the November general election at which the fates of forty-one constitutional amendments, all supported by the Governor, were at stake. Actively aided by the urban press, anti-Longs concentrated their fire on five astutely-labeled "power-grab amendments" which gave Earl control over the Dock Board (Port of New Orleans) and the State University and enlarged

[15]Birmingham (Ala.) *Post*, September 3, 1948, quoted by Key, *Southern Politics*, 177.

the authority of the Board of Liquidation of the State Debt. Those
five amendments, together with four additional measures opposed by
anti-Longs, were defeated because of urban hostility. The vote on
the first constitutional amendment on the ballot, that dealing with
the Board of Liquidation, typified the pattern. With a total vote of
only 329,286, the six most-urban parishes cited in Table 23 cast half
the state's vote and went 71.1 per cent against the amendment.[16]
Since only 63.2 per cent of the vote of the rest of the state favored
the amendment, it was defeated by 54.0 per cent of the total vote.
Only twenty-four parishes returned majorities against the amendment. Of those twenty-four parishes, twenty-two had been in the
lower half of all parishes in support of Russell Long in the Senate
primary some two months earlier.

The November election provided yet another indication of the
degree of urban antipathy to Longism. The Republican rival to
Russell Long secured 25 per cent of the state's vote. The vote cast
by the six most-urban parishes comprised slightly less than half the
total vote, went one-third Republican, and therefore supplied Long's
opponent with two-thirds of his state vote. Heightened support for
Republicanism, however, should be understood within the context
of the new game of presidential politics which engrossed Louisiana
in 1948.

Economics and race:
the Dixiecrats and the presidential election of 1948

It would seem at first glance that a majority of Louisiana voters
should not have been receptive to the States' Rights movement which
stormed the South with varying success in the presidential election
of 1948. Voters habituated to welfare politics at the state level were
not likely to become aroused, assuming a logic to political behavior,
over the epithet of "socialism" hurled by conservatives at the national
Democratic administration. Yet Truman was defeated in Louisiana
in 1948.

[16] With reference to urban domination of the election, Earl commented, "When
a full expression of the people is not obtained, the Longs have never had a
chance to carry an election in Louisiana." New Orleans *Times-Picayune,* November 11, 1948.

Basic to the explanation of this turn of events is a conclusion suggested earlier in connection with the renomination of Ellender in 1942 and that of Overton in 1944, namely that bifactional voting attitudes, productive of clarity in politics, have not persisted in contests other than those for high state office. Within the context of state factionalism the cry of "socialism" was discounted in class perspective by Longites who lacked developed local home-rule ideologies; on the national front, by contrast, states' rights beliefs were held by many citizens at all levels, many of whom undoubtedly were ignorant of the conservative policy implications of that position. The issue of tidelands oil, moreover, offered Louisiana citizens—and Dixiecrat leaders—a tangible point of departure for berating the Roosevelt-Truman administrations for going too far down the leftward winding road.

Most crucially, the Dixiecrats played upon a cross-factional issue which lurked behind the one-party politics of all of the deep South— the problem of the Negro, his place and his rights. In view of the stress upon the Yankee threat to Louisiana's racial equilibrium and of the maneuver of the Dixiecrats in capturing the label of the state Democratic party for the Thurmond-Wright ticket, it was not unexpected that patterns of voting behavior in the presidential election failed to coincide with past bifactionalism. Nonetheless, an economic hard core of anti-Trumanism was discernible amidst the generalized arousal of whites on the racial issue. The Louisiana Dixiecrat movement, in short, while created and financed largely by the upper economic stratum, obscured its origins and intent by appealing to the pride and fear of all whites and thereby rode to success on a potent mixture of economics and race.

Grumblings in Louisiana about the national party antedated 1948 and fuzzily identified bifactional attitudes on the issue of revolt. It will be recalled that Sam Jones spoke warmly of a Southern third-party movement on the assumption that an assertion of the region's political power was prerequisite to its economic progress. The 1944 Louisiana delegation revealed sympathies for Harry Byrd of Virginia at the National Convention, and subsequently, five electors resigned rather than pledge themselves to support of the Roosevelt-Truman ticket. On the other hand, in the 1944 gubernatorial campaign Earl attacked Jones's preachments of party revolt, and Maestri and the Ring stood behind Roosevelt within the 1944 state Democratic delegation. After the 1948 Dixiecratic movement gained momentum in Louisiana, however, Earl abandoned any aggressive defense of Truman and sought to straddle the conflict, with considerable success, by remaining neutral between the rival presidential factions.[17] Russell Long also refused to risk his political prestige by taking sides in the presidential contest, but his later actions left little doubt as to his pro-national administration sympathies.[18] Indeed, no major Louisiana politician or group took up the cudgels for the national party in 1948; the Longs, the Choctaws, and Mayor Morrison were avowedly neutral, and when Alben Barkley landed at Moisant Airport at New Orleans only one major politician, Choctaw Assessor Comiskey of the Third Ward, was there to greet him.

The refusal of nominal Trumanites to stand up and be counted emphasized that the Dixiecrats captured Louisiana by default, a fact all the more surprising in view of the belated start of the movement. At the Democratic National Convention in July, Louisiana neither supported Dixiecrat Ben Laney of Arkansas nor followed Mississippi's and Alabama's walkout over the party's adoption of a civil rights program. The conservative urban press remained noticeably cool toward the idea of a regional political movement.[19] Not until September 10 did Louisiana become a serious partner in Southern revolt, and then by an action which virtually gave over its ten electoral votes to Thurmond and Wright. States' Righters, headed by business conservatives like John U. Barr[20] and Leander Perez,

[17] Earl marked himself as a nominal Trumanite who neither would actively oppose nor aid the States' Righters. In the 1948 regular session, Earl vetoed a bill which would have facilitated the filing of a Dixiecrat ticket in opposition to Truman. The Governor was conspicuously absent from the ranks of the state delegation to the National Convention and from attendance at the State Central Committee session at which the Thurmond ticket was made the official state Democratic party slate. In reference to the latter action, Earl was quoted later as observing, "They did it. I had no part in it." New Orleans *Times-Picayune*, September 21, 1948.

[18] In his resolutely pro-Stevenson stand in 1952, Russell Long termed Perez " . . . a delegate responsible for denying the people the right to vote for the Democratic nominee for President . . . a disservice to the Democratic party." Russell commented that he had failed to block Perez's actions in 1948 only because he was unwilling to jeopardize his own victory at the general election. New Orleans *Item*, August 3, 1952.

[19] The Baton Rouge *State-Times*, July 24, 1948, for example, editorialized that "the Dixiecrats aren't going anywhere, nor are they likely to take many voters with them on their wanderings between now and November."

[20] Barr headed the Louisiana Citizens' Committee which had urged the passage

persuaded the Democratic State Central Committee to assign the state Democratic party emblem, the rooster, to the Dixiecrat slate. Since August 31 was the last day for qualifying presidential candidates and their slates of electors, the Committee's action, taken with malice aforethought, denied the Truman-Barkley ticket a place on the ballot. The Committee justified its action in terms of those governmental principles and racial fears which were the stump appeals of Dixiecrats in every Southern state.

It is within the province and authority, and it is the duty, of the Democratic State Central Committee to nominate presidential electors for the Democratic party of Louisiana to support candidates for President and Vice-President who will preserve the traditions of the people of this state and protect their right of self-government and all other states' rights in accordance with our American way of constitutional government, as opposed to candidates for said offices who are pledged to support the enactment of federal laws to regiment our people, to destroy their rights of state government and to force upon them foreign ideologies such as the Russian 'all races law' here called F. E. P. C.[21]

In response to the protests of the national party, of Louisiana organized labor, and of the urban press,[22] Earl called a special session of the Legislature on September 22 and proposed a bill permitting the Democratic National Committee or a group of one hundred state voters to nominate a slate of Truman electors on a "National Democratic" ticket. As amended by the Dixiecrats and finally enacted, the measure allowed one hundred Louisiana voters to place Truman's name on the ballot, but under no party name which included the term "Democratic." To lessen the likelihood that the confusion

of anti-labor legislation during the 1946 legislative session. In late 1955, Barr became chairman of the executive committee of a newly-formed Federation for Constitutional Government, a Southern group dedicated to delaying the implementation of the United States Supreme Court's racial desegregation school ruling and hardly less dedicated to far right-wing economic doctrines. The propensity of racial politics for making strange bedfellows was illustrated by the fact that Leander Perez and Sam H. Jones, bitter enemies from 1940 to 1944, were members of that organization's advisory committee for Louisiana. New York *Times*, December 30, 1955.

[21] New Orleans *Times-Picayune*, September 11, 1948.

[22] See the editorials in the Shreveport *Times*, September 15, 1948; New Orleans *Times-Picayune*, September 11, 1948; New Orleans *Item*, September 22, 1948; and Baton Rouge *Morning Advocate*, September 12, 1948, all urging fair play for the national party ticket. For an opposite viewpoint, consult the Shreveport *Journal*, editorial, September 11, 1948.

of voters might work to the advantage of the Republican candidates for senator and Third District congressman, the Democratic candidates for those posts, Russell Long and E. E. Willis, were permitted to be certified under the Truman column as well as the Democratic column.

The presidential campaign was most emphatically not a hotly contested affair. Organized labor and Negro groups worked quietly for Truman, while the Dixiecrats monopolized what little there was of political oratory. The Dixiecrat success undoubtedly was due to their possession of the state party label, to the undercover nature of the pro-Truman campaign, and to the effective disguise of conservative resentment against the economic policies of the New Deal through an appeal to racial anxieties.[23] Although supported by a sizeable plurality of Louisiana's voters (Table 24), the Dixiecrat movement was more a shrewdly managed coup by conservative leaders than a grass-roots rebellion against the national party in power since 1932.

Figure 11, when compared with Figure 10 (Russell Long), clearly indicates a pattern of relative parish response not similar to state bifactionalism. Analysis of the parish election data reveals that the traditionally anti-Long parishes were no more anti-Truman than

TABLE 24. The Louisiana Vote in the Presidential Election of 1948

	Orleans	Other	State	% State	Parishes Carried by Majority	Parishes Carried by Plurality
States Rights	50,234	154,056	204,290	49.1	44	8
Truman	41,900	94,444	136,344	32.7	5	6
Republican	29,442	43,215	72,657	17.5	0	1
Progressive	2,203	832	3,035	.7	0	0
Total	123,779	292,547	416,326	100.0	49	15

SOURCE: *World Almanac* (1950), 494, and Alexander Heard and Donald S. Strong, *Southern Primaries and Elections*, 77.

[23] One interviewee expressed to the author his firm opinion that the Dixiecrat movement in Louisiana was in the nature of a popular uprising. Unhappily for his argument he inadvertently concluded, "If the Truman group had kept the [state party] label, then the States' Righters would have made an active campaign to educate and arouse the people. Many voters in Louisiana blindly vote the Democratic label." In 1952, when the Ike-tending *Times-Picayune* wrestled with the problem of whether the rooster ought to be given to the Stevenson-Sparkman ticket, it observed that such action "will be equivalent to delivering to the ticket tens of thousands of votes which are almost automatically cast under the rooster." July 30, 1952.

the rest of the state: the six most-urban parishes cast 49.2 per cent of the total vote; went 35.7 per cent for Truman; and therefore gave Truman 54.4 per cent of his state vote. It is suggested, nonetheless, that evidence derived from more detailed voting data provides an important link between the voting pattern in the presidential election and that of customary state bifactionalism.

The Longite urban lower classes may have been less receptive to the beating of racial drums than their country brethren and therefore have registered a relatively stronger pro-Truman score than did rural Longites. The (economic) logic of the state's bifactionalism, in

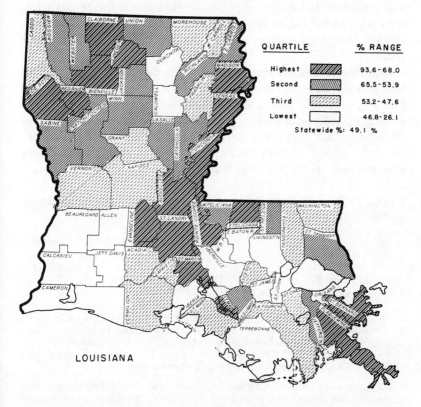

FIGURE 11. Quartile map: proportion of parish vote cast for Thurmond-Wright electors, presidential election of 1948.

SOURCE: same as that for Table 24.

other words, may have been restricted in operation to the less racially sensitive urban areas. Perry Howard's study of Baton Rouge precincts lends support to this view. ". . . the pattern of voting behavior [in the presidential election of 1948] again follows closely the ecological pattern [of Baton Rouge]. The 'regular' Democratic candidate [Truman] was strong in the 'working class' area while the 'middle class' vote favored the States' Rights candidate, Thurmond, or the Republican candidate, Dewey."[24] Using rank-order correlation coefficients by precincts between candidates in the 1948 gubernatorial primary and the presidential election in Baton Rouge, Howard concluded: "The strong $+.899$ coefficient of the Truman-Morrison vote demonstrated rather emphatically that Baton Rouge labor follows labor in the nation generally in being pro-Fair Deal Democrat. . . . We computed a strong $+.720$ correlation between Dewey and Jones. . . ."[25]

On a statewide basis, confirmation of the thesis that bifactionalism offered a partial explanation of the presidential voting pattern may be had by contrasting ward behavior in Russell Long's Senate primary of August, 1948, with that in Truman's race in November. As Table 25 indicates, virtually all of the anti-Long wards were anti-Truman, while the strong Truman wards, necessarily therefore, were drawn from the ranks of the pro-Long wards.

TABLE 25. Ward Voting Behavior in Democratic Senatorial Primary and in Presidential Election, 1948

	No. of Wards That Gave Truman	
	Less Than 50% of Ward Vote	50% or More of Ward Vote
98 wards, gave R. Long less than 50%............	92	6
388 wards, gave R. Long more than 50%.........	320	68
Total* _____	412	74

*The wards of the following parishes are not included: Orleans (17 wards), East Baton Rouge (10), Vernon (8), St. Bernard (7), and Plaquemines (10). The latter two and Orleans have been omitted because of the dominant influence of machine politics, East Baton Rouge because of Perry Howard's study cited above, and Vernon because the election data were missing.

SOURCE: ward data compiled and computed from unpublished precinct data made available through the courtesy of the office of the Secretary of State of Louisiana.

[24] "An Analysis of Voting Behavior in Baton Rouge," *loc. cit.*, 96.
[25] *Ibid.*, 99.

It would thus appear reasonable to conclude that the Dixiecrats secured the support of most of the anti-Longs, presumably in good part because of shared economic attitudes, and of thousands of Long-ites for racial reasons outside the context of customary factionalism. The close relationship of racial fear to Dixiecrat support has been well established by competent students. "In state after state the Dixiecrats won their greatest support among the whites who live closest to large numbers of Negroes. . . . Many of them [whites] have little in common with the leaders of the Dixiecrats except a susceptibility to Negrophobia."[26] Louisiana proved no exception to that pattern: of the sixteen parishes which in 1940 had the highest proportions of Negro population, eight were in the highest quartile of Dixiecrat support, four in the second quartile, one in the third, and three in the lowest.

If the above interpretation is correct, then the Louisiana revolt of 1948 was cut from a cloth as old as the institution of Southern slavery itself. Once again the conservatives were able to stampede their class opponents into support of conservative objectives by arousing racial anxieties. Even Long's Louisiana, welfare-prone and uncommitted to political Negro-baiting, proved vulnerable to that hoary tactic.

*Compromise and cupidity—and voter reaction:
the events of 1950–51*

The decline of Earl Long's political stock, evident in the events of 1948 following the close of the regular session of the Legislature, was accentuated further in January, 1950, when the voters of New Orleans returned Mayor Morrison and his ticket to office by large majorities. Justifiably fearful for Russell Long's renomination in the Senate primary of 1950, the Governor led his Legislature along the paths of compromise in an effort to woo back thousands of voters who had ceased supporting him after February, 1948. The junior Senator's easy renomination attested to the success of those tactics. Earl, however, apparently was misled by Russell's victory and turned back to the methods of 1948, in what was widely interpreted as an attempt to extend his term of office through the mechanism of a constitutional convention. So much opposition from without and

[26] Alexander Heard, *A Two-Party South?* (Chapel Hill, 1952), 27, 164.

within his faction was aroused that the effort had to be shelved gracelessly. The immediate consequence of Long's cupidity was popular rejection of his proposed mammoth bond issue in the November, 1950, election. The ultimate impact of his blunder was noticeable in the 1952 state-office primaries, in which the Long faction fragmented into rival cliques, and Earl Long's candidate was overwhelmingly defeated.

The results of the New Orleans mayoralty contest of January, 1950, proved to Long that there were sharp limits to the utility of punitive laws. The Choctaws and Long's Orleans organization backed a middle-of-the-road businessman, Charles C. Zatarain, against the popular reformer-incumbent, Chep Morrison.[27] The Governor, unsubtly dangling bait before the city's voters, observed, "If harmony prevailed between the city and state and the city and state saw eye to eye more might be done for the city."[28] Morrison made political capital out of the Longite assaults upon the city and stressed his substantial record of reform and liberalism, attested to by the campaign support of the *Times-Picayune*, on the one hand, and the endorsement of him by organized labor and Negro groups on the other. Morrison garnered nearly two-thirds of the record total of 183,744 votes cast, and he captured five of the seven council seats in the first primary. Reform victory spelled the end of the Choctaws, thus ironically reversing the historic pattern of Ring-Longite conflict of the early 1930's. Denied city patronage since 1946, gradually losing ground in the struggle over parish jobs, and dependent upon the state administration for survival, the Choctaws were forced to accept a merger with Long's city group in March, 1951, which created the Regular Louisiana Democratic Organization.

Governor Long interpreted Morrison's renomination—in the face of the change in the structure of city government which hopefully had sought to rig the city elections in favor of the Ring—as a danger sign to nephew Russell's bid for a full-term Senate seat. At a special session in March, 1950, Earl had surplus funds from beer tax revenues allocated to the school lunch program and farm-to-market roads and had the date of the Congressional primary pushed back to

[27] Zatarain was a member of the Louisiana Tax Commission originally appointed by Jones and reappointed by Davis and by Long. Maestri also announced against Morrison but withdrew when Earl failed to back him.

[28] New Orleans *Item*, September 29, 1949.

July 25 to avoid conflict with harvest time in the rural areas. But the new Longite theme was one of conciliation and compromise. At the 1950 regular session the Governor proposed no new taxes: ". . . we in Louisiana have, at this time, reached a point where I feel that our economy can stand no new taxes . . . ."[29] Biennial appropriations of $480,000,000 were adopted, some $15,000,000 more than those of 1948–50, but anti-Longs gained concessions in the fields of old-age assistance, free school lunches, and aid to municipalities.[30] Urban efforts to enact a strict stock-fence law and an automobile financial responsibility measure, however, were rebuffed. Earl also resisted, with uniform success, anti-Long measures which sought to repeal or reduce various taxes, to increase the size of the legislative majority required to enact tax increases, and to install voting machines in every precinct in the state.

The solicitude of the state administration for the plight of New Orleans, which it had caused by legislation two years earlier, was quite apparent. Control of the Police Department was returned to the mayor, and additional revenues were provided through cigarette tax and highway fund allocations and through permissive legislation on city taxation of mechanical amusement machines. The Legislature eliminated the appropriation for continuance of the partisan Port Survey Commission,[31] and Long defeated a move to repeal the allocation of .45 of one cent of the gasoline tax to the retirement of the debt of the Dock Board.[32] Of the greatest importance, after much dispute, a home rule bill was enacted for New Orleans which ultimately would lessen the city's reliance upon the state Legislature and minimize New Orleans' direct stake in the outcome of state contests.[33]

[29] Baton Rouge *State-Times*, May 16, 1950.

[30] The eligibility requirements for old-age assistance were tightened, while the term "free" was eliminated from the school lunch program and provision made for voluntary payment by those children whose parents were able to do so. Municipal taxing powers were enlarged.

[31] The Board of Liquidation of the State Debt, however, later authorized an appropriation of $25,000 for the commission.

[32] Senator Oliver withdrew the measure upon notification of Long's opposition to it. This prompted the New Orleans *Item* in its editorial of June 5, 1950, to liken the behavior of the "independent" Legislature to that of "trained seals." A majority of the Senate subsequently called *Item* publisher Stern and editor Fritchey before them and threatened the latter with a contempt citation, but, despite much chest-beating, the senators found no way to discipline a free press for its straightforward opinions which bore more than a casual relation to fact.

[33] The details of the measure are beyond the scope of this study. Simply put,

The capstone of the new, respectable Earl Longism was the Governor's espousal of a civil service constitutional amendment, complete with Hatch Act prohibitions upon political activities, a measure also supported by the Louisiana Civil Service League.[34] Longite defection, however, was evident immediately. "Civil service is a hypocrite's bill," charged Representative deNux of Avoyelles. "My good friends who worked for me when I was elected—I'm not going to kick them out and kiss those who fought me. Federal civil service? I know who makes the appointments in Avoyelles parish. I make them. Tell me that's not political?"[35] Representatives DeNux and Vallee (Jefferson Davis Parish) openly circulated a round robin against the bill, and on June 27 the constitutional amendment failed to pass by a wide margin, 47y–46n. The opposition was composed almost entirely of Longites and Choctaws. The singularity of factional "revolt" on that one issue lent support to anti-Long doubts as to Earl's sincerity in proposing the measure. While the Governor undoubtedly was unwilling to jeopardize the full support of parish leaders necessary to Russell's re-election, by insisting upon enactment of a bill properly the property of the opposition faction, it was no small concession for the Longite chieftain to endorse what he had had repealed a scant two years before.

To be too good would be to be anti-Long, and therefore some old habits were indulged in by the Longites. Opining that "nickel-and-diming . . . would never pay for projects like that Mississippi River bridge at Orleans,"[36] Earl proposed—and the Legislature acquiesced

the bill declared the present charter to be a home rule charter and gave the city the right to adopt any form of government it chose and the power to operate that government. The Legislature was prohibited, except by general law, from amending the charter. The bill provided for an election in November, 1952, for the purpose of choosing between the present charter and any other proposed alternatives. At that election, the voters of New Orleans endorsed a strong-mayor form of city government to be effective in 1954.

[34] Earl combined his advocacy of civil service in 1950 with the charge that Jones's civil service from 1940 to 1948 was a sham. Its central defect, charged Long, was its omission of effective prohibitions upon political activities of employees (Baton Rouge State-Times, June 20, 1950). The Louisiana Civil Service League, of course, adjusted its tactics to fit the circumstances. When Jones's civil service was endangered in 1948, the League praised it as perfect, but when the League rewrote the measure in 1952 for Kennon's adoption, Hatch Act political bans were included.

[35] Baton Rouge Morning Advocate, June 14, 1950.

[36] New Orleans Times-Picayune, May 10, 1950.

in—passage of the largest bond issue in the history of the state: a
$140,000,000 issue which had been secured by bonding the proceeds
of the additional two-cent gasoline tax of 1948, and earmarked for
the widening of highways and for the construction of a bridge and
tunnel in New Orleans. The Governor was granted broad removal
powers over all public officers appointed by him, with certain specified exceptions.[37] Legislators also dealt kindly with themselves by
permitting public officials to apply for state contracts which were let
by competitive bidding. This open invitation to graft Earl vetoed,
no doubt in appreciation of Senator Tooke's (Caddo) jibe, "This is
the best piece of [anti-Russell Long] legislation that's going to be
distributed in this campaign."[38]

The moderacy of Longism in the 1950 regular session was directly
related to the Senate campaign going on at the same time. Earl's
tactics paid handsome electoral dividends. After two years in office,
Russell Long had proved his soundness on Southern issues and had
followed a mild liberalism which argued well for his renomination
on his own merits. Thanks to Earl's tactics in 1950, Russell did not
have to face an aroused anti-Longism like that of 1948. Sam Jones
expressed a willingness to forgive and forget insofar as Russell was
concerned,[39] and Mayor Morrison probably would have done likewise but for the pressure exerted upon him by his reform backers.[40]

The candidate agreed upon by the anti-Longs was Malcolm Lafargue, United States Attorney for the western district of Louisiana,
whose assets on paper proved to be ephemeral as the campaign progressed.[41] Although inveighing vigorously against creeping socialism

[37] The exceptions included those who were appointed upon the recommendation of, or from lists submitted by, others, those whose terms of office were fixed
in the state Constitution, and those who were required by the Constitution to be
appointed by and with the consent of the Senate. Although the original bill
merely enabled the Governor to fire at will the members of all boards of mental
and hospital institutions except New Orleans Charity, after amendment the
grant of power was so broad as to jeopardize state receipt of federal funds in
certain areas. At Long's insistence, in order to meet minimum federal requirements, the Legislature passed a clarifying resolution empowering the Governor
to suspend the provisions of the act when, in his opinion, it was impracticable to
apply its provisions.
[38] Baton Rouge *Morning Advocate*, July 6, 1950.
[39] Column by Margaret Dixon, *ibid.*, March 19, 1950.
[40] Perhaps Morrison's easy victory in 1950 misled his backers into believing
that he could deliver something like that majority vote to Russell Long's opponent, whoever he was.
[41] It was thought that Lafargue, a French Protestant born in Cajun country and

of state and national varieties, Lafargue was unable to shake popular confidence in the person of Russell Long, a cross-factional trust which was explained in moderate terms by Uncle Earl.

> Russell Long has two year's seniority . . . and has a good record. He is a good boy. The fact is, I say, not because he is my nephew (I have several nephews), he is one of the most conscientious, tolerant, uncontrollable young men I have ever known in my life and is most respectful of the rights of other people.
>
> He will vote for what he thinks is right, regardless of what I say (I have already tried him) and what you say or what any pressure group says. He is an improvement on his uncle and his father, Huey P. Long. He is better educated and respects the other man's opinion more.[42]

In the primary of July 25, Russell Long secured 68.5 per cent of the total of 524,859 votes cast and carried fifty-five parishes by better than a two-to-one vote. Russell's victory in every parish but Plaquemines[43] was a dramatic tribute to his Senate performance and to Governor Long's strategy during the first half of 1950.

The Governor's interpretation of Russell's outstanding victory and his actions which followed as a consequence of that interpretation constituted a turning point in the Earl Long administration. Earl read into Russell's re-election a blanket endorsement of his state administration of a cross-factional magnitude comparable to that which Earl himself enjoyed in the gubernatorial primaries of early 1948. Seeking, Kingfish-like, to transmute extraordinary majority support into the foundations of a personal regime, Earl attempted to call a constitutional convention to extend his faction's term of office without a vote of the people.

Although Louisiana stood in need of a new constitution,[44] the

resident in Shreveport, would make a strong statewide candidate. Actually, he was an unknown whose political beginnings were traceable to Longite affiliations in the days of Leche. By trying to "beat somebody with nobody," the anti-Longs restricted their appeal to their own factional die-hards.

[42] New Orleans *Item*, May 21, 1950.

[43] Perez had broken with the Longs over their lack of support of the Dixiecrat movement. Plaquemines voters, as ever, followed Perez' lead and gave 93.7 per cent of their vote to Lafargue.

[44] The Constitution had been amended some three hundred times since 1921; and since 1946, the Louisiana State Law Institute had been working on a new model organic law. An able discussion of the problem may be found in Kimbrough Owen, "The Need for Constitutional Revision in Louisiana," *Louisiana Law Review*, VIII (1947–48), 1–104.

brazenness of the Governor's real objective gave popular ammunition to those opposed either to a new constitution or to one written under the auspices of the Long faction. The Commissioner of Agriculture and the Register of the Land Office, for example, were denied constitutional status in the Louisiana Law Institute's working draft and therefore were hostile to the calling of a constitutional convention. The urban press, acting as spokesmen for the conservatives, voiced general fears about the contents of an organic law sponsored by the Long faction. The port interests of New Orleans, in particular, questioned Earl's motives, arguing that getting control of the Dock Board stood high upon the list of Earl's aims.[45] Long's shifting convention proposals were never calculated to give the lie to those charges.

The Governor's call for a constitutional convention, as enacted in the regular session of 1950 and revised in the special session of the following August, included several controversial provisions on which the opposition concentrated.[46] Under either of Long's methods for fixing the composition of the convention, the Long faction probably would control a majority of the delegates. Historically, it was not unusual for the sitting governor and his faction to be in control of a constitutional convention. An acute problem arose, however, when Earl also adhered to the weight of precedent by not submitting the convention's product to the vote of the people, a point of view which should be understood in the light of the outcome of the constitutional amendments election of 1948. Strangely commented the leader of the faction of the common man, "With all respects to our people—and they are as good as any in the world—unfortunately there is much ignorance. We are doing everything we can to improve this. But the lawyers themselves don't know what a constitution means."[47] Longite Representative Vallee bluntly concurred, "My people down in Bayou Chene don't know the difference between a constitution and a free pass to a football game."[48]

---

[45] It was significant that the Greater Louisiana Citizens' Committee, an *ad hoc* group formed to combat Long's convention proposals, was organized by representatives of the New Orleans Chamber of Commerce, the International Trade Mart, the Board of Trade, and Greater New Orleans, Inc.

[46] A brief chronological treatment of Earl's proposals may be found in William C. Havard, "The Abortive Louisiana Constitutional Convention of 1951," *Journal of Politics,* XIII (November, 1951), 708–10.

[47] Baton Rouge *State-Times,* August 7, 1950.

[48] *Loc. cit.*

Anti-Long protests persuaded the Governor to adopt a compromise in the August session, if the following odd provision could be so designated: the new constitution would be adjudged ratified, regardless of the division of the vote, unless a minimum of 500,000 votes were cast in the referendum on the Constitution. Another phase of the compromise dealt with the problem of the extension of the terms of office of current state officials, a controversy which arose, it should be noted, after Russell Long's primary, for the original bill passed by the regular session prohibited convention action on that topic. The August special session permitted the convention to deal with that topic and passed a resolution calling upon the convention to submit any term-of-office extensions to a referendum in which the customary majority vote would be determinative.

The foregoing two provisions, argued Earl Long, meant that he could not keep his faction from the polls to assure ratification of the new constitution without at the same time jeopardizing ratification of the separate term-extension resolution. The obvious rejoinder to all this hocus-pocus was that the legislative resolution had no binding force whatsoever upon the convention and could be disregarded by the Longite majority of delegates. In spite of Earl's protestations of innocence, there were many ways to provide for the convention's fair handling of the problem of extending the terms of current state officials. The devious plan Long promoted, naturally enough, was suspected of harboring devious aims.

The Governor's carryings-on threatened to disrupt his own faction in addition to enlarging and solidifying the ranks of the anti-Longs. Former Senator Feazel, Russell Long, labor leader Lige Williams, Choctaw Dudley Desmare, and Clem Sehrt, Long's leader in New Orleans, all warned Earl that he had gone too far this time. Long capitulated. In a one-day special session, held September 12, 1950, the Legislature nullified the call for a constitutional convention by adopting a resolution suspending the law. The political damage, however, was done. Despite retention of his control over a subservient Legislature, Earl had split with many of his influential backers and had shaken the confidence of many outside of the confirmed Longite voters.

The effects of Earl's cupidity were apparent immediately in the constitutional amendments election of November 7, 1950. The key Longite measure, the $140,000,000 road bond issue, was defeated by

150,808 votes to 100,126, the anti-Longs carrying forty-five parishes, including Earl's own parish of Winn. Seeking to redress the factional balance, Long spoke seriously in March, 1951, of running for lieutenant-governor in the coming primaries and, in June, called a special session to distribute some vote-bait funds for highways and state institutions. Little enthusiasm greeted either move, and Earl grudgingly adjusted to the current facts of political life: Earl Longism was in danger of mass repudiation.

An appraisal of Earl Long and the 1952 gubernatorial primaries

Earl Long, though an adept rural politician skilled in personalized politics, was no second Kingfish. "Earl is trying mighty hard to wear Huey's shoes, but he sort of rattles around in them. He hasn't got Huey's brains and he hasn't got Huey's finesse. Where Huey was fiery, this fellow is just loud. Where Huey outsmarted his opposition, Earl just slams into the center of the line."[49] Yet there were important similarities in their performances. Both claimed to head the same class movement, both tilted with the urban press, and both did mighty battle with the New Orleans enemy, though the nature of the latter had undergone striking change from 1934 to 1948. Each was a devotee of spoils politics and of tax-and-spend governmental policies. Each controlled his Legislature and sought to erect an edifice of personal power. Based on their records, however, it must be concluded that Earl outstripped the Kingfish only in the magnitude of state taxation and expenditure. Huey's younger brother never scaled the dizzy heights of adulation and dictatorship that the Kingfish did.

Nonetheless, the programs of economic liberalism associated with the "do-something" Long faction had been given impetus under Earl's leadership; and, by 1952, the full impact of the heavy spending of the state administration was felt in the diverse areas of welfare, highways, public schools, hospitals, school lunches, and veterans' bonuses. Had Earl not indulged ineptly, following Russell's renomination, in hankerings for greater power, the opposition would have been restricted to the awkward position of attacking Longite taxes while pledging to retain Longite benefits. As it happened, Earl

[49] The observations of a Louisiana reporter as quoted by Cabell Phillips, "The Lengthening Shadow of Huey Long," *New York Times Magazine* (November 7, 1948), 79.

aggravated the resentments caused by his taxes by exposing his actions to the charge of personal and factional gain. As Earl was to discover sadly, there was no place in the Louisiana political spectrum for crude half-measures, for a "little Huey Long."

Insofar as the platforms of the 1952 gubernatorial aspirants functioned as sensitive indices of popular attitudes, Earl Long was to be repudiated at the same time that liberal Longism was to be retained but not expanded. Eight anti-Longs and one pro-Long competed for governor on the basis of programs which were distinguished more by their similarities than their differences. The voter had to rely upon a factional sense of smell to assign similarly-talking entrants their appropriate spot on the political spectrum.

On one side, clearly labeled as the candidate of the state administration, stood District Judge Carlos G. Spaht of Baton Rouge, a World War II veteran and former head of the State University alumni group. While Earl's selection of an able judge without known Longite standing or statewide recognition reflected his awareness of the intensity of anti-Longism in the state, the vigorous campaign he conducted on Spaht's behalf denied the latter any independent standing. Throughout the campaign Spaht was referred to simply, and devastatingly, as "Earl's boy."

Three dissident Longites also competed for the highest state office. Lieutenant-Governor William J. Dodd—a loyal Long leader from 1948 to 1951 who had failed to secure Earl's blessing for the 1952 campaign for reasons never divulged—angrily stumped the state claiming the Longite nomination as a matter of implicit right. Lucille May Grace, the long-time Register of the Land Office allegedly possessed of a large personal following, became the first woman in Louisiana to run for the office of chief executive. Miss Grace had broken with Earl over the constitutional convention issue, and now backed by Perez, stressed her record of opposition to Truman and to the tidelands oil "grab" in her bid for office. The third sometime Longite candidate was Dudley LeBlanc, now a patent-medicine manufacturer of great wealth, who pitched his campaign on the proposition that the state's greatest need was for a sure-fire huckster to sell its industrial virtues to an outside commercial world suspicious of Longite Louisiana.[50]

---

[50] Unfortunately for Dudley, he sold his Hadacol patent-medicine firm during the campaign, and shortly afterwards the Federal Trade Commission charged the

Three candidates with consistent anti-Long records also filed for the gubernatorial office. In terms of influential backing, the candidacy of liberal Second District Congressman T. Hale Boggs appeared the most formidable. Though hitherto associated only with the reform faction, Boggs gathered a curious group of supporters behind him: Sam Jones; Mayor Morrison of New Orleans; Senator Russell Long; former Senator Feazel; and Congressman Jimmie Morrison. As additional departures from tradition, Boggs was a Catholic and a resident of New Orleans, two near-insurmountable handicaps for a gubernatorial aspirant, according to the folklore of Louisiana politicians. Seeking to explain and capitalize upon the unorthodox features of his candidacy, Boggs attempted to emulate Davis' "forgive and forget" approach, but attacks from his rivals forced him quickly to turn to the more usual Louisiana campaign conduct. The most conservative anti-Long entrant was James M. McLemore, an Alexandria cattleman backed by the New Orleans *Times-Picayune.* Depicting his entrance into politics as part of a "Citizens' Revolt," McLemore resolutely berated the Long and Truman administrations for their "socialistic biases." Judge Robert Kennon, back for his third try against the Longs, espoused a mild anti-Trumanism and spent most of his campaign attacking state Longism and spelling out his pledges of tax reductions and good-government reforms in greater detail than other candidates.

Two non-serious candidacies increased the total of gubernatorial entrants to nine. Cliff Liles, sergeant-at-arms of the state Legislature, conducted a limited campaign on the single argument that a legalization of gambling would provide $400,000,000 of state revenues annually and would permit the elimination of most current state taxes. Kermit Parker, a New Orleans druggist, became the first Negro since Reconstruction days to offer himself for high state office. His candidacy was a personal matter; he was disavowed by all major Negro organizations. Interestingly enough, Parker's platform was moderate, and except for a greater stress upon the welfare functions of the state, was indistinguishable from the programs advocated by white candidates.

concern with "false and malicious" advertising and the company filed bankruptcy proceedings. LeBlanc tried several times to secure the post of lieutenant-governor on the ticket of some of his rivals but, meeting with no success, was forced to remain in the race until the bitter end.

The multiplicity of candidates suggested a range of public policy alternatives which was, however, not the case. Each of the candidates, Earl's man included, agreed that Louisiana could stand no additional taxation and that tax reductions were in order. Longite Spaht was perhaps the most honest of all in his insistence that, if past benefits were to be maintained, no specific taxes could be decreased until a thorough study of state finances had been undertaken. Kennon, Dodd, and Grace pledged a two-cent reduction in the gasoline tax; McLemore promised repeal of the state property tax; and Grace further promised a cut in the taxes on beer and cigarettes. All candidates expressed the desire to place the highway program on a pay-as-you-go basis. Perhaps the measure of the tax-consciousness evident in the campaign was the proposal of state legislator A. O. Rappelet of Terrebonne—who later withdrew from the gubernatorial race—to the effect that all tax increases voted on by the Legislature would have to be ratified by the people before becoming law.

On the question of benefits, in contrast to taxation, all candidates were loathe to quarrel with the substantial record of the Long administration. Although Spaht remained moderate in his promises, his mentor, the Governor, revived the old tactic of pledging a special session to distribute $17,000,000 for welfare and highways if Spaht was nominated. LeBlanc promised a free college education to all, $75 old-age pensions, and a bonus to World War I veterans. Bill Dodd became the most expansive promiser of largesse when he, straight-faced, adopted Rappelet's planks upon the latter's withdrawal from the race and his declaration of support for Dodd's candidacy. In addition to specifying tax reductions, Rappelet pledged a free college education to all, a $60 old-age pension, a bonus to veterans of the Korean War, a minimum hourly wage of one dollar for state highway workers, and a state bounty of fifty cents per muskrat.

Each of the major candidates favored civil service imbedded in the Constitution, home rule, financial aid to municipalities, a cost-of-living salary increase for state personnel, an independent Legislature, the appointment of a trained penologist to revamp the administration of Angola State Penitentiary,[51] varying degrees of

[51] Long's administration had been no more guilty of poor prison direction than that of his predecessors, but Earl had invited unfavorable publicity by refusing to carry out the reforms recommended by a citizen investigatory committee.

anti-Trumanism, and a vigorous fight for state control of tidelands oil. In spite of the advocacy of an occasional unique pledge, the dominant theme common to all was that each could better administer current state programs with less politicking and with greater efficiency.

The voters' factional identification of the many contestants was complicated further by the bewildering barrage of charges and countercharges they leveled against each other. Earl Long and Dodd engaged in a running feud, causing many to speculate how much each could tell about the other, if either dared. Kennon, Grace, McLemore, and Dodd chorused that the split between uncle Earl and nephew Russell was a subterfuge and that Spaht and Boggs were, in the horse-racing terminology frequently employed, Earl's "double-entry." Miss Grace charged Boggs with being the candidate of the Truman administration as well. LeBlanc's attempts to get on the Dodd state ticket as his candidate for lieutenant-governor were known publicly, while early in the campaign McLemore expressed a willingness to place Miss Grace on his state ticket. Late in the campaign, McLemore came under suspicion for his past business dealings with Longite backers and for attracting the support of Perez, who had earlier jettisoned Miss Grace.

The most extreme attack was leveled by Perez, a leader of the Louisiana Dixiecrats and the boss of Plaquemines Parish, who worked through the medium of Miss Grace to get at Hale Boggs. Boggs's eligibility to run for governor was challenged partly on the grounds that he had engaged in pro-Communist activity as an undergraduate at the Tulane University in 1936–37. The charges, if true, would have resulted in the disqualification of Boggs as a party candidate under the rules of the Democratic party. Although the Democratic State Central Committee and the courts held for Boggs, their decisions were based upon technicalities, thus depriving him of a decisive refutation of the substance of the accusation. Moreover, since Earl Long had bossed the meeting of the committee at which the favorable vote for Boggs was taken, the "double-entry" charge was reinforced. Although Perez' action doubtless ended whatever chance of success Miss Grace might have had—and Perez shortly afterwards shifted his support to McLemore—his objective of helping to defeat the main "Trumanite" candidate was achieved.

The task of the voter was simplified in only two respects. The incumbents of four minor state offices, comprising the secretary of state, treasurer, superintendent of education, and commissioner of agriculture, were renominated without opposition. All state tickets, therefore, were short, embracing a total of five posts at most. Second, even the anti-Long candidates conceded that Spaht would make the runoff primary—the main question, therefore, was which of the numerous anti-Longs would be accorded plurality support. As it turned out, the most liberal anti-Long not involved in the welter of campaign accusations became Spaht's rival for the runoff.

Table 26 reports the results of the January 15 primary, omitting separate treatment of the minor candidacies of Grace, Liles, and

TABLE 26. The Louisiana Vote in the 1952 Democratic Gubernatorial First Primary

	Orleans	Other	State	% State	Parishes Carried by Majority	Plurality
Spaht	42,723	131,264	173,987	22.8	2	20
Kennon	33,754	129,680	163,434	21.5	1	16
Boggs	54,043	88,499	142,542	18.7	1	2
McLemore	17,408	98,997	116,405	15.3	1	12
Dodd	12,082	78,843	90,925	11.9	1	2
LeBlanc	3,067	59,839	62,906	8.3	0	6
Other	2,952	8,583	11,535	1.5	0	0
Total	166,029	595,705	761,734	100.0	6	58

SOURCE: adapted from "Louisiana Voter Participation in the Democratic Primary Election, January 15, 1952," *News Analysis*, No. 6, Supplement, January 30, 1952, Public Affairs Research Council of Louisiana, Inc.

Parker. The multiplicity of candidates produced a wide distribution of the vote: in forty parishes, no candidate received as much as 35 per cent of the vote; and the combined votes of the winning candidates, Spaht and Kennon, fell considerably short of half of the total vote cast. Ticket voting also suffered, with the highly unusual consequence that Kennon's candidate for lieutenant-governor lost out to Boggs's affiliate. For the second primary, Kennon endorsed Boggs's man and later appointed his defeated running-mate as head of the State Department of Commerce and Industry. Dodd, LeBlanc, and Boggs each had mostly a localized appeal, while McLemore showed surprising strength, particularly in some of the anti-Long areas of north Louisiana and in Calcasieu. Spaht's greatest support lay in the northern uplands and in the south-central parishes, while Kennon had scattered south Louisiana strength, the northwestern area of his local influence, and led his rivals in the Florida parishes.

The first primary predicted Earl's repudiation, notwithstanding the fact that more than half the total vote remained to be apportioned between Spaht and Kennon in the runoff. In addition to the slimness of Spaht's plurality, the strong non-Orleans performance of the "pure" anti-Longs, Kennon and McLemore, when compared to that of Boggs and Dodd, lent factional significance to the scattered distribution of votes among competing anti-Long candidates. A high rate of turnover in state legislative contests also emphasized electoral dissatisfaction with Earl Longism.

Scrambling on the bandwagon, all seven defeated candidates, Mayor Morrison, and Congressman Morrison declared their active support for Kennon. Neither Sam Jones nor Russell Long, because of personal hostility to Kennon, took any part in the runoff primary. Several urban papers went so far as to demand that Earl force Spaht to withdraw and to concede the election.[52] Increasingly desperate, Earl spoke of calling a special session to grant a $100 bonus to old-age pensioners, but he abandoned the plan on Spaht's insistence. The inevitable climax came on February 19 and is reported in Table 27.

TABLE 27. The Louisiana Vote in the 1952 Democratic Gubernatorial Second Primary

	Orleans	Other	State	% State	Parishes Carried by Majority
Kennon	106,070	376,232	482,302	61.4	53
Spaht	60,225	242,518	302,743	38.6	11
Total	166,295	618,750	785,045	100.0	64

SOURCE: adapted from "Louisiana Voter Participation in the Democratic Second Primary Election, February 19, 1952," News Analysis, No. 7, Supplement, March 5, 1952, Public Affairs Research Council of Louisiana, Inc.

The six most-urban parishes, casting 42.4 per cent of the total vote, went 36.0 per cent for Spaht; the rest of the state went only 40.3 per cent for Spaht. A comparison of the foregoing figures with the statistics in Table 23 is most revealing. Compared with that of Russell

---

[52] See the editorials in the Baton Rouge State-Times and the Shreveport Journal of January 18, 1952, and in the New Orleans Item of January 17, 1952. The Times-Picayune, with greater logic, insisted that Spaht remain in the race so that the Long faction could be defeated decisively in the second primary.

Long in 1948, the decline in Spaht's proportion of the non-urban vote was far sharper than the decline in his proportion of the vote of the six most-urban parishes. Compared with Earl Long's runoff in 1948, Spaht's proportion in both categories had dropped precipitously, but the decline was greater for the non-urban areas. Thus, Earl's early alienation of urbanites, which nearly caused Russell Long's defeat in 1948, combined with his later alienation of non-urbanites to bring about the overwhelming rejection of Spaht in 1952.

Nonetheless, the centers of Long and anti-Long strength remained fairly constant (Figure 12). Of the sixteen parishes in Spaht's highest

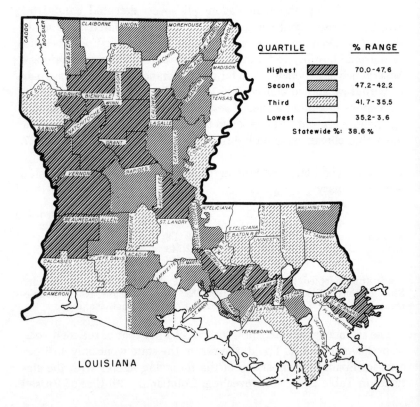

FIGURE 12. Quartile map: proportion of parish vote cast for Spaht, 1952 Democratic gubernatorial second primary.

SOURCE: same as that for Table 27.

quartile, ten had been in Russell Long's highest quartile in 1948, another four in Long's second quartile; ten in Spaht's lowest quartile were also in Long's lowest quartile, another four parishes in his third quartile. The elements of continuity were thus more pervading than those of change with regard to relative parish performance on bifactionalism.[53]

The Kennon victory was complete in that his state ticket took office with him, and a majority of legislators were newcomers. Of the incumbents who had tried for re-election, thirty-four were defeated and thirty-six were victorious in the House; twelve were defeated and fourteen re-elected in the Senate. In New Orleans, reform legislators outnumbered Long-Choctaw affiliates by two-to-one, reducing Orleans' Ring representation in the Legislature to minimal size for the first time since that organization was founded. Indeed, to face with greater effectiveness what appeared to be a bleak future, the Ring announced its withdrawal from Earl's Regular Louisiana Democratic Organization and its rebirth as an independent political organization. The Democratic State Central Committee completed the rout of Longites by dismissing Earl from his post as Democratic National Committeeman.

Longism thus had been rebuffed by a large majority of voters for the first time since 1928. Upon the actions of the Kennon administration rested the fate of the formerly dominant faction in state politics.

The first phase of the Kennon administration

As a consequence of the thoroughness of Kennon's victory, he was able to effect his program with less legislative opposition, both in numbers and in intensity, than had been the case with Sam Jones. In the reform spirit, however, Kennon circulated his major proposals before the session began and then submitted them early in the ses-

[53] For a more detailed statistical treatment of the 1952 gubernatorial primaries, see Rudolf Heberle, George Hillery, Jr., and Frank Lovrich, "Continuity and Change in Voting Behavior in the 1952 Primaries in Louisiana," *The Southwestern Social Science Quarterly*, XXXIII (March, 1953), 328–42. The authors conclude also that the forces of continuity in the Louisiana scene are more dominant than those of change, at least for the immediate future. Unfortunately, that study ignores the political consequences of Earl's programs from 1948 to 1952, and therefore is compelled to attribute Spaht's poor showing to inner

sion to encourage thoughtful amendment where necessary. On balance, the few minor setbacks to the state administration were of less importance than the fostering of the renewed independence of the Legislature. Governor Kennon fulfilled his good-government promises, sensibly violated some of his fiscal pledges rather than curtail necessary state services, and fought successfully in November—against half-hearted Longite opposition—for popular ratification of essential constitutional amendments. The only major factional wrangle concerned the presidential election, in which Kennon carried through on the anti-Trumanism of his gubernatorial campaign by endorsing Eisenhower, while the Longs backed Adlai Stevenson. By the close of the first phase of his administration, Kennon appeared as if he might be following the middle way of "benefits without degradation" with greater success than Jones or Davis.

Kennon's handling of state finances in the regular session of 1952 was as creditable as could be expected in view of his commitment to maintain Longite services. In redemption of his pledges, the gasoline tax rate was reduced two cents, state income tax exemptions were increased, and $20,000,000 were slashed from highway expenditures. The mere maintenance of Longite benefits, however, made mandatory an increase in the level of state spending. The enacted general appropriation bill was $23,000,000 higher than Earl's had been, with the bulk of the added funds allocated to education, hospitals, and the Angola prison. Use of the General Fund surplus and an upward revision of estimated yields from current taxes made up the difference between incoming revenues and outgoing appropriations.[54] At the same time, over urban-parish opposition, a $9,750,000 bond issue was authorized, secured by an existent tax, and allocated to the improvement of the Angola penitentiary, mental institutions, and one white and one Negro state college. Though the *Times-Picayune* and other tax-conscious anti-Longs grumbled that Kennon had violated his

Longite dissension compounded by the multiplication of competing ex-Longite candidates. Perhaps so, but what of the sharp decline in Longite support given to Russell Long in mid-1948 when he and Kennon were the only candidates? It may be, though it is still too early to tell, that heavy-taxing and buccaneering Longism has narrowed its appeal to "have-not" groups, which constitute a decreasing proportion of the state's population.

[54] Kennon's financial advisers, like those of Earl, erred on the side of pessimism. By mid-1953 state surpluses were sufficiently large to permit the calling of a special session to distribute the windfall.

campaign pledges, the Governor was politically astute in rejecting the conservative's view of state finances that had hampered the Jonesian reformers.

The Kennon administration, as expected, took giant strides in the field of good government. A civil service measure, written by the Louisiana Civil Service League and including firm bans on political activities, was enacted in the form of a constitutional amendment. The movement to "take politics out of politics," having captured the University and Dock Boards, reached out to embrace the key departments of welfare, institutions, and highways. By the terms of Kennon-sponsored constitutional amendments those departments were to be administered by citizen boards whose personnel were subject neither to gubernatorial nor popular control.[55] The Budget Office was reorganized and the offices of Auditor and Supervisor of Public Funds consolidated. A competent penologist was appointed to head Angola. The parole board was revamped and Long's Alcoholic Beverage Control Board abolished. Another measure provided that all public boards had to transact their "final and binding actions" in open session.

As a reaction to past abuses, a constitutional amendment was enacted which required an affirmative vote by three-fourths of each legislative chamber in order to appropriate funds at special sessions called by outgoing governors within a stipulated time period before and after the gubernatorial primaries. Voting machines were made mandatory for all precincts, the state to bear the costs, while permanent registration was authorized for Orleans, East Baton Rouge, and Caddo. And at long last, poll-commissioner assistance to illiterate voters was prohibited, based upon the passage of a companion measure which required that each candidate's name on a ballot bear a number.

In view of the high proportion of the state budget allocated to public welfare functions, public inspection of the state welfare rolls was provided for, and the requirements for receipt of old-age pensions were slightly tightened to deny eligibility to those who sold or transferred title to their real property in the five-year period prior

---

[55] These reforms, pledged by Kennon during his campaign, were central to his program of reducing the power of the governor. The administrative workability and political accountability of the citizen boards, however, were equally important considerations to which Kennon gave inadequate attention.

to their applications for the purpose of qualifying for old-age assistance. Symptomatic of Louisiana's coming of age were the establishment of a Legislative Council and the enactment of a home-rule
constitutional amendment permitting cities to vote themselves home-
rule charters. Other important measures failed of passage, such as
legislative reapportionment, a split legislative session, and a stock-
fence law, but on the whole the anti-Long Legislature, by its own
action or in co-operation with Kennon, had performed well. The
voters apparently agreed in that judgment for a large majority endorsed all thirty-four constitutional amendments in the election of
November, 1952.

A regrouping of political forces occasioned by the presidential
election of 1952 shattered the factional tranquillity under Kennon.
Leading an uninstructed delegation to the Democratic National Convention in late July, the Governor voiced stubborn resentment
against an imposition of a loyalty oath upon constituent state delegations and refused to pledge his support to the national ticket.[56]
Senator Russell Long, on the other hand, dramatically broke with
the delegation, declared his willingness to sign the party oath, and
later endorsed the Stevenson-Sparkman ticket. Meeting in late August,
the Louisiana Democratic State Central Committee, unlike 1948,
blessed the national party ticket with the state party emblem of the
rooster, but warned that its action conveyed no positive endorsement
of either the Democratic ticket or its platform. At the same time, a
Perez-backed motion was defeated which would have sanctioned a
third-ticket device under which the voter could stamp the ballot for
Republican presidential electors and for Democratic state and Congressional candidates.

In early September, Kennon announced for Eisenhower, citing
Truman's Fair Deal and corruption and Stevenson's pronouncements
on tidelands oil, on F.E.P.C., and on the Senate filibuster as inimical
to Southern and Louisiana interests. The Louisiana Republican party,
recently rejuvenated from a patronage club status by the "new
guard" leadership of John Minor Wisdom, happily accepted a

---

[56] For a fuller account of the relations between Louisiana and national Democrats, consult Paul T. David, Malcolm Moos, and Ralph M. Goldman (eds.),
Presidential Nominating Politics in 1952, Vol. III, *The South* (Baltimore, 1954),
278–87; L. Vaughn Howard and David R. Deener, *Presidential Politics in Louisiana, 1952*, Tulane Studies in Political Science, Vol. I (New Orleans, 1954).

partnership with Kennon under which it withdrew its Congressional candidates. Perez, other Dixiecrat elements of 1948, and Dudley LeBlanc rallied in support of Eisenhower. Although the *Times-Picayune* could never bring itself to take the fateful step of deserting the Democratic party, its sympathies were clearly with the Republican ticket. In contrast to 1948, the national party candidates did not lack influential support: Earl Long; senators Long and Ellender; all Louisiana congressmen; the Choctaws; Lige Williams and organized labor; organized Negro groups; and the New Orleans *Item* openly backed Stevenson. Mayor Morrison, anxious to alienate neither his reform nor his lower-class backing, repeated his neutral performance of 1948.

Table 28 reports the results of the presidential election of November 4. The six most-urban parishes cast 50.5 per cent of the total vote and went 50.6 per cent for the Democrats; the rest of the state went 55.1 per cent Democratic. That margin of difference between urban and non-urban areas suggests a possible linkage with state bifactionalism which further investigation bears out.

TABLE 28. The Louisiana Vote in the Presidential Election of 1952

	Orleans	Other	State	% State	Parishes Carried by Majority
Stevenson (Dem.)	89,999	255,028	345,027	52.9	49
Eisenhower (Rep.)	85,572	221,353	306,925	47.1	15
Total	175,571	476,381	651,952	100.0	64

SOURCE: computed from *World Almanac* (1954), 593–94.

Comparison of relative parish response to Stevenson (Figure 13) with that to Spaht (Figure 12) and to the Dixiecrats (Figure 11) yields the results indicated in Table 29. It will be seen that a signifi-

TABLE 29. Bifactionalism in Presidential Politics: the Distribution of Parishes in Stevenson's Highest and Lowest Quartiles, 1952, for Spaht (1952) and for the Dixiecrats (1948)

Sixteen Parishes in	No. of Parishes in Each Quartile of Support			
	High	2nd	3rd	Low
Highest Stevenson Quartile, for Spaht	10	4	2	0
Lowest Stevenson Quartile, for Dixiecrats	9	2	3	2
Lowest Stevenson Quartile, for Spaht	2	0	3	11
Highest Stevenson Quartile, for Dixiecrats	2	2	6	6

SOURCE: Figures 11, 12, 13.

cant relationship exists between the centers of support and opposition in the presidential election of 1952 and those in both the gubernatorial runoff primary of 1952 and the presidential election of 1948, but the former provides the stronger correlation of the two.[57]

Stevenson's victory thus highlighted the persistence of those basic

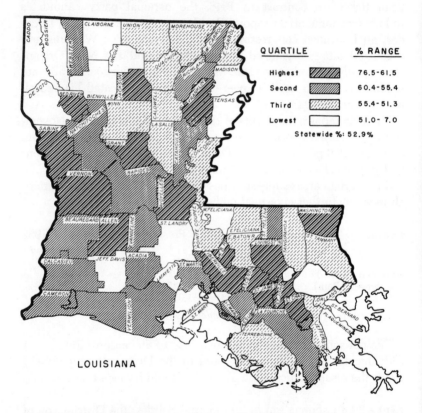

FIGURE 13. Quartile map: proportion of parish vote cast for Stevenson-Sparkman electors, presidential election of 1952.

SOURCE: same as that for Table 28.

[57] For more detailed analyses of the presidential election of 1952 in Louisiana, see Rudolf Heberle and Perry H. Howard, "An Ecological Analysis of Political Tendencies in Louisiana: The Presidential Elections of 1952," *Social Forces*, XXXII (May, 1954), 344–50; Howard and Deener, *Presidential Politics in Louisiana, 1952*, 91–97; Donald S. Strong, "The Presidential Election in the South, 1952," *Journal of Politics*, XVII (August, 1955), 359–60.

political tendencies which underlay the development and crystalliza-
tion of Louisiana bifactionalism. If two-party politics is to come to
Louisiana, more than likely it will stem from the stubborn cleavage
within the Democrats which can provide each party with its core
of supporters and its fixed directions of policy.

CHAPTER 9

The character of recent Louisiana politics

THE PRINCIPAL HAZARD for one who would understand Longite Louisiana is a quick dismissal of the last three decades of state politics as the product of a dictatorial demagogue whose political fortunes rested on the gullibility and ignorance of the citizenry. A politics of class protest which in turn developed a structured politics of deep meaning has been the basic theme of this study: ante-bellum dirt farmers, the Populists, Huey and Earl Long were integral parts of that movement.

Compared to the factional chaos of some other Southern states, recent Louisiana politics has been distinguished by a cohesive bifactionalism and by the dominance of the governor in state politics, both of which were due in some measure to the operation of a "ticket" system comparable to the practice of party slates in two-party states. As a consequence of a well-organized politics, electoral mandates have been translated into enacted programs, and the product of Longite politics, logically enough, has reflected rural liberalism.

The clarity of recent politics, quite remarkable for a one-party system, has led to the claim that Louisiana's bifactionalism is " 'just the same damn thing' as a two-party system."[1] An intensive examination of the validity of that judgment serves both as a systematic analysis of Louisiana politics and as a beginning answer to the question of the extent to which bifactional rivalry can serve as a democratic alternative to two-party competition. It should be noted, however, that few investigations as yet have been undertaken which attempt to measure the degree to which the assumptions and claims made on behalf of the two-party system in the United States have been realized in the actual operation of the varieties of competitive

---

[1] An observation of Louisiana local politicians as quoted by Key, *Southern Politics,* 168.

party politics existent. It would follow that some of the general conclusions reached here on the *relative* inadequacies of Louisiana's bifactionalism are subject to revaluation subsequent to further analyses of the politics of two-party states.

Bifactional loyalties of the voters

The sound and fury of Longite politics had sufficient substantive meaning to provide Louisiana with a well-organized politics of rational interest-voting. Huey's program and performance vitalized state politics and created a conscious, persistent bifactionalism. The voting strength of the two major factions came from distinct groups, each of which displayed a continuity of political attitudes going back to the muted class conflicts of the previous century. The basic cleavages among the voters appeared to be closely related to the antagonisms between city and rural dwellers and to those between dirt farmers and wealthier planters.

The centers of Long and anti-Long strength, as displayed in the maps in this study, have been determined by application of the simple statistical technique of a quartile ranking of parishes by the proportion of the vote each cast for the Long candidate. Figure 14 summarizes the results obtained for eight selected primaries from 1928 through 1952.[2] Those forty-eight of the state's sixty-four parishes which placed in either the upper or lower half of all parishes in at least six of the eight primaries are considered to comprise the core areas, respectively, of Longism and anti-Longism.

The heart of Longism lay in the cut-over uplands of northern and west-central Louisiana, populated by relatively few Negroes and by many poorer white farmers. In addition, sparsely settled Cameron Parish, at the southwestern tip of the state, and the bossed parishes of St. Bernard and Plaquemines, in the southeast, nearly always accorded Long candidates relatively high support. Several of the sugar-growing parishes in south Louisiana also have backed the Longs, although not as intensively as the upland regions. The rural

[2] The eight primary elections selected are:

1928 Gub., Huey	1944 Lt. Gub., 2nd, Earl
1930 Sen., Huey	1948 Gub., 2nd, Earl
1936 Gub., Leche	1948 Sen., Russell
1940 Gub., 2nd, Earl	1952 Gub., 2nd, Spaht

class basis of bifactionalism could be observed most clearly within those parishes which contained both plantation and hill-farming lands, in which pro-Longism increased as the fertility of the soil decreased. Evidence was available even on a parish basis, as in the case of the northeast Delta, where the influx of white farmers from

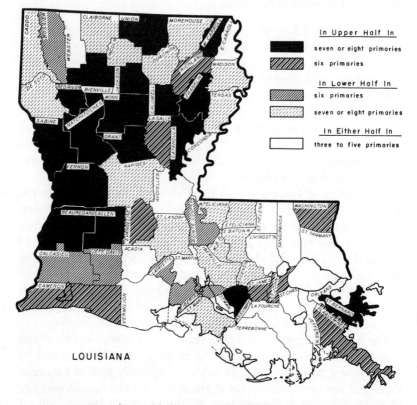

FIGURE 14. Core areas of Longism and anti-Longism: parishes consistently in upper or lower half of all parishes ranked according to proportion of parish vote cast for Long candidates in eight selected primary elections, 1928-1952.

SOURCE: Figures 3, 4, 6, 7, 9, 10, 12, and, for Earl Long's runoff primary race for lieutenant governor, *Compilation of Primary Election Returns of the Democratic Party, State of Louisiana*, elections held January 18 and February 29, 1944, issued by Secretary of State. See footnote 2 for a listing of the eight primary elections selected.

neighboring states diluted the once-high anti-Longism of East Carroll and Concordia. The political success of Longism thus lay in its ability to capture and reinforce the allegiance of those rural groups which twice before had embarked vainly upon a politics of protest.

The core areas of persistent anti-Long sentiment encompassed the urban parishes, Orleans excepted, the plantation areas of the upper Mississippi and Red River deltas, West and East Feliciana, and most of the Sugar Bowl parishes. That even small-scale urbanism and anti-Longism went hand in hand may be shown by an examination of the voting behavior of wards containing the parish seats in fifty-three parishes (Table 30). Conservative urbanites thus were the allies of planters and well-to-do farmers in common opposition to Longism, a combination of political forces that continued the pattern of nineteenth-century politics.

TABLE 30. The Persistence of Anti-Longism in Lesser Urban Areas: Quartile Position of Support of Longism of Fifty-Three Urban Wards Containing Parish Seats Among All Wards of the State, in Selected Democratic Primary Elections, 1928–1952*

Long Candidate and Primary Election	No. of Wards in Each Quartile of Support			
	High	2nd	3rd	Low
Huey Long, 1928, Gov.	1	9	27	16
Earl Long, 1940, Gov., 2nd	4	8	19	22
Earl Long, 1944, Lt. Gov., 2nd	2	7	20	24
Russell Long, 1948, Sen.	3	4	13	33
Carlos Spaht, 1952, Gov., 2nd	6	10	17	20

*The major urban parishes of Orleans, East Baton Rouge, Caddo, and Jefferson and the bossed parishes of Plaquemines and St. Bernard have been omitted. In addition, the seats of the following parishes were not incorporated areas and therefore were omitted: St. Charles, St. James, St. John, Cameron, and Livingston.

SOURCE: for the 1948 primary, unpublished election data on file at the office of the Secretary of State of Louisiana; for the other primaries, the appropriate *Compilation of Primary Election Returns of the Democratic Party, State of Louisiana.*

An informal investigation undertaken by the writer with the cooperation of respondents in every parish affirms the prevalence of interest-voting and the existence of meaningful bifactionalism in recent Louisiana politics. Analysis of the ward data in primary elections from 1928 to 1952 revealed that, in many parishes, one or several wards consistently were stronger or weaker in support of

Longism than was the parish. In an effort to secure an explanation for the political behavior of such wards, questionnaires were sent to veteran parish officials whose offices were subject to little turnover. Some of the more enlightening replies are quoted below, exactly as received. The discussion of the more pro-Long ward or wards is listed first, followed by that of the more anti-Long ward. Perhaps worthy of special note is the bias against Longism evident in many of the comments—most of the officials queried resided in small urban areas.

Avoyelles
". . . the First Ward . . . is somewhat like the parishes of North Louisiana, inasmuch as it is mostly cut-over-pine-land of poor productivity. . . ."
"The Tenth Ward is the most industrialized ward of the parish. With its rich alluvial soil, gas, oil wells, carbon plants and other industries, makes the standard of living much higher than the First Ward. . . ."

Beauregard
"Ward 7—cut over land—and farming—many people have *quit farming* to get on *welfare.*"
"Ward 3—(DeRidder). Industrial ward—smaller percentage on *welfare,* generally better educated, and do not swallow quite as much Long propaganda."

Bossier
"Ward 4 is an upland Ward and has very few resident taxpayers, in fact since the homestead exemption law, I doubt if there is 25 resident tax payers in the ward. . . ."
"Ward 1, being a Red River bottom area exclusively, and made up of principally large land owners, are not too easily let into a political talespin, falling for all the promises of tax exemptions etc. They know that when tax money is spent that somebody is paying the bill."

Caddo
"Ward 3. People of modest means reside in this ward, many of them tenant-farmers or operators of small mercantile establishments. A large number are on the welfare rolls. Ward 9. This ward has, perhaps, a larger per capita showing of white indigents than any other ward of the parish. It has always been pro-Long in its political attitude. . . ."
"Ward 1. This ward lies within the area having the richest soil of any part of Caddo parish. Most of the businessmen and agricul-

turalists are well-to-do, speaking in general terms, there being but few white tenant farmers within the ward. Practically none of the white residents are on the welfare rolls."

East Carroll

"Ward 7 is comprised of a majority of small white farmers, having most of their State, Parish, School and Levee Taxes paid for by the Homestead exemption. They and their leaders have come in here since the threat of Mississippi River overflows has diminished. They were rapped up in Houey Long and all that he stood for. No town in that Ward, just a community has built up around the school."

"Ward 3. This Ward is made up mostly of the Town of Lake Providence. Here is where practically all the independent or anti-Long people reside and vote. These people are independent making their own living without handouts, subsidies, and all other gifts and are on the rugged individual type. A group of fairly large plantation owners live in town and do a lot to shape the opinion of the vote. It is not one or two leaders but a sizable group who think and feel alike."

Morehouse

"Ward 9 is of small population, poor soil area, and the people have consistently followed one political leadership. That leader has always been aligned with the Long faction and what he says pretty well goes. No improvement is shown in way of living and are more or less set in their one way of thinking and living."

"Ward 6 comprises a plantation area of parish and a population of people who pretty well think for themselves. They are people who improve themselves and way of living."

St. Charles

"Ward 4 is on the west side—not industrialized and people are life-long residents of parish. Are more inclined to follow the parish administration."

"Ward 3 is on the east side of the parish. It is the location of the Shell Oil refinery, Katy Terminal and carshop—highly industrialized. Many voters are from out of the parish and the state."

Terrebonne

"In Ward 10 there are small *individual* landowners as voters."
"In Ward 2 there are large landowners as voters."

West Carroll

"Ward 2 is a rural Ward; Ward 4 has in it the town of Oak Grove. It is well-known that the greatest number of Long votes were from the country. Oak Grove is the Parish site of West Carroll Parish. There were some strong supporters of the Long faction in Oak Grove, but just not as many of them as there were in the more rural wards."

The general pattern of urban antipathy to Longism should not obscure the fact that organized labor, predominantly urban, has tended to be pro-Long. Labor's claims of political power, however, contained more boast than reality, so that increasing industrialism in Louisiana does not necessarily signify an increase in the potential of pro-Long votes in the cities.

Organized labor in Louisiana has been handicapped in its growth by the nature of the state's industrial economy, with particular reference to such factors as the inadequate development of secondary industry, the raw-material orientation of much of the state's manufacturing and its high proportion of rural workers, the concentration of wage-earners in medium-size plants, the rural heritage of many non-agricultural workers, and the presence of Negroes in the industrial labor force.[3] The membership of organized labor was concentrated in urban areas; in 1948, for example, 153 of the 170 state AFL unions represented at the annual state convention came from Alexandria, Baton Rouge, New Orleans, Bogalusa, Lake Charles, Monroe, and Shreveport. Union membership figures relative to potential membership were not prepossessing: in 1949, about 110,000 workers were members of either the AFL, the CIO, or of an independent union, a figure which represented 18 per cent of the non-agricultural work force.[4]

Even this numerically weak labor movement had its traditional conflict between the AFL and the CIO. The former, larger in size and greater in political power, expended much of its energies in personalized patronage politics in which victory was conceived in terms of placing AFL men in certain state labor posts. "Friendly" labor appointments were deemed satisfactory substitutes for the formulation of a positive labor program. This short-sighted view was partly responsible for the failure to correct the inadequacies of state policy in the fields of minimum wages, child labor, and workmen's compensation. One student of Southern labor, with reference to the

[3] An able analysis of Louisiana trade-unionism is that of A. S. Freedman, "Social Aspects of Recent Labor Growth in Louisiana," unpublished Master's thesis, Louisiana State University, Baton Rouge, 1950.
[4] Ibid., 156.

prewar period, ranked Louisiana's performance as medium for the South and medium-to-low for the nation.[5]

Organized labor has participated openly in state politics only recently, and then with mixed success and failure. In 1937, the State Federation of Labor called upon its members to contribute one dollar apiece for the purpose of "protecting ourselves in the Legislature and for electing our friends to public office."[6] In 1940, the State Federation supported Earl Long's gubernatorial candidacy over the protest of many locals against such active partisanship,[7] and Sam Jones, after his victory, pointedly remarked to a labor convention, "Keep your organization out of politics."[8] Brought together in common opposition to anti-labor measures proposed in the 1946 regular session of the Legislature, the rival labor confederations jointly supported Earl Long in 1948 but failed subsequently to unseat the seven congressmen who had voted for the passage of the Taft-Hartley Act in 1947 or to defeat Senator Ellender.[9] Labor was split in its endorsements in the 1952 gubernatorial primaries, with some backing going to Spaht, Dodd, Boggs, and LeBlanc.

The pro-Long tendencies of the officials of organized labor reflected no deep resentment of Jones, Davis, or Mayor Morrison of New Orleans. Labor's moderate demands ran no more counter to reformism than to Long's rural liberalism. Through 1952 at least, no faction had ever suppressed or persecuted Louisiana labor, which in itself accounted in good part for the inability of unions to marshall a united bloc of votes. In the absence of external attack, there has been no solidification of a labor vote as such. As one close observer of Louisiana labor related to the author, "The white labor vote is hardly ever a bloc vote. Labor solidarity tends to increase only if there is a labor issue in the campaign. In the 1948 state election, by way of example, while Earl secured 66 per cent of the state's vote,

[5] Addison T. Cutler, "Labor Legislation in Thirteen Southern States," *Southern Economic Journal*, vii (January, 1941), 314–15.

[6] From the address of President Lige Williams of the State Federation of Labor, *Proceedings of the Louisiana State Federation of Labor*, Thirty-Sixth Annual Convention (1948), shorthand transcription printed by Earle J. Christenberry, New Orleans, 383.

[7] New Orleans *Times-Picayune*, December 12, 13, 1939.

[8] Baton Rouge *State-Times*, April 4, 1940.

[9] Both Long and Ellender supported passage of the Taft-Hartley bill and voted to override the President's veto; Sixth District Congressman Morrison did not vote on the bill.

labor probably went about 80 per cent for Long. But if a vital labor issue is absent from the campaign, and the state divides 55–45 per cent, then labor would do well to divide 60–40 per cent."

The special case of the Negro

In contrast to labor, the Negro's recent participation in state politics has introduced a most cohesive bloc vote. The reasons, of course, lie in the depressed status of the Negro and in the history of white treatment of the Negro in racial terms without regard to class distinctions. No basic alteration of the preceding judgment is required by the notation that the Louisiana Negro's lot probably was better than that of Negroes in other deep South states.[10] Louisiana politicians, for example, did not usually resort to "nigger-baiting" in campaigns, and the Negro's share in the social service programs of Louisiana was high. Politically, the Louisiana Negro was impotent from 1898 until the late 1940's, when federal Supreme Court decisions began to be translated into tangible racial gains. In October, 1951, the Democratic State Central Committee belatedly dropped the requirement that a voter or candidate in party primaries "shall be a white person," and substituted, "he shall be registered as a member of the Democratic party."

Urban Negroes constituted nearly two-thirds of the 108,096 Negro registered voters in the state as of October, 1952. Eighteen parishes had no Negro registered voters in January, 1952; by October, 1954, that number was down to four, consisting of the three Delta parishes of Madison, Tensas, and East Carroll, and West Feliciana, possessed of a tight political organization headed by Sheriff Teddy Martin. White fears that Negroes would rush the registration offices, however, have not been realized: in October, 1952, Negroes comprised only 10.2 per cent of the total of registered voters, a figure which represented less than 25 per cent of the Negro voting-age population, in contrast to 82 per cent of the white voting-age population who were registered to vote. Negro leaders uniformly reported to

[10] In the November, 1954, general election, for example, a constitutional amendment designed to maintain racial segregation in the public schools in circumvention of the desegregation ruling of the United States Supreme Court was endorsed by a majority of voters in every parish. The total state vote on the amendment was 217,992 to 46,929.

this writer in early 1952 that racial apathy, not overeagerness, was
their main obstacle to more effective political action. The October,
1954, data bear out that judgment: there were 118,183 Negro registered voters, representing 13.6 per cent of the total of registered
voters.[11]

TABLE 31. Factional Loyalties of Louisiana Negroes in the 1952
Democratic Gubernatorial Primaries, for Seventeen Precincts
in Eight Parishes

Parish, Ward and Precinct	Negro % of Reg. Voters	First Primary Spaht % (or others) of Precinct Vote		Second Primary Spaht % of Precinct Vote
Acadia, VI, 6	98%	87%		94%
Caddo, IV, 43	66	17	(Boggs, 41%; Parker, 30%)	93
Calcasieu				
VII, 5	100	93		96
VI, 4	67	26	(Dodd, 18%; McLemore, 16%)	70
III, 4	71	15	(Dodd, 34%; Boggs, 17%)	75
Jefferson, VIII, 13	98	6	(Boggs, 81%)	22
St. John, I, 1	78	89		87
Rapides				
I, 5	69	70		80
I, 22	86	80		92
East Baton Rouge				
I, 4	72	35	(Dodd, 29%; Boggs, 18%)	80
I, 29	84	36	(Dodd, 26%; Boggs, 26%)	87
I, 42	88	44	(Dodd, 30%; Boggs, 16%)	89
Orleans				
II, 8	82	43	(Boggs, 40%)	74
V, 5	91	33	(Boggs, 43%)	69
VII, 18	93	10	(Boggs, 61%)	54
X, 17	94	25	(Boggs, 54%)	76
XI, 13	84	22	(Boggs, 50%)	67

SOURCE: registration data for Orleans and East Baton Rouge from personal
examination of registration records; remaining registration data through correspondence with parish registrars of voters. Since precinct registation figures are
not published, it is not known what proportion of the state's "Negro precincts" is
represented by the seventeen precincts above on which adequate information was
obtained. Election data from *Compilation of Primary Election Returns of the
Democratic Party, State of Louisiana*, elections held January 15 and February 19,
1952, issued by the Secretary of State.

[11] The foregoing data are drawn from *Report of the Secretary of State to the
Governor of Louisiana*, 1953–54, and from two studies of the Public Affairs
Research Council of Louisiana, Inc.: "The Changing Louisiana Electorate,
1940–1952," *PAR Report* No. 5, January 14, 1952; "Louisiana Voter Participation in the November 4, 1952, Election," *PAR Report* No. 8, January 20, 1953.

White expectations that the Negro vote would tend to be a bloc vote have proven true. Table 31 shows the political behavior of seventeen precincts predominantly Negro in composition in the 1952 gubernatorial primaries. Realistic inferences can be made only in conjunction with a consideration of the workings of Negro political organizations and of parish politics in Louisiana. Because New Orleans is a special entity in Negro as well as in white politics, it will be accorded separate treatment.

Louisiana Negroes outside of New Orleans supported with near-unanimity the candidacies of Earl Long in 1948 and Russell Long in 1948 and 1950. The service-state philosophy of Longism, particularly as applied to old-age pensions and free hospital care, provided a partial explanation. In 1949–50, for example, 79,013 Negroes and 49,448 whites were admitted to the state's general hospitals for free in-patient services. Organized labor, influential in increasing Negro registration in some parishes, such as in the rice-mill sections of Acadia and the sugar-mill sections of St. John, also helped channel the Negro vote to the Longs. The relationship however has hardly been as close as one interviewee asserted: "Nine times out of ten, if Lige Williams [head of the State Federation of Labor] takes a stand for labor, the Negro vote follows." The apparent coolness of the Longs toward the Dixiecrat movement was yet another factor. Strangely enough, however, the core emotional appeal of Longism to the Negro lay in the fact that Huey Long was of heroic stature to them as well as to rural whites. Among the comments most frequently offered to this writer were that Huey never indulged in baiting the Negro nor excluded them from Share-Our-Wealth blueprints, and that he hired Negroes as highway laborers and Negro women as nurses for New Orleans Charity Hospital.

In the 1952 gubernatorial primary (see Table 31), the "liberal" candidacies of Spaht (Earl's man), Dodd (Earl's lieutenant-governor), and Boggs (a pro-Truman Congressman backed by Russell Long) met with Negro favor. The candidacy of Kermit Parker, a New Orleans Negro, enjoyed little Negro support. In the runoff primary, the Negro vote went largely to Spaht in spite of the apparent certainty of his defeat. Continued support of Spaht was viewed by Negro leaders as establishing the proposition that the Negro would keep faith with that white faction which kept faith with the Negro. Runoff-primary support of Kennon, it was urged, would lend cre-

dence to the charge that the Negro was so fickle in his political loyalties that his demands could be ignored by the major factions. At the
same time, token Negro groups declared for Kennon in order to
obligate the new administration to some extent to the Negro electorate. Organized labor also has used that technique, which is anala-
gous to that of contributions by business firms to the campaign chests
of all important state factions.

Negro support of Long has been less cohesive in those parishes
whose highly organized politics have introduced cross-loyalties which
discouraged a choice among competing state candidates simply on
the basis of past records and current pledges. In Jefferson Parish, for
example (see Table 31), Negroes supported Spaht in neither primary, preferring to follow the lead of Sheriff "King" Clancy, who
backed Boggs and then Kennon. The other Negro precincts in Table
31 which gave far less than a united vote to Spaht hailed from New
Orleans, where the rivalry of three Negro organizations illustrated
the conflicting pressures upon Negro loyalties.

The Progressive Voters League, with a peak membership of about
1,500 up to 1952, was more or less allied with the city reform administration, having supported Chep Morrison and Lafargue in 1950,
Boggs and Kennon in 1952. The People's Defense League, with a
mid-1952 membership of slightly less than 5,000, was wedded to the
Long state administration, having backed Long candidates in city
and state contests from 1948 through 1952. The League justified its
pro-Longism partly in terms of the strategic importance of the office
of the Orleans registrar of voters, a gubernatorial appointee, to the
political power of the Orleans Negro. It was generally understood,
for example, that Governor Long had encouraged Negro registration
in Orleans in 1948-49, only to encourage later a purging of the rolls,
when city Negroes voted predominantly for Morrison instead of
Zatarain in the mayoralty election of early 1950.

The third Negro group was the Crescent City Independent Voters
League, whose leader was the president of Local 1419 of the Long-
shoreman's Union, and which was formed ostensibly in protest
against the support of Lafargue in the 1950 Senate primary by the
Progressive Voters League. As of mid-1952, more than 80 per cent
of the Negro union's 3,500 members were registered voters. With a
base of power independent of politics, the organization's leaders
have been the most free-wheeling, backing Mayor Morrison and

Russell Long in 1950, Dodd and Spaht in 1952. Although at odds in parish and state politics, the three rival groups have worked together for the national Democratic party: the five Orleans precincts cited in Table 31 gave from 89 to 94 per cent of the vote to Stevenson in 1952.

As illustrated by the competition for racial leadership in New Orleans, the pro-Long tendencies of Negro voters were not a function of any integrated statewide organization. The bulk of the Negro vote was marshalled by separate local organizations whose members, understandably enough, were bound together by a high degree of caste and class consciousness. Past Negro support of the Longs, after all, made such good interest-voting sense as to justify the comment of one informant that Louisiana Negro leadership had not as yet (1952) been tested because of the natural gravitation of the Negro vote to the Longs.

On the basis of their record through 1952, it would seem fair to conclude that Negroes were not wedded indissolubly either to the Long faction or to labor. Rather, Negro groups were loyal to the pursuit of certain racial and class goals the achievement of which required, in their view, a maximization of their political power through bloc voting. A Negro organization's endorsement of a candidate was preceded usually by a searching interrogation of all candidates and was concluded usually by the striking of a *quid pro quo* agreement with the endorsee. By avoiding fixed factional alignments and by maintaining honest leadership, Negro groups could place themselves in a flexible and strategic fashion within the state's bifactionalism. In the 1952 gubernatorial runoff, for example, Baton Rouge Negroes supported Spaht but endorsed Kennon-aligned Percy Roberts for the state Legislature. Again, in the 1950 New Orleans mayoralty, some Negro groups aligned with Morrison, but they denied support to Criminal Sheriff John Grosch, who ran for renomination on the Morrison city ticket.

Among the major problems facing the Negro in Louisiana politics are the recency of his acquisition of the power to vote and the battle for racial leadership among ambitious competitors. In New Orleans, through 1952, mutual distrust among rival organizations had hampered unified action. It was significant also that none of the three city groups had established any working arrangements of consequence with Negro organizations in other parishes. The competition for leadership at times produced reckless actions: Negro candidates for the state Legislature were entered in Orleans in 1952, and Kermit Parker's gubernatorial candidacy was interpreted by some as his dramatic bid for leadership of city Negroes.[12] One informant soberly predicted to this writer, "Negro political leadership will not be dependable until leaders are economically independent of politics, jobs, and bribes."

Another problem which might have been expected to arise had not materialized by 1952. Negro bloc voting for the Long faction had not evoked (overt) hostile reaction on the part of white politicians. A cynical explanation would stress the natural reluctance of officeseekers to alienate large, cohesive blocs of voters, particularly in the wide-open melee of the first primary. A glance at Table 31 is instructive in this connection in terms of the number of candidates supported by various groups of Negroes. More important, the Negro's entry into politics has been smoothed by the over-all moderation of his demands and by his failure to storm registrars' offices or to insist upon a pro rata racial allotment of parish posts. Finally, and perhaps most crucially, the Negro bloc vote was not a decisive factor in the lopsided gubernatorial primaries of 1948 and 1952 nor in those of 1950, in which Mayor Morrison and Senator Russell Long were renominated. If it should occur that the Louisiana Negro consistently becomes a balance of power in state bifactionalism comparable to his role in the 1952 presidential campaign, then very likely both Negro demands and white reaction may undergo sharp change. In the initial transitional phase from 1948 to 1952, however, the bloc vote of the Negro has been accommodated without much friction within the Democratic politics of bifactional Louisiana.

Rural liberalism

It was not only the vituperativeness of Huey's campaigns which accounted for the sharp increase in voter turnout during and after

[12] In no ward in Orleans, in March, 1952, did Negroes comprise as much as one-third of the total of registered voters. Consequently a Negro candidate would have to secure extra-racial backing to win, unless there were several major competing white entrants. The running of Negro candidates was justified by some informants as a necessary maneuver to increase Negro registration and voting, by others it was viewed as a reflection of inter-organizational Negro rivalry. A few informants believed that Earl Long might have sponsored Parker's candidacy in an effort to cut into the Negro vote for Boggs in New Orleans.

his term of office.[18] The sound and fury of politics signified something, namely a pursuit of rural liberalism which marked the administrations of the Kingfish and brother Earl as the same broad movement of class protest. Longism's advocacy of policies benefiting lower-class agrarians took several forms, including positive aid, protection from attack, and hostility to pro-urban programs and urban governmental ideologies.

Of direct aid to the poorer rural whites were homestead tax exemptions and gasoline tax exemptions for the commercial use of boats and tractors. To avoid stigmatizing public aid programs as "pauperism," the Longs retained lenient eligibility requirements for free hospital care and instituted a free school lunch program, available to all regardless of need. State employment of dental trailers, of a free ambulance service, and of a contract hospital system enabled even the most isolated farmer to make use of public medical facilities. The expanding highway network benefited all citizens, while equal state payments to each parish for road purposes obviously gave relatively greater aid to the rural sections. State assistance was forthcoming also to those poorer parishes which were unable to raise a specified minimum of revenues through taxation or were unable to support an adequate public educational system.

Examples of Longite protection of rural interests from attack range from Huey's fight against tick-eradication bills to Earl's hostility to a stock-fence law, to drivers' license laws, and to a uniform automobile financial responsibility measure. The other side of Longism's dedication to rural liberalism was its antipathy to the fostering of urban programs. Appropriate examples would include the failure to obey the constitutional mandate to reapportion the Legislature every ten years and a distaste for good-government measures reflecting the urban-business mentality, such as those dealing with voting machines, statewide planning to attract industry, civil service, and administrative reorganization.

The Longite assaults on urban areas, in particular, underscored the inadequate legal protection given to municipalities by the Constitution and their fiscal plight during the period of recent politics. Financially, the municipalities were the step-children of the state:

---

[18] Consult Key, *Southern Politics,* 523–24, for a statistical analysis of voter turnout.

a legislative commission observed in 1946 that "the State has given no aid whatever to our municipal governments."[14] To make matters worse, under the Constitution and laws of the state, the tax income of municipalities was specifically limited, and the Legislature not infrequently imposed additional burdens upon city governments, such as setting minimum wages for firemen. The consequence was, as the Louisiana Municipal Association stated in 1945, "there is not a city in Louisiana that has sufficient funds from its general and license taxes to properly supply the normal functions of municipal government."[15] Since 1946, however, progress has been made. Municipalities have come in for a share of abundant state revenues since the latter half of the Davis administration. Shreveport, Baton Rouge, and New Orleans currently possess home-rule charters, and a general home-rule constitutional amendment was endorsed by the voters in late 1952. Home rule, of course, is a means rather than a solution. Nevertheless, it is a sign of Louisiana's political maturity that henceforth cities will work out their problems freer from legislative interference than in the past.

The financial costs of Longite liberalism were high, particularly for a relatively poor state such as Louisiana. The presentation of comparative state data in support of that conclusion, however, is a complex business. The customary figures take into account neither the type or quality of services rendered nor the fact that in some jurisdictions local governments perform functions which elsewhere are the province of state governments. In Louisiana, for example, the state maintains a higher proportion of total road mileage than do most other states, monopolizes the fields of public welfare and public hospital care, and expends a greater proportion of its revenues for state aid to local governments.

However, while the following figures may err in the particular rank-position assigned to Louisiana, the general conclusion of the high cost of Longite liberalism relative to the income of the state's citizens is more than amply supported. Compared to other states, Louisiana ranked (in 1949) thirty-ninth in per-capita income payments to individuals ($1,002), and (in fiscal 1949–50) third in per-

[14] Louisiana Revenue Code Commission, *Preliminary Report* (1946), 149.
[15] Legislative Committee of the Louisiana Municipal Association, "A Statement to the Revenue Code Commission," *Louisiana Municipal Review,* viii (November-December, 1945), 138–39.

capita state government expenditures ($140.58). When the ratios of the two indices are ranked for all states, Louisiana had the highest ratio (13.98 per cent) of state government expenditure to income in the nation.[16] The state taxation and state debt rankings suggested by the foregoing data are borne out: Louisiana ranked (in fiscal 1949–50) first in per-capita state taxes[17] and (as of June 30, 1950) second in per-capita state debt.[18]

From 1940 to 1947, education, welfare, and highways, in that order, constituted the major expenditures of the state government of Louisiana. In fiscal 1948–49, the principal beneficiaries of Earl's expanded liberalism were the areas of welfare (30.9 per cent of state expenditures), schools (29.2 per cent), and highways (14.8 per cent). Indeed, Earl's benefits placed Louisiana in the ranks of the high-taxing and high-spending states as judged by absolute dollar figures as well as by per-capita ranking. By doubling highway and education payments and quadrupling welfare expenditures, Earl went through more than $1,300,000,000 of state and federal funds in his four years as governor, one and one-half times the total combined expenditures of the Jones and Davis administrations.

The time has come when Louisiana politicians will have to take a hard look at the long-term economic development of the state before embarking upon and extending programs which are as costly financially as they are popular politically. In devoting nearly one-third of its expenditures to the least productive element of the community, Louisiana, in 1949, led the nation with 80 per cent of those over 65 years of age on the old-age pension rolls.[19] And the past misappropriation of public funds tends to become fixed as governors make

[16] Public Affairs Research Council of Louisiana, Inc., "Comparison of State Government Expenditures, 1950," PAR Report, No. 2, June 29, 1951. The reaction to this PAR report included some argument over the propriety of including, for comparative purposes, certain items within state government expenditures—see the letter of J. H. Rester, State Commissioner of Administration, New Orleans Times-Picayune, July 11, 1951. The Times-Picayune editorial of July 12, 1951, after discussing the controversy, concluded that the central finding remained valid, namely, "the Louisiana government spends far more in proportion to the income of the people than any other state."

[17] As reported by the Tax Foundation, Inc., and reprinted in the New Orleans Times-Picayune, December 28, 1951.

[18] Public Affairs Research Council of Louisiana, Inc., "The Debt of the Louisiana State Government, 1950 and 1951," PAR Report, No. 6, March 31, 1952.

[19] New Orleans Bureau of Governmental Research, "The Old Age Assistance Program in Louisiana," State Problems, No. 10, June 27, 1949, 4.

RECENT LOUISIANA POLITICS

their taxes palatable and pressure groups safeguard their legislative gains by assigning revenues from specified taxes to enumerated purposes, as, for example, the yield of the sales tax to payment of old-age pensions. The practical effect of the drive of interest groups to insulate their benefits from the vagaries of factional politics is to convert dedications to continuing appropriations, to hamstring both the governor and the Legislature in any serious attempt to re-direct the assignment of existent state funds. Louisiana citizens might recall that welfare politics, no less than do-nothingism, runs the risk of becoming dominated by the vested interests it creates and nurtures.

Personal followings and bifactionalism

Bifactional politics, to approach the organizational influence of a party system, should tend to discourage personal and localistic candidacies for governor which are unrelated to the state's political dualism. Certainly there ought not to be room in Louisiana's bipolarized factionalism to permit an allegedly "personal" leader to deliver his allegedly "personal" following to the support of the gubernatorial candidate of his choice in the runoff primary. Yet experienced Louisiana politicians do compete for the backing of one or more of the lesser leaders who are eliminated in the gubernatorial first primary. And V. O. Key has concluded that ". . . some [Louisiana] leaders have a following that can, at least at times, be voted fairly solidly for another candidate."[20] The question of the existence of transferable personal followings deserves the fullest exploration because of its crucial implications of the inadequacy of the one-party bifactional system.

The reader, perhaps, should be apprised of the statistical technique used in the analysis of this question, particularly for an informed reading of the next four tables. The capacity of a politician to deliver a personal following may be tested in those situations where a major candidate eliminated in the gubernatorial first primary declared his support for one of the two candidates in the runoff primary. Here one may examine the voting data with an eye to

[20] Key, Southern Politics, 173.

selecting all wards in which there was essentially a three-way race in the first primary, involving the two runoff candidates and the defeated candidate, whose alleged personal leadership is being tested. Inspection of the voting data for those wards for the second primary would permit conclusions about the distribution of the eliminated candidate's vote.

The above technique, with some minor refinements, underlies Tables 32–35 in this section. At least two important assumptions are made which reflect the fact that the distribution of the vote of the eliminated candidate cannot be gauged unless other things remain roughly equal from the first to the second primary. The assumptions are: (1) that virtually all the voters in the second primary voted in the first primary (for example, that 50,000 first-primary voters did not drop out to be replaced by an equal number who were voting for the first time in the second primary); and (2) that the voters who supported either of the two leading candidates in the first primary voted the same way in the second primary. Common sense and an indirect check of voting data suggest the reasonableness of both assumptions. The first assumption may be tested indirectly by inspection of the data in the third and fourth columns in the four tables which follow: the total gain in the ward vote for the runoff candidates in the second primary over the first should approximate the number of votes cast for the eliminated candidate in the first primary, making some allowance for the minimum ward vote for other candidates eliminated in the first primary.

The gubernatorial campaign of 1940 is the first state-office primary in recent Louisiana politics to meet the conditions required. It will be recalled that Earl Long (226,385 votes) and Jones (154,936) made the runoff, and in the interim between primaries Noe (116,564) declared his support of and actively stumped for Jones. James H. Morrison (48,243) and H. Vincent Moseley (7,595) also were eliminated in the first primary. In the second primary Jones defeated Long, 284,437 to 265,403 votes.

The runoff-primary distribution of Noe's first-primary vote may be gauged by isolating those wards in which Noe received more than 35 per cent of the first-primary vote, and Morrison and Moseley together less than 3 per cent of that vote, and in which more than 200 votes were cast in the first primary. Seventeen wards from thirteen parishes, located largely in north Louisiana, the section of Noe's

TABLE 32. The Transferability of Personal Followings: the Distribution of Noe's First-Primary Vote to Long and Jones in the Second Primary, 1940, for Selected Wards

Parish	Ward	Noe's % of First Primary Vote	Noe's First Primary Vote	Combined Jones-Long Gain in Second Primary over First	Jones's % of
				J-L Gain	J-L Gain
Caldwell	8	59.3%	128	139	59.0%
Catahoula	3	51.7	135	143	54.5
Jackson	5	50.5	112	100	72.0
Evangeline	5	48.0	557	506	81.3
Avoyelles	5	45.6	264	238	80.8
Winn	10	45.2	114	80	78.7
Grant	8	43.4	261	266	74.5
Webster	1	42.9	297	289	54.7
Rapides	10	40.1	502	537	79.9
West Carroll	5	39.9	237	257	71.0
Winn	8	39.4	145	142	98.7
Avoyelles	1	38.8	290	375	61.6
Bienville	7	37.7	163	192	66.7
Jackson	1	37.5	182	153	93.5
Allen	3	37.3	104	91	75.8
West Carroll	4	36.2	493	497	76.5
Beauregard	5	35.4	180	183	70.0
Total	---	-----	4,164	4,188	73.7%

SOURCE: computed from *Compilation of Primary Election Returns of the Democratic Party, State of Louisiana,* elections held January 16 and February 20, 1940, issued by the Secretary of State.

greatest support, meet the standards specified.[21] As a reading of Table 32 indicates, about three-quarters of Noe's first-primary voters transferred their support to Jones in the runoff, and the pro-Jones direction of the vote was common to each ward analyzed.

Before conclusions on the existence and deliverability of personal

[21] Two additional wards meet the qualifications of a three-cornered race and a high Noe vote but have not been included because they failed to meet the assumptions underlying use of the statistical technique here employed. In precinct 1 of ward 6 of Jefferson Parish, consisting of Barataria and Lafitte, the assumption of the constancy of Long voters from the first to the second primary was not valid. That precinct cast 434 votes for Long in the first primary and 204 votes for him in the runoff; 25 votes for Jones in the first primary and 737 for him in the runoff. Although further investigation would be required, such a voting pattern strongly suggests a tightly organized or bossed district. In ward 1 of Evangeline Parish, the assumption that the combined Jones-Long gain in the second primary over the first would approximate Noe's first-primary vote was not borne out—hence no estimate of the distribution of Noe's first-primary vote is possible in that case.

factions may be reached, however, it first must be ascertained
whether the Noe voters supported Jones because of Noe's leadership
or for some other reason.[22] An analysis of the runoff-primary distribution of Morrison's first-primary vote throws considerable light on that
problem. Table 23 includes all wards which gave Morrison more
than 40 per cent and Noe and Moseley combined less than 6 per cent
of the vote cast in the 1940 first primary. In Table 33, as in Tables 32
and 35, each of the wards chosen cast over 200 votes in the first
primary. Fourteen wards, located in eight parishes, meet the criteria
indicated.[23]

TABLE 33. The Transferability of Personal Followings: the
Distribution of Morrison's First-Primary Vote to Long and Jones
in the Second Primary, 1940, for Selected Wards

Parish	Ward	Morrison's % of First Primary Vote	Morrison's First Primary Vote	Combined Jones-Long Gain in Second Primary over First	
				J-L Gain	Jones's % of J-L Gain
Ascension	10	62.6%	634	582	74.6%
St. James	8	60.2	260	259	66.7
St. James	1	60.0	263	273	77.3
Livingston	6	56.8	368	397	68.7
St. James	2	55.6	148	152	69.1
Pointe Coupee	5	50.2	106	108	100.0
Pointe Coupee	7	49.5	140	138	88.4
St. James	9	47.8	505	530	67.0
Lafourche	6	47.1	154	182	74.7
St. John	4	43.7	340	351	77.7
Terrebonne	7	43.6	230	269	78.5
St. Charles	2	43.5	276	292	75.3
Terrebonne	5	42.4	112	112	86.6
St. John	5	42.2	365	360	73.1
Total	----	------	3,901	4,005	74.5%

SOURCE: computed from *Compilation of Primary Election Returns of the
Democratic Party, State of Louisiana,* elections held January 16 and February
20, 1940, issued by the Secretary of State.

[22] Using parish voting data and a somewhat different statistical technique,
Key, *Southern Politics,* 174–75, also concluded that Jones secured the bulk of
Noe's first-primary vote. Key's mistaken inference from that finding came from
failing to probe further in the manner undertaken in the text above.
[23] Ward 4 of St. Charles Parish also meets the criteria for inclusion, but the
returns from one of its two precincts were missing for the runoff, thus making a
comparison between the primaries impossible.

Morrison, like Noe, campaigned against Earl Long in the first primary. In sharp contrast to Noe, however, Morrison did not support Jones and even implied a personal preference for Earl Long before the runoff. Nevertheless, as worked out in Table 33, roughly the same proportion of Morrison's vote went to Jones as that uncovered for Noe's votes, and the Morrison vote in each of the wards studied also went in the same factional direction in the runoff.

Although the analysis of the distribution of Morrison's vote does not eliminate the possibility that Noe had a transferable personal following, it does render questionable any positive conclusions on the deliverability of Noe's voters when based solely on the data on Noe. In the light of recent Louisiana politics, it seems to this writer more reasonable to conclude that Noe had no personal following to deliver. There was nothing in his brief political career as state senator and acting governor which would account for the large country parish organization of over 100,000 votes imputed to his personal leadership. Another explanation of Noe's role in the 1940 primaries may be suggested. He was less the personal leader of a devoted following than the temporary product of transitory circumstance. His was the voice of those Longites outraged by the Long organization's betrayal of Huey and consequently hostile to Earl's candidacy. Their customary antipathy to an anti-Long candidate was muted by Jones's reiteration that his "pappy was for Huey" and by his pledge to retain and expand liberal governmental benefits. Under such conditions the majority of those who voted for Noe naturally gravitated to Jones; a better test of Noe's alleged factional headship would have occurred had he endorsed Earl Long for the runoff primary.

Another opportunity to test the proposition that some Louisiana politicians are able to control the votes of a deliverable personal following is offered by the events of the gubernatorial runoff primary of 1944, in which Davis defeated Morgan. Dudley LeBlanc had run unsuccessfully in the first primary on an anti-Jones plank, securing 40,392 votes concentrated, in a "friends and neighbors" fashion, in several Cajun parishes. Before the second primary, LeBlanc reversed his factional affiliation and came out for Davis.

A satisfactory measure of LeBlanc's influence may be had by examining parish data in those cases where LeBlanc secured about half the first-primary vote and all other candidates, not including Davis or Morgan, secured in combination a relatively small proportion of the vote. For the three parishes which pass those standards, the share of the first-primary vote going to candidates other than the three named was as follows: Vermilion, 6.4 per cent; Acadia, 8.3 per cent; Lafayette, 8.4 per cent. All of the first-primary vote for candidates other than LeBlanc, Davis, or Morgan is credited arbitrarily to Morgan for the runoff, thus giving LeBlanc every chance to prove possession of a deliverable following. (For example, in Vermilion Parish 783 votes were cast in the first primary for candidates other than the three indicated. Those 783 votes have been subtracted from the combined Davis-Morgan gain (8,299 votes) in the second primary over the first, yielding the figure 7,516 which appears in Table 34. Davis' share of the latter figure is then computed (50.0 per cent). This technique deliberately commits the error of assuming that all votes for other candidates in the first primary were cast for Morgan

TABLE 34. The Transferability of Personal Followings: the Distribution of LeBlanc's First-Primary Vote to Davis and Morgan in the Second Primary, 1944, for Selected Parishes

Parish	LeBlanc's % of First Primary Vote	LeBlanc's First Primary Vote	Combined Davis-Morgan Gain in Second Primary over First, Minus First-Primary Vote of All Candidates Other than Davis, Morgan, and LeBlanc	
			D-M Gain	Davis' % of D-M Gain
Vermilion	58.6%	7,172	7,516	50.0%
Acadia	55.7	5,829	5,880	54.9
Lafayette	47.3	5,260	5,869	50.2
Total		18,261	19,265	51.6%

SOURCE: computed from *Compilation of Primary Election Returns of the Democratic Party, State of Louisiana*, elections held January 18 and February 29, 1944, issued by the Secretary of State.

in the second primary. The effect is to isolate the LeBlanc vote and to credit LeBlanc for all of Davis' gain in the runoff).

Davis' share of LeBlanc's votes, as determined by the biased method described above, was less than the proportion of the total state vote he attracted (53.6 per cent). Thus Dudley LeBlanc, reputed king of the Cajuns, obviously had no deliverable following of any magnitude in 1944.

The 1948 gubernatorial campaign provides a third and final test of the existence of deliverable personal followings. Jimmie Morrison, the Choctaw candidate who competed with Earl Long for leadership of the Long faction, urged support for Sam Jones in the interim between primaries. The distribution of Morrison's vote in the runoff may be determined by the usual method, in this case by employing all wards in which the Kennon vote was less than 5 per cent and the Morrison vote more than 35 per cent in the first primary. Fifteen wards from seven parishes conform to those requirements. As indicated in Table 35, four out of every five Morrison voters supported Earl Long, not Jones, and the Longite direction of Morrison's vote held constant for each of the wards examined.[24]

The degree of deliverability of a personal following in recent

TABLE 35. The Transferability of Personal Followings: the Distribution of Morrison's First-Primary Vote to Long and Jones in the Second Primary, 1948, for Selected Wards

Parish	Ward	Morrison's % of First Primary Vote	Morrison's First Primary Vote	Combined Jones-Long Gain in Second Primary over First J-L Gain	Jones's % of J-L Gain
Livingston	5	82.1%	435	326	18.4%
Ascension	10	74.0	799	898	29.4
Livingston	6	72.3	578	522	19.2
Livingston	10	71.4	177	183	11.5
Tangipahoa	6	70.5	1,480	1,651	21.4
Livingston	3	70.2	377	378	17.2
Livingston	4	68.7	800	862	16.0
Tangipahoa	8	61.0	293	315	18.7
Iberville	8	60.7	458	455	10.3
Lafourche	6	58.6	529	559	24.0
St. Tammany	6	58.6	351	380	19.8
Livingston	8	58.0	188	195	29.7
Tangipahoa	5	56.4	562	595	16.5
St. John	6	54.5	316	351	11.4
Iberville	5	46.1	131	108	14.8
Total	....	......	7,474	7,778	19.5%

SOURCE: computed from *Compilation of Primary Election Returns of the Democratic Party, State of Louisiana,* elections held January 20 and February 24, 1948, issued by the Secretary of State.

[24] Key, *Southern Politics,* 174, footnote 34, noted Morrison's inability to deliver his following, but Key implied that the exception of Morrison helped prove the general rule of transferable followings by resorting to the following speculation: " . . . Morrison's 1948 vote consisted in considerable measure, not of his own following, but of support from the New Orleans 'Old Regular' organization, which further analysis would probably show was able in the second primary to deliver its vote against Jones, the ally of deLesseps Morrison, mayor of New

Louisiana politics has been subjected to three tests: anti-Jones LeBlanc (1944) and Longite Morrison (1948) could not commit their first-primary supporters to anti-Longism; while defecting Longite Noe (1940) merely activated defecting Longite voters in a natural anti-Long direction. The bifactionalism bequeathed by Huey Long to the state of Louisiana is too pervading to permit the existence of many purely personal followings. While the open procedures of the Democratic first primary invite the entrance of candidates other than the leaders of the two major factions, and "native-son" voting is not uncommon in the first primary, such candidacies are offered always with reference to bifactional politics. Noe ran on an anti-Long plank, Morrison as a Longite, and LeBlanc on an anti-Jones platform. Such third candidacies are those of competing Longite and anti-Long leaders, each of whom commands some local following in support of his personal and *factional* candidacy, a candidacy which represents persistent issues and attitudes over and above the attraction of personality. Indeed, the phrase "third candidacies" is quite misleading, for the purpose of the first primary is precisely to determine which of the rival factional leaders commands majority allegiance within each of the two major factions. It should not be overlooked that Louisiana's Democratic gubernatorial first primary apparently produces leaders of two opposing political groups no less regularly than do the party primaries in two-party states.

What are the comparative strengths of the competing pulls of personality and faction? Similar to a two-party system, Louisiana's bifactional system permits some play for personal loyalties. Morrison, for example, is assured of some votes on a "friends and neighbors" basis, regardless of whether he supports either or neither of the dominant factions. Such a truly personal following is, however, of minimal proportions because of the voters' greater concern with faction. Thus Morrison could not expect to attract anything like the same sources of localistic (Florida parishes) support in the same degree, irrespective of whether he allied himself with or against the Longites. When Morrison is pro-Long, many pro-Long voters in the

Orleans and foe of the 'Old Regulars.'" While the Orleans vote for Morrison behaved in the second primary as Key predicted, the fact remains that two-thirds of Morrison's vote (68,502 of 101,754 votes) came from parishes other than Orleans. It should be noted that Table 35 consists entirely of non-Orleans wards. Because of the dominant influence of the "old regulars" in city politics, no wards from Orleans have been included in the tables in this section.

Florida parishes will go along with native-son Morrison in the first primary rather than with a rival Longite candidate from another part of the state; proportionately much fewer of the anti-Longs in the region will do so.

Loyalty to the person of Morrison, therefore, far from being unconditional and blind, is conditional upon a more basic commitment to the factional system itself. Morrison's supporters in 1940 and in 1948, consonant with their primary allegiance to faction, moved consistently in the same factional direction in the first and second primary in bland disregard of the opposite factional tack taken by their "personal leader." Noe, in 1940, by asking his supporters to vote in the second primary for the candidate most of them were going to support anyway, merely created the illusion of a following both personal and deliverable. However, LeBlanc's performance in 1944 deviated somewhat from this pattern, thereby implying that his was a more likely example of personal leadership. But, in contradiction to LeBlanc's endorsement of Davis in the runoff primary, his first-primary supporters split almost evenly for both factions.

The practical conclusions for state politicians are obvious: neither Noe nor Morrison had true personal followings at all, and LeBlanc had but limited influence over his Cajun supporters.[25] There would be considerably less clamor in Louisiana about the frequency and evil of second-primary "sell-outs" if it were realized clearly that no leader to date had anything much to sell. The broader implication of the foregoing analysis is also clear: the fact that the runoff-primary influence of the losing candidate in the first primary is overshadowed by the orientation of his followers toward the bifactional system supports Louisiana's claim to possession of something like a two-party system.

The operation of the ticket system

Extensive employment by the major factions of the "ticket system," Louisiana's equivalent of party slates, together with a cohesive bifac-

---

[25] It would be relevant to note that reputed personal leadership virtually vanishes when the leader himself is not a candidate. In the 1952 gubernatorial first primary, for example, while non-candidate James Morrison stumped for reform candidate Boggs, the Florida parishes went overwhelmingly for reform candidate Kennon.

tionalism and the dominance of the governor in state politics, comprise the three distinctive traits of Louisiana's one-party system as contrasted with the rest of the one-party South. All three characteristics are interdependent, and have been interacting to create a facsimile of a smoothly operating two-party system. Louisiana governors, for example, possessed no unique formal powers, yet, unlike many other Southern governors, they usually were undisputed masters of both the bureaucracy and the Legislature. The explanation lies in the Longite development of a disciplined bifactional politics and in the Longite intensification of the use of the ticket system in state and parish politics.

The pervasiveness of the ticket system preserves the logical structure of bifactionalism for the voter and provides some of the cement of factional unity underlying legislative and administrative cooperation with the governor. Joint factional candidacies have been the rule in recent Louisiana state politics; every candidate is not for himself alone. At the state-office level, serious contenders for the nine elective posts affiliate with one or more of several state slates, campaign together, and present their candidacies as a ticket unit to the electorate. Many of the candidates for state legislative posts and for parish offices see fit to align themselves publicly (and many more privately) with a state ticket, and, on occasion, state bifactionalism penetrates to the ward level of police jury contests. A detailed analysis of the Louisiana ticket system, therefore, should illuminate the factional base of gubernatorial power and provide some answers to the question of how closely bifactionalism approaches the workings of a two-party system.[26]

The state ticket system. The practice of state-office candidates campaigning jointly on public slates antedated Huey Long and most probably originated in the early days of the Choctaws, who created the state ticket they supported and forced their opponents to adopt some sort of counterslate. Many potential candidates for state offices sounded out the New Orleans city machine before deciding whether or not to run, and the Choctaws created the equivalent of a state ticket by their endorsements of candidates for each state office. Before the Kingfish, however, ticket campaigning and ticket voting

[26] The analysis is based, for the most part, on an extensive questionnaire, interview, and research project on the ticket aspects of the 1948 and 1952 gubernatorial primaries undertaken by the writer.

were confined largely to the New Orleans area. The 1932 state primary, according to old-timer interviewees, marked the first time that a full state ticket campaigned as a unit in the parishes outside of New Orleans. Since 1932, all major candidates for state office have run on state tickets.

The utility of the ticket device to the parties concerned is clear. From the point of view of the gubernatorial candidate, a state ticket offers him the opportunity of broadening his appeal to all sections of the state through the skillful creation of a "balanced" slate which adequately recognizes the politically relevant diversity within the state. The customary running-mate of a north Louisiana Protestant gubernatorial candidate, for example, is a south Louisiana Catholic for lieutenant-governor. From the perspective of a lesser ticket member, no matter how large he believes his personal following to be, an alliance with a major faction provides him with the statewide organization indispensable to a serious candidacy. It is not uncommon, however, for some state tickets to be "bob-tailed," i.e., not to include an affiliated candidate for every one of the nine statewide offices, and for some to include candidates for lesser state office who are also endorsed by another rival ticket. For all the participants on a ticket its core value is monetary: each candidate secures the benefit of a fully-organized campaign at cut-rate prices.

A state ticket is in reality a gubernatorial ticket, since the candidate for governor both heads and dominates it. It is an "Earl Long ticket" or a "Sam Jones ticket" that is presented to the voters. The affiliated candidates devote much of their oratory on the stump to urging support for their gubernatorial ally and for the full ticket, and often they have little of substance to say on their own behalf. The latter situation is particularly true for certain of the elective posts: what can candidates for auditor, treasurer, and register of the State Land Office publicly pledge by way of dramatic, winning appeal? A frequent complaint of Louisianians is that the ticket organization of candidacies at times allows the poorly qualified candidate to secure office on the coattails of the governor, but that defect is more than counterbalanced by the heightened possibility of a rational politics through use of the ticket device.

The degree to which the state ticket system injects order into one-party politics is ultimately a function of the behavior of individual voters. In Key's informed judgment, "In Louisiana . . . the voters mark a straight ticket about as consistently as they do at a general election in a two-party state."[27] Ticket voting is, naturally, strongest in the runoff primary when the number of factional slates is reduced to two, and it is considerably weaker in the more bewildering melee of the first primary.

Generally, the chances of success are slim for an "independent" candidate without a place on a major state ticket. On the other hand, affiliation with a losing ticket sometimes may be overcome, particularly by long-time incumbents of lesser state posts running for renomination who have personal friendships over the state, such as Harry Wilson (Commissioner of Agriculture), T. H. Harris (Superintendent of Education), Lucille May Grace (Register of the Land Office), L. B. Baynard (Auditor), and A. P. Tugwell (Treasurer). However, these "personal followings" provide no exception to the previous analysis of deliverable followings, for they are nontransferable and, moreover, evaporate when the veteran incumbent ambitiously seeks the highest state office. For example, Miss Grace, running for governor in 1952, polled 4,832 votes. Continued re-election to lesser state office has not been the route to the Executive Mansion. Hence the system of state tickets dominated by gubernatorial candidates provides some basis for post-election gubernatorial control over the elective department heads.

Affiliation with a state ticket by local candidates. The issues of tremendous popular concern put forward by Longism, together with the deep penetration of state politics as practiced by the Kingfish, argued for an extension of bifactionalism into local politics. A provision of the state primary-election law encouraged state tickets and local candidates to enter some sort of working agreement to insure adequate poll-commissioner representation for each. Under that provision, only candidates for local offices could submit the names of poll commissioners and watchers for the first primary; their selection for the second primary was controlled by the gubernatorial candidates participating in the runoff.[28] Affiliation with a state ticket

[27] Key, *Southern Politics*, 170.

[28] *Revised Statutes of Louisiana, 1950*, Title 18, Chapter 2, Sections 340, 357, 358. Under Act 97 of 1922, which was controlling until 1940 with the exception of Huey's brief innovations from 1934 to 1937, local candidates controlled the selection of commissioners in both primaries. Act 46 of 1940, Jones's change in the primary-election law, established the procedure as described in the text. The system forced gubernatorial candidates, in order to secure fair representation

by a local candidate satisfied the former's need for grass-roots organization and enabled the latter to meet more easily the financial costs of campaigning. Such utilitarian pressures appear to be at the heart of the extension of the state ticket into parish politics.

There seems to be a sectional pattern in the practice of parish candidate alliance with a state ticket. Public affiliations are confined largely to Catholic south Louisiana, where high rates of illiteracy enhance the strategic role of poll commissioners and where politics is so highly organized that running for parish and ward offices on local tickets is traditional.[29] In north Louisiana the tie-ups between local candidates and a state faction, though not uncommon, are less frequently publicized.[30] Like the consumption of liquor, perhaps, the action is concluded behind barn doors.

Factional leanings of local candidates are often known anyway, particularly in those parishes where bifactional preferences have been quite definite. For example, in the "independent" parish of Caddo the majority of legislative candidates in the 1952 primaries were known to be anti-Long, although there were no local tickets and only one local candidate publicly affiliated himself with a state ticket.[31] The situation is the same in Longite strongholds—for example, Red River Parish, about which an informant related, "A majority of the local candidates are Long supporters, but with few

among election-day personnel in the first primary, to make overtures to local candidates who controlled the selection of such personnel. The significance of this power may be gauged by the following form letter issued under the name of Earl Long and dated January——, 1940: "Dear Mr.——: I am glad to note that you were drawn as an Election Commissioner. I am sure that you realize the heavy responsibility that rests on your shoulders. Anything that you can do to see that I get a square deal in this election will be appreciated and remembered. If I can render you any assistance, do not hesitate to call on me." Wisdom Collection of Long Materials, Howard Tilton Memorial Library, the Tulane University, New Orleans.

[29] Most, though not all, of the parishes in which legislative candidates aligned with a state ticket in 1952 had a firm tradition of local tickets. The sheriff usually heads a local ticket, and its rationale again lies in the practical benefits accruing to each of the participants.

[30] The author's data indicate some exceptions: Union, Catahoula, Rapides, St. Helena, and Livingston parishes had both public local tickets and open local candidate alignment in either or both 1948 and 1952.

[31] An informant related that in the 1952 runoff primary Kennon's headquarters in Shreveport would suggest to the inquiring voter support of designated candidates for the state Legislature, none of whom had affiliated publicly with the Kennon ticket.

exceptions, none have been backed by a state ticket." In most cases the factional preferences of local candidates are common knowledge, at least to the political insiders if not to the public at large, a conclusion attested to by the following replies to the writer's questionnaires with regard to the 1948 and 1952 state-office primaries sent to selected parish officials.

> *East Feliciana, 1948.* "There were no public alignments of local candidates with state factions. . . . Of course, several candidates were known to have belonged to certain state factions, but they all ran for office on the public theory that they were independent of factionalism."

> *Ouachita, 1948.* "None of the candidates were publicly aligned with state tickets or other local candidates. (We do not have local tickets.) Of course there were candidates in different races who were encouraged by local leaders of state tickets to enter respective races. This was not generally known to the public."

> *Tensas, 1948.* ". . . not any of the local candidates . . . were aligned with any of the State candidates. In some instances it was generally known that several of the Parish candidates were against the administration at that time, or were for the administration at that time, but they were not aligned in any manner with respect to posters, ads, or tickets."

> *Lincoln, 1952.* "There were numerous secret alliances but for some reason the 'local ticket' practice prevailing in many Louisiana parishes has never . . . been employed in this parish."

The clearest factional guideposts to the voter obviously are provided by the open alliances between state tickets and local candidates. Several examples of forthright public endorsements of state tickets by parish officeseekers may be cited.

> We, the undersigned, do hereby certify that at a caucus held in the office of the Governor, Sunday, October 13, 1935, the above-named candidates for parish and district offices [in Pointe Coupee Parish] did agree and pledge themselves to support all candidates on the Long-Allen state ticket, and did further agree and pledge themselves to support each other for parish and district offices. . . .[32]

In his political advertisement as candidate for coroner, East Baton Rouge Parish, in the 1944 primary, Dr. F. U. Darby stated:

[32] *Pointe Coupee Banner,* November 21, 1935.

My politics are not secret. I am supporting Jimmie H. Davis for Governor and am a candidate on the Parish Ticket.[33]

In his political advertisement for renomination as sheriff of Iberia Parish in 1948, Gilbert Ozenne declared:

I have endorsed the candidacy of Earl K. Long for Governor. My opponent lacks the political courage to acknowledge that he was supported and endorsed by the Sam Jones faction. I solicit the vote and support of all qualified voters regardless of political affiliations.[34]

Affiliation is a two-way affair, so gubernatorial tickets also spread the factional word. In a political circular distributed by the Louisiana Democratic Association, Longite Governor Leche began:

In order that the people of Louisiana may have correct information as to who bears the endorsement of the Louisiana Democratic Association in all second primaries, we the undersigned [the state ticket members] now make the statement that the following candidates for their respective [parish and local] offices have been endorsed. . . .[35]

Reform candidate Sam Jones urged publicly before the 1940 first primary:

Wherever you have a Sam Jones candidate for either House or Senate be sure to vote for him. If it should happen that none of the candidates have endorsed me, vote for an anti-administration independent candidate. . . .[36]

Since the objective of the ticket system is to aid the candidacies of each of its co-participants, public endorsements between state tickets and local candidates tend to be delayed until after the first primary. Neither state nor parish politicians care to restrict their appeal to the following of one of many candidates or to gamble on who will make the runoff primary. These considerations are controlling in the case of wide-open parish and gubernatorial contests with a multiplicity of rivals. Conversely, pre-first-primary alignments are common when one of the gubernatorial candidates seems likely to sweep

[33] Baton Rouge *Morning Advocate,* January 16, 1944.
[34] New Iberia *Daily Iberian,* February 23, 1948.
[35] Political circular in Conway Scrapbook of Huey Long Materials, Vol. 7, 95, Louisiana State Library, Baton Rouge.
[36] Baton Rouge *State-Times,* January 12, 1940.

the parish or when local incumbents are unopposed for renomination. Nevertheless, if, as a general rule, the state ticket affiliations of local candidates are not revealed until the interim between primaries, the commitments and arrangements between the two parties very often have been discussed, if not decided upon, before the first primary.[37]

Many informants suggested to the writer another uniformity in the variety of parish candidate links with state politics, namely, that the incumbent parish administration tended to align with the incumbent state administration, while challengers of the parish incumbents tended to affiliate with major anti-administration state tickets. The proposition appears logical in that the state administration over the course of four years establishes working relationships with the courthouse cliques and maintains some disciplinary powers over local regimes for the three months following the gubernatorial primaries, such as the enforcement of state anti-gambling laws, the supervision of tax assessments, and the like. On the basis of evidence gathered by the writer, however, this political rule of thumb appears to be in error. Since the sheriff is usually the leader of the parish organization, under the suggested rule the majority of sheriffs who affiliated with a state ticket in their races for renomination would have supported Jones in 1948 and Spaht in 1952. A computation of the data contained in replies to the writer's questionnaires contradicts that suggested pattern (see Table 36).

TABLE 36. The Pattern of Affiliation with State Tickets by Sheriffs Running for Renomination, 1948 and 1952 Democratic Gubernatorial First and Second Primaries

	1948 Primary	1952 Primary
No. of parishes in which the sheriff ran for renomination	55	52
No. of sheriffs neutral in gubernatorial race	20	33
No. of sheriffs aligned anti-Long	6	5
No. of sheriffs aligned pro-Long	29	14

[37] For example, according to information received by the author, in Rapides Parish in the 1952 primary, Boggs, Kennon, and McLemore (all anti-Longs) jointly and secretly backed three candidates for the House. Two of them made the runoff and then were endorsed openly by Kennon. Frequently these arrangements include a commitment by the gubernatorial candidate, should he make the runoff, to reappoint the poll commissioners named by the local candidate for the first primary.

In the light of the utilitarian motivations for ticket alignments, the following interpretation seems most appropriate. Most sheriffs who affiliate publicly with state factions tend to align with the Longites. This may well be a passing phenomenon, since many of the sheriffs are veteran incumbents who have ties with the stable Longite leaders going back to the 1930's, and the Longs have been known for their skillful politicking in the country parishes. The general tendency noted is subject, however, to at least two major qualifications. Parish organizations are loathe to endorse state tickets unpopular in the parish or unlikely to win, statewide, in the runoff primary. In the 1952 primaries, the sheriffs were subjected to conflicting pressures for alignment with the result that many refused to affiliate openly with either state faction. While the sheriffs' actions suggest some of the inadequacies of the ticket system which next deserve comment, it might be noted that local candidates in a two-party state also have been known to remain discreetly silent when faced with a national or state party ticket unpopular in their district.

Limitations of the ticket system. The penetration of local politics by the state ticket system does not carry with it an extension of the great issues of state politics: the contests for parish office are dominated by local matters. Most local candidates, even those publicly aligned with a state faction, restrict their campaigning to local issues. Of fifty-five contests for sheriff in 1952 on which adequate information was secured by the writer, forty-eight were characterized as revolving largely around items of local concern.

As a result, straight-ticket voting from governor on down through parish clerk of court occurs only in some of the highly organized or bossed parishes, and it is not unusual for voters to support at the same time a parish ticket and the state ticket it opposed. One south Louisiana sheriff informed the writer:

> The [parish] ticket supported Spaht in both primaries [1952] and carried Spaht in both primaries. However, a number of staunch supporters of the parish ticket just 'couldn't see' Spaht and voted Kennon. This had no effect on the local issue. Local voters are either for or against [us] politically, but when it comes to state tickets, they vote how they please, with no effect on the local issues. . . . Voters are entirely free to choose their state candidates. . . .

In another south Louisiana parish, "La Vieille Faction" has con-

trolled public office for more than twenty-five years and uniformly
has supported Longite candidates at state primaries, yet the parish
did not place among those high in support of Longism from 1928 to
1952.[38]

As a final point, while state legislative candidates campaign more
in the mold of state bifactionalism than do the candidates for other
parish offices, the difference is not one of kind. Of the fifty-five House
races in 1952 on which adequate data were obtained, thirty-three
were confined to local issues, with state ticket alignment adjudged as
having little to no influence on the outcome. Campaign tie-ups between the governor and legislators, then, account only in part for the
later co-operation of a large majority of the latter with the governor.

An appraisal of Louisiana's bifactionalism

Bifactionalism and the ticket system have served, with considerable effectiveness, as Louisiana's substitutes for a two-party system.
Unlike several sister Southern states, Louisiana's politics has not
been characterized by a chaotic multifactionalism, by a bewildering
succession of transitory state factions without continuity in program,
leadership, or voter loyalty. Localism and a "friends and neighbors"
influence have been reduced to minimal proportions within a polar-
ized politics of pro- and anti-Longism. The voter is offered a meaningful choice between factions embracing alternative leaders and
programs, while the victorious faction normally is assured of a working control of the administrative and legislative branches to effectuate its pledges made to the voters. Huey Long thus gave Louisiana
a structured and organized politics, a politics that made sense.[39]

[38] So strong was La Vieille Faction's grip upon the parish that the quadrennial
appearance of a rival slate was held to be motivated by the desire to control
parish patronage in the event the anti-Longs should capture the governorship. If
true, here would be a Democratic factional analogy to the role of the Louisiana
Republican party prior to 1952.

[39] Two additional bits of evidence relative to competition for office and turnover in office might be mentioned in support of the general conclusion that the
development of Longism strengthened the democratic operation of Louisiana's
one-party politics. In his study of primary-election returns for state and local
offices in the South for the period 1900–48, Cortez A. M. Ewing found that
Louisiana had both the lowest proportion of unopposed nominations of the states

Although vastly superior to one-party confusion, Louisiana's bifactionalism is considerably inferior to two-party politics, or at least to the claims put forward on behalf of the two-party system in the United States. A summary review of some of the major divergences will, I trust, support that conclusion.

Louisiana's ticket system, together with its bifactionalism, has been adjudged by Key to ". . . more closely approach the reality of a party system than do the factions of any other Southern state."[40] It is useful to an understanding of the differences between the systems to point out that bifactionalism approached the organizational thoroughness of a two-party system only in the despotic days of the Kingfish. The Louisiana ticket system as analyzed is neither cohesive nor penetrating enough to provide the basis for a permanent state factional machine on a par with stable party control—resort must be had to a control of parish governments and of election machinery and to high-handed attempts to extend factional dominance for longer than a single term of office, as indulged in by the brothers Long. The state ticket device permits no governor-oriented machine at the state level because of the hard fact that the governor, alone of the elective state officers, is not eligible for immediate re-election. On the parish level, selfish political considerations, not the friendly links between local officials and Longite leaders, determine the choice of ticket alignments. The fact that a parish organization supported Earl Long in 1940 will have some but not decisive weight in its decision whether or not to support him in 1944 or 1948. In times of stress, as in the case of Longite Spaht, who was soundly beaten in the gubernatorial contest of 1952, the hollowness of what passes for a durable Longite machine stands revealed.

Courthouse groupings, therefore, provide no certain permanent local organization for any state faction, much less a solid political base comparable to the ward and precinct organization of parties. Every four years there is a wild, fresh scramble by state tickets for parish candidate and local ticket support. The popularized notion of an Earl Long machine, therefore, does not square with the rationale

operating under the double-primary system and the highest proportion of incumbents who failed of Democratic renomination of all the Southern states. *Primary Elections in the South* (Norman, Oklahoma, 1953), 51, 67, 70.

[40] Key, *Southern Politics*, 169. Key is correct in pointing out that Louisiana's bifactionalism fails to approximate, in absolute terms, a bipartisan scheme.

and operation of the ticket system in Louisiana politics. These judgments have even greater validity for the anti-Long faction, which suffers from inability to maintain a grass-roots organization in the period between quadrennial elections. Louisiana's experience raises the question of whether bifactionalism, in the absence of a functioning rival party, can ever hope to attain a quasi-party system without degenerating into factional dictatorship.

Apart from Huey's regime, the measure of the difference between bifactional and party schemes is the increasing fuzziness of the former as it extends beyond the arena of state-office politics, as in the limitations of the ticket system already examined. No matter how lightly party attachments may be viewed, the labels in a party system give identification and some meaning to candidacies and thereby provide clarification for the voter. By contrast, Louisiana senators and congressmen often develop their own followings and are judged by the voters by standards independent of bifactionalism. For this reason senators often may "interfere" in state elections even to the point of changing, as Overton and Russell Long have done, their factional affiliation without much fear of electoral retaliation several years later. The late Senator Overton and Senator Ellender both traced their political lineage to close personal support of Huey Long, and yet, except for their original primary election, neither had serious difficulty in being returned to office. The 1948 and 1950 primaries of Russell Long illustrate the same point. In similar fashion bifactional linkage to presidential politics customarily has been weak, although the electoral pattern in the 1952 presidential election bore more than a casual relationship to state bifactionalism.

Notwithstanding the durability of Louisiana's two major factions, neither has established a stable and satisfactory process of recruitment of its leaders without reference to party primary battles. Years ago the Choctaws informally performed that function; the Long faction in 1932 and 1936, and the anti-Longs in 1940, also chose their standard-bearers before the first primary. But for the most part the fairly constant Longite and anti-Long groups are wooed by competing would-be leaders, as in 1944, 1948, and 1952. The determination of factional leadership by open competition in the primaries presents many serious problems, not the least of which is the frequent inability of natural allies to consolidate their forces in the brief five or six weeks following a first-primary campaign in which they were railing bitterly at each other. Bandwagon pressure, by discouraging open affiliation between state and parish allies, also handicaps the effectiveness of the primary as the selector of factional leaders. For example, anti-Long parish candidates were reluctant to tie up with Jones in 1948, and many parish Longites similarly spurned alliance with Spaht in 1952. Finally, in the absence of a regularized path to leadership usually supplied by a party system, it has become almost traditional for Louisiana's governors and lieutenant-governors to have a falling out during their term of office.

A final grave inadequacy of Louisiana's bifactionalism is that it produces less constancy on the part of factional chieftains than of the voters. Factional defection is not limited to politicians in control of their local bailiwicks, such as Leander Perez, veteran Longite boss of Plaquemines Parish, who deserted the Longs in 1948 because of their coolness to the States' Rights movement. Major politicians like Noe, James Morrison, Overton, and LeBlanc have been on all sides of the factional fence. The cross-factional support accorded the gubernatorial candidacy of Hale Boggs in the 1952 primary rarely would be duplicated in a two-party setting: reform leaders ex-Governor Jones and Mayor Morrison of New Orleans, sometime Longite Congressman James Morrison, and Longites ex-Senator Feazel and Senator Russell Long. Here again the very lack of party labels is not compensated for by the persistence of bifactionalism; loyalty to faction appears less rigid and demanding than loyalty to party.[41]

A concluding word about the future of Louisiana politics may not be inappropriate. In mid-1952 many of the author's informants were of the opinion that Huey Long's class revolution of 1928 had run its full course.[42] After all, not only had Earl Long's candidate been

[41] One finding from the data collected by the author bears directly on this point. In spite of the high degree of non-performance and even double-dealing engaged in by many of the parish candidates who affiliate with a state ticket, in only one case was an affiliate termed a factional deserter. In the situation referred to, a legislative candidate from a south Louisiana parish supported Longite Spaht in the first primary in 1952, made the runoff primary, and then "flopped" (as my informant put it) to support Kennon against Spaht in the gubernatorial runoff primary. Both the legislative candidate in question and Kennon failed to carry the parish.

[42] Anti-Longs, however, repeated their error of 1940 and 1944 again in 1952, namely, underestimating the staying power of the Long faction. The results of the 1956 gubernatorial first primary hardly suggest the demise of bifactionalism. Earl Long carried 51 parishes by majority vote and won the nomination with 51.4 per cent of the vote cast. Fourteen of the 17 most pro-Long parishes shown

defeated but Huey's son had backed an anti-Long candidate on the proposition that "the time had come to forgive and forget old factional bitterness." The analysis of recent Louisiana politics here undertaken suggests that the disappearance, whether gradual or sudden, of the bifactional pattern might well be viewed with something less than optimism. Louisiana's bifactionalism, however defective, has injected order and clarity into the confusion of one-party politics. Those who cheer the passing of Longism and the Long faction might pause to consider that the political system most likely to follow the state's bifactionalism will be unstructured multifactionalism, not competitive party politics.

in Figure 14 (above, p. 250) again placed in the upper half of all parishes ranked according to percentage of the popular vote for Long; 13 of the 17 most anti-Long parishes as indicated in Figure 14 again placed in the lower half.

Bibliographical essay

I. PRIMARY SOURCES

A. BASIC LEGAL AND LEGISLATIVE STATE DOCUMENTS

Acts of Louisiana, 1920–52; *Revised Statutes of Louisiana,* 1950; *Constitution of Louisiana,* amended through 1952; *Official Journal of the Proceedings of the House of Representatives* and *of the Senate of Louisiana,* all regular and special sessions, 1928–52. All the references in this study to factional alignments of legislators on bills or in particular sessions are based upon analysis of the relevant *Official Journal.* With the exception of the impeachment session (Fifth Extra Session, beginning March 20, 1929), the *Journals* contain no record of debate or speeches.

B. OFFICIAL REPORTS OF STATE AGENCIES

Commissioner of Agriculture and Immigration, 1940–50; *Department of Education,* 1929–50; *Department of Finance,* 1940–48; *Division of Administration,* 1948–51; *Executive Budget,* 1950–52; *Louisiana Tax Commission,* 1940–50; *Department of Highways,* Statistical and Technical Supplement, 1948–49; *Department of Institutions,* 1940–47; *State Hospital Board,* Annual Statistical Report, 1949–50; *Department of Public Welfare,* 1939–51; *Department of Public Works,* 1944–50; *State Department of Civil Service,* 1943–47.

C. ELECTION AND OTHER POLITICAL DATA

Louisiana elections are the most fully reported in the South and compare favorably with any state in the nation. Parish returns are broken down into precincts in each of the *Compilation of Primary Election Returns of the Democratic Party, State of Louisiana,* the more recent of which bear the inscription, "issued by the Secretary of State of Louisiana." These *Compilations* cover all the state-office contests for each of the gubernatorial primaries from 1920 to 1952 and the various federal and state posts competed for in the primaries held in 1918, 1926, 1930, and 1950. The biennial *Report of the Secretary of State to the Governor* contains parish data on registered voters, including party affiliation, race, sex, and literacy and disability, parish election returns on constitutional amendments, on general elections for state-office and federal posts, and, at times, on Democratic primary contests for Senate and House. The *Reports* used in this study cover the period 1935–52.

The parish returns for all Democratic gubernatorial and senatorial primaries from 1920 through 1948 are readily available in Alexander Heard and Donald S. Strong, *Southern Primaries and Elections* (University, Alabama, 1950), 69–77. For some of those primaries the percentage of the vote received in each parish by some or all the candidates is included. Since I have made use of Heard and Strong's computations, the reader may check the sources cited for each table to ascertain which primaries have been computed in their book.

Unpublished precinct returns for the Democratic primary held August 31, 1948, are on file at the office of the Secretary of State of Louisiana. At that primary, Russell Long and Allen Ellender were nominated to the United States Senate. Through the courtesy of the office of the Secretary of State of Louisiana, I was permitted to compile precinct returns for the presidential election of November 2, 1948, from the official voting tally sheets mailed to the Secretary of State by poll commissioners from each of the state's precincts, some two thousand in number. Also on file at the office of the Secretary of State are unpublished parish returns for the Democratic primary contests for state legislators, 1948 and 1952, which are contained in reports of the various Democratic party committees.

Questionnaires were sent to various parish respondents to secure information on the factional affiliation of candidates for the state Legislature and for various parish offices in the 1948 and 1952 gubernatorial primaries, and to seek explanations for the political behavior of deviant wards. Since anonymity was promised to them to encourage their co-operation, their names do not appear in any part of this study. In addition, the co-operation of several parish registrars of voters was solicited and obtained in connection with registration data on predominantly Negro precincts reported in Table 31.

D. NEWSPAPERS AND VARIOUS COLLECTIONS OF PRESS CLIPPINGS

Virtually all the copies of the various *Progresses* published from 1930 to 1940 are on microfilm at Louisiana State University Library. The Department of Government at Louisiana State University possesses a useful file of clippings on the Scandals of 1939–40. In the Louisiana Room of the L.S.U. Library may be found a large file of editorials culled from the nation's press which comment upon the assassination of Huey Long. The Lucille May Grace Scrapbook Collection, about ten volumes, unnumbered, in the personal possession of Miss Grace, Register of the State Land Office from 1931–52, consists mainly of clippings from the urban press, considerable country press commentary, and some political circulars. All major events in state politics, particularly from 1940 to 1950, are well covered.

The E. A. Conway Scrapbook Collection of Long Materials, thirteen volumes, with numbered pages, at the Louisiana State Library in Baton Rouge, includes press clippings from urban dailies, some political circulars, and some copies of the *Progress*. The first five volumes cover 1928–32, the remainder deal with 1935–40. The William B. Wisdom Collection of Huey Long Materials, at the Tulane University, New Orleans, is a potpourri of newspaper clippings, *Progresses*, secondary materials, and all too few letters concerning Huey and Earl Long.

In addition to the press materials contained in the above sources, this study relied upon a fairly systematic reading of the Baton Rouge *State-Times*, the New Orleans *Times-Picayune*, and the New Orleans *Item*.

E. MISCELLANY

The material on Governor Parker (1920–24) to be found in Governor's Correspondence, Department of Archives, Louisiana State University, is of little use to this study because it was apparently too well-screened prior to its submission to the library for public use.

The valuable testimony offered in the course of the investigation into Overton's 1932 nomination may be found in United States Senate, *Hearings of the Special Committee on the Investigation of Campaign Expenditures*, 72nd Congress, 2nd Session (1932), and *Report*, No. 191, 73rd Congress, 2nd Session (1934).

II. INTERVIEWS

Most of the interviews listed below were held in Louisiana during late 1951 or early 1952, after the bulk of formal research had been accomplished. For the most part, these interviews were of incalculable aid to me in the insights, information, and interpretations suggested by the various informants. In keeping with my pledge to them, at no point in this study is any quoted statement or observation assigned to a specific source.

A. PRESS REPRESENTATIVES

Everett M. Clinton, James W. Gillis, George W. Healy, Jr., Bernard L. Krebs of the New Orleans *Times-Picayune; Hermann B. Deutsch, William Monroe, Edward W. Stagg* of the New Orleans *Item;* Mrs. *Margaret Dixon* and *C. P. Liter* of the Baton Rouge *Morning Advocate* and the Baton Rouge *State-Times; William Fitzpatrick* of the New Orleans *States; Harry Leddingham* of the Associated Press.

B. ACADEMICS

Drs. *Fred C. Cole, Robert French, Lawrence V. Howard, William W. Shaw,* and *George E. Simmons* of the Tulane University, in New Orleans;

Dr. *William Kolb* of Newcomb College, New Orleans; Dr. *Joseph Fichter*, S.J., of Loyola University, New Orleans; Drs. *Fred C. Frey* and *Robert J. Harris* of Louisiana State University, Baton Rouge.

C. NEGRO LEADERS

Jackson V. Acox of the Progressive Voters League; Rev. *A. L. Alexander* and *Dave A. Dennis* of the Crescent City Independent Voters League; *Ernest Wright* of the People's Defense League, all of New Orleans. Dr. *Felton Clark*, President of Southern University, Baton Rouge, and Dr. *Albert W. Dent*, President of Dillard University, New Orleans. Dr. *George Snowden*, State Division of Employment Security; *A. P. Tureaud*, National Association for the Advancement of Colored People, New Orleans; *J. Westbrook McPherson*, New Orleans Urban League; *Louis Berry* of Orleans; *Edward Jackson* and *John G. Lewis* of Baton Rouge.

D. SPOKESMEN FOR ORGANIZED LABOR

Aubrey Hirsch, attorney for the State Federation of Labor, Baton Rouge; Dr. *Vincent O'Connell*, S.J., Notre Dame Seminary, and Dr. *Louis Twomey*, S.J., Loyola University, both in New Orleans; *Robert L. Soule* of the New Orleans Central Trades and Labor Council; *Robert Stearns* of the Congress of Industrial Organizations Council, New Orleans.

E. REPUBLICANS

Harrison G. Bagwell, defeated candidate for governor, 1952, and a leader of the pro-Eisenhower "new guard" Republicans in Baton Rouge; *J. E. Perkins*, Negro Republican leader in Baton Rouge.

F. ELECTED PUBLIC OFFICIALS, PRESENT AND PAST

Former Governor *Sam H. Jones;* Lieutenant-Governor *William J. Dodd;* Miss *Lucille May Grace*, Register of the Land Office; *Bolivar Kemp*, Attorney General; *Wade O. Martin, Jr.*, Secretary of State; *A. P. Tugwell*, State Treasurer. Congressmen *T. Hale Boggs*, Second District, and *F. Edward Hebert*, First District; former Congressmen *James Domengeaux*, Third District, and *Jared Y. Sanders, Jr.*, Sixth District.

Wade O. Martin, Sr., Public Service Commission and a political leader of St. Martin Parish; state Senator *Robert Ainsworth*, president pro tempore, 1952 session; state representatives *Algie Brown* and *James Gardner* of Caddo, *James Eubank* of Rapides; District Judge *Coleman Lindsey* of Baton Rouge; District Attorney *Leander Perez* of Plaquemines and St. Bernard parishes, political leader of the former parish and a Dixiecrat leader in 1948; District Judge *Carlos Spaht* of Baton Rouge, defeated candidate for governor, 1952; former District Attorney *John Fred Odom* of Baton Rouge, the official charged with the investigation of Huey's death;

Sheldon W. Smelley, assessor of Bienville Parish; veteran New Orleans political leaders Captain *William A. Bisso, Sr., Edward Haggerty, Sr., George Montgomery, Sr., A. Miles Pratt,* and *Francis Williams.*

G. OTHER GOVERNMENT OFFICIALS

Ronald Cocreham, Executive Secretary under Governor Jones and Collector of Revenue under Davis; *Alden Muller,* Assistant City Attorney of Orleans and a ward leader of Mayor Morrison's political organization; *G. T. Owen,* Executive Counsel to Sam Jones, 1940–42; *J. J. Reily,* Commissioner of Finance under Davis; *Jesse H. Bankston,* Director of the State Hospital Board, 1948–52; *Harry Henderlite,* veteran Chief Highway Engineer, State Highway Commission; *Lee Laycock,* clerk of the Louisiana House of Representatives; *Clarence O. Roberts,* Assistant Director, Merit System Council; *Homer H. Russell,* Chief Budget Accountant, Division of Administration.

H. ALL OTHER INTERVIEWS

H. Vincent Moseley, defeated candidate for governor, 1940 and 1944; *Jess Funderburck, Jr.,* defeated candidate for state Legislature, from Vernon Parish, 1952; *J. A. Logan,* District Engineer, Federal Bureau of Public Roads, Baton Rouge; New Orleans civic leaders *J. Blanc Monroe, Jacob Morrison, Mrs. Edgar B. Stern,* and *Lester Kabacoff; Val Mogensen* and *Louis E. Newman* of the Bureau of Governmental Research in New Orleans; *Charles E. Dunbar, Jr.,* of the Louisiana Civil Service League; public relations men *Scott Wilson* and *David McGuire* of New Orleans; *Bruce Tucker,* staff office head to Senator Russell Long; informed students of the Southern and Louisiana scene *Harnett T. Kane* of New Orleans, *Hodding Carter* and *David Cohn* of Greenville, Mississippi, Dr. *Alexander Heard* of the University of North Carolina, and Dr. *Donald S. Strong* of the University of Alabama.

III. SECONDARY SOURCES

The bibliography which follows is neither exhaustive of the field nor inclusive of all materials utilized for this study. Most of the substantial works, as distinct from the polemical and the impressionistic, in the literature on Louisiana politics and Longism are included.

A. LOUISIANA HISTORY

With but a few exceptions, neither the general nor special histories of Louisiana are very satisfactory. Of the former, perhaps the most useful is Henry E. Chambers, *History of Louisiana,* 3 vols., (Chicago, 1925). The ablest account for the time-period indicated by its title is Roger W.

Shugg's *Origins of Class Struggle in Louisiana, 1840–1875* (Baton Rouge, 1939), a source heavily relied upon in this study. The decade of the 1850's is well treated in the serialized articles of James K. Greer, "Louisiana Politics, 1845–1861," *Louisiana Historical Quarterly*, xii–xiii (1929–30), and a special aspect thereof in Harry L. Coles, Jr., "Some Notes on Slave-ownership and Landownership in Louisiana, 1850–1860," *Journal of Southern History*, ix (August, 1943), 381–94. Secession sentiment is gauged in John C. Merrill, Jr., "Louisiana Public Opinion on Secession, 1859–1860," unpublished Master's thesis, Louisiana State University (Baton Rouge, 1950), and in Roger W. Shugg's "A Suppressed Coopera-tionist Protest Against Secession," *Louisiana Historical Quarterly*, xix (January, 1936), 199–204. Lane C. Kendall's six articles entitled "The Interregnum in Louisiana in 1861," *Louisiana Historical Quarterly*, xvi–xvii (1933–34), and Jefferson D. Bragg's *Louisiana in the Confederacy* (Baton Rouge, 1941), cover the Civil War phase.

The researcher must make the best of outdated or inadequate treat-ments of Reconstruction, Restoration, and Populism in Louisiana. On the first, the studies by Ella Lonn, *Reconstruction in Louisiana: (After 1868)* (New York, 1918), and John R. Ficklen, *History of Reconstruction in Louisiana (Through 1868)* (Baltimore, 1910) are standard. Henry Clay Warmoth's biased memories are informative: *War, Politics, and Recon-struction* (New York, 1930). More recent studies, such as Willie M. Cas-key's *Secession and Restoration of Louisiana* (Baton Rouge, 1938), and Garnie W. McGinty's *Louisiana Redeemed: The Overthrow of Carpetbag Rule, 1876–1880* (New Orleans, 1941) shed little new light. Two useful articles are those of William E. Highsmith, "Some Aspects of Reconstruc-tion in the Heart of Louisiana," *Journal of Southern History*, xiii (Novem-ber, 1947), 460–91; and T. Harry Williams, "The Louisiana Unification Movement of 1873," *Journal of Southern History*, xi (August, 1945), 349–69. On the place of the Louisiana Lottery, consult Berthold C. Alwes, "The History of the Louisiana State Lottery Company," *Louisiana Histori-cal Quarterly*, xxvii (October, 1944), 964–1118; and R. H. Wiggins, "The Louisiana Press and the Lottery," *Louisiana Historical Quarterly*, xxxi (July, 1948), 716–844.

Published analysis of Populism is restricted to Melvin J. White, "Popul-ism in Louisiana During the Nineties," *The Mississippi Valley Historical Review*, v (June, 1918), 3–19, and to Lucia E. Daniel, "The Louisiana People's Party," *Louisiana Historical Quarterly*, xxvi (October, 1943), 1055–1149. See also, for an account of earlier urban unrest, Roger W. Shugg, "The New Orleans General Strike of 1892," *Louisiana Historical Quarterly*, xxi (April, 1938), 547–59. Of more limited use is James S. Penny, "The People's Party Press During the Louisiana Political Upheaval of the 1890's," unpublished Master's thesis, Louisiana State University, (Baton Rouge, 1942).

The standard—and only—study of the New Orleans Choctaws is George M. Reynolds, *Machine Politics in New Orleans, 1897–1926* (New York,

1936). It is thorough but unduly skimpy on election analysis. Consult, also, the chapter on Behrman in Harold Zink, *City Bosses in the United States* (Durham, 1930). The elementary remarks of Choctaw secretary and ward leader Dudley G. Desmare, "History of the Old Regular Organization," *Louisiana Police Jury Review*, XI (April, 1947), 99ff., provide some flavor of the machine. Of less use to a political study are John S. Kendall's *History of New Orleans* (Chicago, 1922), and Harold Sinclair's *The Port of New Orleans* (New York, 1942).

It might be noted that the *Louisiana Historical Quarterly*, for the last ten years or so, has reprinted, substantially without revision, Master's theses written for the Tulane University and for Louisiana State University. Those of the studies which deal with politics are stronger on facts than on interpretations, for the most part. Some of the more thoughtful of them are cited individually within this bibliographical essay.

B. BASIC DATA ON LOUISIANA

Three excellent studies provide necessary information on some raw materials of politics: T. Lynn Smith and Homer L. Hitt, *The People of Louisiana* (Baton Rouge, 1952); Yvonne Phillips, "Land-Use Patterns in Louisiana," unpublished Master's thesis, Louisiana State University (Baton Rouge, 1950); and John S. Kyser, "Evolution of Louisiana Parishes in Relation to Population Growth and Movements," unpublished doctoral thesis, Louisiana State University (Baton Rouge, 1938). For all sorts of data on agricultural resources, consult the Bulletins of the Agricultural Experiment Station, Louisiana State University. The industrial economy of Louisiana is analyzed in Stanley W. Preston, "Survey of Louisiana Manufacturing, 1929–1939," *Louisiana Business Bulletin*, VIII (December, 1946), 5–30; William H. Baughn and William D. Ross, "Changes in the Louisiana Manufacturing Economy Between 1939 and 1947," *Louisiana Business Bulletin*, XIII (April, 1951), 7–83; and Rudolf Heberle, *The Labor Force in Louisiana* (Baton Rouge, 1948). Also consult the relevant data in C. B. Hoover and B. U. Ratchford, *Economic Resources and Policies of the South* (New York, 1951); and other issues of the *Louisiana Business Bulletin* for special studies.

Some studies of a sociological nature on selected aspects of the Louisiana scene are of value. An excellent analysis of trade-unionism may be found in A. S. Freedman, "Social Aspects of Recent Labor Growth in Louisiana," unpublished Master's thesis, Louisiana State University (Baton Rouge, 1950). The difference in social patterns of living between dirt farmers and planters may be examined in Roy E. Hyde, "Social Stratification Among Cotton Farmers in the Hills and Delta of Louisiana," unpublished doctoral thesis, Louisiana State University (Baton Rouge, 1942); Edgar A. Shuller, "Social and Economic Status in a Louisiana Hill Community," *Rural Sociology*, V (March, 1940), 69–83; and Joseph S. Vandiver, "A Demographic Comparison of Plantation and Non-Plantation

Counties in the Cotton Belt," unpublished doctoral thesis, Louisiana State University (Baton Rouge, 1948).

Investigations of the Cajuns include Harlan W. Gilmore's articles in *Social Forces:* "Social Isolation of French Speaking People of Rural Louisiana," xii (October, 1933), 78–84, and "Family-Capitalism in a Community of Rural Louisiana," xv (October, 1936), 71–75; T. Lynn Smith and Vernon Parenton, "Acculturation Among the Louisiana French," *American Journal of Sociology,* xxxxiv (November, 1938), 355–65. Examples of nationality conflicts are studied in Lewis W. Newton, "Creoles and Anglo-Americans in Old Louisiana," *Southwestern Political and Social Science Quarterly,* xiv (June, 1933), 31–48; and John E. Coxe, "The New Orleans Mafia Incident," *Louisiana Historical Quarterly,* xx (October, 1937), 1066–1109.

Neither Louisiana Negroes nor Catholics have come in for adequate analysis. On the former, see Charles B. Rousseve, *The Negro in Louisiana; Aspects of His Culture and Literature* (New Orleans, 1937), and the unpublished study conducted for the New Orleans Urban League in early 1950 by Warren M. Banner and J. Harvey Kerns, "A Review of the Economic and Cultural Problems of New Orleans, Louisiana, as they relate to conditions in the Negro population." Roger Baudier's *The Catholic Church in Louisiana* (New Orleans, 1931) is an "official," descriptive history; Father Joseph H. Fichter's provocative *Southern Parish* (Chicago, 1951) attempts to measure the failure of Catholic doctrine to be translated into everyday action by Catholic parishioners in an anonymous district actually located in New Orleans.

C. CONSTITUTIONAL STRUCTURE, FORMAL GOVERNMENT,
   AND ELECTION LAWS

The constitutional structure and formal government of Louisiana are most adequately explored fields due to the efforts of the Louisiana State Law Institute in its Constitution Revision Project of 1947–51. The Central Research Staff of the Institute prepared seventy-four mimeographed studies on Louisiana and on comparative state data on governmental, legal, and constitutional topics, and additionally amassed seven volumes of explanatory notes and materials. Although the constitutional convention was not held, the Institute has secured a legislative appropriation to publish its Explanatory Notes in the near future. On the need for a new constitution, see an article by the late Kimbrough Owen, "The Need for Constitutional Revision in Louisiana," *Louisiana Law Review,* viii (1947–48), 1–104. On the ease of securing amendments to the current Constitution of 1921, consult Alden L. Powell, "Amending the Louisiana Constitution," *Southwestern Social Science Quarterly,* xviii (June, 1937), 25–34, and the occasional reports on the problem issued by the New Orleans Bureau of Governmental Research.

A useful but outdated analysis is that of Melvin Evans, *A Study in the State Government of Louisiana* (Baton Rouge, 1931). Formal aspects of gubernatorial power are treated in James W. Prothro, "A Study of Constitutional Developments in the Office of the Governor of Louisiana," unpublished Master's thesis, Louisiana State University (Baton Rouge, 1948); and Ben B. Taylor, Jr., "A Study of the Appointive and Removal Powers of the Governor of Louisiana," unpublished Master's thesis, Louisiana State University (Baton Rouge, 1935). Coleman B. Ransone, Jr., *The Office of Governor in the South* (University, Alabama, 1951), offers valuable insights on a more informal basis.

Roderick L. Carleton's *The Reorganization and Consolidation of State Administration in Louisiana* (Baton Rouge, 1937), F. J. Mechlin and C. S. Hyneman, *The Administrative System of the State of Louisiana*, Louisiana State University Bureau of Government Research (Baton Rouge, 1940), and a 1951 report on the executive branch by the Public Affairs Research Council of Louisiana testify to the chaotic structure of state administration. A superior study of a unique governmental agency is that of the New Orleans Bureau of Governmental Research, *Louisiana's "Little Legislature": A Study of the Board of Liquidation of the State Debt*, Monograph No. 1 (New Orleans, 1945). Another old but useful study is Ben R. Miller's *The Louisiana Judiciary* (Baton Rouge, 1932); more recent and attuned to political implications is Emmett Asseff's *Legislative Apportionment in Louisiana*, Louisiana State University Bureau of Government Research (Baton Rouge, 1950).

Studies of local government are varied and ample: Roderick L. Carleton, *Local Government and Administration in Louisiana* (Baton Rouge, 1935); the relevant portions, written by Emmett Asseff, in Paul W. Wager, (ed.), *County Government Across the Nation* (Chapel Hill, 1950); Jesse H. Bankston, "Origins and Duties of the Police Jury in Louisiana," *Louisiana Police Jury Review*, IV (April, 1940), 71–74; R. Taylor Cole, "The Police Jury of Louisiana," *Southwestern Political and Social Science Quarterly*, XI (June, 1930), 93–95; and four publications of the Louisiana State University Bureau of Government Research including Clarence Scheps, *Central Control of Municipal Accounts in Louisiana* (1941); Emmett Asseff, *Special Districts in Louisiana* (1951); Asseff and Highsaw, *Civil Service in the Local Units of Government* (1951); and Asseff, Highsaw, and Looper, *State Supervision of Local Finance in Louisiana* (1951). Consult also Research Study No. 1 of the Public Affairs Research Council of Louisiana, entitled *Home Rule for Louisiana Municipalities* (1952); and the issues of the *Louisiana Police Jury Review* and the *Louisiana Municipal Review*.

A presentation and discussion of Louisiana election laws and party organization may be found in Reynold's *Machine Politics* cited earlier, in V. O. Key, Jr., *Southern Politics* (New York, 1949), and in two Louisiana State University Bureau of Government Research studies by Alden L.

Powell and Emmett Asseff, *Registration of Voters in Louisiana* (1951), and *Party Organization and Nominations in Louisiana* (1952).

D. THE POLITICAL PROCESS IN THE SOUTH

V. O. Key's *Southern Politics* (New York, 1949) is the indispensable starting-off point and may be supplemented usefully by Paul Lewinson, *Race, Class and Party* (New York, 1932); Gunnar Myrdal, *An American Dilemma* (New York, 1944); Alexander Heard, *A Two-Party South?* (Chapel Hill, 1952); Jasper B. Shannon, *Toward a New Politics in the South* (Nashville, 1949); Ransone, *The Office of Governor in the South,* cited earlier; William A. Percy, *Lanterns on the Levee* (New York, 1941); Wilbur J. Cash, *The Mind of the South* (New York, 1941); William G. Carleton's "The Conservative South—A Political Myth," *Virginia Quarterly Review,* xxii (Spring, 1946), 179–92, and "The Southern Politician—1900 and 1950," *Journal of Politics,* xiii (May, 1951), 215–31; Cortez A. M. Ewing, "Southern Governors," *Journal of Politics,* x (May, 1948), 385–409; Alden L. Powell, "Politics and Political Parties: A Critique of Recent Literature," *Journal of Politics,* iv (February, 1942), 95–106; and Herman C. Nixon, "Politics of the Hills," *Journal of Politics,* viii (May, 1946), 123–33.

Thoughtful and challenging evaluations of "poor white" Southern leaders are contained in Daniel M. Robison, "From Tillman to Long: Some Striking Leaders of the Rural South," *Journal of Southern History,* iii (August, 1937), 289–310; Rupert B. Vance, "Rebels and Agrarians All," *The Southern Review,* iv (Summer, 1938), 261–64; and Gerald W. Johnson, "Live Demagogues or Dead Gentlemen," *Virginia Quarterly Review,* xii (1936), 1–14.

E. THE POLITICAL PROCESS IN LOUISIANA

In contrast to the plethora of materials on Huey Long there has been but a minimal amount of systematic analysis of Louisiana politics. Key's *Southern Politics* again provides the point of departure, although an earlier study of Harold F. Gosnell, *Grass Roots Politics* (Washington, D. C., 1942), contains a helpful chapter on the Louisiana scene. Professor Rudolf Heberle of the Department of Sociology at Louisiana State University is undertaking a long-range exploration of the "ecology" of Louisiana politics, which has resulted, to date, in the following articles and studies: Heberle, "On Political Ecology," *Social Forces,* xxxi (October, 1952), 1–9; Heberle and Bertrand, "Factors Motivating Voting Behavior in a One-Party State: A Case Study of the 1948 Louisiana Gubernatorial Primaries," *Social Forces,* xxvii (May, 1949), 343–50; Heberle, Hillery, and Lovrich, "Continuity and Change in Voting Behavior in the 1952 Primaries in Louisiana," *Southwestern Social Science Quarterly,* xxxiii (March, 1953), 328–42; Perry H. Howard, "The Political Ecology of Louisiana," unpub-

lished Master's thesis, Louisiana State University (Baton Rouge, 1951);
Howard, "An Analysis of Voting Behavior in Baton Rouge," *The Proceed-
ings of the Louisiana Academy of Sciences*, xv (August, 1952), 84–100;
Heberle and Howard, "An Ecological Analysis of Political Tendencies in
Louisiana: The Presidential Elections of 1952," *Social Forces*, xxxii
(May, 1954), 344–50. On the latter topic, consult also L. Vaughan
Howard and David R. Deener, *Presidential Politics in Louisiana, 1952,*
Tulane Studies in Political Science, Vol. I (New Orleans, 1954); Donald
S. Strong, "The Presidential Election in the South, 1952," *Journal of
Politics*, xvii (August, 1955), 359–60. The publications of the New
Orleans Bureau of Governmental Research and of the Public Affairs
Research Council of Louisiana should also be consulted.

F. HUEY LONG

Huey's autobiography, *Every Man a King* (New Orleans, 1933), designed to enhance the appeal of Share-Our-Wealth, is appropriately soft-
spoken. His *My First Days in the White House* (Harrisburg, 1935), is a
curious, tongue-in-cheek prediction of coming events, while his national
platform is spelled out in his *Share Our Wealth; Every Man a King*
(Washington, D. C., 1935). The best of the full-length biographies are
Forrest Davis, *Huey Long, A Candid Biography* (New York, 1935); Carleton Beals, *The Story of Huey P. Long* (Philadelphia, 1935); and Hermann
B. Deutsch, "The Kingdom of the Kingfish," serialized in the New Orleans
Item, July 19–September 20, 1939. Considerably inferior are Thomas O.
Harris, *The Kingfish: Huey P. Long, Dictator* (New Orleans, 1938) and
Webster Smith, *The Kingfish: A Biography of Huey P. Long* (New York,
1933). The first part of Harnett T. Kane's *Louisiana Hayride* (New York,
1941) and one chapter in Reinhard H. Luthin, *American Demagogues,
Twentieth Century* (Boston, 1954) attempt capsule treatments of Huey's
regime.

Samples of Huey's oratory may be found in B. A. Botkin (ed.), *A Treas-
ury of Southern Folklore* (New York, 1949) and of his taste in humor in
Hugh M. Blain, *Favorite Huey Long Stories* (Baton Rouge, 1937). Arthur
M. Shaw recently has recalled his initial exposure to Long's magnetism
before a crowd in "The First Time I Saw Huey," *Southwest Review*, xxxv
(Winter, 1950), 59–63.

A running commentary on phases of Huey's career is provided by Hod-
ding Carter in several articles in the *New Republic*, "Kingfish to Craw-
fish," lxxvii (January 24, 1934), 302–305; "Kingfish on His Way," lxxxi
(November 21, 1934), 40–42; and "How Come Huey Long?," lxxxii
(February 13, 1935), 11–15; by Walter Davenport in *Collier's*, "Yes, Your
Excellency," lxxxvi (December 13, 1930), 22ff.; "Catching Up With
Huey," xcii (June 1, 1933), 12ff.; "Huey Long Gets Away With It," xcii
(June 17, 1933), 10ff.; and "Too High and Too Mighty," xcv (January
13, 1935), 7ff.; and by Hermann B. Deutsch in the *Saturday Evening Post,*

"Hattie and Huey," ccv (October 15, 1932), 6ff.; "Prelude to a Heterocrat," ccviii (September 7, 1935), 5ff.; "Paradox in Pajamas," ccviii (October 5, 1935), 14ff.; and "Huey Long, the Last Phase," ccviii (October 12, 1935), 27ff.

Superior brief evaluations of Huey Longism include: Raymond Gram Swing's *Forerunners of American Fascism* (New York, 1935) and three articles he wrote for *The Nation:* "The Menace of Huey Long," cxl (January 9, 16, 23, 1935), 36–39, 69–71, 98–100; Unofficial Observer (John F. Carter), *American Messiahs* (New York, 1935); Raymond Moley, *Twenty-Seven Masters of Politics* (New York, 1949); Allan A. Michie and Frank Ryhlick, *Dixie Demagogues* (New York, 1939); Hodding Carter, "Huey Long's Louisiana Hayride," *American Mercury*, lxviii (April, 1949), 435–47; and several articles by Hamilton Basso, "Huey Long and His Background," *Harper's Magazine*, clxx (May, 1935), 663–73; "Death and Legacy of Huey Long," *New Republic*, lxxxv (January 1, 1936), 215–18; "Huey's Louisiana Heritage," *New Republic*, c (August 30, 1939), 99–100; and "The Huey Long Legend," *Life*, xxi (December 9, 1946), 106–21.

There are some useful analyses of parts of the Long record as well. Hodding Carter's personal reminiscences about suppression of the country press under the Kingfish may be found in Isabel Leighton (ed.), *The Aspirin Age, 1919–1941* (New York, 1949). Huey's omission of benefits for Negroes is catalogued in Carleton Beals and A. Plenn, "Louisiana's Black Utopia," *The Nation*, cxli (October 30, 1935), 503–505. Tulane Professor of Law Newman F. Baker analyzes the legal basis of the 1929 conflict in "Some Legal Aspects of Impeachment in Louisiana," *Southwestern Political and Social Science Quarterly*, x (March, 1930), 359–87. Huey as political technician is examined by Emile B. Ader, "An Analysis of the Campaign Techniques and Appeals of Huey Long," unpublished Master's thesis, Tulane University (New Orleans, 1942); Elsie B. Stallworth, "A Survey of the Louisiana *Progresses* of the 1930's," unpublished Master's thesis, Louisiana State University (Baton Rouge, 1948); and Burton L. Hotaling, "Huey P. Long as Journalist and Propagandist," *Journalism Quarterly*, xx (March, 1943), 21–29.

Leo G. Douthit offers some useful detail in his "The Governorship of Huey Long," unpublished Master's thesis, Tulane University (New Orleans, 1947). Anti-Long Hilda P. Hammond warmly retells her vain effort to persuade the Senate to unseat Overton and Long in *Let Freedom Ring* (New York, 1936). Huey's Senate obstructionism is related in Franklin L. Burdette, *Filibustering in the Senate* (Princeton, 1940); his threat to the Roosevelt administration in James A. Farley, *Behind the Ballots* (New York, 1938); and his ultimate prison fate is sworn to by Internal Revenue official Elmer L. Irey, *The Tax Dodgers* (New York, 1948). A superior bibliography of materials on Huey Long may be found in Reinhard H. Luthin, *American Demagogues, Twentieth Century* (Boston, 1954), 345–49.

G. POST-HUEY POLITICS AND POLITICIANS

Pre-Scandals estimates of Huey's successors may be found in F. Raymond Daniell, "Huey's Heirs," *Saturday Evening Post*, ccx (February 12, 1938), 5ff., and in Walter Davenport, "Robes of the Kingfish," *Collier's*, xcvi (November 23, 1935), 12ff. Harnett T. Kane's *Louisiana Hayride* (New York, 1941) is a delightful and thorough telling of the Scandals which maintains the proper balance of awe and levity. Kane may be supplemented by Alva Johnston's articles for the *Saturday Evening Post*, ccxii: "Louisiana Revolution," (May 11, 1940), 16ff.; "The Camera Trapped Them," (June 15, 1940), 22ff.; and "They Sent a Letter," (June 22, 1940), 29ff.; and by George E. Simmons, "Crusading Newspapers in Louisiana," *Journalism Quarterly*, xvi (December, 1939), 328–33. The moral decay induced by the decade of rule of Huey and his heirs is uncovered through polls in George Gallup and Saul F. Rae, *The Pulse of Democracy* (New York, 1940).

On the high hopes for the Jones administration held by outsiders, see James E. Crown, "Louisiana's David Who Slew the Giant That Was the Long Machine," *New York Times Magazine*, (March 3, 1940), 7ff., and Tom Dutton, "Sam Houston Jones: Louisiana's Liberator," *Christian Science Monitor Magazine*, (April 27, 1940), 3ff. Harlan W. Gilmore, "Louisiana Clings to Reform," *National Municipal Review*, xxxiii (April, 1944), 164–69, and Jacob M. Morrison, "Long Shadows over Louisiana," *Southwest Review*, xxix (Winter, 1944), 121–35, offer a favorable verdict on Jones's record, while the disappointments of purist reformers are voiced by W. V. Holloway, "The Crash of the Long Machine and Its Aftermath," *Journal of Politics*, iii (August, 1941), 348–62. Robert J. Harris, "Some Common Fallacies Concerning Good Government," *Louisiana Municipal Review*, v (May-June, 1943), 65–66, succinctly punctures the tax-conscious tone of anti-Longism.

Sam Jones details his own position on natural gas policy in "Louisiana's Natural Gas Policy," *Louisiana Police Jury Review*, x (April, 1946), 18ff. and on Southern discontents with the national Democratic party in "Will Dixie Bolt the New Deal?" *Saturday Evening Post*, ccxv (March 6, 1943), 20ff. Administrative reorganization under Jones is evaluated in Robert H. Weaver, *Administrative Reorganization in Louisiana*, Louisiana State University Bureau of Government Research (Baton Rouge, 1951); Charles S. Hyneman, "Political and Administrative Reform in the 1940 Legislature," *Louisiana Law Review*, iii (November, 1940), 1–54; and Donald H. Morrison, "Administrative Reorganization in Louisiana," *Louisiana Municipal Review*, iii (September-October, 1940), 9ff.

The legislative record of the decade 1940–50 is available, in non-political terms, in James A. Bugea, Carlos E. Lazarus, and William T. Pegues, "The Louisiana Legislation of 1940," *Louisiana Law Review*, iii (1940–41), 98–199; M. G. Dakin, "Louisiana Tax Legislation of 1940," *Louisiana Law Review*, iii (1940-41), 55–97; Carlos E. Lazarus, "Louisiana Legislation of 1946," *Louisiana Law Review*, vii (1946-47), 23–114; Student

Board, Louisiana Law Review, "Louisiana Legislation of 1948," *Louisiana Law Review*, IX (1948–49), 18–141; and Student Symposium, Louisiana Law Review, "Louisiana Legislation of 1950," *Louisiana Law Review*, XI (1950–51), 22–94. The New Orleans Bureau of Governmental Research has reported the contents and progress of major legislation for each session since 1940, while the Public Affairs Research Council of Louisiana has analyzed the special sessions held in 1951 and 1953.

For an account of the impact of Long's punitive legislation of 1948, see Lennox L. Moak and Helen R. Moak, "The Rape of New Orleans," *National Municipal Review*, XXXVII (September, 1948), 412–15, and for a discussion of a turning point of the Earl Long administration see William C. Havard, "The Abortive Louisiana Constitutional Convention of 1951," *Journal of Politics*, XIII (November, 1951), 697–711. The principles of the Dixiecrats are extolled by Leander H. Perez, "Are You a States' Righter?" *Louisiana Police Jury Review*, XIV (April, 1950), 9ff. The 1952 intra-Democratic story may be found in the section on Louisiana in Paul T. David, Malcolm Moos, and Ralph M. Goldman (eds.), *Presidential Nominating Politics in 1952*, Vol. III, *The South* (Baltimore, 1954), 278–87.

Congressman Jimmie Morrison is the subject of Robert L. Taylor's "Minnow Who Would be Kingfish," *Saturday Evening Post*, CCXVI (January 8, 1944), 20ff.; while Perez is critically dissected in Lester Velie's "Kingfish of the Dixiecrats," *Collier's*, CXXIV (December 17, 24, 1949), 9ff., 21ff., and in Hodding Carter, "Dixiecrat Boss of the Bayous," *The Reporter*, II (January 17, 1950), 10–12. Chep Morrison is thoughtfully treated by James Sharp, "Morrison of New Orleans," *The Reporter*, II (February 28, 1950), 29–31; aso useful are Ralph G. Martin, "New Orleans Has Its Face Lifted," *New Republic*, CXVI (June 2, 1947), 16–19, and Ralph Wallace, "Chep Morrison, Mayor," *Forum*, CIX (May, 1948), 271–75.

H. STUDIES OF STATE POLICIES AND PROGRAMS

Insofar as much of what is inherently simple legislative matter becomes imbedded in the state Constitution, the Constitution Revision Project materials of the Louisiana State Law Institute are valuable sources in this area. Special studies and reports by the New Orleans Bureau of Governmental Research, the Public Affairs Research Council of Louisiana, the Louisiana Police Jury Association, the Louisiana Municipal Association and other like bodies, and, of course, the official reports of state agencies, should also be consulted.

Edwin W. Fay, *The History of Education in Louisiana* (Washington, D. C., 1898), and T. H. Harris, *The Story of Education in Louisiana* (New Orleans, 1924), are both outdated and somewhat inadequate. More useful to a study of recent politics are Marcus M. Wilkerson, *Thomas Duckett Boyd* (Baton Rouge, 1935), and Guy C. Mitchell, "Growth of State Control of Public Education in Louisiana," unpublished doctoral thesis, University of Michigan (Ann Arbor, 1942). Don Wharton, "L.S.U.: The School Huey Built," *Scribner's Magazine,* CII (September, 1937), 33ff., offers an intelligent evaluation of the good and bad in the Kingfish's devotion to "my school." The most recent thorough evaluation of public education in Louisiana is the report of the Louisiana Educational Survey Commission, *Elementary and Secondary Education,* 7 vols. (Baton Rouge, 1942). The Commission's findings are summarized in Carleton Washburne, *Louisiana Looks At Its Schools* (Baton Rouge, 1942). Additional educational surveys were made in 1946, and the recently created Legislative Council is currently undertaking another look at the field.

The *Preliminary Report* (April 10, 1946), *Report* (March 10, 1948), and *Projet of a Revenue Code for the State of Louisiana* (May 11, 1948) of the Louisiana Revenue Code Commission is a major source for an understanding of state finances and state debt. Also useful are the four *Reports* (1932–33) of the Louisiana Tax Reform Commission and the *Louisiana State Tax Handbook* (1952 and 1953), published by the Public Affairs Research Council of Louisiana. The Louisiana Revenue Code Commission's *Supplemental Report: Natural Gas Taxation* (May 30, 1946) is exhaustive, while severance taxation is analyzed by T. N. Farris, "Severance Taxation in Louisiana," *Louisiana Business Bulletin,* II (April, September, 1938), 5–54, 5–37, and by Leslie Moses, "The Growth of Severance Taxation in Louisiana and Its Relation to the Oil and Gas Industry," *Tulane Law Review,* XVII (1943), 602–19.

Aspects of state tax exemption policy are examined in Clarence A. Boonstra, "Characteristics Surrounding Rural Homestead Exemptions in Louisiana," *Southwestern Social Science Quarterly,* XX (June, 1939), 58–67; Charles A. Reynard, "Louisiana Homestead Tax Exemption—An Unlitigated Constitutional Provision," *Louisiana Law Review,* X (1949–50), 405–30; and William D. Ross, "Tax Exemption in Louisiana as a Device for Encouraging Industrial Development," *Southwestern Social Science Quarterly,* XXXIV (June, 1953), 14–23.

Donald V. Wilson, *Public Social Services in Louisiana* (Monroe, La., 1943) is a competent survey of the field. On the welfare phase consult Elizabeth Wisner, *Public Welfare Administration in Louisiana* (Chicago, 1930); E. J. Eberling, "Old Age and Survivors' Insurance and Old Age Assistance in the South," *Southern Economic Journal,* XV (July, 1948), 54–66; and a 1949 report of the New Orleans Bureau of Governmental Research and a 1954 report of the Public Affairs Research Council on old-age pensions in Louisiana. On the state's hospital facilities see the summary statements of Jesse H. Bankston, then Director of the State Hospital Board, "Public Facilities for Medical Care in Louisiana," *Louisiana Police Jury Review,* XIII (April, 1949), 125ff., and the detailed analysis by Stella O'Conner, "The Charity Hospital of Louisiana at New Orleans: An Administrative and Financial History, 1736–1941," *Louisiana Historical Quarterly,* XXXI (January, 1948), 5–109.

Louisiana labor is closely studied in A. S. Freedman's "Social Aspects of Recent Labor Growth in Louisiana," previously cited; the *Proceedings of the Annual Convention of the State Federation of Labor* are also valuable. Relevant sections are contained in Addison T. Cutler, "Labor Legislation in the Thirteen Southern States," *Southern Economic Journal,* VII (January, 1941), 297–316, and in Frank T. De Vyver, "The Present Status of Labor Unions in the South," *Southern Economic Journal,* XVI (July, 1949), 1–22.

Natural resource policy is analyzed in R. Nolan Moose and Kaliste J. Saloom, Jr., "The Oil and Gas Conservation Movement in Louisiana," *Tulane Law Review,* XVI (1942), 199–227, and Leslie Moses, "Louisiana's Oil and Gas Conservation Law," *Tulane Law Review,* XXIV (1950), 311–18.

Eloquent pleas on behalf of the plight of Louisiana's cities are offered by Edgar J. Davies, "Is Municipal Home Rule the Solution to Problems?," *Louisiana Municipal Review,* XI (May, 1948), 10–11; Legislative Committee of the Louisiana Municipal Association, "A Statement to the Revenue Code Commission," *Louisiana Municipal Review,* VIII (November-December, 1945), 138–43; and Frank H. Peterman, "The Financial Need of Municipalities in Louisiana," *Louisiana Police Jury Review,* XII (April, 1948), 63ff.

Index

Abolitionism: 6, 7
Acadia Parish: 258, 270
Acadians, the: 32
Adams, J. Emory: 139
AFL: 254
Agrarian protest: 16–20
Agricultural production: 2, 16, 27
Alcoholic Beverage Control Board: 212, 212n., 243
Alexandria, Louisiana: 20, 30, 88, 93, 93n., 254
Allen, Oscar K.: 82n., 86, 88, 96, 110, 125n., 158, 182, 196; calling out of militia by, 91, 94; death of, 125; and gubernatorial primary (1932), 76, 77, 77n., 78; and public education, 104; and senatorial primary (1936), 118–25, 118n.; support of Huey Long by, 46n.; and taxation of refined oil, 95; and tick-eradication, 69n.; will of, 106n.
Allen Parish: 78, 187, 190
American Bar Association: 122n.
American Federation of Musicians: 194n.
American Institute of Public Opinion: 115n.
American Legion: 70, 140
American Political Science Review: ix
American Progress: 85, 85n., 101, 101n., 119, 122n., 129, 133, 133n.–134n., 145n.; *see also Louisiana Progress*
Amite News-Digest: 184, 184n.
Angola State Penitentiary: 48, 64n., 236, 242, 243
Ansell, Samuel T.: 81n.
Antoine's Restaurant: 127n.
Anzalone, Charles: 212
Apportionment, legislative: 3–4, 23, 23n., table, p. 4
Arkansas, Huey Long's influence in: 85
Arkansas Southern Railroad: 45
Asseff, Emmett: viii
Astor, Vincent: 86
Aswell, James: 180n.
Atkinson, Mrs. Tom: viii
Aucoin, Lee: 171
Automobile license fees: 44, 44n., 89, 89n., 121, 161, 179
Avoyelles Parish: 252

Banks, Nathaniel P.: 13
Barkley, Alben W.: 220
Barr, John U.: 220, 220n.–221n.
Baton Rouge, Louisiana: 30, 62n., 93, 94, 136n., 148, 204, 224, 254, 263; "battle of the airport" in, 95
Bauer, R. Norman: 155
Baynard, L. B.: 189, 189n., 276
Beauregard Parish: 140, 187, 252
Beckcom, George E.: 130
Behrman, Martin: 41, 50, 52n.
Bell, John: 7, 10, 10n.
Benjamin, Judah: 5, 7
Bienville Hotel: 139
Bifactionalism: 125, 175n., 181, 187–88, 190, 194, 196–97, 198, 205, 214, 215, 219, 222–23, 245, 247, 249–56; appraisal of, 282–86; as equiva-

304

314